CRITICAL INSIGHTS

Margaret Atwood

CRITICAL
INSIGHTS

Margaret Atwood

Editor
J. Brooks Bouson
Loyola University Chicago

SALEM PRESS
A Division of EBSCO Publishing
Ipswich, Massachusetts

Library of Congress Cataloging-in-Publication Data
Margaret Atwood / editor, J. Brooks Bouson.
    p. cm. -- (Critical insights)
  Includes bibliographical references and index.
  ISBN 978-1-4298-3721-7 (hardcover)
  1. Atwood, Margaret, 1939---Criticism and interpretation. 2. Women and literature--Canada--History--20th century. I. Bouson, J. Brooks.
  PR9199.3.A8Z7475 2012
  818'.5409--dc23
                        2012009730

Contents _____

Resources

About This Volume

J. Brooks Bouson

An author whose work has attracted an ever-growing popular audience over the years even as it has given rise to a lively—and global—critical conversation, Canadian writer Margaret Atwood has long been interested in her readers. "It isn't the writer who decides whether or not his work is relevant. Instead, it's the reader," according to Atwood, who feels that there is "only one real question" that can be asked about any literary work—whether it is "alive" or "dead" (*Negotiating* 122, 140). For Atwood, a work is "alive" if it can "grow and change" through its interactions with its readers; indeed, "books must travel from reader to reader in order to stay alive" (*Negotiating* 140, 146). We can find ample evidence of just how alive and well-traveled Atwood's books are in the essays collected in this volume. Bringing together the critical insights of well-established and emerging Atwood scholars from the United States, Canada, England, Germany, and Israel and analyzing Atwood's poetry, novels, short stories, and short fictions from various critical and theoretical perspectives, this collection offers testimony to the shape-shifting and ever-vital complexity of Atwood's globally acclaimed writings.

The author of over forty works—including over a dozen novels and over a dozen books of poetry as well as collections of short stories and short fictions, works of literary criticism, and collections of her essays and reviews—Atwood is indisputably Canada's best-known contemporary writer and her works are taught in colleges and universities all over the world in a variety of courses, including women's literature, contemporary literature, world and comparative literature, women's studies, Canadian studies, environmental studies, and science fiction (see Wilson 1; Rosenthal 42). The "Critical Contexts" chapters that begin this volume offer a useful point of entry to the study of Atwood's writings. Atwood, who began writing at a time when there was not a "clearly established" Canadian literary tradition or canon, helped to "'invent' Canadian literature as a critical concept" and develop its literary tradition, as Heidi Slettedahl Macpherson remarks in her chapter entitled "'On Being a Woman Writer': Atwood's Canadian and Feminist Contexts." As Macpherson investigates Atwood's literary and cultural criticism, she places emphasis on Atwood's Canadian context and her changing stance on feminism. "Atwood's work," writes Macpherson, "must be seen as, in some ways, arising from the second-wave feminist movement," and while Atwood "does not consistently call herself a feminist," commentators often do. "These two strands—Atwood's engagement with and construction of Canada as a critical space, and her historical positioning as a writer preoccupied with women's issues . . . during a period when such 'women's issues' came to the fore—offer two of the most important critical contexts for her work." An author who has "long used her art to examine the ways in which culture . . . structures the world we inhabit," Atwood remains engaged in her women-centered works with "the reinvention of femaleness and femininity and with the recovery of female agency and female strength."

Even as Atwood's writings have appealed to a wide reading public, they are critically challenging works that have given rise to an ever-growing and lively scholarly conversation, as Coral Ann Howells shows in her chapter "The Critical Reception of Atwood's Works: A Chronological Survey." Providing a comprehensive survey of the critical response to Atwood over the past forty years, Howells finds both "patterns of continuity and shifts of emphasis" in the critical reaction to Atwood's works. For even as some of the initial focuses of Atwood criticism in the 1970s—such as Atwood's relation to the Canadian literary tradition, her engagement with feminism, and her interest in the Canadian wilderness and in environmental issues—have remained key concerns, Atwood scholarship has also evolved in response not only to Atwood's "continuous experimentalism with genres and literary conventions" but also to the new critical perspectives that opened up in the 1980s as critics have placed increasing emphasis in the study of

Atwood on "postmodernism, narratology, and generic hybridity, post-colonialism, [and] ecocriticism" and as they have offered "revisions in feminist approaches" in the analysis of Atwood's works and have shifted from "Atwood's Canadianness to her concern with global issues." As Howells skillfully charts a way through the "complex maze" and "changing contexts" of Atwoodian scholarship, identifying along the way "key topics and dominant trends from one decade to the next," she offers an invaluable and trustworthy guide to the "changing narrative of Atwoodian criticism."

In the "Critical Lens" and "Comparison/Contrast" chapters included in the "Critical Contexts" introduction to Atwood's writings, we find examples of the contemporary critical approaches to Atwood described by Howells. Earl Ingersoll, in his "Critical Lens" chapter entitled "Whodunit: The Mystery/Detective Story Framework in Atwood's *Alias Grace* and *The Blind Assassin*," draws on narratology and postmodern theory as he demonstrates the usefulness of the detective novel format—which promises that readers will learn, by the novel's end, the "truth" of "whodunit" and thus the guilt or innocence of the murder suspects—in reading two consecutive and paired novels by Atwood, *Alias Grace* (1996) and *The Blind Assassin* (2000), works in which Atwood "skillfully shapes her reader's perceptions of meaning" by providing an opening ending to *Alias Grace* and a definitive ending to *The Blind Assassin*. In *Alias Grace*, just as the psychoanalyst/detective Dr. Simon Jordan probes Grace's unconscious memories in an attempt to determine if she was a willing accomplice to a grisly double murder, so "readers are drawn along as 'detectives'" and are enticed to "sift through Grace's account looking for clues to her innocence or guilt." But like Dr. Jordan, readers become "frustrated detectives" and are "left at the end as uncertain of Grace's culpability as they were at the beginning." Iris Chase Griffen, the elderly narrator of *The Blind Assassin*, draws readers into a mystery in the opening sentence of her narrative by reporting on the tragic death of her sister Laura, who, in an apparent suicide, drove a car over a bridge over a half century earlier.

Because Iris appears to know the circumstances surrounding Laura's suicide and seems determined, as she writes her memoir, on setting the record straight, readers of *The Blind Assassin* may believe that "the truth" will be revealed at the end, and, indeed, because Iris confesses to her own culpability in precipitating her sister's act, we have "greater confidence" than we have at the end of *Alias Grace* that we know "whodunit." Yet even as we come to understand "Iris's role as the 'blind assassin' of Laura," we also know that both Iris and Laura were "blindly sacrificed" by their own father while Laura was "knowingly made into a sexual sacrifice by Richard Griffen." Thus, in Atwood's whodunits we find that mysteries "persist" in a way that resonates with the " 'truth' of our experience."

Atwood's skillful and complex use of the detective novel framework in her paired novels *Alias Grace* and *The Blind Assassin* offers evidence that she is a writer who, as Shuli Barzilai aptly remarks, shows no signs of the "anxieties of influence and of authorship" that afflict some writers. Rather than feeling inhibited by her popular and literary forerunners, Atwood draws openly on inherited literary models as Barzilai shows in her "Comparison and Contrast" chapter "From H. G. Wells's Island to Margaret Atwood's Paradice: Bio-perversity and Its Ramifications," which explores the ways that Atwood's 2003 novel *Oryx and Crake* relies on but also extends beyond H. G. Wells's 1896 science-fiction novel *The Island of Doctor Moreau*. Even as Atwood adheres to many of the salient motifs of Wells's novel, such as the scientific hubris of the mad scientist character who creates hybrid animals and endeavors to remake humankind, she also moves away from Wells's account of Doctor Moreau's island kingdom as contained and isolated in her postapocalyptic and global vision of "not only the systematic destruction of most human and nonhuman animals but also of the habitable environment." Arguing that Atwood's "Introduction" to the Penguin Classics reissue of Wells's novel suggests "diverse ways" of approaching *Oryx and Crake*, Barzilai shows how Atwood's observation that Wells's novel has generic ties to the romance, the fable, and the adventure story can be applied to *Oryx and Crake* as Atwood "examines patterns established in the past for her present departures." And like Wells's *The Island of Doctor Moreau*, Atwood's *Oryx and Crake* has an "ethical dimension" as it offers "an analogous cautionary message"—that "lack of care, consideration, and respect for nonhuman animals and, generally, for all nature leads to desolation and catastrophe." As Atwood plays with and against Wells's novel, she "looks back on her precursor's work with an appreciation untrammeled by the dual anxieties of influence and authorship" that trouble and adversely affect other writers as they draw on the works of their literary heritage.

Confirmation that Atwood shows no signs of the kind of writerly anxiety that inhibits other writers is found in the eleven critical readings included in this volume, which highlight the remarkable range, irrepressible inventiveness, and evolving complexity of Atwood's poetry, critical works, short stories and short fictions, and novels. Kathryrn VanSpanckeren, in "Margaret Atwood's Poetry: Voice and Vision," offers a comprehensive overview of and fresh perspective on Atwood's poetry, paying attention not only to the distinctive Atwoodian voice that emerges in Atwood's verse but also to Atwood's enduring vision and concerns. In her chronological survey of Atwood's poetry and reappraisal of Atwood's poetic development, VanSpanckeren provides close readings of many well-known poems and poetic sequences by Atwood and traces the movement of Atwood's poetry "from personal concerns—identity and the tension between her desire for love and her commitment to art—to increasingly larger topics: Canada's national identity, women's struggle for equality, threats to citizens from repressive regimes and unjust wars, the need for artistic freedom of expression, and, most recently, the dangers of environmental decline in an era of global climate change." As a "latter-day romantic," Atwood "believes, with the romantics, that poetry is music, and that the poetic imagination is capable of transforming the world," writes VanSpanckeren, who finds that Atwood's verse, even as it offers readers entrance into the "essence" of Atwood's "philosophical and ethical vision," remains remarkable for its "musical intermingling of voice and meaning." Also focusing on Atwood's poetry, Tomoko Kuribayashi, in " 'Consider the Body': Remaking the Myth of Female Sexuality in Margaret Atwood's Poems in *Morning in the Burned House*," demonstrates how Atwood uses first-person female speakers from classical mythology or from the recent popular or celebrity culture to stage the intergenerational conflict between second- and third-wave feminists around the issue of women's sexual self-expression and embodied experience by asking whether a woman who presents herself in a sexually explicit way is asserting her sexual autonomy or capitulating to male expectations. As Atwood covers "the entire spectrum of ways in which women view their sexual desires, experiences, and/or expectations" in poems like "Manet's Olympia," "Miss July Grows Older," "Ava Gardner Reincarnated as a Magnolia," "Daphne and Laura and So Forth," and "Helen of Troy Does Counter Dancing," she reveals "the inextricable links between women's victimization and empowerment and their sexuality." Please note that page numbers rather than line numbers are given in the citations for Atwood's poetry in this volume

Reingard Nischik, who also emphasizes Atwood's treatment of gender, offers a comprehensive and chronological survey of Atwood's seven collections of short stories and short fictions in "Gender and Genre in Atwood's Short Stories and Short Fictions." Remarking that Atwood "belongs to the rare species of writers who have excelled in practically all literary genres," Nischik states that the "very versatility and variability of genre that characterizes Atwood's oeuvre as a whole" can be seen in her short prose where she is "at her most experimental." As Nischik highlights the process that she calls "engendering genre," she illustrates the way gender and genre "intertwine in a combination of complicity and critique" in Atwood's works. In her overview, Nischik begins by tracing the movement in Atwood's short story collections from a focus on characters in unfulfilling or disintegrating relationships in *Dancing Girls, and Other Stories* (1977), to family-oriented stories in *Bluebeard's Egg* (1983), to stories that dramatize characters in their workplaces in *Wilderness Tips* (1991). Nischik then moves on to an examination of Atwood's postmodern explorations of "new generic territories" in her collections of short fictions, prose poems, and fictional essays in *Murder in the Dark: Short Fictions and Prose Poems* (1983), *Good Bones* (1992), and *The Tent* (2006), which include short texts that are difficult to classify and that offer examples of "Atwood's contribution to the postmodern development of generic hybridization," including the hybrid "essay-fiction" format used to great effect in *The Tent*. And finally, Nischik offers commentary on Atwood's short-story collection *Moral Disorder* (2006), which "marks another generic debut" because Atwood links "the individual stories thematically in such an integrative way" that this work is accurately described as Atwood's "first short-story cycle."

We find further compelling evidence of Atwood's exceptional "versatility and variability" in the remaining critical essays included in this collection, which range from discussions of Atwood's postcolonialism and ecofeminism, to her novelistic portrayals of female victims and villainesses, to her experiments with the gothic and her use of fairy tales, folklore, and religion in her novels, to her forays into the past in her historical novels and into the future in her speculative dystopian and postapocalyptic works. In her chapter "Atwood and the Gothic," Carol Margaret Davison investigates Atwood's long fascination with the gothic. After providing a detailed introduction to the history and anatomy of gothic literature, Davison discusses Atwood's engagement with the gothic not only in her gothic-inflected works of criticism, such as *Survival: A Thematic Guide to Canadian Literature* (1972), *Strange Things: The Malevolent North in Canadian Literature* (1995), and *Negotiating with the Dead: A Writer on Writing* (2002), but also in her poetry and novels, such as *The Journals of Susanna Moodie* (1970), *Surfacing* (1972), and *Lady Oracle* (1976), where, as she has experimented variously with the Canadian gothic, the postcolonial gothic, the female gothic, and gothic parody, she has also been concerned with questions of history and with national and gender identity. Just as Atwood, in her critical works, "may be credited with laying some crucial groundwork for the serious study of Canadian gothic literature," writes Davison, so Atwood, in her various literary experiments with gothic forms, "has been vital in adapting an Old World gothic mode to address New World gothic issues and concerns within a Canadian context."

In the same way that Atwood's writings have helped spur interest in the study of the Canadian gothic, so her critical work *Survival* and her novel *Surfacing* have drawn attention to the issue of Canadian postcolonialism, as Laura Wright shows in " 'This Is Border Country': Atwood's *Surfacing* and Postcolonial Identity." Engaging with theoretical accounts that ask if Canadian literature can be read through the lens of contemporary postcolonial theory, Wright elaborates on the ways in which Atwood's novel *Surfacing* both situates Canadian identity within "an enmeshed matrix of colonial dominance" and "cultural subjection" even as it complicates a binary understanding of postcolonial identity by placing the narrator in "border country," the space that is at once "between and outside categorization and language." Drawing a connection between *Survival* and *Surfacing*, Wright argues that Canadian literature can be read as postcolonial "largely because of *Survival* and because of Atwood's project in *Surfacing*." Indeed, *Surfacing*'s "careful deconstruction" of "imperial, gendered, and national" power politics "furthers Atwood's supposition, which is stated and codified in *Survival*, that Canada is a victim, that Canada is a colony, and that it is possible to imagine Canada as, therefore, a postcolonial survivor, a country, like Atwood's narrator in *Surfacing*, seeking to articulate and map the unspeakable and liminal space of the border."

Like Wright, Michael P. Murphy also examines Atwood's critique of oppressive power structures. In his essay "Hanging (onto) Words: Language, Religion, and Spirituality in Atwood's *The Handmaid's Tale*," Murphy illuminates the "relational spirituality" espoused in *The Handmaid's Tale*, a work that "admonishes readers to be mindful of the political power of speech" and to reflect on "the connections among language, community and political meaning." Emphasizing in

The Handmaid's Tale that "our social systems fail if language fails to mean," Atwood shows how the Gilead regime is able to gain control over women, in part, "by making use of the disconnection between language and meaning" and by using "fear-based and misguided interpretations of scripture" to provide religious justification not only for the sexual enslavement of the Handmaids but also for the state-sanctioned violence of the Salvaging and Particicution scapegoating rituals. If "personalist theologian Martin Buber would diagnose the spiritually wounded Gilead as an exemplary case of what he calls the 'I-it' relationship," what Atwood's Handmaid Offred seeks is the "I-Thou" encounter described by Buber in which "authentic persons" relate to each other "in true community." Just as Murphy finds in Offred's "hunger" for the "linguistic intimacy" of an "I-Thou" encounter evidence of the "connection between speaking and being," so he describes Offred's narrative as "a kind of spiritual handbook, a diary" that records the development of her "interior life."

Like *The Handmaid's Tale*'s Offred, who is a well-known Atwoodian female victim, other female characters in Atwood's novels, including the Surfacer-narrator in *Surfacing*, Rennie in *Bodily Harm*, and Iris in *The Blind Assassin*, are vulnerable to "physical, sexual, and psychological violence in situations of male domination," as Laurie Vickroy shows in "Sexual Trauma, Ethics, and the Reader in the Works of Margaret Atwood." Drawing on the work of contemporary trauma specialists as she examines Atwood's ongoing interest in the "gendered effects of the oppression of women," Vickroy ponders the plight of Atwood's victim-survivors, who end up "ethically or emotionally compromised by their fears of male violence and exploitation." If Atwood's trauma-survivor characters may appear deeply flawed— for they may seem to be "overly passive and emotionally paralyzed, unreliable and overly defensive, unheroic and even unethical"—their failures, as Vickroy shows, are classic "manifestations of trauma." While trauma can "break down the human spirit" and deprive victims of "memory, identity, and vitality," Atwood also reveals that "recovery is possible" as her victim characters—Iris, the Surfacer, Rennie, and Offred—"begin to reclaim themselves from tainted identities and from ascriptions of power."

Even as Atwood has created a cast of well-known female victims in her novels, she has also insisted that "literature cannot do without bad behavior," as Sarah Appleton remarks in "Freed from the Salt Mines of Virtue: Wicked Women in Margaret Atwood's Novels," her investigation of Atwood's various depictions of the villainess in characters such as *The Handmaid's Tale*'s wicked stepmother character, Serena Joy; *Cat's Eye*'s child character Cordelia, who torments another girl; *The Blind Assassin*'s Iris, who enacts the role of the treacherous sister; and *The Robber Bride*'s Zenia, who is the false friend and sexual rival who betrays and victimizes her women friends and takes their men. If Atwood includes in her works "stories of female treachery, betrayal, deceit, lies, vindictiveness, and a whole host of similar evils," she also insists that her wicked women act as mirrors or doubles for the virtuous characters, allowing the characters—and readers—to "explore the necessity of sometimes acting badly."

Just as Atwood has revived the villainess character in her novels, so she has helped reinvent the Canadian historical novel through her novelistic reclamations of Canadian women's history. In "The 'Historical Turn' in Margaret Atwood's *The Blind Assassin* and *Alias Grace*," Alice Ridout places Atwood's historical novels within the broader context of recent theoretical work on the historical novel's relationship to gender, postmodernism, nationalism, and postcolonialism. Presenting Canada as a location for historical fiction, *Alias Grace* and *The Blind Assassin* not only draw on and play with gendered expectations of the woman's historical romance, they also use postmodern strategies of historiographic metafiction as they tell the stories of two women: *Alias Grace*'s poor Irish immigrant, Grace Marks, and *The Blind Assassin*'s upper-class society wife, Iris Chase Griffen. Concerned with the erasure of women's history from male-authorized versions of public history, both works juxtapose many different voices and texts to disrupt the linear or masculine version of history and both works reveal that women's history is private and hidden from public or official versions of history. Because at the end of *Alias Grace* we do not know if Grace was a willing accomplice to murder, readers "come away with the central mystery unsolved and without one authoritative version of the truth." And while *The Blind Assassin*'s elderly memoirist Iris "plots her way into public discourse through writing and re-writing history," the novel also places emphasis on "the ways in which we can only know history via textual traces, such as Laura's encoded notebooks."

If Atwood, in *Alias Grace* and *The Blind Assassin*, demonstrates what Ridout calls an interesting "historical turn," in her dystopian novels Atwood looks to the near future to comment on our present historical moment. Karen Stein, in "Surviving the Waterless Flood: Feminism and Ecofeminism in Margaret Atwood's *The Handmaid's Tale*, *Oryx and Crake*, and *The Year of the Flood*," traces Atwood's evolving ecofeminist concerns. Stein explains that as a "relatively new branch of feminist theory," ecofeminism seeks "to analyze structures of domination and to promote corrective approaches to achieve both environmental justice and social equality." In her speculative dystopian novels, Atwood has an ecofeminist agenda as she depicts "social hierarchies that, having lost imaginative contact with and respect for nature, abuse women and the environment." As Atwood envisions the dire consequences of the male domination of both nature and women in *The Handmaid's Tale*, she describes how the widespread sexual sterility caused by environmental pollution leads to the sexual enslavement of the Handmaids. In her postapocalyptic companion novels *Oryx and Crake* and *The Year of the Flood*, Atwood depicts a futuristic world where unbridled scientific experiments by a cadre of mostly male scientists has led to a nightmarish world in which new hybrid and predatory species run wild and most of the human population has been killed off by a bioengineered virus created by the genius-scientist Crake, who has designed a genetically modified species to replace humankind. If Atwood's voice is "admonitory" in *Oryx and Crake* and *The Year of the Flood*, writes Stein, "it is also satirical, as she utilizes feminist and ecofeminist ethics to critique the wastefulness, arrogance, and greed of contemporary society," and even as Atwood warns us that "we may be heedlessly destroying the planet and heading toward a posthuman future," she "holds out hope" that apocalyptic novels like hers might lead us "to rethink our consumerist, exploitative behavior" and "to formulate more balanced and egalitarian approaches to nature and society."

Atwood's speculative novels *Oryx and Crake* and *The Year of the Flood* not only convey important political messages, they are also carefully crafted works that, in typical Atwoodian fashion, make a complex use of fairy tale and folkloric intertexts, as Sharon R. Wilson demonstrates in "Postapocalyptic Vision: Flood Myths and Other Folklore in Atwood's *Oryx and Crake* and *The Year of the Flood*." As Atwood envisions a possible end of the world in these novels, writes Wilson, she uses folkloric and other intertexts both to illustrate the "blindness" of her characters and to show "what postapocalyptic vision could be like." Just as Atwood uses the Frankenstein and Faust legends as intertexts in *Oryx and Crake* to describe Crake's creation of a humanoid species to replace humankind, so in her companion novel *The Year of the Flood*, which overlaps the action of *Oryx and Crake*, Atwood draws on flood stories, in particular the Genesis story of Noah and the flood, to tell the story of the Waterless Flood—that is, Crake's pandemic virus—that destroys humanity. Constituting a "plural Noah" (*Year of the Flood* 91), the God's Gardeners, a religious environmentalist group, not only foretell the coming Waterless Flood but they "feel responsible for replenishing the earth after a second 'flood' caused by short-sighted as well as corrupt human beings." But while Atwood expresses her environmental concerns in *The Year of the Flood*, she also satirizes the cult-like religion of the Gardeners. And instead of "directly voicing her concerns over genetic splicing, species extinction, apocalypse, and general blindness," Atwood presents the "oral histories" of her characters, especially Toby and Ren, who are "familiar Atwoodian Scheherazades, that is, narrator-characters who tell their stories partly as a survival technique." As

Wilson illuminates Atwood's complex use of "legends, fairy-tale allusions, animal folklore, folk remedies, sermons, stories about the saints, and songs as folk allusions or intertexts," she also shows how *The Year of the Flood*, in its open-ended closure, offers some hope to readers by suggesting that human life will continue beyond the apocalypse.

Atwood has admitted that she is an "addicted reader" (Macpherson 4); likewise, many Atwood scholars would confess to being "addicted" readers of Atwood who take deep pleasure not only in their first reading—and multiple rereadings—of an Atwood work but also in writing about her works. Reflecting on the title she selected for one of her collections of occasional pieces—*Writing with Intent*—Atwood, as is her wont, remarks on the various dictionary meanings of the word *intent*. "It can mean a state of mind or will, but it can also mean an inclination of spirit or soul. And, as a word, *intent* is joined at the hip with *intense*. 'Eager,' 'keen,' and 'resolved' are also mentioned in its dictionary definition. 'Having the mind strenuously bent upon something,' says the *Shorter Oxford*, and that certainly describes the feeling you need to have—or that I need to have—when writing these kinds of pieces" (Introduction xvii). Readers and critics of Atwood know well the state of mind Atwood is describing. "Once you start making lists or devising rules for stories, or for any other kind of writing," Atwood insists, "some writer will be sure to happen along and casually break every abstract rule you or anyone else has ever thought up, and take your breath away in the process. The word *should* is a dangerous one to use when speaking of writing. It's a kind of challenge to the deviousness and inventiveness and audacity and perversity of the creative spirit" ("Reading Blind" 68). Atwood is an author who has long taken away the collective breath of her readers and critics with her own devious and inventive, and at times audacious and perverse, and yet morally engaged works. Just as readers of Atwood find themselves reading with intent, so Atwood scholars find themselves reading and writing with intent as they grapple with the unending critical challenges of Atwood's irrepressible and inimitable art.

Works Cited

Atwood, Margaret. Introduction. *Writing with Intent* xiii–xvii.

_____. *Negotiating with the Dead: A Writer on Writing*. Cambridge, UK: Cambridge UP, 2002.

_____. "Reading Blind: *The Best American Short Stories 1989*." *Writing with Intent* 68–79.

_____. *Writing with Intent: Essays, Reviews, Personal Prose: 1983–2005*. New York: Carroll, 2005.

Macpherson, Heidi Slettedahl. *The Cambridge Introduction to Margaret Atwood*. Cambridge, UK: Cambridge UP, 2010.

Rosenthal, Caroline. "Canonizing Atwood: Her Impact on Teaching in the US, Canada, and Europe." *Margaret Atwood: Works and Impact*. Ed. Reingard Nischik. Rochester, NY: Camden, 2000. 41–56.

Wilson, Sharon. Preface. *Approaches to Teaching Atwood's* The Handmaid's Tale *and Other Works*. Eds. Sharon Wilson, Thomas Friedman, and Shannon Hengen. New York: MLA, 1996. 1–2.

CAREER, LIFE, AND INFLUENCE

On Margaret Atwood _____

Canadian author Margaret Atwood, in the years since the publication of her first novel *The Edible Woman* (1969), her poetry collections *The Journals of Susanna Moodie* (1970) and *Power Politics* (1971), and her first critical work *Survival: A Thematic Guide to Canadian Literature* (1972), has evolved from a Canadian cult figure and national author into a globally acclaimed writer and a well-known cultural ambassador for Canada. An international best-selling and prize-winning author whose books have been translated into over forty languages, Atwood is the author of over forty works, including over a dozen novels and over a dozen books of poetry as well as collections of short stories and short fictions, works of literary criticism, and collections of her essays and reviews. Canada's best-known contemporary author, Atwood has both a wide popular audience and an ever-growing academic following. Not only is Atwood the "most frequently studied Canadian writer at the university level" (Nischik, "Flagpoles" 2), but her works have attracted intense academic interest and given rise to an academic association solely devoted to the critical analysis of her poetry, novels, stories, and literary criticism—The Margaret Atwood Society—as literary scholars from all over the world have studied her writings.

"Any author whose work . . . can be found in both airport newspaper shops *and* on graduate school syllabi all over the world must be doing something right," as commentators have remarked of Atwood's writings (cited by Pache 120). An author who produces critically complex works that nevertheless appeal to a wide reading public, Atwood is often praised for her shrewd and often wryly ironic and witty commentary on contemporary culture and for her unabashed and self-confident risk-taking in her writing. Over the years, Atwood has focused not only on feminist and postfeminist concerns in her novelistic and poetic investigations of female victims and survivors, but also, in her recent works, on humanist and posthumanist concerns as she questions the very survival of humanity in an era of excessive consumerism, unbridled biotechnological experimentation, and unprecedented environmental destruction. Considered one of our preeminent feminist writers, Atwood has explored the power politics of male-female relations in her poetry, beginning in *Power Politics* and *You Are Happy* (1974), and in her novels, beginning with *The Edible Woman* (1969), and continuing in *Surfacing* (1972), *Lady Oracle* (1976), and most famously in *The Handmaid's Tale* (1985). Atwood has also created a cast of well-known villainess characters in her works including the novels *Cat's Eye* (1988), *The Robber Bride* (1993), *Alias Grace* (1996), and *The Blind Assassin* (2000). Lauded for both her evolving feminism and ecofeminism, especially in futuristic dystopian novels *Oryx and Crake* (2003) and *The Year of the Flood* (2009), Atwood sounds dire warnings against current trends in contemporary society that put the future of humanity in jeopardy.

"Art," according to Atwood, "is what you can get away with," and over the years Atwood has delighted in getting away with what she calls "*genre* crossover[s]," in which she throws various fictional forms, such as detective stories, war stories, and ghost stories, into her "cauldron and stir[s]" ("Spotty-Handed Villainesses" 130, 131). An author who revels in "genre crossovers," Atwood has long dazzled and exhilarated her readers with her irrepressible deviousness and inventiveness as she has drawn on, often with subversive, parodic intent, traditional and popular fictional plots and formulas: the bildungsroman in *Lady Oracle* and *Künstlerroman* in *Cat's Eye*; the wilderness quest novel and ghost story in *Surfacing*; the female gothic novel in *The Edible Woman*, *Lady Oracle*, and *Bodily Harm*; the detective novel and spy thriller in *Bodily Harm*; the incest survivor story as well as war and vampire stories in *The Robber Bride*; the feminist memoir and science fiction stories in *The Blind Assassin*; the historical novel and detective novel in *The Blind Assassin* and *Alias Grace*; and the dystopian and postapocalyptic novel in *The Handmaid's Tale*, *Oryx and Crake*, and *The Year of the Flood*. Atwood also incorporates into her writings the kinds of literary and popular intertexts and allusions that challenge and delight critics and scholars, ranging from classic British literature, to folk and fairy tales, to the fashions and obsessions of our contemporary popular and consumer culture.

Yet even as Atwood carefully designs her interwoven texts in a kind of audacious, even flamboyant, textual inventiveness, she also grounds her novels, including her futuristic dystopian works, in the rich stuff of everyday life. And she is also driven by the compulsion to tell what she calls "Ancient Mariner stories"—stories that "seize hold" of storyteller-authors and "torment them until they've grabbed a batch of unsuspecting Wedding-Guests with their skinny hands and held them with their glittering eyes or else their glittering prose, and told them a tale they cannot choose but hear" ("In Search" 175). As writers tell stories about human nature—about "pride, envy, avarice, lust, sloth, gluttony, and anger"; about "truth and lies, and disguises and revelations"; about "crime and punishment" and "love and forgiveness and long-suffering and charity"; and about "sin and retribution and sometimes even redemption"—their stories must have an Ancient Mariner "sense of urgency" and "must be told with as much intentness as if the teller's life depended on it" ("In Search" 175; "Reading Blind" 75). An author who firmly believes in the seductive powers of storytelling, Atwood describes how writers must "negotiate with the dead"—with the writers who preceded them and with their ancestors—as they go from "*now* to *once upon a time*" and "descend to where the stories are kept" and then bring back their "treasure" to the "land of the living," which is "the realm of the audience, the realm of the readers, the realm of change" (*Negotiating* 178–79). If Atwood often describes herself as a storyteller-writer who is part author-trickster and con-artist illusionist, she also is an author-moralist who expresses her moral imagination in her art. And as Atwood sets out to delight and fascinate but also to teach in her accessible yet carefully designed works, she writes for her readers aware that "the process of reading is part of the process of writing, the necessary completion without which writing can hardly be said to exist" ("End to Audience" 345).

"Great Unexpectations": Coming of Age as a Writer

In the humorous stories that Atwood tells about her coming of age as a writer, she describes what she calls her "great unexpectations," for at the outset of her writing career, as she has often explained, she found herself at a double disadvantage because she was both a Canadian and a woman. Born in 1939 in a very unliterary and provincial Canadian culture, Atwood became intimately familiar with the Canadian wilderness during her childhood when her family spent every summer in the Canadian north woods where her father, an entomologist, conducted research on forest insects. Evidence of the formative influence of Atwood's experiences in the Canadian wilderness on her artistic imagination is found in her remark that for Canadians "the north is at the back of our minds, always": "Turning to face north, face the north, we enter our own unconscious. Always, in retrospect, the journey north has the quality of dream" ("True North" 33). Just as Atwood was shaped by her experiences in the Canadian north woods, so she was influenced by her experiences in what she describes as the "stodgy provincial" city world of Toronto, which began in 1946 when her father became a faculty member at the University of Toronto (*Negotiating* 10). Growing up in Toronto during the postwar Baby Boom era when "marriage and four kids were the ideal," Atwood, by age ten, began to become "corrupted" by the popular culture of the time—by "Patti Page, the Singing Rage" and the "sniffling radio soap-operas," and "night-time serials such as *The Green Hornet* and *Inner Sanctum*"—and she also recalls how, up until the age of sixteen, her reading in school focused on classic British texts, such as Shakespeare's *Romeo and Juliet* and Eliot's *The Mill on the Floss*, while what she read out of school ranged from Sherlock Holmes to *True Romance* magazines to pulp science fiction to *Peyton Place* (*Negotiating* 10, 11). "Given such conditions," Atwood remarks, "how is it that I became a writer? It wasn't a likely thing for me to have done, nor was it something I chose." Instead, "it simply happened, suddenly, in 1956, while I was crossing the football field on the way home from school. I wrote a poem in my head and then I wrote it down, and after that writing was the only thing I wanted to do" (*Negotiating* 14).

Despite her determination, Atwood faced a potentially difficult coming of age as an artist, for during her formative years as a writer the Canadian literary scene was an inhospitable place for an aspiring young author like her. When in 1960 the nineteen-year-old Atwood was in her junior year at the University of Toronto's Victoria College, she was "scared to death" when she reflected on the difficulties that confronted her as a writer. As she recalls, "the prospects for being a Canadian and a writer, both at the same time, in 1960, were dim"; indeed, Canadian writers were viewed as "a freak of nature, like duck-billed platypuses," for "logically they ought not to exist, and when they did so anyway, they were just pathetic imitations of the real thing" ("Great Unexpectations" xiii). In addition, Atwood was an aspiring *woman* writer, which had some advantages since in Canada the male writer was considered "a sissy" while writing "was not quite so unthinkable for a woman, ranking as it did with flower painting and making roses out of wool" ("Great Unexpectations" xiv).

But as Atwood soon discovered, as she confronted the disabling myths of the woman writer current at the time, "the advantages of being a Canadian woman writer were canceled out by the disadvantages of being a woman writer," for according to the socially constructed roles open to the female artist in the late 1950s and early 1960s, women writers were doomed to suffer ("Great Unexpectations" xiv). "Stern and dedicated creatures," they were expected to forgo marriage and a normal home life "in favor of warped virginity or seedy loose living, or suicide—suffering of one kind or another" (*Negotiating* 15). Moreover, when Atwood read Robert Graves's book *The White Goddess*, she was "further terrified" to learn that a woman might have the chance to become a poet only if she took on the role of the White Goddess and "spent her time seducing men and then doing them in"—activities that "sounded a little strenuous, and appeared to rule out domestic bliss" ("Great Unexpectations" xv). After Atwood published her first two books of poetry at a time when "Sylvia Plath and Anne Sexton had been setting new, high standards in self-destructiveness" for women poets, she confronted yet another cultural myth of the female artist—that of the suicidal female poet—as she found others asking her not "whether" but "when" she was going to commit suicide ("Great Unexpectations" xvi). "Unless you were willing to put your life on the line—or rather, dispose of it altogether—you would not be taken quite seriously as a woman poet. Or so the mythology decreed. Luckily I wrote fiction as well as poetry. Though there are some suicidal novelists too, I did feel that prose had a balancing effect. More meat and potatoes on the plate, you could say, and fewer cut-off heads" (*Negotiating* 89–90).

Just as the cultural myths surrounding the female artist were potentially disabling to Atwood, so was the cultural injunction for beginning women writers from her generation who were told, in the prefeminist 1950s and early 1960s, "If you can't say something nice, don't say anything at all." Offering subversive feminist commentary on this era, Atwood recounts the kinds of sexist insults women of her generation heard from men: "Put a paper bag over their heads and they're all the same. She's just mad because she's a woman. Nothing wrong with her that a good screw won't fix." Women were also told that there were "certain 'right,' 'normal' ways to be women" while other ways were "wrong," and while the "right ways were limited in number," the "wrong ways were endless" ("If You Can't" 15). When Atwood began writing, she faced an openly sexist male reviewing establishment that placed a "double bind" on women writers who were told that "if women said nice things, they were being female, therefore weak, and therefore bad writers," while if they "didn't say nice things they weren't proper women." Thus, Atwood had to ignore not only her socialization to please others by being nice but also the available theories about how women "ought" to write. "The alternative," as she remarks, "was silence" ("If You Can't" 18).

"I first became aware of the constellation of attitudes or wave of energy loosely known as 'The Women's Movement' in 1969," writes

Atwood, who recalls the early and mid-1970s as a time when there was "a grand fermentation of ideas," a "vitality, an urgency, in writing by women that surpassed anything men as a group were coming up with" as the "unsaid was being said" ("If You Can't" 19, 20). The "heady stuff" of the women's movement affected Atwood's writing. "How could it not? It affected everyone, in one way or another. It affected ways of looking, ways of feeling, ways of saying, the entire spectrum of assumption and perceived possibility" ("If You Can't" 20). Yet as feminism has hardened into a new political orthodoxy, Atwood has viewed with "some alarm the attempts being made to dictate to women writers, on ideological grounds, various 'acceptable' modes of approach, style, form, language, subject or voice. . . . In fiction, those who write from the abstract theory on down instead of from the specific earth up all too often end by producing work that resembles a filled-in colouring book" ("If You Can't" 22). While women writers do not want to be "overlooked and undervalued" because they are women, they also do not "wish to be defined solely by gender, or constrained by loyalties to it alone—an attitude that may puzzle, hurt, or enrage those whose political priorities cause them to view writing as a tool, a means to an end, rather than as a vocation subject to a Muse who will desert you if you break trust with your calling" ("*Women Writers*" 83).

If Atwood's "brand of feminism is self-interrogating" because of her caution about "investing in any single feminist ideology," she nevertheless can be numbered among those women writers who have "shattered male plots" even as her novels resist "the assumptions of many contemporary feminist writers and critics" (McWilliams 94). Refusing to adhere to an ideological hard line or to write from some "abstract theory on down," Atwood, instead, writes about women not out of a sense of political obligation, but because women, in all their infinite variations, "interest" her: "Women are not Woman. They come in all shapes, sizes, colors, classes, ages and degrees of moral rectitude. . . . Some of them are wonderful. Some of them are awful. To deny them this is to deny them their humanity and to restrict their area of moral choice to the size of a teacup" ("If You Can't" 22). As Atwood creates in her works a compelling cast of female characters, she explores what first drew her as a student to the study of women writers: her deep curiosity about the multiple and complex lives of women.

Survivalwoman: Atwood's Rise to Canadian Cultural Ambassador

Although Atwood, when she began to write, found the Canadian literary scene largely inhospitable and was aware of the "absence of an inherited Canadian literary tradition with which she might identify," when she took on the Canadian cultural nationalist role in her 1972 book of literary criticism *Survival: A Thematic Guide to Canadian Literature,* she "found herself in the unusual position of playing a major role in forging the means by which she could write with confidence as a Canadian woman writer" (McWilliams 43, 48). Indeed, at a time when there was "historical anxiety about the visibility and viability of Canadian literature and culture," *Survival* marked "a moment of unprecedented assertiveness and confidence in the Canadian literary tradition" (McWilliams 42). In *Survival,* which Atwood describes as "a cross between a personal statement . . . and a political manifesto," she seeks to reveal the "shape of Canadian literature" and uncover what she calls a "national habit of mind" as she investigates what she has referred to as the "great Canadian victim complex" (*Survival* 13; Gibson 11). Finding a "superabundance of victims in Canadian literature," Atwood states: "Stick a pin in Canadian literature at random, and nine times out of ten you'll hit a victim" (*Survival* 39). As Atwood develops her thematic study of various "victim positions," which range from denying that one is a victim to becoming a "creative non-victim" (*Survival* 36–39), she also asserts that the "central symbol for Canada . . . is undoubtedly Survival" and she finds evidence for this in stories of "those who made it back, from the awful experience—the North, the snowstorm, the sinking ship—that killed everyone else" (*Survival* 32, 33).

Reflecting almost thirty years later on the uproar caused by the publication of *Survival*, Atwood remarks, "Who could have suspected that this modest cultural artifact would have got so thoroughly up the noses of my elders and betters?" ("Survival" 54). In its first year, *Survival* sold ten times the 3,000 copies it was projected to sell, and "suddenly CanLit was everybody's business" ("Survival" 55). Those who had been cultivating the "neglected pumpkin patch" of CanLit over the "meager years were affronted because a mere chit of a girl had appropriated a pumpkin they regarded as theirs" while others were "affronted" because Atwood had "obnoxiously pointed out that there was in fact a pumpkin to appropriate" as she set out to prove what were considered "radical" ideas when she wrote the book but are now taken "for granted": that there is such a thing as Canadian literature and that it is "not just a second-rate version" of British or American literature ("Survival" 55, 56). Over the years, *Survival* has been criticized, especially in Canada, for offering, in its focus on Canadian victimhood, a "negative image of Canada and its literary tradition," and for attempting to represent "a national literature and culture according to a notion of [a] unified national character" (Goetsch 175; McWilliams 44)—an idea that seems outdated in an era of Canadian multiculturalism. Yet the book continues to be influential and Atwood, herself, has come to be viewed as "the figurehead of CanLit" (Moss 24). Indeed, many twenty-first-century Canadian studies courses begin with *Survival*, and while Atwood's cultural nationalism is "commonly rejected in Canada, it sometimes still holds sway abroad." And as Atwood has become known as "an ambassador of Canada in the world," she has also become associated with "transnational-nationalism" and is viewed as an author who "touches on 'global' concerns that transcend national borders" (Moss 28).

If Atwood, at the outset of her career, had what she calls "great unexpectations," over the years she has become both a Canadian national icon and a global literary celebrity. Yet for Atwood, such a celebrity status has come with a cost. Calling attention, yet again, to the cultural myths of the female artist, Atwood recounts the various ways the media and her reviewers have represented her because of her growing star status—"Witch, man-hater, man-freezing Medusa, man-devouring monster. The Ice Goddess, the Snow Queen" ("If You Can't" 20). Yet while Atwood has felt much "uneasiness" about the ways the media has portrayed her, she has cannily taken "preemptive critical strikes" and "skewered" these portrayals by assembling lists of the mythological versions of her (as a witch, a medusa, a monster) invented by the media (York, "Slightly Uneasy Eminence" 40–41). And as the media has focused attention over the years on Atwood's physical appearance—especially her trademark mass of curly hair—she has mocked her "celebrity commodification" by presenting herself, in cartoon-images on her website, as a "short woman with squiggles for hair" (York, *Literary Celebrity* 102, 103). Similarly, in a comic strip series she produced in the mid-1970s, Atwood offered an "ironic" cartoon image of herself as the author of *Survival* in her creation of Survivalwoman—a female and Canadian superhero cartoon character depicted as a small woman with curly hair (Nischik, *Engendering Genre* 206; see also 202–27).

"The author is the name on the books. I'm the other one," remarks Atwood as she comments on her double nature as Peggy the person and Margaret Atwood the author (*Negotiating* 37). "When writers have spoken consciously of their own double natures, they're likely to say that one half does the living, the other half the writing," Atwood states in *Negotiating with the Dead: A Writer on Writing* as she describes the "two entities" within the writer: "the person who exists when no writing is going forward—the one who walks the dog, eats bran for regularity, takes the car in to be washed, and so forth—and that other, more shadowy and altogether more equivocal personage who shares the same body, and who, when no one is looking, takes it over and uses it to commit the actual writing" (37, 35). Atwood's uneasy relationship with her celebrity identity is evident in her advice to readers in *Negotiating with the Dead*: "Pay no attention to the facsimiles of the writer that appear on talkshows, in newspaper interviews, and the like—they ought not to have anything to do with what goes on between you, the reader, and the page you are reading, where an invisible hand has previously left some marks for you to decipher" (125–26). If we find in Atwood's writings a recurring notion of the writer "as double, as split personality," it is the "workings of celebrity" that exacerbate the split between Atwood the public writer and Atwood the private individual (York, *Literary Celebrity* 121). Although her celebrity status has come with a cost, Atwood has put her literary stardom to good use. Atwood, who views "Canadian nationalism and the concern for women's rights as part of a larger, non-exclusive picture" (*Second Words* 282), has become known over the years not only as a Canadian transnational-nationalist but also as a feminist and an environmentalist who has used her public platform as a global Canadian celebrity and citizen to speak out in support of global feminist, human rights, and environmental causes.

"We'll All Become Stories": Atwood's Storyteller-Witnesses

"As a storyteller," writes Atwood, "all I can do is to tell the kinds of stories I wish to tell or think I ought to tell and hope that someone or other will want to listen to them, which is, and has been for some time, the plight of the writer in a postromantic society" ("End to Audience" 335). Just as Atwood is driven to tell what she calls "Ancient Mariner stories"—the kinds of stories that "seize hold of" and "torment" the writer and that the listener "cannot choose but hear" ("In Search" 175)—so she also strives to capture a "voice" that speaks to her readers. Insisting that "even when we read silently, we read with the ear," Atwood explains that story must have "a speaking voice." As she states, "Surely every written story is, in the final analysis, a score for voice" ("Reading Blind" 71). Thus as Atwood tells novelistic stories using a range of speaking voices, from the morally serious and fatalistic to the flamboyantly comic and subversively sardonic, she creates a series of consummate storyteller-witnesses in her works, from

Lady Oracle's gothic novelist and poet Joan Foster, to *Bodily Harm*'s lifestyles reporter Rennie Wilford, to *The Handmaid's Tale*'s sexual and state slave Offred, to *The Robber Bride*'s academic historian Tony and con artist Zenia, to *The Blind Assassin*'s elderly and dying memoirist Iris Chase Griffen, to *Oryx and Crake*'s Jimmy-Snowman and *The Year of the Flood*'s Toby, both survivors of a pandemic virus that has wiped out most of humanity.

As Atwood plots and replots the classic female gothic novel in her antigothic novel *Lady Oracle*, she tells the story of Joan Foster who, even though she lives in the postromantic 1970s, is seduced by gothic plots. A masterful and duplicitous Atwoodian storyteller and a self-described "escape artist" (367), Joan is attempting to run away from her various identities—her "Fat Lady" identity, which is based on her tormenting memories of her fat girl past; her secret identity as Louisa K. Delacourt, the author of popular gothic novels; and her very public identity as the cult-figure poet Lady Oracle—and she also is trying to break free of her entanglement in the gothic romance plot. As a gothic novelist, Joan prides herself on being a "professional" about fantasy lives while other women, including her readers, are "merely amateurs" (241). Yet she, too, becomes plagued by gothic fears, imagining that her husband Arthur might be the unknown tormentor sending her death threats. And just as Joan thinks that Arthur is trying to get rid of her, so in her gothic novel-in-progress, *Stalked by Love*, Felicia, the wife of Redmond, fears that Redmond wants to dispose of her and replace her with a new wife, the young and virginal Charlotte. Joan is aware that showing sympathy for Felicia is "against the rules" of the gothic novel and would "foul up the plot," which demands that the wife-character must be "eventually either mad or dead, or both." Yet she wonders how she can possibly sacrifice Felicia for Charlotte: "I was getting tired of Charlotte, with her intact virtue and her tidy ways. Wearing her was like wearing a hair shirt, she made me itchy, I wanted her to fall into a mud puddle, have menstrual cramps, sweat, burp, fart" (352). Even as Atwood offers a parody of the gothic novel in *Lady Oracle*, she also explores the staying power of gothic fantasies in the lives of many women, who look to men for rescue but may also come to fear the smothering dominance of men as they are "stalked by love."

While gothic fears also plague *Bodily Harm*'s Rennie Wilford and *The Handmaid's Tale*'s Offred, Atwood's mood is grim as she reflects on postfeminism in *Bodily Harm* and on the antifeminist, conservative backlash that arose in the 1980s in *The Handmaid's Tale*. Described by Atwood as an "anti-thriller" (Draine 379), *Bodily Harm*, which was published in 1981, draws on the conventions of the spy thriller and the detective novel as it tells the story of postfeminist Rennie Wilford, a Toronto lifestyles reporter. During the second-wave feminism of the early 1970s when Rennie was in college, her goal was to become a socially responsible reporter and expose political abuses in her journalism, but she ends up instead as a lifestyles reporter. Not only does postfeminist Rennie accept an assignment to write an article on pornography as an art form, but she also attempts to please her lover by transforming herself into a pornographic object and participating in his sadistic sexual games—games in which she is cast in the role of the passive female victim. After undergoing a partial mastectomy and then discovering a coiled rope on her bed left by an unknown intruder, Rennie escapes to a Caribbean island, where she has taken on an assignment to write a fluff travel piece. Rennie thinks she has left her murderous pursuer and Gothic terrors behind only to end up in a prison cell after a violent political coup. There are "only people with power and people without power," Rennie is told in the Caribbean (240), and when the imprisoned Rennie becomes an eyewitness to police brutality, she discovers the horrible truth behind this political dictum. A "spectator, a voyeur" who has used her tourist vision to distance herself from the suffering of others (125), Rennie is forced to confront the brutal reality of power politics when her cellmate Lora is savagely beaten in front of her. No longer a superficial lifestyles writer, Rennie becomes one of Atwood's storyteller-witnesses. A morally responsible reporter once again, Rennie, who is still in prison as the novel ends, determines that she "will pick her time; then she will report" (301).

Like *Bodily Harm*, Atwood's futuristic dystopian novel*The Handmaid's Tale* is addressed to postfeminist women. "All fictions begin with the question *What if* " Atwood remarks, describing *The Handmaid's Tale* as "speculative fiction" in which she asks *what if* Christian fundamentalists were to take over the United States ("Writing Utopia" 97, 93). Offering a chilling account of what might happen, Atwood tells the story of Offred, a thirty-three-year-old Handmaid in the Republic of Gilead, a theocracy established in the United States by New Right fundamentalists after they overthrow the government in a violent political coup. The Handmaids are fertile women in a world of mass sterility who are stripped of their individuality and then used for breeding purposes. A "refugee from the past," Offred recalls her pre-Gilead life in a society where women felt as if they were "free to shape and reshape forever the ever-expanding perimeters" of their lives (294). Offred is part of the "transitional generation" of women who are forced to undergo a brutal reeducation process. "For the ones who come after you," she is told, "it will be easier. They will accept their duties with willing hearts": they will freely submit, Offred recognizes, because "they will have no memories, of any other way" (151). A compelling storyteller-witness, Atwood's Handmaid not only tries to hold on to her memories of her pre-Gilead past—that is, our present—through her storytelling, but she also attempts to retain a sense of her individual identity and her connection with imagined others. While Offred is "sorry there is so much pain" in her story (343), she is driven to go on with her account. "I keep on going with this sad and hungry and sordid, this limping and mutilated story, because after all I want you to hear it. . . . By telling you anything at all I'm at least believing in you, I believe you're there, I believe you into being. Because I'm telling you this story I will your existence. I tell, therefore you are" (344). Speaking with a deep sense of urgency, Offred, who as a Handmaid is condemned to a life of silence, tells her story not only as she resists the

Gileadean regime but also as she bears witness for those women who come after her.

While in feminist works like *Bodily Harm* and *The Handmaid's Tale*, Atwood speaks to a postfeminist generation as she exposes the potential power politics of gender relations, in *The Robber Bride*, she explores the potential power dynamics of female relations through her portrayal of the audacious villainess Zenia. While Atwood remarks that she has derived "benefits" from the women's movement, which has offered "a sharp-eyed examination of the way power works in gender relations" and has exposed "much of this as socially constructed," she also has bridled under the restrictions feminist ideology has placed on women writers like her, especially the notion that it is "somehow *unfeminist* to depict a woman behaving badly" and that heroines must be "essentially spotless of soul" as they struggle against, flee from, or are victimized by male oppression ("Spotty-Handed Villainesses" 132, 126, 132). In *The Robber Bride*, which is set in the early 1990s, Atwood weaves together in a complex triple narration the stories of three middle-aged friends—the academic and military historian Tony, the New Ager spiritualist Charis, and the wealthy businesswoman Roz—who have been brought together by their painful encounters with Zenia, who, in her role as the robber bride, has stolen the men of the three women

If Zenia is the betrayer and sexual rival of the three women, she is also the embodiment of their hidden badness as she acts out their secret fantasies of power and revenge, for not only are women fantasies for men, but they are also "fantasies for other women" and thus the "Zenias of this world" have "slipped sideways" into the "dreams of women" (388). And Zenia is also a masterful and duplicitous storyteller who creates custom-made stories and identities designed to appeal to each woman as she befriends them in order to con them, presenting herself as extremely intelligent to the intellectual Tony, as a sexual victim and battered woman to the sexually traumatized Charis, and as a smart career woman to the successful businesswoman Roz.

Linking her storyteller-character to the novelist, Atwood states, "Zenia is, among other things, an illusionist. She tells stories so plausible that each of her listeners believes her. . . . But isn't this the goal of every novelist—to deceive? Doesn't every novelist play Zenia to every reader's willing dupe?" And just as writers, while aware that their stories are "a pack of lies" also feel "there is another kind of truth concealed" in their stories, so perhaps the "arch-liar" Zenia "tells a form of truth" (Introduction). Atwood's three women characters not only learn a deep truth about themselves—about their own hidden badness—through their encounters with the storyteller Zenia, they also become storytellers themselves. As Tony realizes at the end of the novel, "That's what they will do, increasingly in their lives: tell stories. Tonight their stories will be about Zenia" (466). In a similar way, as readers of Atwood's novel, we are prompted to assume the storyteller role and tell stories about Zenia as we struggle to understand Atwood's novel and the meaning and function of the villainess Zenia not only in the lives of Tony, Charis, and Roz but also in the dreams and fantasies of contemporary women.

Returning in *The Blind Assassin* to an issue that has long troubled her—the power politics of gender relations—Atwood incorporates into her novel a broad social history of Canada, especially during the first and second world wars, as she tells the story of two sisters, Iris and Laura Chase. A masterful storyteller, the frail and elderly Iris writes her memoir—a "commemoration of wounds endured . . . and resented" (508)—in the final year of her life near the end of the twentieth century. "It's the fashion now, bean-spilling: people spill their own beans and also those of other people, they spill every bean they have and even some they don't have," Iris reflects at one point, mocking the contemporary confessional culture found on daytime television talk shows (448). Yet Iris too is driven to confess, for she is a memory-haunted woman who feels morally culpable for the untimely demise of her sister Laura, whose death in 1945 at the age of twenty-five was an apparent suicide. As Iris reviews the past, she describes her own sexual sacrifice when she entered into a paternally arranged marriage to the wealthy and autocratic Richard Griffen. A man who preferred sexual "conquest to cooperation" and who got "a bargain—two for the price of one"—when he married Iris, Richard expressed his ownership rights over the two sisters by physically abusing Iris and sexually abusing Laura (371, 505). Even as the elderly memoirist Iris confesses to her own destructive blindness to Laura's plight, she seeks a listener-witness. "Why is it we want so badly to memorialize ourselves? Even while we're still alive," Iris asks as she writes her memoir. "At the very least we want a witness. We can't stand the idea of our own voices falling silent finally, like a radio running down" (95). Iris wants what we all "want," which is to "leave a message" that "cannot be cancelled out" (420). A storyteller-witness who attests to the sexual self-sacrifice of women from her generation, Iris writes for and wills her manuscript to her granddaughter Sabrina—and thus to future generations of young women—as she leaves behind "a message" that "cannot be cancelled out" in the written account of her life that will survive after her death. "What is it that I'll want from you? . . . Only a listener, perhaps; only someone who will see me." As Iris ends her account, she leaves herself in the "hands" of Sabrina—and her readers. "What choice do I have? By the time you read this last page, that—if anywhere—is the only place I will be" (521).

Like *The Handmaid's Tale*, *Oryx and Crake* is "speculative fiction" in Atwood's view, and it, too, grows out of a "what if" scenario. Commenting that "every novel begins with a *what if* and then sets forth its axioms," Atwood explains that the "*what if* of *Oryx and Crake* is simply, *What if we continue down the road we're already on? How slippery is the slope?*" ("Writing *Oryx and Crake*" 285–86). Describing in her futuristic novel an environmentally devastated and corporation-controlled world, she expresses humanist and posthumanist concerns as she questions the very survival of humanity in an era of pandemic viruses and unregulated biotechnological experiments in which scientists are free to use genetic engineering to tamper with the "building blocks of life" (57). Like Offred in *The Handmaid's Tale, Oryx and Crake*'s Jimmy-Snowman, who divides his identity into his preapocalyptic past as Jimmy and his postapocalyptic present as Snowman, is a compelling storyteller-witness. Believing that he is the last human survivor of a global pandemic virus that has wiped out humanity, Jimmy-Snowman wishes he had a listener as he ruminates over the past. "Things happened, I had no idea, it was out of my control! What could I have done? Just someone, anyone, listen to me please!" (45). A "castaway of sorts," Jimmy-Snowman thinks about keeping a journal only to realize that while a castaway assumes he will have a "future reader"—someone who will find his writings and learn what happened to him—the only reader he can imagine is "in the past" (41). Left alone in a vast global graveyard by his genius-scientist friend Crake so he can act as the guide of the Crakers—the bioengineered and environmentally-friendly hominids created by Crake to replace humanity—Jimmy-Snowman comes to acknowledge his own "willed" ignorance (184) and thus his culpability as he broods over the past, realizing, belatedly, that he acted as an unwitting partner in Crake's deadly genocidal endgame. "All it takes . . . is the elimination of one generation. One generation of anything. . . . Break the link in time between one generation and the next, and it's game over forever" (223), as Jimmy-Snowman recalls Crake once telling him as he prepared his Extinctathon game plan to destroy humanity. "Sitting in judgment on the world . . . but why had that been his right?" (341), asks Jimmy-Snowman as he reflects on the scientific hubris and imperialism of Crake, who viewed his doomsday game plan as an "elegant concept" (295).

If in *Oryx and Crake* Atwood focuses on the Compound world of Jimmy-Snowman and Crake—gated communities where elite scientists and corporate business people live—in *The Year of the Flood,* in contrast, she centers her story on the pleebland world where the nonaffluent masses live as she tells the stories of Ren and Toby, two former members of the God's Gardeners, an ecoreligious cult and resistance group, and two survivors of the pandemic virus created by Crake.

Offering a feminist re-telling and re-visioning of *Oryx and Crake*'s male-centered apocalyptic end-of-the-world story, in *The Year of the Flood* Atwood describes in graphic detail the degrading and gruesomely violent environment that Toby and Ren inhabit where unprotected women easily become the prey of predatory men. Literalizing a metaphor that has long interested her—the male consumption of women—Atwood describes how Toby comes under the influence of Blanco, a man who views women as sexual objects to be used and abused and then cannibalized: that is, literally turned into meat. Even as Atwood focuses on female victims and survivors in *The Year of the Flood*, she continues to express her humanist and posthumanist concerns as she questions whether or not humankind will survive in the twenty-first century. "Ours is a fall into greed: why do we think that everything on Earth belongs to us, while in reality we belong to Everything? . . . God's commandment to 'replenish the Earth' did not mean we should fill it to overflowing with ourselves, thus wiping out everything else," says Adam One, the leader of the God's Gardeners (52–53). Like Jimmy-Snowman, Toby is a survivor-witness who, as she reflects on her past, recognizes her own willed ignorance, her own refusal to pay heed to the warning signs of the coming apocalypse. When people discussed the "wrongness" in the world—*"We're using up the Earth. It's almost gone"*—individuals like Toby "tuned them out, because what they were saying was both so obvious and so unthinkable" (239). Warning us that we might be on a slippery slope that will lead us to the unspeakable catastrophe of mass human extinction and a genetically engineered posthuman future, Atwood challenges her readers to think the unthinkable in both *Oryx and Crake* and *The Year of the Flood* as she expresses her long-held fears about the potentially deadly consequences of environmental destruction and unchecked genetic experimentation as scientists sit "in judgment on the world" and play games with the genetic "building blocks of life."

An author who feels that "fiction writing is the guardian of the moral and ethical sense of the community" ("End to Audience" 346), Atwood, as she conveys her sense of the "wrongness" in the world in her works, also expresses her deep and abiding interest in her readers. "One of my university professors," Atwood recalls, "used to say that there was only one real question to be asked about any work, and that was—is it alive, or is it dead?" For Atwood a text is "alive" if it can "grow and change" through its interactions with its readers (*Negotiating* 140). As the "original invisible man," the writer is "not there at all but also very solidly there" when the reader is reading. "At least we have the impression that he or she is right here, in the same room with us—we can hear the voice. . . . Or we can hear *a* voice. Or so it seems" (*Negotiating* 148). For Atwood, if we love books as objects "and ignore the human element in them—that is, their voices," we are "committing an error of the soul" (*Negotiating* 145). If "writing is writing down, and what is written down is a score for voice," remarks Atwood, what the "voice" does most often is tell a story, and "however you tell it, there's a plot" (*Negotiating* 158). As Atwood, in her art, explores the multiple and complex social and personal lives of women, she is driven by the need to tell stories. "Where are we without our plots?" asks Atwood's character Nell in the 2006 short story sequence *Moral Disorder*, and, as Nell also recognizes, "in the end, we'll all become stories" (202, 188). Just as Atwood is driven by the storytelling compulsion, so she seduces both her readers and her critics not only with her irrepressible and mesmerizing storytelling but also with the Atwoodian voice—the very human element that we connect with when we enter the storied world of her novels and have the impression that, like her storyteller-characters, Atwood herself is somehow in the same room with us telling us stories we cannot choose but hear. "From listening to the stories of others, we learn to tell our own" ("Reading Blind" 79), according to Atwood, an author who makes us aware of the storied nature of our own lives and how we, too, in the end will "all become stories."

Works Cited

Atwood, Margaret. *The Blind Assassin*. New York: Doubleday, 2000.

_____. *Bodily Harm*. 1981. New York: Bantam, 1983.

_____. "An End to Audience?" *Second Words* 334–57.

_____. "Great Unexpectations: An Autobiographical Forward." *Margaret Atwood: Vision and Forms*. Ed. Kathryn VanSpanckeren and Jan Garden Castro. Carbondale: Southern Illinois UP, 1988. xiii–xvi.

_____. *The Handmaid's Tale*. 1985. New York: Ballantine, 1987.

_____. "If You Can't Say Something Nice, Don't Say Anything at All." *Language in Her Eye: Views on Writing and Gender by Canadian Women Writing in English*. Ed. Libby Scheier, Sarah Sheard, Eleanor Wachtel. Toronto: Coach, 1990. 15–25.

_____. "In Search of *Alias Grace*: On Writing Canadian Historical Fiction." *Writing with Intent* 158–76.

_____. Introduction. *The Robber Bride*. Signed First Edition. Franklin Center, PA: Franklin Library, 1993. n. pag.

_____. *Lady Oracle*. 1976. New York: Ballantine, 1987.

_____. *Moral Disorder and Other Stories*. New York: Doubleday, 2006.

_____. *Negotiating with the Dead: A Writer on Writing*. Cambridge, UK: Cambridge UP, 2002.

_____. *Oryx and Crake*. New York: Doubleday, 2003.

_____. "Reading Blind: *The Best American Short Stories 1989*." *Writing with Intent* 68–79.

_____. *The Robber Bride*. New York: Doubleday–Bantam, 1993.

_____. *Second Words: Selected Critical Prose*. 1982. Boston: Beacon, 1984.

_____. "Spotty-Handed Villainesses: Problems of Female Bad Behavior in the Creation of Literature." *Writing with Intent* 125–38.

_____. *Survival: A Thematic Guide to Canadian Literature*. Toronto: Anansi, 1972.

_____. "Survival, Then and Now." *Maclean's* 112.26 (1 July 1999): 54–58.

_____. "True North." *Writing with Intent* 31–45.

_____. "*Women Writers at Work: The Paris Review Interviews*." *Writing with Intent* 80–88.

_____. "Writing *Oryx and Crake*." *Writing with Intent* 284–86.

_____. "Writing Utopia." *Writing with Intent* 92–100.

_____. *Writing with Intent: Essays, Reviews, Personal Prose: 1983–2005*. New York: Carroll, 2005.

_____. *The Year of the Flood*. New York: Doubleday, 2009.

Draine, Betsy. "An Interview with Margaret Atwood." *Interviews with Contemporary Writers: Second Series, 1972–1982*. Ed. L.S. Dembo. Madison: U of Wisconsin P, 1983. 366–81.

Gibson, Graeme. "Dissecting the Way a Writer Works." Interview with Atwood. *Waltzing Again: New and Selected Conversations with Margaret Atwood*. Ed. Earl Ingersoll. Princeton, NJ: Ontario Review, 2006. 1–17.

Goetsch, Paul. "Margaret Atwood: A Canadian Nationalist." Nischik, *Margaret Atwood* 166–79.

McWilliams, Ellen. *Margaret Atwood and the Female Bildungsroman*. Farnham, Eng: Ashgate, 2009.

Moss, Laura. "Margaret Atwood: Branding an Icon Abroad." *Margaret Atwood: The Open Eye*. Ed. John Moss and Tobi Kozakewich. Ottawa: U of Ottawa P, 2006. 19–33.

Nischik, Reingard. *Engendering Genre: The Works of Margaret Atwood*. Ottawa: U of Ottawa P, 2009.

_____. "'Flagpoles and Entrance Doors': Introduction." Nischik, *Margaret Atwood* 1–12.

_____, ed. *Margaret Atwood: Works and Impact*. Rochester, NY: Camden, 2000.

Pache, Walter. "'A Certain Frivolity': Margaret Atwood's Literary Criticism." Nischik, *Margaret Atwood* 120–35.

York, Lorraine. *Literary Celebrity in Canada*. Toronto: U of Toronto P, 2007.

_____. "'A Slightly Uneasy Eminence': The Celebrity of Margaret Atwood." *Margaret Atwood: The Open Eye*. Ed. John Moss and Tobi Kozakewich. Ottawa: U of Ottawa P, 2006. 35–47.

Biography of Margaret Atwood _____

Shannon Hengen

Canadian author Margaret Atwood, who was born in 1939, grew up in a country that, in terms of having a national identity, barely existed. Becoming a Confederation in 1867 but remaining a British colony until the repatriation of its Constitution in 1982, Canada retained many of the traits of what the influential literary critic Northrop Frye—who was Atwood's professor at the University of Toronto in the late 1950s and early 1960s—famously called the "garrison mentality." The "garrison mentality," as Frye explained, developed during the settlement of Canada when the settlers lived in small communities and, finding themselves surrounded by a "huge, unthinking, menacing" wilderness, banded together, forming a "closely knit and beleaguered society . . . [with] a dominating herd-mind in which nothing original [could] grow" ("Conclusion" 830–31).

As Frye's infamous and unflattering description of the Canadian national character indicates, the Canada that Atwood grew up in suffered from a kind of cultural inferiority complex, and thus Canadians had a tendency to believe, as Atwood puts it, that the "Great Good Place was, culturally speaking, elsewhere" ("Survival, Then and Now" 56). When Atwood in the late 1960s and early 1970s traveled the country giving poetry readings, she recalls being repeatedly asked two questions by members of the audience: " 'Is there any Canadian literature?' and, 'Supposing there is, isn't it just a second-rate copy of real literature, which comes from England and the United States?'" ("Survival, Then and Now" 56). But even as Frye emphasized Canada's colonial status, evident in its "garrison mentality," he also made a "revolutionary" statement that had a deep impact on Atwood as he spoke, in a reverent way, of the boundlessness of the artistic imagination: "the center of reality is wherever one happens to be, and its circumference is whatever one's imagination can make sense of" (qtd. in *Negotiating* 23). As Atwood recalls, Frye's pronouncement gave courage to young writers of her generation who were entering the Canadian literary scene, making them aware that they "didn't have to be from London or Paris or New York" to become artists (*Negotiating* 23).

If, when Atwood began to think about making her living as a writer in the late 1950s when she was twenty, Canadian writers were assumed by their fellow Canadians to be "not only inferior, but pitiable, pathetic, and pretentious" (*Negotiating* 67), then she and her generation of young artists had the unique opportunity to help shape the Canadian cultural consciousness that would allow them to mature as Canadian artists. As Rosemary Sullivan writes: "Canadians would discover that, largely because of the nationalist movement from 1965 to the end of the 1970s, which changed perceptions [,] . . . Canada had become a place where writing was possible" (301). Spurred by the emerging Canadian cultural nationalism of the 1960s and 1970s, small presses that published only Canadian writing began to appear; the Canada Council, a government funding body for artists, was created; Canadian artists, especially fiction writers, gathered together to form a sense of shared purpose as they determined to give voice to Canadian experience.

Not only was Atwood directly involved in the growth of one of those small presses, the prestigious House of Anansi Press in Toronto, but later she would also help form and run the Writers' Union of Canada as well as the Canadian chapter of PEN International, a group dedicated to freedom of speech for writers everywhere. Perhaps most significantly, she published *Survival: A Thematic Guide to Canadian Literature* (1972) with Anansi Press. In *Survival*, Atwood offered a critical study and outline of the country's central works of fiction and poetry organized around her thesis that bare survival had predominated as a theme in Canadian literature, resulting in a sense of collective victimhood. Although controversial, the book nevertheless sold well by providing one of the first comprehensive treatments of Canadian literature. As Nathalie Cooke remarks, "*Survival* was both a result of the rising tide of Canadian nationalism and a catalyst for it. . . . For Atwood, *Survival* was more than a book of criticism: it was a statement of belonging. . . .

Over the course of the next decade, she would not only discover Canada but also become one of those who created it in myth and in narrative" (196–97).

Atwood's identification as a Canadian nationalist was, in part, strengthened by her experiences as a student in the United States in the 1960s. Following her undergraduate years at the University of Toronto's Victoria College where she completed an honors BA in English in 1961, Atwood began her graduate studies at Harvard University's Radcliffe College. Atwood completed her MA degree in 1962 and worked on her doctorate at Harvard from 1965 to 1967, although she left Harvard before defending her dissertation on Victorian fantasy writers. It was during the time that Atwood spent in the United States that she began to perceive differences between that country and hers. As she writes in her essay, "Canadian-American Relations": "Canadians and Americans may look alike, but the contents of their heads are quite different. Americans experience themselves, individually, as small toads in the biggest and most powerful puddle in the world. Their sense of power comes from identifying with the puddle. Canadians as individuals may have more power within the puddle, since there are fewer toads in it; it's the puddle that's seen as powerless" (380). To Atwood, twenty-first-century Canadians remain "a cautious people" who are "less flamboyant" than their neighbors in the United States (Interview). Her view of Canada as a more stable country, less prone to the excesses exhibited by the United States, such as the rise of the American fundamentalist New Right in the 1980s, was one of the reasons she set her novel, *The Handmaid's Tale* (1985), in the United States.

Atwood published her first volume of poetry, *The Circle Game* (1966), when she was twenty-seven, and it won the prestigious Governor General's Literary Award in 1967. Atwood's perception of the ways that social conventions inhibit human behavior, which emerged in these early poems, has continued as a persistent idea throughout her career as a writer. Atwood came of age as a writer in the mid- to late-1960s at a time when her country was in the process of emerging from a colonial habit of mind, and at the same time she began to see clearly that a rich imaginative life thrived beneath the dull, cautious surface of the Canada of her youth. We find a poetic expression of this in Atwood's often-anthologized poem, "This Is a Photograph of Me," in which the speaker says: "(The photograph was taken / the day after I drowned. // I am in the lake, in the centre / of the picture, just under the surface . . . .)" (17). As Atwood insists, if we look "just under the surface" of our routine, prescribed behaviors, we can find the imaginative core of our shared humanity.

Atwood's signature ability to express the underside of consciousness colors much of her work, a result, perhaps, of her unique early life. Her father was a forest entomologist whose work took him and his young family into the bush of northern Ontario and Quebec when Atwood was a child. She describes having been brought by her parents via packsack into the woods at age six months, commenting that "this landscape became my home town" (*Negotiating* 7). She would not live permanently in a city until approximately age eight when her family settled in Toronto with the appointment of her father as a professor at the University of Toronto. Thus she developed a uniquely keen sense of duality from her contrasting experiences of a subsistence-level life in the bush with its attendant freedoms and a convention-ridden life in the city with its restricting codes. Just as the influences on Atwood have been both familial and cultural, so the two spheres are seen to interpenetrate in her work. How we live our private lives affects our culture and, in turn, our culture, in many ways both obvious and subtle, affects our private lives, as Atwood shows in her art.

Raised by a gifted story-telling mother, Atwood and her older brother spent hours making and telling fantastic tales as children together in the bush. Her love of and facility with a good tale later connected with the rise of Canadian nationalism to produce one of the world's most popular novelists. Her family's stories habitually referred to their roots in eastern maritime Canada, particularly Nova Scotia, to such an extent that her relatives, separated by a large distance from her and rarely seen, achieved a kind of mythic status in Atwood's young imagination. She comments on her first inklings of the relationship between the ordinary and mythic levels of consciousness this way: "what we consider real is also imagined: every life lived is also an inner life, a life created" (*Negotiating* 7). Thus, as Atwood insists, the personal and cultural interpenetrate.

Atwood's work shows concern with these issues of double consciousness (ordinary/mythic, city/wilderness, imperial/colonial, personal/cultural) that have been informed not only by her having matured in a country just coming of age, and by growing up in an unusual family, but also by the rise of international movements in contemporary times. During the course of her career, Atwood has had a long-term association with causes like feminism and environmentalism and has joined those who are voicing resistance to globalization. As Atwood has come to define her role as writer in connection with large social and political concerns, she has become known as "one of the most respected critics and chroniclers of our times" (Cooke 330). Coming to reject the romantic cliché of the suffering artist, Atwood, instead, views the artist as someone who is "meant to actively shape society, and not be its victim" (Sullivan 219). Thus Atwood, who early in her career helped shape the Canadian cultural consciousness in the 1960s and 1970s, has moved to other pressing issues in her role as a global Canadian citizen. And yet even as she voices her concerns about the rampant consumerism and environmental carnage occurring in contemporary times, she speaks to us in her distinctively reasoned, clear, witty, and often prophetic voice.

Over the years, Atwood has taken up political causes, but she has also steered away from any overt type of politicizing in her art. In an article for Canada's *Saturday Night* magazine in 2001, Atwood articulates candidly her ideological relationship with the feminist movement; her statement might as rightly describe her relationship with all *isms*: "Writing and *isms* are two different things. Those who pledge their first loyalties to *isms* often hate and fear artists and their perverse loyalty to their art, because art is uncontrollable and has a habit of exploring the shadow side, the unspoken, the unthought. From the point of view of those who want a neatly ordered universe, writers are messy and undependable" (32). As a "chronicler of our times," Atwood records. She does not propagandize.

Atwood's concerns have broadened with time just as her national and international influence has grown. Her novel *Surfacing* (1972) has been described as a ghost story about nature gods in the Canadian north (Sullivan 288). Her fiction of the 1980s moves to a Caribbean island as she explores the horrors of power politics in *Bodily Harm* (1981) and to a theocratic futuristic dystopia in the former United States in *The Handmaid's Tale.* In the 1990s and the early 2000s, Atwood offers a revisionist Canadian history in *Alias Grace* (1996) and *The Blind Assassin* (2000), and in the first decade of the twenty-first century, she has focused on how the unethical use of science may lead to a nightmarish posthuman future in *Oryx and Crake* (2003) and *The Year of the Flood* (2009). Over the years, Atwood has gained a large international following. According to Rosemary Sullivan, Atwood's global appeal "has something to do with her empathy for her reader" and her ability "to connect with something real in people's lives" (323–24). When Atwood sees prejudice against women, she describes it just as frankly as she describes contemporary society's abuse of nature, its worship of technology, and its rampant consumerist greed. Lauded in 2010 as "the public intellectual par excellence of the new century" in Canada (Adams F6), Atwood herself claims that she is "not a real activist" (Interview). Again, as always, her double consciousness comes through.

Atwood has a large popular audience and she also has won many prestigious awards over the years for her critically acclaimed works. Her official self-titled website lists her numerous awards, including a Guggenheim Fellowship, two Governor General's Awards, one for poetry and one for fiction, the Giller Prize, the Booker Prize, the Arthur C. Clarke Award for Best Science Fiction; she has also received twenty honorary degrees from such universities as Harvard, University of

Toronto, Sorbonne Nouvelle, and Cambridge. Atwood's website also lists her publications, which include seventeen volumes of poetry, seven volumes of short fiction, thirteen novels, seven children's books, nine works of nonfiction, five edited books, one theatre piece, and numerous smaller publications. While traveling to many countries to read from her work, she maintains her home in Toronto, Ontario, Canada with her partner of many years, the writer and ornithologist Graeme Gibson.

What rarely emerges in any official documentation of Atwood's life and works is her refreshing, irrepressible, and inventive sense of humor. In a CBC interview, for example, Atwood turns her views of the governing Canadian political party into a campaign for Turnip for Prime Minister. Her reasons? To paraphrase her, a turnip is an ordinary vegetable that knows its roots, doesn't have any gender issues, and takes a long time to think things through. The other thing that official accounts rarely acknowledge is Atwood's reverence for art. Drawing on Lewis Hyde's notion that art is a gift that cannot be commodified, Atwood states that art comes not from "the realm of market exchange," but from "the realm of gift." "A gift," she explains, "is not weighed and measured, nor can it be bought. It can't be expected or demanded; rather it is granted, or else not. In theological terms, it's a grace, proceeding from the fullness of being" (*Negotiating* 69–70). Like Hyde who feels that art comes from beyond the individual ego of the artist, Atwood claims that writers "learn from ancestors in all their forms," including the writers who have "preceded" them as they "learn from the dead." "Writers, she insists, must go from "*now* to *once upon a time*" as they "descend to where the stories are kept" and bring back the gift of story—the "treasure"—to the "land of the living" (*Negotiating* 178). We read Atwood to understand the limits both of human kindness and human cruelty, thoughtfulness and stupidity, in the context of her recurring concern with nature, power politics, art, and lost or forgotten parts of ourselves. Who *are* we as humans in an ever-changing world? This is the question Atwood continues to ask as she offers us the gift of her writing with boldness, creativity, and intelligence.

Works Cited

Adams, James. "Decade Nation Builders." *The Globe and Mail* [Canada]. 1 January 2010. F6.

Atwood, Margaret. "Canadian-American Relations: Surviving the Eighties." *Second Words: Selected Critical Prose*. Toronto: Anansi, 1982. 371–92.

_____. *The Circle Game*. Toronto: Anansi, 1966.

_____. "If You Can't Say Something Nice, Don't Say Anything at All." *Saturday Night* [Canada]. 6 & 13 January 2001: 26–29, 32–33. (Rpt. In *Language in Her Eye: Views on Writing and Gender by Canadian Women Writing in English*. Ed. Libby Scheier, Sarah Sheard, and Eleanor Wachtel. Toronto: Coach House, 1990. 15–25)

_____. Interview with Carol Off. *As It Happens*. CBC Radio One. Canada. 25 Apr. 2011.

_____. *Negotiating with the Dead: A Writer on Writing*. Cambridge, UK: Cambridge UP, 2002.

_____. "Survival, Then and Now." *Maclean's* 1 July 1999: 54–58.

Cooke, Nathalie. *Margaret Atwood: A Biography*. Toronto: ECW, 1998.

Frye, Northrop. "Conclusion." *Literary History of Canada: Canadian Literature in English*. Ed. Carl F. Klinck. Toronto: U of Toronto P, 1965, 1966, 1967. 821–49.

Hyde, Lewis. *The Gift: Imagination and the Erotic Life of Property*. New York: Vintage, 1983.

Sullivan, Rosemary. *The Red Shoes: Margaret Atwood, Starting Out*. Toronto: Harper, 1998.

CRITICAL
CONTEXTS

"On Being a Woman Writer": Atwood's Canadian and Feminist Contexts

Heidi Slettedahl Macpherson

> When you begin to write you're in love with the language, the act of creation, with yourself partly; but as you go on, the writing—if you follow it—will take you places you never intended to go and show you things you would never otherwise have seen. I began as a profoundly apolitical writer, but then I began to do what all novelists and some poets do: I began to describe the world around me.
>
> (Atwood, *Second Words* 15)

Margaret Atwood began her writing career at a time when Canadian literature did not have a clearly established canon or identity. In fact, she has been credited with helping to "invent" Canadian literature as a critical concept, both because she herself is a prolific poet, novelist and short story writer, but also because she has published books of literary and cultural criticism throughout her long career. As she noted in the early 1970s, "Until recently, reading Canadian literature has been for me and for everyone else who did it a personal interest, since it was not taught, required or even mentioned (except with derision) in the public sphere" (*Survival* 13). That attitude has clearly changed, not only because of Atwood's own position as a very important cultural icon, but also because of the preeminence of contemporary Canadian writers on the world literary stage. Atwood's contemporaries include Alice Munro, Carol Shields, Margaret Laurence, and Marian Engel, among others; Joan Barfoot and Michael Ondaatje are only a few years younger than she is. With these other writers, Atwood is in the fortunate position of "participating in a developing literary tradition, rather than reacting to an already-established one" (Irvine 242). In order to understand the work of Margaret Atwood, it is necessary to understand her central position in Canadian literature, as well as the way in which she herself creates a critical context for her own work. In addition, Atwood's work must be seen as, in some ways, arising from the second-wave feminist movement (the period roughly from the early 1960s to the 1980s, though some argue the second wave continues to this day). Atwood herself does not consistently call herself a feminist. Others do, however, and her work is fully engaged with the reinvention of femaleness and femininity and with the recovery of female agency and female strength. These two strands—Atwood's engagement with and construction of Canada as a critical space, and her historical positioning as a writer preoccupied with women's issues (broadly defined) during a period when such "women's issues" came to the fore—offer two of the most important critical contexts for her work. Thus, these two issues will be the focus of this chapter.

While there are difficulties with assuming that a particular nation produces a particular kind of literature, literary histories often attempt to locate connections between literary works and national authors in order to establish thematic commonality. In a similar way, literary historians may link together various works in establishing a national canon in order to prove continuity of subject across time and space (sometimes to the exclusion of other works that do not "fit" the framework). In her book *Nationalism and Literature: The Politics of Culture in Canada and the United States*, Sarah Corse argues that "national literatures exist not because they unconsciously reflect 'real' national differences, but because they are integral to the process of constructing national differences" (12). In other words, there is something imaginary—but very influential—about suggesting that national literatures speak with the same tongue. Of course, Canada's two official languages and its diverse immigrant population, not to mention its indigenous one, make this singular speaking voice problematic, but it is nevertheless a powerful idea. If, as has been argued, Canada and its English-speaking authors have striven for differentiation not only from their southern neighbor the United States but also from the United Kingdom, then one can see why developing a narrative of "Canadianness" has been seen as a necessary stage in the construction of the nation's literature.

Atwood has played a significant role in this construction, from her first nonfiction book on Canadian literature, *Survival* (1972), through to her recent collection of essays and journalism, *Curious Pursuits: Occasional Writing, 1970–2005* (2005).

Atwood published *Survival* in 1972, the same year that she published her breakthrough novel *Surfacing*, which in some ways acts as a companion piece to her critical work, though Atwood denies that they were written to bolster each other. In *Survival*, Atwood proposes that Canadian literature is thematically based on victimhood and survival and that Canada's harsh climate (among other things) contributes to this focus. Atwood offers selective readings of Canadian literature that support this stance and develops as well her theory of the four basic victim positions represented in such literature. Part of her aim, as she explains, is to make explicit what she felt was implicit in Canadian literature and culture, for in her view, "if a country or a culture lacks such mirrors it has no way of knowing what it looks like; it must travel blind" (*Survival* 15–16). Images of blindness and sight are common within Atwood's work, and the idea of literature as a reflection (of reality, of a country, of a gender) has been a common, though debated, idea throughout literary history.

Lay readers and students found much of interest in *Survival*, but professional literary critics have taken issue with Atwood's thematic focus, finding it reductive and exclusive. Atwood metaphorically shrugs her shoulders at this, noting that she never claimed to be a professional critic. In fact, in the introduction to the book, she is quite explicit about what the book is and what it is not: "I'm a writer rather than an academic or an expert," she asserts, "and I've taken my examples where I've found them, not through study or research but in the course of my own reading" (*Survival* 11).

Atwood's emphasis on her own reading as a basis for her critical understanding appears to be career-long. In her 2005 collection, *Curious Pursuits*, Atwood continues to use her own reading as the basis for her critical stance. She argues that her own curiosity is as much a trigger for her reading and writing as anything else: "if something doesn't arouse my curiosity, I'm not likely to write about it. Though perhaps 'curious' as a word carries too light a weight: my curiosities are (I hope) not idle ones" (*Curious Pursuits* xv).[1] The collection covers thirty-five years of essays, analysis, and even obituaries, and it is of interest to readers primarily because it shows just what Atwood has been reading and thinking about. This recent collection of her nonfiction work as well as two earlier ones—*Second Words* (1982) and *Negotiating with the Dead: A Writer on Writing* (2002)—give valuable insight into the contexts for and of her writing, not least because she writes about her own writing experience and details her own critical preoccupations. There is as well some overlap between *Second Words* and *Curious Pursuits* in that the very best of the essays in the former are reissued in the latter. All of the collections deal in some way with Atwood as a *woman* writer, and this context requires further exploration, both in relation to significant essays that she has written and in relation to other critics' views of her and her work.

Atwood called her early collection of essays *Second Words* not only to indicate her primary focus on creative writing, but also because "a writer has to write something before a critic can criticize it" (*Second Words* 11). Thus, for Atwood, criticism necessarily comes *second* and, in her view, is of secondary importance. Part of what she writes about in this collection is her own sense of being a woman who writes, a topic that continues to preoccupy her. With essay titles like "On Being a Woman Writer: Paradoxes and Dilemmas," "The Curse of Eve—Or, What I Learned in School," and "Writing the Male Character," among others, essays in the collection take issue with—and try to explore— what it means to be a woman writer in the latter part of the twentieth century. In her essay "On Being a Woman Writer," which was first published in 1976, Atwood explores not only the impossibility of slicing off aspects of one's identity, but also of the cultural context of women's work. Thus she notes: "As writers, women writers are like other writers" but, "[a]s biological specimens and as citizens . . .

women are like other women: subject to the same discriminatory laws, encountering the same demeaning attitudes, burdened with the same good reasons for not walking through the park alone after dark. They too have bodies" (*SW* 194). Furthermore, she notes: "categories like Woman, White, Canadian, Writer are only ways of looking at a thing, and the thing itself is whole, entire and indivisible. *Paradox*: Woman and Writer are separate categories; but in any individual woman writer, they are inseparable" (*SW* 195, italics in original). Atwood identifies the ways in which women writers' work is reviewed; in the 1970s, there was more systematic and overt discrimination than today (though the phenomenon has yet to go away). Women's writing was often described in "feminine" terms: "She can be bad but female, a carrier of the 'feminine sensibility' virus; or she can be 'good' in male-adjective terms, but sexless" (*SW* 198)—in other words, she could be seen to *write like a man*, a "compliment" that stripped a woman of her gender and belittled her own contribution to literature.

Atwood also has explored the phenomenon of the interview,[2] where the focus is often on the woman author herself and not on her work. Certainly throughout Atwood's long career members of the media have attempted to define her or contain her within stereotypes. In the essay, "The Curse of Eve," Atwood identifies a series of media portrayals of her: "Margaret the Magician, Margaret the Medusa, Margaret the Man-eater, clawing her way to success over the corpses of many hapless men" (*SW* 227). In each of these media constructions, Atwood is made "other" in some way: she is depicted as monstrous or as super (or sub) human. Atwood's fiction also engages with such imagery. When, for example, the young Joan Foster in Atwood's 1976 novel *Lady Oracle* finds herself oddly re-created as a woman poet, she imagines that others see her as "a female monster, larger than life . . . striding down the hill, her hair standing on end with electrical force, volts of malevolent energy shooting from her fingers" (*Lady Oracle* 336). Years later, Elaine Risley, the middle-aged painter in Atwood's 1988 novel *Cat's Eye* similarly deals tetchily with fame. On a flyer for her exhibit of her paintings, "Risley in Retrospect," Elaine sees that someone has defaced her photo with a moustache. "A public face, a face worth defacing. This is an accomplishment. I have made something of myself, something or other, after all" (*Cat's Eye* 20), she claims, though she is also deeply uncomfortable with the spotlight. When she is being interviewed, Elaine likens the experience to a trip to the dentist, "mouth gracelessly open while some stranger with a light and mirror gazes down my throat at something I can't see" (*Cat's Eye* 89).

Atwood herself is a canny interviewee, with much experience in the media limelight; as a result, she is rarely caught off guard. Lorraine York argues that Atwood maintains "a self-conscious awareness of the terms of her own celebrity," which she parodies not only within her literary work but through her cartoons and sketches. As a result, she utilizes "critical pre-emptive strikes of a particularly clever sort" (100). In fact, it could be said that she controls any interview she gives, and in an interview I conducted in Toronto in 2007, she laughingly referred to her own appearance and the media's preoccupation with her curly hair. She told me I needed to include reference to it in the book I was writing: "Now I have the hair criticism. I get criticism of the book, criticism of the ascribed personality and then criticism of the hair. (Laughter) That's why you have to have a chapter on hair."[3] In the same way that she (humorously) directed my writing, she directed the entire interview away from my primary topic, her experience of literary celebrity, and onto safer and more familiar ground where she offered up commentary that provided echoes of her previous interviews, including, for example, her (varied) stance on feminism. Atwood's rather exasperated reply to my question was as follows:

> Well, yeah, what is feminist? There we have a very broad range of definitions which I've gone over countless times. Do I mean that you have to have hairy legs, wear overalls and boots and kick men off a cliff? No. Do I think that women should have equality under the law? Yes. Does equality

mean exact sameness in all respects? No. How much further do we need to go? (Personal interview)

Atwood did admit to some early negative reactions to some of her work, even by feminists themselves, who were not, it seems, prepared for her intricate analysis of all human relationships and her refusal to set up clear victims and villains:

> In the age of high feminism, which took place in 1978 or 9, I used to get attacked for having female characters that were not perfect in every respect, that behaved badly and had emotions such as jealousy, anger, malevolence, and the whole box of tricks, and to those people I say, *I guess you never went to school. I guess you don't remember little Betsy from when you were eleven, who made your life such hell, or I guess you don't remember being little Betsy yourself.* Yes, women are not exempt, and have unpleasant emotions, but that's no reason why they should be deprived of property, identity, their children, their lives . . . it's just that people for a while, in that swing reaction that takes place, wanted to have all women as victims, hard done by, virtuous, pure and nice, kind and gentle, and if they did have bad personality traits it was the fault of the patriarchy, but I think that view has kind of dissipated by now, and anyway it was a view that deprived women of responsibility for their own actions and behaviour. (Personal interview)

Atwood's perspective on creating female characters is that one should be free to imagine their many and varied personalities. As she noted in "The Curse of Eve," one of the problems with trying to do so was the lack of examples of a fictional woman who "makes decisions, performs actions, causes as well as endures events, and has perhaps even some ambition, some creative power." Atwood plaintively asks, "What stories does my culture have to tell me about such women?" (*SW* 223); the answer seemed to be, *Not very many.* A few years later, Atwood attempted to explore the difficulties of "Writing the Male

Character" and argued that in some respects, the critical tables had been turned: now it was the case that critics felt women writers were being unfair in their depiction of men. Atwood has the same response: "it seems to me that a good, that is, a successfully-written, character in a novel is not at all the same as a 'good,' that is, a morally good, character in real life" (*SW* 420). Atwood further argues, "Maybe it's time to do away with judgment by role-model and bring back The Human Condition, this time acknowledging that there may in fact be more than one of them" (*SW* 422)

That Atwood felt the need to respond, in print, to these issues indicates their importance, as well as the historical and cultural contexts in which she was writing during the last few decades of the twentieth century. In the early part of the twenty-first century, Atwood returned to some of these issues in her collection of lectures, *Negotiating with the Dead* (2002). In a series of questions extending across several pages, Atwood revisits the question of the role of a woman writer: "If you're a woman and a writer, does that combination of gender and vocation automatically make you a feminist, and what does that mean, exactly?" (106). Atwood continues, "And even if you aren't an F-word feminist in any strict ideological sense, will nervous critics wallop you over the head for being one, simply because you exemplify that suspicious character, A Woman Who Writes? If, that is, you put any female characters in your books who aren't happy, and any men who aren't good. Well, probably they will. It's happened before" (107).

It seems, therefore, that questions over a woman writer's place (and allegiances) remain as important to Atwood in the twenty-first century as they were when she first began writing, despite changes in societal norms. Over the years, Atwood has responded robustly to this issue. Rather than creating the type of female characters lauded by feminists—the good heroine who must struggle against oppressive and victimizing males—Atwood instead has reveled in the creation of female villains and has frequently depicted women's bad behaviour, including the cruelty of little girls in *Cat's Eye*. Her most famous female villains include Cordelia, who, unlike her Shakespearean namesake, is a cruel bully and later a defeated one; Grace in *Alias Grace* (1996), a celebrated murderess (or is she?), who argues that if the general public wants a monster, she will oblige, because "they ought to be provided with one" (*Alias Grace* 33); and Zenia in *The Robber Bride* (1993) who callously and ruthlessly exposes the weak spots of her women friends—Tony, Charis, and Roz—and not only betrays their friendship but steals their men. It is not accidental that in *The Robber Bride*, Roz's twin daughters go through a childhood phase in which they insist, when an adult is reading fairy tales to them, that all of the characters must be female: thus the big bad wolf is feminized, as are the three little pigs, and the robber bridegroom is transformed into a robber bride, whose victims are all women. The twins "opt for women in every single role'" (*Robber Bride* 294), a perspective one senses Atwood offers her approval of, wholeheartedly.

Atwood has also experimented with rewriting apparently virtuous women, rewriting *The Odyssey* from a female perspective in *The Penelopiad* (2005) Having argued that "sinister women act, virtuous women are acted upon," she felt it was time to explore the story from another angle, as she noted in our interview:

> Well, let us just look at the trio, the ancient trio, always brought up as three, of Penelope, Clytemnestra and Helen, all of whom are related, and the ancients always mention them: you know, evil bad Clytemnestra killed her husband; wicked, naughty Helen ran off with another man; but virtuous Penelope stayed at home and wove and wept. So which of the three is most famous? It's not Penelope.

In fact, Atwood rewrites Helen of Troy as well, making her into a lap dancer in a poem collected in *Morning in the Burned House* (1995). In the same interview she suggested:

Well, that's what she'd be doing if she were she alive today. She'd be either that or a movie star, one or the other, but we never heard that she was particularly smart. No, simply this supernatural beauty, and that's all anyone ever says about her. It must have been, at some point in her life, pretty annoying, because that's how I do it as well. Whereas poor Penelope, all they say about her is that she's really smart.

Clearly Atwood is exercised by the place and positioning of women, not only in her own culture, but in previous and distant ones as well. In two of her well-known essays—"Spotty-Handed Villainesses: Problems of Female Bad Behaviour in the Creation of Literature" and "In Search of *Alias Grace*: On Writing Canadian Historical Fiction"—Atwood considers villainesses to be "disruptive to static order" (*CP* 172) and therefore, by her assessment, *good*. Atwood recalls how, as feminism hardened into an orthodoxy, there were some types of newly discovered and feminist-sanctioned "bad behaviours" available to authors writing the female character: the female character could "rebel against social strictures" and "flout authority" and "do new bad-good things, such as leaving her husband and even deserting her children" (*CP* 180). Yet even as women writers were able to explore this newly created space, they were, at the same time, constrained by feminist ideology and its insistence that the good feminist heroine had to be "essentially spotless of soul" as she struggled against "male oppression" (*CP* 179). Atwood utterly rejects the notion that writing about female badness is somehow "antifeminist" and is "tantamount to aiding and abetting the enemy, namely the male power structure" (*CP* 180). Aware that there have always been "spellbinding evil parts for women" in literature, Atwood insists that literature "cannot do without bad behaviour" (*CP* 181). Indeed, she argues that female villains serve important functions since they can "act as keys to doors we need to open and as mirrors in which we can see more than just a pretty face" (*CP* 182).

Atwood's interest in writing a distinctly Canadian example of the female villain led to her fictional re-creation of a famous Canadian murder mystery in her 1996 novel *Alias Grace*, which retells the story of a notorious 1843 double murder case that was widely reported in the news at the time. Grace Marks, who was sixteen when the murders were committed, was convicted as an accessory to the crime. In her essay "In Search of *Alias Grace*: On Writing Canadian Historical Fiction," Atwood remarks that for Canadian writers of her generation, the "lure of the Canadian past . . . has been partly the lure of the unmentionable—the mysteries, the buried, the forgotten, the discarded, the taboo" (*CP* 218). As Atwood reflects on the appeal of historical fiction, she also sheds light on her own art as she describes the way that historical fiction "appeals to the little cultural anthropologist in each one of us": "It's such fun to snoop, as it were; to peek in the windows. What did they eat, back then? . . . What did they think about? What lies did they tell, and why? Who were they really?" (*CP* 221). But Atwood also insists that "fiction is where individual memory and experience and collective memory and experience come together, in greater or lesser proportions" (*CP* 209). Indeed, she insists, "We have to write out of who we are and where and when we are, whether we like it or not, and disguise it how we may" (*CP* 210). Thus, even as Atwood insists that she carefully drew on historical documents in writing *Alias Grace*, her foray into historical fiction still has a very contemporary Atwoodian feel to it. And even as Atwood takes the opportunity to act as a cultural anthropologist as she looks into the past in *Alias Grace*, she also examines the shaping power of culture on female identity—an issue that has long interested her. While Atwood is aware that she cannot escape her historical and cultural contexts, she has had the rare opportunity to help reinvent Canadian literature. Something of a cultural historian herself, Atwood has long used her art to examine the ways in which culture (which can sometimes appear invisible) structures the world we inhabit.

In order to explore this further, the remainder of this chapter will focus on Atwood's 1988 novel *Cat's Eye*. While it is not Atwood's most famous novel, it is one that carefully explores the power of culture to form, deform, and transform an individual woman's life. As such, it melds together the two foci of this chapter: the influence of Canadianness at a particular historical juncture, and the inescapability of gender as a signifying force in the lives of women. The novel offers two differing accounts of Toronto—it is a dull and provincial town when Elaine spends her girlhood there but is transformed into a "world-class" (14) city when the middle-aged Elaine returns for a retrospective exhibition of her art—and neither construction wholly matches Elaine's own painstakingly reconstructed sense of place.

Past and present are intertwined in the novel; it is not accidental that the present tense of the novel includes a retrospective exhibition of Elaine's artwork. The novel itself does much the same thing, revisiting spaces and individuals in order to find meaning or connection, and indeed, as Coral Ann Howells argues, *Cat's Eye* can be read "as Atwood's own retrospective glance back at the imaginative territory of her earlier fictions" (110). Some familiar strains include the position of the woman artist (explored in *Surfacing* and *Lady Oracle* as well as numerous short stories); women's discomfort with other women, particularly in groups (which is evident in almost all her fiction); and an overt grappling with what feminism might mean to the woman artist. When the middle-aged Elaine returns to Toronto for an exhibition of her paintings, she is subjected to an interview in which a young female journalist wishes to characterize and categorize her work. Elaine's automatic position is a defensive one: "Probably she's out to get me. Probably she'll succeed" (88). Like Grace Marks of *Alias Grace*, Elaine conceals more than she reveals while being questioned, refusing to answer in ways that make good copy. Asked about feminism's influence, Elaine retorts, "'I'm too old to have invented it and you're too young to understand it, so what's the point of discussing it at all?'" (90). She also refuses to reveal her victimization at the hands of male mentors and artists—though it is fair to say she is more victimized by women, hence her automatically wary and prickly approach to being questioned.

Elaine's feeling when she is with the women at the Toronto gallery—that she is "outnumbered, as if they are a species" of which she is "not a member" (87)—is telling. For as Elaine recalls her past, she remembers being castigated for her lack of femininity, for not belonging, for having to learn what other little girls believed to be natural behavior: "Playing with girls is different and at first I feel strange as I do it, self-conscious, as if I'm only doing an imitation of a girl. But I soon get more used to it" (52). Having grown up in the Canadian bush where her sole playmate was her brother and where she lived as much outdoors as indoors, Elaine is unprepared for the rituals of girlhood in the Toronto society of the 1940s and 1950s. "Until we moved to Toronto I was happy" (21), Elaine states as she describes her early life in the Canadian north woods where her entomologist father undertook research on forest insects. But when she goes to school for the first time at the age of eight and is introduced to the world of girls, she feels "awkward" in their presence: "I know the unspoken rules of boys, but with girls I sense that I am always on the verge of some unforeseen, calamitous blunder" (47).

This is a feeling that never leaves Elaine, in part because her education into femininity is a vicious one once Cordelia enters the frame. Cordelia becomes the unofficial leader of Elaine's small group of friends and uses bullying and exclusion to control Elaine's behaviour. As Elaine's young girlfriends repeatedly tell her she is "not measuring up" and will have to "improve," she becomes plagued by worry: "I worry about what I've said today, the expression on my face, how I walk, what I wear, because all of these things need improvement" (118). "Stand up straight! People are looking! . . . Don't move your arms like that" Cordelia says to Elaine (119–20). Speaking with the voice of patriarchy, Cordelia forces Elaine to scrutinize herself and to find herself wanting.

In *Cat's Eye*, as June Deery argues, Atwood "painstakingly reconstructs how Elaine's friends/enemies instruct her in femininity" and while this may seem to be "an account of infra-female interaction . . . the male voice is ever present" (476). But because Elaine consistently blames women for her feelings of inferiority, she ignores instances where men also behave badly and she fails to see how connected men and women are in relation to regulating behaviour. As an adult, she works with a collective of women artists and attends consciousness-raising events with them, but her unease with women in general makes these events uncomfortable for her:

> I am awkward and uncertain, because whatever I do say might be the wrong thing. I have not suffered enough, I haven't paid my dues, I have no right to speak. I feel as if I am standing outside a closed door while decisions are being made, disapproving judgments are being pronounced, inside, about me. At the same time I want to please (344–45).

These feelings replicate precisely her feelings as a child when she felt as if she were on the outside, looking in. When she and other female painters decide to have a woman-only group show, they sense the problems of doing so at that particular historical junction of the 1970s: "This is risky business, and we know it. Jody says we could get trashed, by the male art establishment. . . . We could get trashed by women as well, for singling ourselves out, putting ourselves forward. We could be called elitist. There are many pitfalls." Everything Elaine does is colored by her gender, whether she calls herself an artist, or a woman artist, whether she subscribes to the view that "great art transcends gender" or that the male establishment's hold on artistic greatness is so tight that "a woman artist can get admired by them only as a sideline, a sort of freaky exception" (347).

Bizarrely, perhaps, it is a woman who attempts to destroy her work—a series of paintings of Mrs. Smeath, the mother of one of her childhood friends—by throwing a bottle of ink over it at the exhibition.

It is significant that Elaine has forgotten why she hates Mrs. Smeath, and obsessively paints her, but Mrs. Smeath condoned her daughter's cruel behaviour towards Elaine. As Lyn Brown argues, "*Cat's Eye* implicitly warns women of the dangers of unconsciously passing on to girls what we, ourselves, have suffered at the hands of patriarchy" (295). Just as bizarrely, perhaps, the woman's destructive act transforms Elaine's own perception of her work: "I will be looked at, now, with respect: paintings that can get bottles of ink thrown at them, that can inspire such outraged violence, such uproar and display, must have an odd revolutionary power. I will seem audacious, and brave. Some dimension of heroism has been added to me" (354).[4]

There are many versions of Elaine's life, some of which she has only limited access to herself. The reader is often more aware than she is, and she remains an unreliable narrator, unable to see the disfiguring effects of her traumatic girlhood on her adult life, or of Toronto mores on her upbringing. "I'm supposed to have accumulated things by now: possessions, responsibilities, achievements, experience and wisdom. I'm supposed to be a person of substance," Elaine reflects (13). Instead, she feels, at times, that she is "without worth," that nothing she does "is of any value" (41). Although June Deery argues that "Atwood's predominant interest is her characters' reconstructions of the past in the light of the present and their coming to understand the past's effect on their present selves" (478), it is not at all clear that Elaine is ever able to understand fully the connections between her past experiences and her present unhappiness. She herself proclaims, "The past has become discontinuous, like stones skipped across water, like postcards: I catch an image of myself, a dark blank, an image, a blank" (302).

Elaine is a dark image, a blank, in part because she is meant to represent more than herself: she is also the figure of the woman artist, struggling with her place in time and her relationship with women, men and feminism. Whatever Atwood's own final take on feminism is, there is no doubt that its presence has colored her work, and that she has been as much shaped by its responses to the cultural condition of women as she has by the wider culture itself. Jane Brown suggests, rightly, that Atwood's work "has always moved women and their concerns from their peripheral places in traditional storytelling to a position of primacy" (197)—whether they are villainesses, or victims of men, or even, as in Elaine's case, victims of other women. When Elaine is with feminists, she reexperiences her childhood bullying at the hands of Cordelia:

> They make me more nervous than ever, because they have a certain way they want me to be, and I am not that way. They want to improve me. At times I feel defiant: what right have they to tell me what to think? I am not Woman, and I'm damned if I'll be shoved into it. *Bitch*, I think silently. *Don't boss me around.* (379, italics in original)

Such vehemence on the part of Elaine offers evidence that Atwood wishes to push the boundaries of the "unsayable" herself; by allowing Elaine to react so aggressively, she claims another territory, where women do not necessarily support each other. As Elaine herself notes, "Sisterhood is a difficult concept for me" (345). Atwood's role here is to explore why, to "take the capital W off Woman" and to offer up a female character who is allowed to have a full range of emotions, some of them unpleasant, "without having her pronounced a monster, a slur, or a bad example" (*SW* 227).

Atwood may have begun her writing career as "a profoundly apolitical writer" (*SW* 15), but she has, during her long career, moved from a position of aesthetic distancing to one of active engagement. She is a member of Amnesty International; she fights for the rights of writers through the Writers' Union of Canada (she is a former vice chair) as well as through her association with PEN International (where she is a vice chair); and she helped to develop a remote signing device, called LongPen, in order to reduce her carbon footprint by enabling remote book signing. In her nonfiction book, *Payback: Debt and the Shadow Side of Wealth* (2008), Atwood engages with the debt we owe the future. Her style in *Payback* is allegorical and ecological as she explains that the future of the planet itself depends on how we re-envision the concepts of wealth and debt, as well as the environmental choices we make. While her deep involvement in ecological issues may have its roots in the time she spent with her family as a child in the Canadian north woods, Atwood has used her celebrity status as a writer to speak out as a committed environmentalist, someone who is deeply concerned for the future of the planet in our era of environmental devastation.

In a similar vein, though Atwood is clearly tired of questions about whether she is a feminist, she writes about feminist issues, not least because she came of age and matured as an artist at a time in which feminism as a literary and political practice has come to the fore. As she has written about the lives of women over the years, she has explored the roles of women (and men) in their own victimhood or in their survival. Her writing is most often based in Canada, but it is accessible worldwide and her readership is clearly global.

In many respects, Atwood *is* her own context; and Canadian literature has benefitted from her active intervention as a lay critic and as a creative writer. In exploring the boundaries and borders of her culture, she has also ranged significantly beyond them, intervening in classical myths and legends and rewriting strong women through her fiction and her poetry. She has written one of the most enduring feminist dystopias, *The Handmaid's Tale* (1985), which is set in the future of what was the United States, and which takes as its main character a woman known only as Offred in order to indicate the way she belongs to Commander Fred in whose house she lives: she is "of-Fred." Offred does not exhibit overt strength but rather passivity. Yet she, too, is worthy of Atwood's attention, even as she lives "in the blank white spaces at the edges of print" (66). While Offred's mother is a stereotypical second-wave feminist, who attends rallies and fights for women's rights, Atwood's focus is on the postfeminist Offred, who rejects her mother's feminism. "You're just a backlash. Flash in the pan. History will absolve me," as Offred's mother once said to her (131). Again, this shows Atwood's commitment to recording not only the extraordinary but also the ordinary woman, and to situating her characters within political and cultural realms that speak to their situations and to ours. Atwood welcomes the way in which the feminist movement has benefitted literature, arguing that it has led to "the expansion of the territory available to writers, both in character and in language; a sharp-eyed examination of the way power works in gender relations, and the exposure of much of this as socially constructed; a vigorous exploration of many hitherto-concealed areas of experience" (*CP* 179). These words could as easily be applied to Atwood's work itself. That she remains so successful says something about the immense range of her work as well as her active engagement with the political contexts of her time.

Notes

1. In the United States, the collection *Writing with Intent* (2005) and in Canada, the collection *Moving Targets* (2004) cover a slightly shorter range but include much of the same material, and her titles are just as evocative.
2. Atwood has been subjected to many an interview; in fact, a whole book, *Waltzing Again* (2006), edited by Earl G. Ingersoll, is made up of Atwood interviews.
3. The interview was conducted on August 8, 2007, at L'Espresso Bar Mercurio, Toronto. For further exploration of this interview, see *The Cambridge Introduction to Margaret Atwood* (2010). Thanks are extended to Rachael Walters for her excellent transcription of the interview and to Margaret Atwood for permission to quote from it. All nonattributed quotations come from this interview.
4. Coral Howells suggests that throughout *Cat's Eye*, Elaine's "individual paintings offer a disruptive commentary figuring events from a different angle from that of the memoir, so that it is only appropriate that they could be collected and shown in a gallery named 'Sub-Versions'" (112).

Works Cited

Atwood, Margaret. *Alias Grace*. London: Bloomsbury, 1996.

_____. *The Blind Assassin*. London: Bloomsbury, 2000.

_____. *Cat's Eye*. 1988. London: Virago, 1990.

_____. *Curious Pursuits: Occasional Writing 1970–2005*. London: Virago, 2005.

_____. *The Handmaid's Tale*. London: Virago, 1985.

_____. *Lady Oracle*. 1976. London: Virago, 1992.

_____. *Negotiating with the Dead: A Writer on Writing*. Cambridge, UK: Cambridge UP, 2002.

_____. *The Robber Bride*. Bloomsbury: London, 1993.

_____. *Payback: Debt as Metaphor and the Shadow Side of Wealth*. London: Bloomsbury, 2008.

_____. Personal interview. 7 Aug. 2007.

_____. *Second Words: Selected Critical Prose*. Toronto: Anansi, 1982.

_____. *Strange Things: The Malevolent North in Canadian Literature*. Oxford: Clarendon, 1995.

_____. *Surfacing*. 1972. London: Virago, 1991.

_____. *Survival: A Thematic Guide to Canadian Literature*. Toronto: McClelland, 1972.

Brown, Jane W. "Constructing the Narrative of Women's Friendship: Margaret Atwood's Reflexive Fictions." *LIT: Literature Interpretation Theory* 6.3–4 (1995): 197–212.

Brown, Lyn Mikel. "The Dangers of Time Travel: Revisioning the Landscape of Girls' Relationships in Margaret Atwood's *Cat's Eye*." *LIT: Literature Interpretation Theory* 6.3–4 (1995): 285–98.

Corse, Sarah M. *Nationalism and Literature: The Politics of Culture in Canada and the United States*. Cambridge, UK: Cambridge UP, 1997.

Deery, June. "Science for Feminists: Margaret Atwood's Body of Knowledge." *Twentieth Century Literature* 43.4 (1997): 470–86.

Howells, Coral Ann. *Margaret Atwood* 2nd ed. Houndmills: Palgrave, 2005.

Ingersoll, Earl G. *Waltzing Again: New and Selected Conversations with Margaret Atwood*. Princeton, NJ: Ontario Rev., 2006.

Irvine, Lorna. "A Psychological Journey: Mothers and Daughters in English-Canadian Fiction." *The Lost Tradition: Mothers and Daughters in Literature*. Eds. Cathy N. Davidson and E. M. Broner. New York: Ungar, 1980. 242–52.

Macpherson, Heidi Slettedahl. *The Cambridge Introduction to Margaret Atwood*. Cambridge: Cambridge UP, 2010.

York, Lorraine. *Literary Celebrity in Canada*. Toronto: U of Toronto P, 2007.

The Critical Reception of Atwood's Works: A Chronological Survey

Coral Ann Howells

This chapter offers a chronological survey of the major critical concerns surrounding the study of Margaret Atwood's work, tracing patterns of continuity and shifts of emphasis during her writing career as poet, novelist, short story writer, and cultural critic over forty years. As Atwood's literary production and international celebrity have increased, so has the academic critical industry surrounding her work, and every student needs a guide through this mass of material in order to locate any particular Atwood text within the broad framework of critical approaches on offer. Critical discussions of Atwood initially focused on her relation to Canadian literary traditions; her engagement with the Canadian wilderness and environmental issues; her feminism; her roles as a historian, mythographer, and satirist; her narrative techniques; and the rhetorical power of her language. All these have remained key topics in Atwood criticism, though Atwood's own continuous experimentalism with genres and literary conventions, combined with the influence of new theoretical perspectives since the 1980s, have opened up new critical directions, shown in an increasing emphasis on postmodernism, narratology, generic hybridity, postcolonialism, ecocriticism, as well as revisions in feminist approaches and a shift from Atwood's Canadianness to her concern with global issues. One remarkable continuity is the enduring scholarly fascination with *The Handmaid's Tale*.

In order to chart a way through the complex maze of Atwoodian scholarship, I have adopted a chronological arrangement in this survey, focusing on selected critical books and edited essay collections as the major pieces of criticism on Atwood published in every decade since the 1970s. The bulk and variety of these publications, especially since 1990, are marks both of Atwood's popularity and the changing contexts within which her work has been received. I will identify key topics and dominant trends from one decade to the next, my aim being to reconstruct the changing narrative of Atwoodian criticism in American, Canadian, and British publications.

1970s

Atwood began her writing career in the 1960s as a poet, winning the Governor General's Award for *The Circle Game* (1966) in Canada's centennial year (1967) when she was a graduate student at Harvard. By the mid-1970s she had published six collections of poetry, three novels, and one bestselling guide to Canadian literature. Her early work immediately gained popular and scholarly attention, for her themes keyed into the new North American feminist movement and the resurgence of cultural nationalism in Canada. That position is neatly summarized in the critical responses to her second novel *Surfacing* (1972), which, as Atwood reported, was reviewed in the United States "almost exclusively as a feminist or ecological treatise. In Canada it was reviewed almost exclusively as a nationalistic one" (Ingersoll, *Conversations* 117). In 1977, Linda Sandler edited the first collection of critical essays on Atwood's work—*Margaret Atwood: A Symposium*—which appeared in *The Malahat Review.* This groundbreaking volume identified key thematic and stylistic features of her early poetry and fiction, mapping major directions for Atwood criticism for decades to come. The main topics were, not surprisingly, Atwood's Canadianness (themes of wilderness, human and animal victims, survival) and her feminism (female victims and conversely women's empowerment), resulting in a critical construct close to the early 1970s feminist slogan, "The Personal Is Political." Most essays analyzed her poetic style, her gothic imagery, her satirical wit, while also her noting her revisions of mythic figures, like Persephone, from a feminist perspective. Here too appeared the first checklist of Atwood criticism and the first report on the newly acquired Atwood papers in the University of Toronto's Fisher Library. The collection showcased the variety of Atwood's appeal, encapsulated in this description of the "various Atwoods" that had been "created" to meet the "cultural needs" of readers and critics: Atwood as "feminist, nationalist, literary witch, mythological poet, satirist, [and] formulator of critical theories" (Sandler 95).

1980s

Atwood's popularity continued to grow throughout the 1980s, especially after 1985 with the publication of her bestseller *The Handmaid's Tale*, which is still her most widely read and studied novel. This was the decade when the first critical books on Atwood appeared, together with four important anthologies. It was also the decade when literary criticism changed under the influence of the new critical theories of structuralism and poststructuralism, while feminist criticism was similarly influenced by French feminist theorists, particularly by Hélène Cixous with her concept of "*écriture féminine*" (a distinctive form of female discourse for writing the body and women's emotions). By the end of the 1980s "postmodernism" had entered the critical vocabulary, and Atwood criticism in this period responded to all these influences.

The first book, Sherrill Grace's *Violent Duality: A Study of Margaret Atwood* (1980) laid out the pattern for much of the Atwood criticism of the 1980s by offering an interpretive guide to Atwood's poetry, novels, and literary criticism to date, while drawing on a range of critical perspectives, including feminist and structuralist ones. For Grace, duality is the key to Atwood's oeuvre: "From *Double Persephone* to *Two Headed Poems,* Atwood explores the concept of duplicity thematically and formally, always with an ironic eye to its common meaning of deceit" (*Violent Duality* 3). Her argument opens the way to consider doubles and split identities, tensions between art and reality, realism and romance, demonstrating that Atwood "reworks, probes, and dramatizes the ability to see double" (134). Grace's argument also includes a feminist analysis of women's entrapment and their quest for freedom, as well as sketching Atwood's fictional modes, including her duplicitous trickster narrators, which have since become part of her novelist signature.

Grace continued to explore Atwood's poetics of duplicity in her essay for Arnold and Cathy Davidson's *The Art of Margaret Atwood: Essays in Criticism* (1981). This collection, like Grace's book, offered a comprehensive assessment of Atwood's early poetry, fiction, and nonfiction, adopting a multiplicity of critical approaches. The essays treated topics similar to those included in the *Malahat* collection, though pushing in more theoretical directions. Perhaps the most valuable essays are those which contextualize Atwood's poetry, first within a specifically Canadian tradition, and then, in the section entitled "Atwood's Haunted Sequences," in relation to British and American gothic traditions. Many contributors adopt feminist approaches in their study of Atwood's sexual politics, while *Surfacing* is already cited as a feminist quest classic. The collection includes the first essays on Atwood's narrative techniques and shows that, even in the early 1980s, there was much critical debate over different interpretations of Atwood's work.

Perhaps the most important example of an explicitly structuralist and deconstructive critical approach to Atwood is the critical collection *Margaret Atwood: Language, Text and System* (1983), edited by Sherrill Grace and Lorraine Weir, which pays careful attention to the stylistic features of language and imagery in Atwood's works, especially to Atwood's metaphors of transformation and metamorphosis. Linda Hutcheon offers the first structuralist analysis of Atwood's four early novels: there are feminist analyses of sexual politics in Atwood's poetry, and a typically structuralist computer-generated analysis of the syntax in *Surfacing*. Grace's own essay extends her previous analysis of the theme of duplicity, relating the concept to what she calls Atwood's "system" (the codes that structure a writer's work), demonstrating how she deconstructs binary oppositions between culture/nature, male/female, victor/victim in her search for "a third way of being outside the either/or alternatives which her system resists" (3).

Two books produced in 1984, one in Canada and one in the United States, both recognized Atwood as the most significant contemporary writer in Canada while taking strikingly different critical approaches to her work. Frank Davey's *Margaret Atwood: A Feminist Poetics* offers a more radical critique than Jerome H. Rosenberg's Twayne's World Authors volume, which is simply titled *Margaret Atwood*. Davey's aim was to interrogate Atwood's "particular combination of ideological assumptions through which much of Canadian writing tends at the moment to be read and evaluated" (*Reading* 64). Following that agenda in his critique of Atwood, he offered a semiotic analysis of her recurrent themes, images, and narrative structures, while his brilliant but controversial chapter, "An Atwood Vocabulary," anatomized precisely those features that have remained constants in her work. He also challenged what he saw as Atwood's excessively feminist ideology, and, not surprisingly, feminist critics chastised him for distorting feminism from his male critical standpoint. By comparison, Rosenberg's Twayne study is uncontentious; he steers away from feminist readings toward what he calls "universal themes," though his masculinist perspective peeps through in his description of the emotional difficulties of every one of Atwood's early female protagonists as a "special psychological quirk" (116) when, in fact, they are the very traumas through which these women need to struggle towards a reintegrated identity. His book remains a useful introduction to Atwood's early work, contextualizing it within the Canadian cultural and political scene of the late 1970s and early 1980s, while tracing the development of her craft up to that time.

Leaping ahead fifteen years to Karen Stein's updated Twayne volume, *Margaret Atwood Revisited* (1999), it is easy to identify radical shifts in critical discourse over that time, during which Atwood had become a significant figure in world literature with her works translated into more than twenty-two languages. Like Rosenberg, Stein presents an overview of Atwood's work (up to her 1996 novel, *Alias Grace*), but her critical agenda is far more specific. It is narratological (in its focus on storytelling), feminist (in its analysis of sexual politics), and mythic (in its discussion of female quests and mythic intertexts). Moreover, Stein's critical vocabulary is vastly different, as this single short extract shows: "Her fictions simultaneously tell stories and comment metafictively on the narrative process, engaging readers with a provocative series of questions: What would happen if we heard the stories of marginalized, usually silent people, especially women? What stories do women tell about themselves? What happens when their stories run counter to literary conventions or societies expectations?" (1) The chapter on Atwood's later novels, "Victims, Tricksters, and Scheherazades" is particularly valuable for its genre analyses of *Cat's Eye* (1988), *The Robber Bride* (1993), and Atwood's postmodern generic subversions in *Alias Grace* with the "quintessential Atwood Scheherazade" figure at its center (109).

To return to the mid-1980s, what difference did *The Handmaid's Tale* make to Atwood criticism? The first dramatic change was a shift in critics' attention away from her poetry to her fiction. Much the same is true today, where it is Atwood the novelist who receives most attention. The second change rested on her use of the dystopian genre, which alerted readers to the wider political dimensions of her work beyond sexual politics to include national politics and a concern for human rights. As Atwood said in a much-quoted interview in 1985: "And what do we mean by 'political'? What we mean is how people relate to a power structure and vice versa" (Ingersoll, *Conversations* 185). The popularity of *The Handmaid's Tale* (1985) made it a reference point for general critical studies of Canadian fiction, such as Coral Ann Howells's *Private and Fictional Words: Canadian Women's Writing of the 1970s and 80s* (1987) and Linda Hutcheon's *The Canadian Postmodern: A Study of Contemporary English-Canadian Fiction* (1988). Hutcheon's analysis sees Grace's "violent dualities" as the perfect postmodern condition of dynamic tension between fixity and flux, or product and process, commenting that "it is its ironic metafictional awareness of this paradox that distinguishes Atwood's postmodernism" (Hutcheon 138). Hutcheon also remarks on Atwood's feminist use and abuse of the masculine dystopian genre that exemplifies the "postmodern paradox of complicity and critique" (146). The methodology provided by her book, which focuses on the analysis of Atwood's narrative strategies, has proved highly influential since the 1990s.

Barbara Hill Rigney's *Margaret Atwood* (1987), the first full-length study of Atwood to be published in Britain, presented Atwood as a cartographer, an image Rigney borrowed from Atwood's *Survival* (1972). Rigney read Atwood's novels as maps for her female protagonists' journeys toward discovery of their own identities, while she viewed Canada as a "green world" that is "essentially 'feminine' in a powerfully 'masculine' world" (Rigney 3). Rigney's parallelism between Atwood's nationalism and her feminism was not new, though her analysis of Atwood's unreliable narrators as failed artists, like her emphasis on the importance of mothers and mothering, opened fresh perspectives for feminist analysis. Refreshingly, she also raised the much neglected topic of Atwood's humor, highlighting her ironic awareness of incongruities, her irreverence, and her critical wit, all of which relate to a dissident feminist critical mode in response to patriarchal oppression.

Two important American critical collections appeared in the late 1980s, one offering a retrospective view of Atwood criticism up to 1987, and the other suggesting directions for further Atwood study. *Critical Essays on Margaret Atwood* (1988), edited by Judith McCombs, assembled over thirty assorted reviews and articles published in American and Canadian journals and newspapers, covering Atwood's poetry and fiction from 1967 through 1987; it also included the first essay on *The Handmaid's Tale.* Many of these essays have long been out of print, and this collection remains a valuable historical resource, for it provides the most comprehensive guide to North American Atwood critical studies up to the late 1980s. Lucy Freibert's essay, "Control and Creativity: The Politics of Risk in Margaret Atwood's *The Handmaid's Tale*," flags the main thematic issues of the novel. Her analysis of Atwood's first work of "speculative fiction" (Atwood has always rejected the "science fiction" label) adopts a feminist approach, arguing that Atwood "deconstructs Western phallocentrism and explores those aspects of French feminist theory that offer women a measure of hope" (McCombs 280–81). Clearly she is alluding to Cixous's pioneering essay "The Laugh of the Medusa" when she argues that Atwood "sets Offred, body and voice, against the body politic and through her condemns the patriarchal tradition" (285). This essay set out a blueprint for hundreds of studies on this novel over the next twenty years.

The title of the 1988 collection *Margaret Atwood: Vision and Forms*, edited by Kathryn VanSpanckeren and Jan Garden Castro, signals new critical directions, with an emphasis on formal analysis and "vision" in its double sense of sight and insight. Two pioneering essays appeared here. VanSpanckeren's "Shamanism in the Works of Margaret Atwood" extended earlier essays on spirituality and mystic quests in Atwood by offering an investigation of shamanic themes, images, and structures in Atwood's poetry and early novels. Though this kind of analysis has not become mainstream, an eerie confirmation of VanSpanckeren's speculations is found in Atwood's discussion of the artist's creative processes in the final chapter of *Negotiating with the Dead: A Writer on Writing* (2002). Atwood's visual artwork was treated for the first time in Sharon R. Wilson's "Sexual Politics in Atwood's Visual Art," complemented by an eight-page color supplement reproducing some of Atwood's Gothic watercolors from the archives of the University of Toronto's Fisher Library. Wilson's argument (which foreshadows her later work on Atwood's use of myths and fairy tales) is again a feminist one, demonstrating a parallel between images of sexual politics in Atwood's paintings and her writings. For a long time Wilson was the only critic who investigated the relation between Atwood's verbal and visual art, though since 2000 Reingard Nischik has been investigating Atwood as cartoonist, again adopting a feminist perspective. Another "first" was this volume's emphasis on Atwood's novels and criticism. The editors, both of whom were already leading American Atwoodians, assembled not only innovative essays but also those addressing major critical issues, notably feminism, landscape and environmentalism, the gothic, and Atwood's use of myth and folklore. The collection also includes discussions of Atwood's political concerns, especially her view of Canada's relation with the United States, a topic brought to the forefront by *The Handmaid's Tale*. Atwood gives her personal views on Canadian-American relations in an autobiographical foreword and in a recorded conversation with students at the University of Tampa in 1987. There are two *Handmaid* essays here, the most significant being Arnold E. Davidson's analysis of Atwood's historiographic interest and her narrative methodologies in "Future Tense: Making History in *The Handmaid's Tale.*"

1990s

The 1990s saw a shift in critical trends away from thematics toward closer examination of Atwood's postmodern narrative techniques, together with more nuanced theoretical approaches that combined feminist perspectives with psychoanalytic and genre criticism. Greater emphasis was being laid on the connections between gender and genre in her work, especially in her fiction. The flood of Atwood criticism since 1990 makes it impossible to be other than highly selective in this survey of a decade, so I shall group these new critical works according to their thematic or generic similarities.

Nineteen ninety-three was a landmark year, with a constellation of four books published in Canada and the United States, all of which might be classified as feminist, but which together illustrate the variety of critical perspectives now available under the "feminist" umbrella. J. Brooks Bouson's *Brutal Choreographies: Oppositional Strategies and Narrative Design in the Novels of Margaret Atwood* (1993) focused, as its subtitle suggests, on violent dualities and power politics, showing how Atwood explores women's contested relations to power through different fictional forms. Women as victims, female revenge fantasies, female madness, female friendships and enmities are all exemplified in Bouson's chronological treatment of Atwood's novels through *Cat's Eye*. Women's relation to power is again the topic of Shannon Hengen's *Margaret Atwood's Power: Mirrors, Reflections and Images in Select*

Fiction and Poetry (1993), though Hengen's emphasis is more widely social and political. She combines feminist and psychoanalytical approaches in her analysis, using theories of narcissism and an exploration of Atwood's mirror imagery. Certainly psychoanalytic theory was a big influence on feminist criticism in the mid-1990s, though most critics concentrated on multiple identities and split subjects, whereas Hengen's approach is more unusual and shows some affinity with Linda Hutcheon's *Narcissistic Narrative: The Metafictional Paradox* (1984). Eleonora Rao's *Strategies for Identity: The Fiction of Margaret Atwood* (1993) interrogates stereotypes of womanhood, using Lacanian psychoanalytic theory to deconstruct the concept of a unified self where the identities of Atwood's female protagonists are represented as unstable constructs. In parallel fashion, Rao views Atwood's narratives through a postmodern lens, examining parody and intertextuality in her cross-generic fictional forms, of which the antigothic fragmented Harlequin romance *Lady Oracle* is a perfect example.

Sharon Wilson's *Margaret Atwood's Fairy-Tale Sexual Politics* adopts a different feminist perspective, reading Atwood through an intertextual lens with emphasis on her revisionary use of classic fairy tales. As Wilson teases out the intertwined tales embedded in every Atwood novel (such as the Little Red Riding Hood story in *The Handmaid's Tale*), she details Atwood's techniques of parody, irony, gender reversals, and plot displacements and offers new insights into Atwood's critique of sexual politics. Again, as in her 1988 essay, Wilson constructs parallels between Atwood's uses of fairy tale and myth in her writings and in her paintings and drawings. Wilson's later book *Myths and Fairy Tales in Contemporary Women's Fiction: From Atwood to Morrison* (2008) pursues similar lines of investigation on a much expanded scale, resituating Atwood in a globalized context of contemporary feminist writers such as Doris Lessing, Iris Murdoch, Jean Rhys, and Keri Hulme, all of whom rework myths and fairy tales in their fictions of women's struggles for empowerment. It is worth noting in this context that in 2008 there also appeared a new collection of essays, *Once Upon a Time: Myth, Fairy Tales and Legends in Margaret Atwood's Writings*, edited by Sarah A. Appleton, which has extended the dimensions of this critical field.

The first British collection, *Margaret Atwood: Writing and Subjectivity: New Critical Essays*, edited by Colin Nicholson, appeared in 1994, with contributors from Britain and Europe as well as from North America. It was the first time that a postcolonial perspective was introduced into Atwood criticism, with Nicholson arguing in his introduction and his essay "Living on the Edges: Constructions of Post-Colonial Subjectivity in Margaret Atwood's Early Poetry" that Atwood "brings into focus both the problematized subjectivity characteristic of postmodernist writing and the postcolonial desire to move from positions of marginalisation" (25). Several essays return to the topic of Atwood as historiographer and archaeologist, a perspective first suggested by Eli Mandel back in 1975 and here developed in Mark Evans's "Versions of History: *The Handmaid's Tale* and Its Dedicatees" and in several poetic analyses. Predictably, there are essays that explore issues of gender and genre while offering investigations of postmodern narrative techniques. However, it is particularly interesting that this collection, which was produced outside North America, presents Atwood's work from a more distanced angle, where the wider political dimensions of her writing are more evident, and where she is seen to be challenging not only myths of femininity but also the national myths of Canada's colonial heritage.

Lorraine York's *Various Atwoods: Essays on the Later Poems, Short Fiction, and Novels* (1995) is important for several reasons, first because it represents an explicit updating of Atwood criticism since the 1980s, and second because it inaugurates the principle of selectivity in an anthology, which is itself a reflection of the growing body of Atwood's work, thanks to her incessant productivity and inventiveness. This collection of thirteen essays is a memorial tribute to Arnold Davidson, coeditor of *The Art of Margaret Atwood* (1981), and several of the original contributors reappear here, offering revisionary readings of their earlier critical positions. Through these essays we can assess the difference that new theoretical perspectives have made to literary criticism, altering the lenses through which traditional Atwood topics are viewed. The focus on Atwood's later works has made space for essays on new topics, such as an analysis of the new Atwood genre of short fiction in *Murder in the Dark* and *Good Bones*, a first essay on *The Robber Bride*, and an interdisciplinary essay on *The Handmaid's Tale* in novel and film.

Two books from 1996 should also be noted: Sonia Mycak's *In Search of the Split Subject: Psychoanalysis, Phenomenology, and the Novels of Margaret Atwood* and Coral Ann Howells's *Margaret Atwood*, which are studies as different from each other as Davey's and Rosenberg's twelve years earlier. Like Davey, Mycak sets out to challenge some received critical opinions, this time regarding Atwood's "violent dualities" in identity formations, and her book presents a densely argued theoretical investigation into the recurrent motif of the "divided self" as it is represented in six of Atwood's novels from *The Edible Woman* (1969) to *The Robber Bride* (but excluding *Surfacing* and *The Handmaid's Tale* for reasons she explains in an appendix). Her book is the epitome of 1990s psychoanalytical criticism, pervaded by the vocabulary of psychoanalysis and phenomenology and containing a formidable glossary of terms like "castration complex," "the imaginary," and "the mirror stage." It offers a precise clinical examination of the ways in which identity is "dislocated, alienated, splintered, and split" (Mycak 9) and though later Atwood critics have not followed Mycak's example, they have drawn selectively from her insights. By contrast, Howells presents a more reader-friendly survey of Atwood's fiction up to *Cat's Eye*, tracing patterns of development and continuity in Atwood's refigurations of "topical topics" like wilderness, survival and environmental issues, the female body, the gothic, and power politics. Taking as her starting point that Atwood is first and foremost who is captivated by language's endless possibilities, Howells focuses on Atwood's textuality and her continuing challenge to generic limits of narrative. As Howells writes, "Atwood is an extremely versatile writer, and in every novel she takes up the conventions of a different narrative form—Gothic romance, fairy tale, spy thriller, science fiction or history—working within those conventions and reshaping them" (6). While Howells refers to a variety of critical approaches, she treats theory lightly in favor of an examination of Atwood's narrative artifice and an evaluation of the significance of shifts in her storytelling perspective. (The book was updated and revised in 2005.)

Any survey of Atwood criticism in the 1990s must end with Reingard Nischik's *Margaret Atwood: Works and Impact* (2000), designed as a retrospective and comprehensive assessment of Atwood's work up to her sixtieth birthday in 1999. The book is arranged in four sections —"Life and Status," "Works," "Approaches," and "Creativity – Transmission – Reception"—and includes contributions from Atwood's literary agents and one of her German translators. The most critically interesting section—entitled "Approaches"—contains seven essays that read Atwood's work through genre theory, gender politics, environmentalism, postcolonialism, myth criticism, and cultural theory. Especially notable as an example of cultural criticism is Lorna Irvine's fascinating essay entitled "Recycling Culture: Kitsch, Camp, and Trash in Margaret Atwood's Fiction." Nischik's volume makes a distinctive and important contribution to international Atwood scholarship at the turn of the century.

2000 and Later

Criticism since 2000 bears witness to Atwood's canonical status, not only within Canada but also in the global literary contexts of feminist, postmodernist, and postcolonial writing, with several books and essay collections recontextualizing her work in broader historical and generic dimensions. Of course, many critics are still focusing their attention solely on Atwood's writings, as comprehensive surveys and selective essay collections continue to appear at a fast rate. In addition, valuable resource materials are provided in Earl G. Ingersoll's updated

Margaret Atwood: Conversations (1990), in *Waltzing Again* (2006), and in Hengen and Thomson's massive reference guide to Atwood criticism, *Margaret Atwood: A Reference Guide 1988–2005* (2007). Indeed, we might have the impression that the Atwood critical industry is continually "in process" of reinventing itself, stimulated by Atwood's own productivity and inventiveness.

The first significant critical collection of the new decade was Sharon Rose Wilson's *Margaret Atwood's Textual Assassinations: Recent Poetry and Fiction* (2003). Its rather sinister title echoes that of *The Blind Assassin*, and the essays included in Wilson's volume link together violence, criminality, and textuality in their explorations of a selection of Atwood's later works. The inspirations for this collection, as Wilson explained in her introduction, were Atwood's own textual "assassinations," a reference to Atwood's disruptions of "traditional genres, plots, narrative voices, structure, techniques and reader expectations" (xiii). This collection pushes the boundaries of Atwood criticism toward ever more sophisticated narrative and poetic analyses, drawing attention to the neglected genre of Atwood's short fictions (sometimes called flash fictions or prose poems), with two essays devoted to them. The emphasis throughout is feminist, postmodernist, and postcolonial as the essays explore Atwood's narrative artifice in discussions of her trickster narrators and the generic hybridity of her later novels. Wilson's essay "Quilting as Narrative Art: Metafictional Construction in *Alias Grace*" is probably the best in the book, offering a formal analysis combined with cultural criticism and archival research. This is not a book for beginners, but for Atwood scholars who are interested in the cutting edge of criticism in this field.

In 2006 Atwood's international appeal was highlighted by the appearance of two new comprehensive essay collections, *Margaret Atwood: The Open Eye*, edited by John Moss and Tobi Kozakewich (which was a selection of papers from the international Atwood symposium held at the University of Ottawa in 2004) and *The Cambridge Companion to Margaret Atwood*, edited by Coral Ann Howells with essays by many international Atwoodian scholars. Both of these collections look at Atwood's works and her biographical and cultural contexts from a variety of different perspectives, and the dialogues between the essays in each volume show how multiple interpretations of a text can be constructed. To take an example, Moss's volume has five essays on *Oryx and Crake* (2003), which is read variously in relation to *Frankenstein* (1818), to feminist theory on absent mothers, to cyborg identities, and to the arts versus science debate. The two essays on that novel in the *Cambridge Companion* take quite different approaches from those in Moss's volume and from each other, one comparing Atwood's revisions of the dystopian genre in *Oryx and Crake* with *The Handmaid's Tale*, and the other seeing *Oryx and Crake* in relation to Atwood's recurrent themes of distorted vision, moral blindness, and survival. Atwood's essays on "Writing Utopia" and "Writing *Oryx and Crake*"—included in *Moving Targets* (2004), *Writing with Intent* (2005), and *Curious Pursuits* (2005)—also provide fascinating authorial insights. Significantly, both Moss and Howells feature essays on Atwood as a celebrity, a topic examined in wider contexts by Graham Huggan in *The Post-Colonial Exotic: Marketing the Margins* (2001) and by Lorraine York in *Literary Celebrity in Canada* (2007).

After forty years of feminist criticism on Atwood, Fiona Tolan's *Margaret Atwood: Feminism and Fiction* (2007) provides a historical analysis, contextualizing Atwood's novels in relation to second-wave feminism as cultural and literary discourse. Tolan combines a historical survey of the main trends in Western feminism since the late 1960s with a critical assessment of Atwood's engagement with that discourse from *The Edible Woman* to *Oryx and Crake*, together with accounts of feminist debates around particular Atwood novels. While acknowledging that Atwood's political interests are by no means confined to feminism, Tolan centers her discussion on "gender, femininity, and sexuality" as "the common political ground that Atwood holds with feminist ideology" (2). The structure of her book is chronological, for as she rightly argues, Atwood's novels are embedded in and responsive to contemporary social contexts, and Tolan's chapter titles signal specific feminist positions appropriate to particular novels, such as "*Life Before Man*: Feminism and Science" and "*The Robber Bride*: The Other Woman in Post-Colonial Discourse." This historicist perspective provides a useful framework for situating Atwoodian feminist criticism, and concludes that "the feminism to be read in Atwood's novels is not the feminism that is to be discovered in feminist textbooks" (3).

Two recent books published in 2009 have expanded generic approaches to Atwood's work in important new ways: *Margaret Atwood and the Female Bildungsroman* by Ellen McWilliams and *Engendering Genre: The Works of Margaret Atwood* by Reingard Nischik. McWilliams approaches Atwood's revisions of the traditionally masculine genre of the bildungsroman from a historical perspective combined with narratological, feminist, and postcolonial perspectives, arguing that Atwood's use of the form represents "the coming of age of a writer, a genre, and a national literature" or, in other words, "Atwood's reclamation of a colonized national and female identity" (1). The book is structured chronologically, beginning with a survey of the German and British foundations of a genre that Atwood inherited, followed by chapter studies of individual fictions from *The Edible Woman* to the short stories in *Moral Disorder* (2006). According to McWilliams, Atwood's renegotiation of the bildungsroman literary model in her autobiographical fictions illustrates a developmental pattern of identity formation and transformation specific to Atwood's individual protagonists and to Canada's emergent national narrative over the past forty years. Nischik's study is far more wide-ranging. In her interdisciplinary study, Nischik adds layers of complexity to debates over the relation between gender and genre as she focuses on Atwood's writings, her cartoons, and comic art (in her mid-1970s *Kanadian Kultchur Komix* and early 1990s *Book Tour Comics/Comix*), and the Hollywood film adaptation of *The Handmaid's Tale*. Nischik's discussion ranges across texts from all Atwoodian genres and though her major concerns are with Atwood's subversions and transformations of genre conventions, her approach is also language centered as she pays close attention to the effects of gender-sensitive linguistic variants within various genres. Two chapters actually open up unfamiliar Atwood genres to critical view in a detailed analysis of the prose poems and short fictions together with a groundbreaking illustrated critical survey of Atwood's comic art and its political implications. This study is the most thorough to date on the stylistic and formal effects of Atwood's gendered perspective on her narrative art.

Assessments, reassessments, and innovations tend to be the main characteristics of Atwood criticism at the present time. J. Brooks Bouson's edited collection *Margaret Atwood: The Robber Bride, The Blind Assassin, Oryx and Crake* (2010) offers nine new critical reevaluations of these three post-1990s novels. Highlighting Atwood's tricksterish narratives as they engage with postmodernist narrative analysis, these essays offer investigations of Atwood's use of gothic parody and magical realism in her works and also discuss her apocalyptic imagination, her environmentalism, her incorporation of trauma in the creation of her characters in Laurie Vickroy's "You're History: Living with Trauma in *The Robber Bride*," and also the recurrent feature of ekphrasis or phototextuality as Shuli Barzilai explains in her essay, " 'If You Look Long Enough': Photography, Memory, and Mourning in *The Blind Assassin*." Many of these critics also comment on Atwood's critique of contemporary culture and changing social fashions and fears, now related, as Hengen's essay title, "Moral/Environmental Debt in *Payback* and *Oryx and Crake*," suggests. Two other essays by J. Brooks Bouson on Atwood's dystopias should be noted here, one on Atwood's bioengineered posthuman future in *Oryx and Crake* (Bouson 2004) and the other on Atwood's return to the postapocalyptic future of *Oryx and Crake* in *The Year of the Flood* (Bouson 2011). *The Cambridge Introduction to Margaret Atwood* by Heidi Slettedahl Macpherson (2010) presents an excellent short critical guide to the Atwood canon and to changing fashions in critical reception, while Gina Wisker's *The Fiction of Margaret Atwood: An Introduction to Critical Views* (2012) follows the Macpherson model with a new study of Atwood's fiction up to *The Year of the Flood* (2009), while also offering an authoritative overview of the key elements and debates in Atwood criticism.

Endings are, as Atwood reminds us, always provisional, just as her novels are open-ended, so I shall end this survey of Atwood criticism since the 1970s by echoing the final words of *The Handmaid's Tale*: "Are there any questions?"

Note

Those interested in doing further research will find the following resources useful: Shannon Hengen and Ashley Thomson's *Margaret Atwood: A Reference Guide 1988–2005* (2007); *Margaret Atwood Studies,* the journal of the Margaret Atwood Society; Atwood's official self-titled website; the Margaret Atwood Society website; and the Atwood papers, which are found in the Thomas Fisher Rare Book Library at the University of Toronto. (Permission is needed to consult these.)

Works Cited

Appleton, Sarah A., ed. *Once Upon a Time: Myth, Fairy Tales and Legends in Margaret Atwood's Writings.* Newcastle upon Tyne, Eng.: Cambridge Scholars, 2008.

Atwood, Margaret. *Curious Pursuits: Occasional Writing 1970–2005.* London: Virago, 2005.

_____. *Moving Targets: Writing with Intent 1982–2004.* Toronto: Anansi, 2004.

_____. *Writing with Intent: Essays, Reviews, Personal Prose: 1983–2005.* New York: Carroll, 2005.

Bouson, J. Brooks. *Brutal Choreographies: Oppositional Strategies and Narrative Design in the Novels of Margaret Atwood.* Amherst: U of Massachusetts P, 1993.

_____. "'It's Game over Forever': Atwood's Satiric Vision of a Bioengineered Posthuman Future in *Oryx and Crake*." *Journal of Commonwealth Literature* 39.3 (2004): 139–56.

_____, ed. *Margaret Atwood: The Robber Bride, The Blind Assassin, Oryx and Crake.* London: Continuum, 2010.

_____. "'We're Using Up the Earth. It's Almost Gone': A Return to the Post-Apocalyptic Future in Margaret Atwood's *The Year of the Flood*." *Journal of Commonwealth Literature* 46.1 (2011): 9–26.

Cixous, Hélène. "The Laugh of the Medusa." Trans. Keith Cohen and Paula Cohen. *New French Feminisms: An Anthology*. Ed. Elaine Marks and Isabelle de Courtivron. Brighton, Sussex, UK: Harvester, 1981. 245–64.

Davey, Frank. *Margaret Atwood: A Feminist Poetics*. Vancouver: Talonbooks, 1984.

Davidson, Arnold E., and Cathy N. Davidson, eds. *The Art of Margaret Atwood: Essays in Criticism*. Toronto: Anansi, 1981.

Grace, Sherrill. *Violent Duality: A Study of Margaret Atwood*. Montreal: Véhicule, 1980.

_____ and Lorraine Weir, eds. *Margaret Atwood: Language, Text and System*. Vancouver: U of British Columbia P, 1983.

Hengen, Shannon. *Margaret Atwood's Power: Mirrors, Reflections, and Images in Select Fiction and Poetry*. Toronto: Second Story, 1993.

Hengen, Shannon, and Ashley Thomson. *Margaret Atwood: A Reference Guide, 1988–2005*. Lanham, MD: Scarecrow, 2007.

Howells, Coral Ann, ed. *The Cambridge Companion to Margaret Atwood*. Cambridge, UK: Cambridge UP, 2006.

_____. *Margaret Atwood*. 2nd ed. New York and Hampshire: Palgrave, 2005.

Huggan, Graham. *The Post-Colonial Exotic: Marketing the Margins*. London and New York: Routledge, 2001.

Hutcheon, Linda. *The Canadian Postmodern: A Study of Contemporary English-Canadian Fiction*. Toronto, New York, and Oxford: Oxford UP, 1988.

_____. *Narcissistic Narrative: The Metafictional Paradox*. New York: Methuen, 1984.

Ingersoll, Earl, ed. *Margaret Atwood: Conversations*. Princeton, NJ: Ontario Rev., 1990.

_____, ed. *Waltzing Again: New and Selected Conversations with Margaret Atwood*. Princeton, NJ: Ontario Rev., 2006.

Macpherson, Heidi Slettedahl. *The Cambridge Introduction to Margaret Atwood*. Cambridge, UK: Cambridge UP, 2010.

McCombs, Judith, ed. *Critical Essays on Margaret Atwood*. Boston: Hall, 1988.

McWilliams, Ellen. *Margaret Atwood and the Female Bildungsroman*. Farnham, Eng. and Burlington, VT: Ashgate, 2009.

Moss, John, and Tobi Kozakewich, eds. *Margaret Atwood: The Open Eye*. Ottawa: Ottawa UP, 2006.

Mycak, Sonia. *In Search of the Split Subject: Psychoanalysis, Phenomenology, and the Novels of Margaret Atwood*. Toronto: ECW, 1996.

Nicholson, Colin, ed. *Margaret Atwood: Writing and Subjectivity: New Critical Essays*. London: Macmillan, 1994.

Nischik, Reingard M. *Engendering Genre: The Works of Margaret Atwood*. Ottawa: U of Ottawa P, 2009.

_____, ed. *Margaret Atwood: Works and Impact*. Rochester, NY: Camden, 2000.

Rao, Eleonora. *Strategies for Identity: The Fiction of Margaret Atwood*. New York: Lang, 1993.

Rigney, Barbara Hill. *Margaret Atwood*. Basingstoke, Hampshire, UK: Macmillan, 1987.

Rosenberg, Jerome K. *Margaret Atwood*. Boston: Twayne, 1987.

Sandler, Linda, ed. *Margaret Atwood: A Symposium*. Spec. issue of *The Malahat Review* 41 (Jan. 1977).

Stein, Karen F. *Margaret Atwood Revisited*. New York: Twayne, 1999.

Tolan, Fiona. *Margaret Atwood: Feminism and Fiction*. Amsterdam and New York: Rodopi, 2007.

VanSpanckeren, Kathryn, and Jan Garden Castro, eds. *Margaret Atwood: Vision and Forms*. Carbondale and Edwardsville: S. Illinois UP, 1988.

Wilson, Sharon Rose. *Margaret Atwood's Fairy-Tale Sexual Politics*. Jackson: U of Mississippi P, 1993.

_____, ed. *Margaret Atwood's Textual Assassinations: Recent Poetry and Fiction*. Columbus: Ohio State U P, 2003.

_____. *Myths and Fairy Tales in Contemporary Women's Fiction: From Atwood to Morrison*. New York: Palgrave, 2008.

Wisker, Gina. *The Fiction of Margaret Atwood: An Introduction to Critical Views*. Basingstoke, Hampshire, UK: Palgrave. 2012.

York, Lorraine M. *Literary Celebrity in Canada*. Toronto: U of Toronto P, 2007.

_____, ed. *Various Atwoods: Essays on the Later Poems, Short Fiction, and Novels*. Concord, ON: Anansi, 1995.

Whodunit: The Mystery/Detective Story Framework in Atwood's *Alias Grace* and *The Blind Assassin*____

Earl Ingersoll

A salient feature of the contemporary novel is its interface with other literary forms. Readers of Margaret Atwood, for example, find her employing narrative strategies from dystopian fiction in *The Handmaid's Tale* (1985) and *Oryx and Crake* (2003), or the memoir in *Alias Grace* (1996) and *The Blind Assassin* (2000). *Alias Grace* and *The Blind Assassin* are also associated with another form of fiction—the mystery or detective novel. Traditionally, the detective story has been consigned to the extraliterary category of popular- or mass-culture fiction, a category that includes well-known popular works such as Dashiell Hammett's *The Maltese Falcon* (1930) and Mickey Spillane's *I, the Jury* (1947). Narrative theorists, however, have pointed out the larger implications of the mystery or detective novel framework. In particular, they have noted the capacity of this framework to open up philosophical and psychological concerns inherent in narratives conventionally read as efforts to discover "the Truth," especially as it is associated with endings.

Because a novel's ending has traditionally determined the reader's perception of meaning, how a novel ends is tantamount to *how* it means. As Brian McHale has argued, modernist fiction such as William Faulkner's *Absalom, Absalom!* (1936) encourages readers to anticipate endings that represent revelations of meaning, in much the same way as detective novels promise answers to the question of "whodunit." But in contemporary postmodernist fiction such as John Fowles's *The French Lieutenant's Woman* (1969), readers often look toward a novel's ending with less confidence that the narrative will let the truth shine forth, since the closures of postmodernist works can be problematic—they may be ambiguous or they may offer multiple endings or even anti-endings. The mystery or detective novel framework is especially helpful in reading the anti–detective novel, *Alias Grace,* and its immediate detective novel successor, *The Blind Assassin,* paired works in which Atwood skillfully shapes her reader's perceptions of meaning by offering a definitive ending to *The Blind Assassin* and an open ending to *Alias Grace.*

Alias Grace and the Enigma of Grace Marks

Atwood's 1996 novel *Alias Grace* is a fictional retelling of a notorious and widely reported nineteenth-century Canadian murder case: the 1843 double murder of Thomas Kinnear and his housekeeper Nancy Montgomery. James McDermott, Kinnear's manservant, was found guilty of murder and executed while Grace Marks, who was sixteen at the time of the crime, was convicted as an accessory to the crime, but her death sentence was commuted to life in prison. After nearly thirty years in prison, she was freed. When Atwood was working on the novel, she carefully examined the historical records on the case, including newspaper stories and eyewitness reports, because she wanted "every major element" in her novel "to be suggested by something in the writing about Grace and her times"("In Search" 174) But because there were a number of gaps and contradictions in the historical record, she was also "free to invent" in her novel and thus, as she remarks, "*Alias Grace* is very much a novel rather than a documentary" ("In Search" 174). Given *Alias Grace*'s focus on a sensational and well-known historical case, readers are confronted at the outset with several possible courses the narrative might take. It might become a historical novel in which Atwood is capitalizing on a grisly murder case to demonstrate to readers that such crimes occurred in her country 150 years ago.[1] On the other hand, *Alias Grace* might be a revisionist story, introducing new evidence to prove that Grace was the innocent victim of a miscarriage of justice. Some readers might be drawn to the latter possibility as the narrative foregrounds the efforts of a "detective," the American physician Simon Jordan, who meets with Grace over a period of months to investigate her involvement in the murders. Once this pursuit of the truth in the whodunit is set in motion, readers are drawn along as detectives, attempting to arrive at "the Truth" before Dr. Jordan discovers

Grace's innocence, preferably, or guilt, if need be. If the popular term *whodunit* is the key concern in the traditional detective story, it is a question without a question mark because it presumes the narrative will, in the end, reveal the guilty person.

Much as mystery or detective fiction has made modern icons of Sam Spade and Mike Hammer, many have argued that the genre has very old and distinguished roots in Western culture. They claim that the very first detective story was *Oedipus Rex* (ca. 427 BC), more commonly identified as *the* classic example of Greek tragedy. To rid his city of a devastating plague, Oedipus accepts the "assignment" of finding out who murdered the king he replaced, only to discover in the end that the murderer he is pursuing is none other than himself. Sigmund Freud may be famous for choosing the Oedipus story to frame his conception of the human psyche, but the father of modern psychology also acknowledged that the psychoanalyst's job is like a detective's: both pay attention to clues, draw conclusions, and attempt to uncover the truth.

It is no coincidence, then, that Atwood chose Dr. Simon Jordan, as the male lead of *Alias Grace.* As a pioneer psychoanalyst, whose energies are invested in the effort to probe the psyche of Grace Marks, he is a fictional forerunner of Freud. Like Freud, Dr. Jordan wants to approach his work with scientific objectivity, but as his interrogation of Grace proceeds, his motives become less objective. For example, he is intent on making a name for himself to start a clinic, and what's worse he eventually finds himself drawn erotically to Grace and begins an adulterous affair with his landlady who is Grace's surrogate. He may tell Grace he is interested only in how her mind works, but if it turns out she was insane when the murders took place, she might be innocent. As a psychoanalyst/detective, Dr. Jordan is driven to find a resolution of the enigma of his subject's innocence or guilt.[2] Even Grace is aware of society's need to identify the person responsible for a crime. "People want a guilty person," she remarks. "If there has been a crime, they want to know who did it. They don't like not knowing" (90–91).

Thus she highlights our immense satisfaction when life imitates the detective story and satisfies our profound desire to believe that the truth can ultimately be ascertained.

The novel's focus is the series of sessions in which Simon Jordan, some sixteen years after the double murders, attempts to gain access to Grace's repressed memories of the events surrounding the murders of her master, Thomas Kinnear, and his housekeeper, Nancy Montgomery. To Simon, Grace's mind is a locked box for which he hopes to find the key. Because Grace claims to have total amnesia of the events surrounding the double murders, Simon's effort—one might even say his *obsession*—is to prod Grace's memories of the cellar where Nancy Montgomery was strangled with Grace's scarf. To further that end, Simon brings root vegetables to their sessions, hoping that a potato or a parsnip will be the "open sesame" to lead her back to memories of the crime scene. Instead, when Grace is asked for her associations, she provides directions for cooking potatoes, or offers sayings such as "Fine words butter no parsnips" (196), thus de-metaphorizing the root vegetables Simon hopes she will associate with the cellar crime scene. Is she a literalist constitutionally unable to see the root vegetables as potential keys? Or, as Simon suspects, is she simply having a laugh at his clumsy efforts to pick the lock of her mind?

Frustrated with her response, Simon—anticipating Freud—asks her to relate her dreams, but she resists. As she says, "I have little enough of my own, no belongings, no possessions, no privacy to speak of, and I need to keep something for myself; and in any case, what use would he have for my dreams, after all?" (101). When Simon responds: "Well, there is more than one way to skin a cat" (101), she plays the literalist: "I am not a cat, Sir" (101). This interchange between the "learned gentleman" Simon and the "humble servant" Grace recalls Hamlet's encounter with the gravedigger who twists the Prince's words to demonstrate he can compete in wit. Grace, however, seems to be performing stupidity as a defensive strategy, encouraging her opponent to delude himself into believing he is smarter than she and thereby exposing his vulnerability to her apparent manipulation:

> And he says, Let us begin at the beginning.
> And I say, The beginning of what, Sir?
> And he says, The beginning of your life.
> I was born, Sir, like anyone else, I say, still annoyed with him. (101)

Having defeated his efforts to lead her down into the cellar of her psyche through association or dream analysis, Grace settles into telling the story of her life in roughly chronological order, inevitably moving toward its climax in the double murders, effecting a compromise between his desire to penetrate her soul and her desire to preserve her psychic virginity.

As Simon eventually acknowledges, Grace becomes a variety of Scheherazade as she tells stories to satisfy a powerful male. The potentially sexual implications of such satisfaction become clearer after she is released from prison and marries Jamie Walsh, who bears such great guilt for testifying against her that he urges Grace to tell him how she suffered as a prisoner, a narrative she knows will arouse him sexually. Given Grace's frequent asides to her listeners/readers, in which she indicates what she is *not* telling Simon, readers may wonder if they *too* are being deluded into believing in their own privileged positions, just as Simon is eventually undone by his misguided belief that he is Grace's superior in intelligence and cleverness. Grace's "memoir," the story of her life, is a synecdoche for Atwood's postmodernist novel *Alias Grace* as a whole. Just as the novel offers a semblance of truth—it is after all based on history, on actual crimes and punishment but is, in fact, no more than a series of texts, or writings—so too Grace's narrative is a fiction that is shaped by her audience—both Simon and the reader—whose desires she satisfies, even though some elements of her account may have no basis in "fact." Like the psychoanalyst/detective Simon Jordan, who must lead his patient/criminal Grace back to her childhood, or wherever her story begins, the reader must assume the role of the detective and sift through Grace's account looking for clues to her innocence or guilt.

Who, then, is this Grace she constructs for Simon and the reader in her autobiography? First, Grace is a survivor and thus an expression of Canada's almost clichéd cultural identity—Survival.[3] An Irish immigrant servant and the daughter of an irresponsible, abusive father and a passive, long-suffering mother, who died at sea when the family was crossing the Atlantic, Grace has survived by her wits. The responsibility of caring for her younger siblings, exacerbated by her mother's death when Grace was twelve years old, has robbed her of a conventional childhood and propelled her into young womanhood at a tender age. At one point she self-consciously departs from her performance of Victorian decorum to share with Simon—he is after all a physician, she tells him—that the onset of puberty meant the horror of unexplained bleeding between her legs. She not so subtly reminds him of her perilous journey through a man's world in which her youthful innocence and beauty exposed her to unwanted advances by men, who were attracted to her because of her virginity but were also ready to rob her of it by force and then pronounce her a slut. Difficult as her mother's death and burial at sea must have been, the death of Grace's friend and fellow servant Mary Whitney, who died from a botched abortion, was even more painful. In her life *story*, Grace describes Mary's death as a classic traumatic event, and Mary's death later appears to be replicated in Nancy Montgomery's murder.

Mary Whitney operates in the narrative, both Grace's and Atwood's, as a powerfully mysterious figure. In a sense, Mary is the fruit of Atwood's creative imagination, a character generated out of the Mary Whitney alias used by Grace Marks as a fugitive. Grace and Mary recall the nineteenth-century fascination with the doppelgänger, or psychological double. Are Grace and Mary, readers might wonder, the twin halves of what the popular imagination conceives of as a split personality? Does Mary have an existence separate from Grace, or is she generated by needs/desires in Grace's psyche? Later nineteenth-century readers were drawn to similarly discordant opposites such as Dr. Jekyll and Mr. Hyde, much as twentieth-century viewers were drawn to figures such as Eve White and Eve Black in the film *The Three Faces of Eve* (1957). Because Grace controls her story, readers do not know with any certainty if Mary is a real person or if she is an alter identity produced by Grace to deal with desires she could not accommodate into her self-concept as an innocent woman. In a culture separating women into the categories of "ladies" and "sluts," how could a "good girl" like Grace deal with desire, sexual or merely acquisitive, without feeling self-divided? And even if Mary Whitney is an actual person, and not simply a character the innocent and vulnerable Grace has constructed, the attachment is so strong that Mary's demise is tantamount to the death of a vital but hidden part of Grace's identity. Mary is daring, savvy, full of street smarts—in short, she is the woman Grace might have been. As an expression of Grace's repressed sexuality, Mary cynically exposes the sexually predatory natures of men, and she engages in the kind of "dirty" talk that the "proper" Grace secretly finds attractive. Even so, Mary is a victim of self-delusion, fooling herself into believing she can trust the "young master," who buys her favors with promises of marriage and a gold wedding band, and then abandons her as a "slut" when she becomes pregnant, because a "lady" would have been a wise virgin and resisted his sexual advances.

The climax of Grace's autobiography toward which Dr. Simon Jordan and the reader are drawn is, of course, the episode of the two murders. Accordingly Simon encourages Grace to provide the key to the locked box of her memory: "It is not a question of your guilt or innocence that concerns me. . . . I am a doctor, not a judge. I simply wish to know what you yourself can actually remember" (307). What she "remembers" is a confusing and ultimately unsatisfying recollection of events that is coupled with vague expressions of her thoughts and feelings. In her account, the inebriated McDermott shared with her his secret plan to attack Nancy with an axe, and strangle her as well, then shoot Mr. Kinnear on his return before running off with the valuables. She indicates McDermott also told her she had to help him and go with him. However, she thought he was "just bragging, about what a fine man he was and what he could do, which was a thing he was prone to when drunk. . . . But at the same time he seemed in earnest, and I was afraid of him; and I had a strong feeling as if it was fated, and it couldn't be avoided, no matter what I did" (309). When Simon asks Grace why she did not warn Nancy, she explains that she did not expect to be believed and that she knew that McDermott would contradict her: "There was only my word for it, which he could easily deny, and say I was nothing but a silly hysterical girl. At the same time, if McDermott really meant it he might have killed the both of us right there and then; and I did not want to be killed" (310). The "best" she could do, she claims, was to delay McDermott's murder of Nancy, hoping Kinnear would return and intervene. In a story frustratingly short on recollections of what happened, Grace's memory ironically allows her to describe in detail the supper she shared with McDermott and Nancy, including the menu. *If*, of course, the menu is not a fiction instead of a recollection.

Desperate for clues as to Grace's guilt or innocence, readers may find themselves examining her narrative with Sherlock Holmes's iconic magnifying glass. In the passage above in which Grace tells Jordan how McDermott seduced/threatened her into the murder plot, she *seems* to unwittingly reveal a couple of hints to her motivation. Terrified that Montgomery would not only fire her but refuse to pay her, and what's worse deny her a reference letter, Grace quickly promised McDermott she would not reveal the secret he was about to share with her. Knowing McDermott's propensity for anger and violence, she must have known that his secret was unlikely to be an effort to sweet-talk Montgomery into keeping them on. Without reflection, Grace gave her promise and hypocritically added she was "bound by it," even though the secret was to commit theft and murder. According to Grace, McDermott told her "he was going to kill Nancy with the axe, and strangle her as well, and shoot Mr. Kinnear when he came back" (309). Granted, Grace is recalling this nightmare experience many years later and her recollection of the actual murder may have shaped her memory of how McDermott proposed to kill Montgomery, but it still challenges the reader's credulity that McDermott claimed ahead of time he would axe and then strangle Montgomery. Was McDermott's committing of the murders influenced by his need to maintain Grace's complicity as an accomplice? Surely if Nancy ordered him and Grace off the property, he could have dispatched the housekeeper with the rifle at any moment before Kinnear returned. If McDermott plans to shoot Kinnear, why would he not also shoot Montgomery? And why would he fail in his effort to axe her to death and be forced to resort to strangulation? Was her murder more impromptu: that is, was it the result of McDermott's anger, fueled by his misogynistic bias that Montgomery, who had seduced a good master with her "womanly wiles," was a dirty slut and therefore she did not deserve the quick, clean death of a bullet? Did McDermott pause in the axe murder and think, If I am going keep Grace as a willing accomplice, I need to implicate her by strangling Montgomery with Grace's scarf, and the grisly butchering of "one of us," a fellow servant who betrayed her social class by offering the master her favors, will be a powerful club to brandish over Grace? Thus it seems less likely that McDermott revealed the details of the murder and more likely that Grace is misremembering to justify her claim that she felt coerced by McDermott to act as his accomplice. She tells Jordan she did not want to die, but she does *not* articulate the greater horror of being butchered, which turned out to be McDermott's method of executing the real object of his rage, the "slut" his master had forced him to obey as his "mistress." Clearly this is no proof of Grace's culpability and even if she was an unwilling accomplice, who of us would not say, "There, but for the grace of God go I—and most of humanity?"

Recounting the visit of the young Jamie Walsh the next afternoon, Grace again describes the menu and the good time she and Nancy had singing, accompanied by Jamie's flute, with McDermott present as a scowling observer. Tellingly Grace recalls: "We sang *The Rose of Tralee*, and I remembered Mary Whitney, and wished very much that she was there, as she would know what to do, and would help me out of my difficulties" (311). That night, she insists, she *did* warn Nancy: "McDermott wants to kill you," but apparently not persuasively, because Nancy laughed it off: "I expect he does. I would not mind killing him, either" (312). Grace says she remembers Mary appearing to her in a dream before waking in sorrow at having lost Mary once again. The question is: Was Mary's appearance more than a dream? Was the dream Grace's strategy for pointing the finger at Mary as the figure who took over her personality, and, as "Alias Grace," helped murder Nancy as McDermott's accomplice? Grace recalls another dream, which seems to describe the actual murder scene:

I saw Nancy, on her knees, with her hair fallen over and the blood running down into her eyes. Around her neck was a white cotton kerchief printed with blue flowers, love-in-a-mist, and it was mine. She was holding out her hands to me for mercy. . . . I wanted to run to her and help her, but I could not (313–14).

When the confused Simon asks if she dreamed this episode before Nancy's death, Grace confirms she did, and it was this recurring nightmare that got her consigned to the insane asylum. "They said they were not dreams at all. . . . They said I was awake. But I do not wish to say any more about it," she remarks to Simon (314). Grace also insists that she did not actually see either murder committed, that she cannot remember parts of what happened, and that she fainted when McDermott shot at her. Thus Grace *needs* to misremember McDermott telling her he *planned* to axe and then strangle Nancy, or else Jordan would legitimately ask how she could have known about events she did not witness, unless McDermott bragged about Nancy's murder while they were fleeing to the border.

"Sooner or later we will get to the bottom of it," Simon Jordan tells Grace, to which she responds, "I hope so, Sir. . . . It would be a great relief to me, to know the whole truth at last" (320). If in his detective role Simon assures Grace that he will help her uncover the "whole truth," it is crucial that this is the last session in which we can be certain that Simon is present while Grace is speaking. As Grace completes her story, she describes her departure with McDermott through to her awaking in the hotel room in Lewiston, New York, where the two were apprehended by the authorities and taken back to Toronto. Surprisingly the two fugitives, even Grace the supposedly coerced accomplice, meekly allow themselves to be taken back to Canada, even though their pursuers "had no real authority," as she later realizes (354). But indeterminacy plagues Grace's narration of these events, since careful examination reveals no evidence of Simon's presence as Grace is speaking. The last segment of Grace's story begins with her assertion that "Dr. Jordan has gone off to Toronto" and quickly proceeds to a hypothetical encounter in which she imagines what she "could say" to Simon (353). Thus, as Grace's storytelling continues—but outside its earlier logical construct of having a listener—it becomes a variety of soliloquy. Any hope that Simon's absence will expedite the reader/detective's learning anything from Grace's revelation is eventually eliminated by her proceeding just as though he were there. The reader begins to suspect Grace is telling her story to provide herself with not *the* truth, but *a* truth she can live with. And these suspicions are reinforced in Simon and Grace's last encounter during the hypnosis session in which he asks her questions while the lid of her consciousness supposedly has been lifted to expose her unconscious. If, however, readers, as frustrated detectives, anticipate that the hypnosis scene will uncover "the whole truth at last" from Grace, they are about as deluded as Mary Whitney was when she believed that the "young master" would marry her and give their child his name.

The dramatic scene of Grace's hypnosis is at least doubly staged. It is a quasi-scientific experiment in which a stage hypnotist is offering the psychoanalytic detective Dr. Simon Jordan[4] a key to penetrate the psyche of a notorious murderess while an audience of detectives looks on. It may also be staged by the hypnotist Dr. Dupont whom Grace knew earlier as Jeremiah the peddler. In that earlier guise, Dupont once told Grace she was "one of us," presumably someone with psychic powers. Jeremiah also proposed that Grace join him as a stage performer and presumably become his lover. Additionally Dupont and Grace are alone together before the hypnosis session and could well have discussed how they would perform this experiment. Yet this can be no more than conjecture on the reader's part because what has become *Atwood*'s story offers no substantial evidence of collusion between Dupont and Grace.

Presumably while Grace is under hypnosis, Mary Whitney exposes herself as Grace's alter identity or double. To muddy the waters further, Atwood's title itself tantalizingly suggests that Grace has become Mary's alias, either as a spirit/demon that captured Grace's soul or as the other that Grace was transformed into under the pressure of participating in murder to avoid becoming another of McDermott's victims. Burkhard Niederhoff argues that performing the role of Mary and talking dirty as Mary did by making lewd comments about another woman's "furry mousehole" (400) would have required more acting ability than readers can expect from Grace ("Ghosts" 131). But what Niederhoff ignores is that after Mary's death, Grace becomes a full-time performer and acts the way others expect her to. He also underestimates how traumatized Grace was by Mary's death. Moreover, the fact that Grace lost Mary soon after losing her mother might explain why she adopted Mary—a woman who could perform the role of the obedient servant while sleeping with the son of the mistress—as a role model.

Janice Fiamengo, in her response to Niederhoff's essay,[5] finds three mutually exclusive options for interpreting Grace's behavior: that Grace is a schizophrenic and so has no awareness of what she might have done while the murders took place; that she is a "deceptive sociopath," who could knowingly murder without guilt or remorse; or that she is a victim, who is trying to survive. Fiamengo's approach of mutual exclusivity may be attractive because it offers an answer of a kind, similar to the anticipated solution to the whodunit. Atwood herself appears to contribute to this sense of a potential definitive answer. For even though she insists that the "true character of the historical Grace Marks remains an enigma" (Author's Afterword 463), Atwood also comments that while she is not saying that there is "no truth to be known," she, nevertheless, has to conclude that "although there undoubtedly was a truth—somebody did kill Nancy Montgomery—truth is sometimes unknowable" ("In Search" 175). In this way, Atwood seems to be confirming Fiamengo's structuralist logic that there is a truth that could be determined. There may, however, be a more interesting poststructuralist approach to the enigma of Grace Marks, one that finds the borders between Fiamengo's options much less solid.

It is conceivable that Grace's schizophrenia resulted from psychic trauma—from the stress of her utter helplessness in her relationship with the psychopathic McDermott, who, if he had not killed Kinnear and Montgomery, might have killed someone else, or if he had safely escaped to the United States might have killed again. It is hardly a stretch to see Grace as McDermott's victim when she has been victimized by virtually everyone else she has encountered, including Mary, who encouraged Grace to believe she was not so much innocent as naive or stupid. As Grace indicates after her release from prison, it is paradoxically victims, not victimizers, who cause trouble. But if Grace *was* a schizophrenic, what made her illness go away? If she was a deceptive sociopath, wasn't she also, at least in part, a victim surviving as best she could while contending with the murderous psychopath McDermott?

In this detective story, the reader/detective comes back to the novel's prologue, "Jagged Edge," in which Grace remembers telling Simon about the peonies she saw while being escorted by the prison guard. These peonies recall the flowers she associates with Nancy. But peonies do not bloom in April, and touching them confirms they are cloth.

In a similar way, as she recalls Nancy "on her knees, with her hair fallen over and the blood running down into her eyes," the image of the bloodied Nancy "scatters into patches of colour, a drift of red cloth petals" (6). The cloth petals are not real but fabrications or texts, like the graphic representations of quilting patterns with which each section of the novel begins. Similarly this novel suggests that "history" also is a text, a quilt, or a bouquet of cloth, or *text*-ual peonies. Detective stories draw us into believing we will find what is frequently undiscoverable in our experience—"the Truth." Thus, paradoxically, cloth peonies are real because they confront us with our immersion in textuality—in the stories we fabricate individually and collectively to survive.

The Blind Assassin and the Mystery of the Human Heart

Because readers of *Alias Grace* are left at the end as uncertain of Grace's culpability as they were at the beginning, those who have just finished *Alias Grace* may suspect that Atwood, once again, is launching her readers on a frustrating pursuit for the truth when they read the provocative opening sentence of her 2000 novel, *The Blind Assassin*: "Ten days after the war ended, my sister Laura drove a car off a bridge" (1). The elderly narrator of *The Blind Assassin*, Iris Chase Griffen, quickly offers sufficient details and conclusions to draw readers into her narrative: The car belonged to Iris, and she does not believe the death was an accident, implying it was suicide. Immediately the reader becomes an observing detective, confronting questions such as: Why does Iris think Laura's death was not an accident? What precipitated Laura's suicide? Was anyone implicated in the suicide? Because Iris alone appears to know what we want to know, readers may worry that this novel could be yet another *Alias Grace* in which they wait with waning hope for disclosures that never come.[6]

Readers' anxieties are not diminished by elements in *The Blind Assassin* that are reminiscent of the earlier novel. Once again the author has delegated responsibility for the narrative to a central character who may know more than she discloses about a death that occurred many years earlier. Even more so than *Alias Grace, The Blind Assassin* is a collection of texts, which presumably have been left by Iris, along with her memoir, in her steamer trunk, Iris's hope chest for the hereafter. Some of them, such as the various newspaper articles that Iris includes in her account, purport to be historical, or "real," while others, such as the science fiction episodes in Laura's romance novel, are blatant fabrications. Iris is more likely to have read these newspaper clippings than Grace is to have read the outside texts used in *Alias Grace*—such as newspaper stories and excerpts from Susanna Moodie's books about the double murders. But the newspaper stories are similarly external to Iris's memoir as is *The Blind Assassin* romance novel, which, as readers eventually learn, was authored by Iris but published under Laura's name. Thus in *The Blind Assassin,* Atwood offers another mélange of texts, recalling the patchwork quilting of *Alias Grace.*[7]

In contrast to the story Grace is making up for Simon Jordan, Iris is engaged in a more overt effort to explain/justify herself, and, in confessing, to set the record straight. One factor that enhances readers' confidence that Iris knows the truth and will eventually reveal it is the couching of her storytelling in a firmer, more empirically based, narrative framework. Not only is Grace speaking her story, but she continues to "speak" even when her listener/audience, Simon, is absent. Grace's circumstances replicate Offred's in *The Handmaid's Tale,* another oral discourse purportedly recorded after the fact but as though Offred were speaking while still in Commander Fred's household. In contrast Iris is *writing* her memoir with eventually one reader in mind, her granddaughter Sabrina, the sole survivor of the family's tragic self-destruction.

Other factors in Iris's storytelling impinge upon the substantiality and credibility of her narrative. When she begins to write her memoir, she is eighty-two, and has a weak heart. Given that she is writing her memoir as an appeal for her granddaughter's understanding and love, Iris certainly has her work cut out for her since she has been no sentimentalized Nana. Iris is racing with time to end her story before Time puts an end to her: "I hasten on, making my way crabwise across the paper. It's a slow race now, between me and my heart, but I intend to get there first. Where is there? The end, or *The End*. One or the other. Both are destinations, of a sort" (222–23). Toward the end, as she sits writing in her garden, readers can imagine her heart stopping and the pages of the manuscript blowing in the wind. Because her story is in our hands as *The Blind Assassin*, however, the manuscript, which she stored in her steamer trunk and willed to Sabrina, must have ended up in the hands of her granddaughter, who had it published. Similarly Iris's advanced age and ill health cut both ways regarding the truth she will tell. Because Iris is leaving her memoir as a legacy to her estranged granddaughter, should she tell all or should she attempt to show herself in the most flattering light? And since writing her memoir also affords her the opportunity to seek revenge on those who victimized her, will Iris have any more objectivity than the rest of us would in remembering those who did her wrong?

These elements set the parameters for the reader's detective work in moving through the saga of the Chase family that Iris constructs to explain why her sister killed herself. Iris's story begins with her parents' generation. Prosperous upper-middle-class Canadians, her parents enjoy the affluence created by her entrepreneur grandfather's founding of the Chase Button Factory. The fall of the Chase family is precipitated by the catastrophe of World War I, as the innocence and comfort of the pre-war years are followed by the colossal death and destruction of the war. Captain Norval Chase, Iris's father, just barely survives the calamity that killed his two soldier brothers and their heartbroken father, leaving Norval physically and psychologically scarred for life. Adding to the Chase family tragedies is the death of Iris's mother in childbirth,[8] which leaves the motherless Laura and Iris unprotected from the men's world, eventually represented by Richard Griffen, the evil capitalist, who admires Hitler. And the two sisters become rivals when, as young women in the 1930s, they both fall in love with Alex Thomas. Called an "armchair pinko" (188) by Richard, Alex is a union organizer and a believer in socialism, an increasingly attractive ideology at a time when the Depression had left many people unemployed and thus exposed to the evils of capitalism.

Following a decade of false prosperity in the 1920s, the Chases in the 1930s face the devastating economic collapse of the Great Depression, another consequence of the war. Almost broken in spirit, the embattled Norval Chase struggles to save the family's fortune and his employees' jobs in a world where new technology and foreign competition make it impossible to survive. Rather than downsize his operations, the benevolent Chase keeps all his workers on the payroll, and the family business collapses. The outcome is the "sacrifice of the virgin"—Norval marries off his eighteen-year-old daughter Iris to the wealthy industrialist Richard Griffen, who is twice her age.

Iris sacrifices herself to marry Richard in the hope of saving the Chase factories. Instead, Richard closes the factories and Iris's brokenhearted father drinks himself to death. "I'd married Richard for nothing, then—I hadn't saved the factories, and I certainly hadn't saved father" (314). Married to Richard, Iris becomes subjected to his sexual brutality. Her life as a society wife of the wealthy and respected industrialist Griffen is one of "placidity and order and everything in its place, with a decorous and sanctioned violence going on underneath everything" (371). Aware that she is expected to uphold the image of middle-class respectability, Iris plays the role of the upper-class society wife even as she has a secret affair with Alex, who has become a fugitive from the law and must support himself by writing pulp fiction. Accordingly Alex becomes the writer figure in the romance novel *The Blind Assassin*. Published in 1947 under Laura's name, it describes a passionate clandestine extramarital affair between an upper-class society wife and a leftist fugitive who makes a living by writing pulp science fiction and tells some of his sci-fi stories to his lover.[9] Good readers/detectives eventually surmise that this woman is not Laura but Iris, who is trapped in a loveless marriage with the sadistic plutocrat

Richard Griffen. With Iris's prompting, readers may also conclude that the father of Iris's daughter Aimee may be Alex, rather than Richard, when Iris highlights his sister Winfred's surprise that the baby has dark rather than blond hair. The nurse may offer the information that babies born with dark hair might lose it to be replaced by lighter colored hair, but Iris may be preparing readers for the "surprise" of her belief that Alex is Aimee's father. As we become more convinced that Iris, not Laura, is the woman in bed with Alex and also the author of the romance novel, the implications of Iris's involvement in her sister's suicide tease us with their potentially explosive consequences.

As Iris continues to demonstrate her strength as a writer, it becomes easier to figure out why she would have published the romance novel under her sister's name.[10] When Iris finally confesses that she wrote the novel, she says that in writing it—as in the writing of her memoir—she was "recording" what she "remembered" and that she wrote because she wanted "a memorial" for Alex and for herself, insisting also that Laura was her spiritual "collaborator" as she was writing it (512–13). Thus, in writing both her memoir and her romance novel, Iris is intent on leaving written memorials of her own love for Alex as well as Laura's. Further evidence of this supposition is Iris's fascination with yet another memorial to Alex and her love—the iconic photograph of Laura, Alex, and herself. Tellingly Laura is mainly "out of the picture"—all that is visible is her hand in Alex's—while all of Iris is visible. For Iris, this photograph represents Eden before the Fall, when the three could be, in some sense, one. As a graphic representation of innocent love, the photograph exists outside time, and therefore, outside life. In contrast, life is a story, a journey or movement toward an ending, happy or otherwise.[11]

This love-triangle story ends in tragedy when the loss of Alex whom both women loved precipitates such suffering that essentially neither sister survives. Laura's suicide is mirrored in Iris's self-destructive behavior—the alcoholism and promiscuity that destroy her reputation and turn her into an unfit mother to raise Aimee. Earlier in the memoir,

Iris was concerned with the truth factor in writing, or storytelling: "The only way you can write the truth is to assume that what you set down will never be read. Not by any other person, and not even by yourself at some later date. Otherwise you begin excusing yourself." She continues: "You must see the writing emerging like a long scroll of ink from the index finger of your right hand; you must see your left hand erasing it. Impossible, of course" (283). By implication Iris is admitting that she is an unreliable narrator, caught in a double bind. She could represent the truth but only for the short time before the writing is erased. Additionally the truth factor is rendered problematic by her recognition she is writing for someone, perhaps her nanny's daughter, Myra, or her granddaughter Sabrina. As Atwood pointed out in *Alias Grace*, truth in storytelling gets contaminated by the presence of an audience whose desire shapes the story's truth.

As readers we must not forget Iris's blunt admission of her unreliability as a narrator as she inevitably confronts her *memory* of the events surrounding Laura's suicide, including "the part that still haunts" her (488). If Iris qualifies for tragic stature, this is the scene of her error in judgment that ultimately costs both sisters their lives. When she examines Laura's writings after the suicide, Iris will finally *know* Richard was the father of the aborted fetus, produced from his multiple rapes of his sister-in-law. If we examine the conversation at Diana Sweets where the sisters meet for the final time and Laura fills Iris in on what has happened since they last saw each other, the issue of knowing is rendered highly problematic by the reluctance of both sisters to speak frankly about Laura's relationships with Alex and with Richard.

Once the conversation gets past the expected chitchat and Iris asks where her sister has been living, Laura tells her Halifax: "It was where the ships came in" (484). There may have been a "reason" for her sister's choice of Halifax, but Iris recalls she "shied away from hearing" it, implying her persistent notion that Laura typically acted irrationally. Before the conversation ends, however, Laura reveals the "reason" and the narrative suggests why Iris chose not to "pursue this." Halifax is the seaport to which Laura expected Alex to return after the war. Iris learns that Laura wrote letters from Halifax, but Richard intercepted them, just as he had torn up Reenie's telegrams announcing his father-in-law's death because he hypocritically did not want the news to spoil the honeymoon for Iris. Laura tells her that Richard is "very evil," implying activity more heinous than intercepting letters, but Iris refuses to believe her. To Laura, Richard is so evil that Iris must take Aimee and herself out of his house, but Iris says her daughter is "pretty stuck on Richard" (485). When Iris tells Laura that Richard said he had to put her away because Laura was delusional and thought she was pregnant, Laura responds, "I *was* pregnant." (485). Unable to credit Laura with no longer being her wacky little sister who believed she could make bargains with God, Iris refuses to believe Laura could have been pregnant, as if her sister is too crazy to know. Iris's incredulity becomes clearer as she asks in a whisper, "Who was the father?" to which Laura fatally and enigmatically responds (like the Delphic Oracle), "If you don't already know, I don't think I can tell you" (486).

Iris's next and equally enigmatic response is delayed by a longish paragraph in which the elderly Iris supplies her supposition that the father was Alex. Tellingly Iris as the narrator never editorializes on her naiveté here in believing that the father has to be Alex because he "was the only man Laura had ever shown any interest in—besides Father, that is, and God" (486). Surely the eighty-two-year-old Iris who is writing her memoir knows that babies result from rape, especially this one, because the elderly Iris who is telling the story already has examined Laura's journal of the rapes. Absent, then, is any evidence that Iris the storyteller senses the dramatic irony in the fact that the "him" she and Laura speak of before Laura's suicide is not the same man. When Iris asks, "Were you in love with him? . . . With— you know," Laura responds, "Not at all. It was horrible, but I had to do it. I had to make the sacrifice. . . . I promised God. I knew if I did that, it would save Alex" (487). Even Laura's additional phrase "from being caught" in response to Iris's "Save Alex from what?" (487) is patently insufficient to dispel Iris's blind refusal to see the obvious. She persists in believing Laura sacrificed herself to Alex who fathered the aborted fetus—which Laura expresses no sorrow in having lost—and all to save Alex from being caught because Richard knew where the fugitive was hiding. Laura, as any perceptive reader should be able to see, is trying to tell her sister the truth. But Iris refuses to *know* it. Instead, when Laura talks about saving Alex, Iris recalls her sister's "crazy" childhood belief that she could bargain with God and save others by sacrificing herself.

The sixty-four-dollar question is "Why?" Is there yet another whodunit in this detective-story framework? Does Iris "whisper" her whodunit question about Laura's aborted child—"Who was the father?" (486)—because it raises the agonizing question of Aimee's paternity? Iris needs to believe that Alex fathered Laura's child because she even more desperately *needs* to believe that Alex also fathered *hers*. Against the implications of what Laura is struggling to tell her, Iris refuses to believe Richard the rapist could have fathered either sister's child. Given that Richard was raping Iris regularly while she was making love with Alex only occasionally, she must believe Alex fathered Aimee as well as Laura's child, even though Laura said, "It was horrible." It may be that Iris "itches" to push Laura "over the edge" (490) because her sister is giving voice to a horrible truth—that much as Iris might want to believe babies are the products of love, they are also, sadly, the sinister fruit of sadistic rape.

This is "the part that still haunts" Iris because more than a half century later she continues to be puzzled by whodunit. Consciously she can reflect on what a loving sister, or even a caring human being, *might have said* that the telegram reporting Alex's death was misaddressed; it should have been sent to Laura. Instead she bludgeons her own sister with the words that became Laura's death sentence: "We'd been lovers, you see—in secret, for quite a long time—and who else did he have?" (488). Who is speaking these words? A less sophisticated woman, such as Grace Marks, might have generated a Mary Whitney to bear the responsibility for them. Looking back, Iris must begin to acknowledge the part she played in driving Laura to commit suicide, but more important what it was that motivated her behavior.

And Laura's "murder" leads to another. When Iris reads Laura's journal of her "affair" with Richard, Iris can no longer shut out the truth her sister was trying to tell her in their final Diana Sweets meeting. Finally, she faces the fact that Richard had sexually exploited Laura by playing on her desperate hope of saving Alex from arrest and possible imprisonment. Ironically Alex might have survived in prison, as he did not in the war. As an act of revenge, Iris publishes *The Blind Assassin* under Laura's name to force Richard out of politics, as the public scandal surrounding the publication of the novel raised questions about Laura's suicide and the clinic where Richard sent her to have the abortion. "You as good as raped her," Iris tells Richard in their final conversation, and soon afterward, Richard is found dead—an apparent suicide—with a copy of *The Blind Assassin* at his elbow (511). Richard's death, although richly deserved, is nothing short of cold-blooded murder, Iris having become "heaven's scourge and minister" in meting out justice to the wicked. Tellingly, however, Iris's memoir begins with the abrupt statement of Laura's death, not Richard's, for his death has no power to "haunt" her, as does Laura's—yet another reminiscence of the earlier novel in which Grace mourns Nancy's death, as she does not Kinnear's. Once again we need to remind ourselves that Atwood has turned over the narrating to Iris, who clearly has *not* been erasing with her left hand.

One of the helpful outcomes of poststructuralist theory has been its analysis of structuralist binaries. Although deconstruction has devolved into a notion of agency in which a poststructuralist deconstructs binaries, Derrida, the "inventor" of deconstruction, thought of binaries as *deconstructing themselves*: that is, it is in the very nature of binaries that they will expose their inevitable hierarchizing of two entities as well as their lack of mutual exclusivity. The end of Iris's story *seems* the polar opposite of Grace's account, which leaves us unsure of her guilt or innocence. We leave Iris's story with greater confidence that we know whodunit because Iris confesses, and yet we are likely to be shocked at Iris's revelation of her guilt. "Without memory, there can be no revenge," Iris writes, describing her memoir as a "commemoration of wounds. . . . Endured, and resented" (508). As readers asking "whodunit?" we recognize, in part, Iris's role as the "blind assassin" of Laura, but we also realize that Iris, like Laura, was blindly sacrificed by her own father, while Laura was knowingly made into a sexual sacrifice by Richard Griffen. In Atwood's whodunit, we find mysteries that persist despite the easy confidence of our knowing that Iris precipitated her sister Laura's suicide by revealing that she was Alex's lover. Similarly Iris exposes her responsibility for Richard's death. But ultimately, Iris's grief, loss, and anger remain to haunt us with the unsolved mysteries of the human heart.

Iris's agency in Laura's demise stays with us after we finish *The Blind Assassin* as a mirror image of our perplexity after we read *Alias Grace*, making Iris's cruel dispensing with her own sister yet another mysterious act like Grace's endlessly enigmatic role in the murder of Nancy Montgomery. When she finishes reading Laura's rape journal, Iris certifies herself as a tragic figure: "That was the whole story. Everything was known. It had been there all along, right before my very eyes. How could I have been so blind?" (500). These are the very words Oedipus, perhaps the original blind assassin, could have uttered in his tragic recognition that the horrors he sought to avert were the very acts he committed in killing a man old enough to be his father and marrying a woman old enough to be his mother.

The traditional mystery/detective novel feeds our hunger for answers, for the illusory security of discovering the truth, while Atwood offers twin novels that resonate for us with the truth of our experience. They give us not mysteries solved, but what the poet W. B. Yeats termed "heart mysteries," revelations of a truth that passes understanding.[12]

Notes

1. Indeed, when Atwood was a student at Harvard in the early 1960s, she discovered that some professors had to hide their nationality and become "closet Canadians" because Americans considered "Canadian-ness" as boring as "mashed potatoes" (Ingersoll, *Conversations* 78).

2. It might be recalled that in the Sophocles play Oedipus relishes the opportunity to solve the mystery of who killed his predecessor because he was chosen king after solving the Sphinx's riddle.

3. In 1972, early in her career, Atwood herself wrote a book—*Survival: A Thematic Guide to Canadian Literature*—in which she identified Canadian culture as centered in "survival."

4. Jordan's given name may allude less to the disciple Simon, called Peter, than to the nursery rhyme "Simple Simon."

5. Niederhoff's *Connotations* essay, "The Return of the Dead in Margaret Atwood's *Surfacing* and *Alias Grace*," provoked a series of responses by scholars such as Fiamengo in *Connotations* 19.1–3 (2009/2010): 53–135.

6. J. Brooks Bouson speaks of *The Blind Assassin* as "an intricately designed literary puzzle" (251).

7. As Bouson notes, in addition to *The Blind Assassin* being a "feminist memoir," Atwood is borrowing from genres such as "the historical novel, the *Künstlerroman*, the female Gothic and romance novel, and pulp science fiction" (252). Hilde Staels adds the bildungsroman to the list of literary forms to which Iris's memoir is indebted (151).

8. Presumably since the Chase Button Factory had been a family business, Mrs. Chase was doing her "woman's work" by attempting to produce a son to take over the business.

9. It should be noted that "sci-fi" is the popular marketing label that most who write SF find abhorrent.

10. Alan Robinson calls his article on *The Blind Assassin* "Alias Laura."

11. Shuli Barzilai does some extensive and provocative "detective work" in examining the ekphrasis of this novel's many photographs, or "phototexts," in an effort to demonstrate Iris was not alone as the "blind assassin" of her sister Laura and that even their father, for example, was implicated in Laura's suicide.

12. In his poem "The Circus Animals' Desertion."

Works Cited

Atwood, Margaret. *Alias Grace*. New York: Doubleday, 1996.

_____. Author's Afterword. *Alias Grace*. By Atwood. New York: Doubleday, 1996. 461–65.

_____. *The Blind Assassin*. New York: Doubleday, 2000.

_____. *The Handmaid's Tale*. New York: Houghton, 1986.

_____. "In Search of *Alias Grace*: On Writing Canadian Historical Fiction." *Writing with Intent: Essays, Reviews, Personal Prose, 1983–2005*. By Atwood. New York: Carroll, 2005. 158–76. (Rpt. of *American Historical Review* (Dec 1998): 1503–16).

_____. *Oryx and Crake*. New York: Doubleday, 2003.

_____. *Survival: A Thematic Guide to Canadian Literature*. Toronto: Anansi, 1972.

Bouson, J. Brooks. " 'A Commemoration of Wounds Endured and Resented': Margaret Atwood's *The Blind Assassin* as Feminist Memoir." *Critique* 44.3 (Spring 2003): 251–69.

Fiamengo, Janice. "Truths of Storytelling: A Response to Burkhard Niederhoff." *Connotations* 19.1–3 (2009/2010): 53–78.

Ingersoll, Earl G., ed. *Margaret Atwood: Conversations*. Princeton: Ontario Rev., 1990.

McHale, Brian. "Change of Dominant from Modernist to Postmodernist Writing." *Approaching Postmodernism*. Ed. Douwe Fokkema and Hans Bertens. Amsterdam and Philadelphia: Benjamins, 1986. 53–79.

Niederhoff, Burkhard. "Ghosts, Knowledge and Truth in Atwood: A Guide to Six Responses." *Connotations* 19.1–3 (2009–2010): 126–35.

_____. "The Return of the Dead in Margaret Atwood's *Surfacing* and *Alias Grace*." *Connotations* 16.1–3 (2006/2007): 60–91.

Robinson, Alan. "Alias Laura: Representations of the Past in Margaret Atwood's *The Blind Assassin*." Modern Language Rev. 101.2 (Apr. 2006): 347–59.

Staels, Hilde. "Atwood's Specular Narrative: The Blind Assassin." *English Studies* 2 (2004): 147–60.

Yeats, W. B. "The Circus Animals' Desertion." *W. B. Yeats: The Poems*. Ed. Richard J. Finneran. New York: Macmillan, 1983. 346–48.

From H. G. Wells's Island to Margaret Atwood's Paradice: Bio-perversity and Its Ramifications_____

Shuli Barzilai

> In our efforts to rise above ourselves we have indeed fallen far, and are falling farther still; for, like the Creation, the Fall, too, is ongoing. Ours is a fall into greed: why do we think that everything on Earth belongs to us, while in reality we belong to Everything?
>
> (Adam One, *The Year of the Flood*, 2009)

Tradition and Two Individual Talents

Margaret Atwood's eclectic and extensive reading is evident everywhere in her writing. Nonetheless, as the more than forty works of poetry, fiction, and nonfiction she has published to date indicate, Atwood shows no signs or symptoms of writerly anxiety. Neither the "immense anxieties of indebtedness" that inhibit (mainly) male poets and critics according to Harold Bloom's *The Anxiety of Influence: A Theory of Poetry* (1973), nor the "anxiety of authorship" that afflicts women writers—an acculturated fear that they cannot create—according to Sandra Gilbert and Susan Gubar's *The Madwoman in the Attic* (1979), seems to constitute an obstacle or blocking factor (Bloom 5; Gilbert and Gubar 73). Rather, with varying degrees of explicitness, Atwood frequently pays tribute to her precursors; her works abound with references to writers who have informed and shaped her artistic vision.

So how has Atwood managed to circumvent or overleap these two hypothesized hurdles, both the anxieties of influence and of authorship, which have indeed adversely affected other creators? In addressing this question, my analysis will focus on the ways in which Atwood's 2003 novel, *Oryx and Crake*, simultaneously draws on and reaches beyond one of her eminent precursors: H. G. Wells's 1896 science-fiction novel, *The Island of Doctor Moreau*. In Wells's novel, a shipwreck survivor named Edward Prendick tells the story of how he was rescued by a boat carrying an odd assortment of animals and, then, was left on a remote island together with the boat's other passengers and cargo. The island is home to Doctor Moreau, a brilliant physiologist whose notoriously cruel experiments on animals forced him to leave England— "The doctor was simply howled out of the country" (34)—and continue his attempts to create human organisms out of nonhuman ones in relative seclusion. Wells wrote his novel during a period when animal vivisection (from the Latin *vivus*, "alive," and *sectio*, "cutting") was a highly contested issue throughout Europe. Indeed, two years after the novel's publication, the writer and suffragette Frances Power Cobbe founded the British Union for the Abolition of Vivisection, an animal protection and advocacy organization that is active to the present day ("Caine"). Atwood's novel, as I shall argue, departs from the topical literary model of *The Island of Doctor Moreau*, even while adhering to many of its prominent motifs and narrative components: the figure of the mad scientist (Wells's Doctor Moreau and his analogue, Atwood's Crake), the ruthless creation of hybrid animal species (such as hyena-swine in *The Island* and pigoons in *Oryx and Crake*), and the hubris, the extreme self-confidence and arrogance, displayed in the scientific endeavor to (re)make humankind, among other analogies.[1]

One of the immediately notable ways in which Atwood "swerves"— to recall Bloom's term—or moves away from Wells's classic dystopian fiction is by transposing the contained and isolated kingdom of Doctor Moreau into a global postapocalyptic setting. In Atwood's revisionary setting, Crake's genetically modified hemorrhagic virus, secretly embedded in the "BlyssPluss" pill, has wiped out almost all the population on the globally warmed and environmentally devastated planet. Crake has replaced humanity with his bioengineered hominids, the "Children of Crake" or "Crakers," an environmentally friendly and peaceable people who are adapted to eat only plant-based foods and have sexual intercourse during limited breeding seasons. The scale of the apocalypse imagined in *Oryx and Crake* thus encompasses not only the systematic destruction of most human and nonhuman animals but also of the habitable environment: "On the eastern horizon there's a grayish haze, lit now with a rosy, deadly glow. . . . [T]he distant ocean grinding against the ersatz reefs of rusted car parts and jumbled bricks and assorted rubble sound almost like holiday traffic" (*Oryx* 3). The nostalgic image of "holiday traffic" in the novel's opening paragraphs evokes a world that no longer exists. This destruction occurred not as a result of the invasion of Earth by malevolent aliens from Mars, as in Wells's *The War of the Worlds* (1898), but rather as a result of the corruption and degeneration that took place within the human breast or, if you will, the human beast.

But before further presenting the multiple textual intersections of *The Island of Doctor Moreau* and *Oryx and Crake*, I want to note several parallelisms that mark the literary careers of H. G. Wells (1866–1946) and Margaret Atwood (b. 1939). Wells in his day, like Atwood in ours, was not only a prolific and widely read author who published in many genres—realistic fiction, speculative or science fiction, short stories, essays, book reviews, and other nonfiction—but also a public figure and an active member of International PEN, the writers' organization that promotes intellectual cooperation among writers and freedom of expression everywhere. For the purposes of this analysis, however, two correlations between these authors are particularly relevant.

First, Atwood may be said to share Wells's view of history as what he called "a race between education and catastrophe" (Wells, *Outline of History* 1169). Both authors often address social and political issues in their writings and, relatedly, some of their works have a prophetic or predictive dimension. In 1901, for instance, Wells published his first major work of nonfiction, *Anticipations of the Reaction of Mechanical and Scientific Progress Upon Human Life and Thought*, a collection of essays describing "the possible effects of scientific and technological progress in the twentieth century" (Parrinder x). In his futuristic novel of 1933, *The Shape of Things to Come*, Wells predicted the outbreak of a second world war in Europe and described its catastrophic aftermaths, including the collapse of central governments and a plague that decimates the human population and nearly wipes out civilization.[2]

The rise of business conglomerates in place of failing governments, worldwide environmental decline, and finally a "plague" in the guise of the BlyssPluss pill cause comparable damage in *Oryx and Crake*. In general, the prophetic-cautionary mode in which Wells often wrote during the first half of the twentieth century corresponds to a prevailing mode in Atwood's writings during the second half of the twentieth and early twenty-first centuries.

Second, although Wells and Atwood are innovative writers who tend to experiment with various forms of narrative, they also do not hesitate to take their precursors' works as avowed models. Just as Atwood's *The Penelopiad* (2005) rewrites Homer's account of Penelope and her maids in *The Odyssey*, so a century earlier Wells's *A Modern Utopia* (1905) brought into play Sir Thomas More's *Utopia* and Plato's *Republic*.[3] In other words, both writers do not appear to be afflicted by their literary heritage, by the burden of their belatedness, but rather openly mine the past for their materials. Moreover, as their prolific output shows, the anxiety of authorship, of being unable to create, that inhibits some writers (especially women writers, as Gilbert and Gubar would argue) has not acted as a blocking agent on them. A case in point is the many ways in which *Oryx and Crake* sustains a dynamic "conversation" with *The Island of Doctor Moreau*.

Variations on the Romance, Fable, and Adventure Story

Two years after the publication of her 2003 novel, Atwood wrote an "Introduction" to the Penguin Classics reissue of Wells's 1896 novel that holds a mirror up to *Oryx and Crake*—that is, in presenting "Ten Ways of Looking at *The Island of Doctor Moreau*," Atwood also suggests to the reader diverse ways of looking at her own recent dystopian narrative. Wells's novel, she observes in the "Introduction," has generic ties with at least three literary traditions: the romance, the fable, and the adventure story (xiii–xix). As Atwood discusses these genres, explicitly in relation to *The Island of Doctor Moreau* and, I am proposing, implicitly in relation to *Oryx and Crake*, a common factor emerges: the crucial place of nonhuman animals in both fictional worlds.

To begin with the romance genre, Atwood delineates this venerable literary form as follows: "Typically a romance begins with a break in ordinary consciousness, traditionally signaled by a shipwreck. . . . Exotic climes are a feature, especially exotic desert islands; so are strange creatures" ("Introduction" xix). Atwood's interest in what characteristically happens in romance is, of course, not purely academic; rather, she examines patterns established in the past as points for her present departures. Knowing the generic rules is necessary for making exceptions.

In *Oryx and Crake*, for example, the focalizer or central viewpoint character, Snowman (formerly known as Jimmy), is analogous to Wells's focalizer, Edward Pendrick, insofar as he is the survivor of a kind of shipwreck: a global catastrophe or world-wreck. In his preapocalyptic life, Jimmy was unsuspectingly vaccinated by Crake so that he would survive the pandemic and serve as a caretaker for the Crakers during their adjustment to the "real" postapocalyptic world. The climes and times are certainly exotic in Atwood's novel, and the break in Snowman's consciousness is indicated not only by his change of name but also by his increasing loss of language and memory: "'In view of the mitigating,' he says. He finds himself standing with his mouth open, trying to remember the rest of the sentence" (*Oryx* 5). But perhaps most strikingly, *Oryx and Crake* retains the romance element of "strange creatures," an element integral to the plot and thematic orientation of *The Island of Doctor Moreau*—with some noteworthy differences examined later in this discussion.

Despite a surface realism, an initial air of probability, *The Island of Doctor Moreau* invites classification not just as a romance but also as a fable. Wells is a fabulist or teller of fables, in Atwood's view, because his narrative contains "something fabulous or invented": namely, "no man ever did or ever will turn animals into human beings by cutting them up and sewing them together again" ("Introduction" xiii–xiv). To this observation, it may be added that Wells's novel belongs, or seems to belong, to the specific genre of the animal fable since it features nonhuman talking creatures: "The characters of fables . . . are usually animals who act and talk just like people whilst retaining their animal traits" ("Aesop's Fables"). These animals, however, speak like people not simply due to compliance with the literary convention in which it is normative; more complexly, their speech is due to a radical departure from this convention.

In the nightmarish world of Wells's *Island*, the talking animals are the outcome of the surgical invasion and refashioning of their brains. "I took a gorilla," Doctor Moreau tells Prendick, his appalled yet riveted listener, and then: "All the week, night and day, I moulded him. With him it was chiefly the brain that needed moulding; much had to be added, much changed. . . . I taught him the rudiments of English, gave him ideas of counting, even made the thing read the alphabet" (76). Clearly alluding to the biblical seven days of creation, he magisterially—and blasphemously—asserts: "I will make a rational creature of my own" (78). Like Atwood's Crake, Moreau is a man with an unholy mission; unlike Crake, however, he does not have modern genetic science at his disposal.

Against this scientific background, it would seem that *Oryx and Crake* cannot be designated a fable per se. The strange creatures it contains are not "fabulous" and beyond the realms of possibility. On the contrary, the pigoons, wolvogs, rakunks, and other hybrid creatures that populate its fictional landscapes are based on actual transgenetic experiments being conducted in major laboratories throughout the world.[4] Such nonhuman animals uphold Atwood's insistence that *Oryx and Crake* be considered "a speculative fiction, not a science fiction proper," for the reason that "it invents nothing we haven't already invented or started to invent" ("Writing *Oryx*" 285). Nonetheless, I would argue, *Oryx and Crake* does belong to the Aesopian tradition of fables in one significant respect. Like *The Island of Doctor Moreau*, Atwood's narrative, too, is "meant to convey some useful lesson" ("Introduction" xiv). The ethical dimension that pervades the two novels entails an analogous cautionary message: lack of care, consideration, and respect for nonhuman animals and, generally, for all nature leads to desolation and catastrophe. In fact, "A Catastrophe" is precisely the title of the climactic chapter in which Doctor Moreau meets his dark and well-deserved destiny.

On the seemingly lighter side, *The Island of Doctor Moreau* and *Oryx and Crake* are both adventure stories. Such stories in bygone days, as Atwood points out, would be likely to feature heroes battling with "fantastic monsters—dragons, gorgons, hydras" ("Introduction" xvi). In Wells's adventure story, however, these fanciful monsters have been replaced by others—the Beast People—engendered by means of the "agency that was seen by many in late Victorian England as the bright, new, shiny salvation of mankind: Science" (xvi–xvii). Once again, the parallels between *The Island of Doctor Moreau* and *Oryx and Crake* are apparent. Atwood envisions a future world abounding in fantastic and yet feasible "monsters" that are the creations of dedicated (albeit also well-remunerated) scientists. At the Watson-Crick Institute, for instance, the mascot stationed at the gates is a bronze statue of the goat/spider: "one of the first successful splices . . . goat crossed with spider to produce high-tensile spider silk filaments in the milk" (*Oryx* 199). Interesting, the reader might say, quite innovative. But information immediately follows intended to curb her nascent enthusiasm: "The main application nowadays was bulletproof vests. The CorpSeCorps swore by the stuff" (199). These mercenary quasi-military units ruthlessly guard, as their very name suggests, the compounds of the huge conglomerates that have effectively replaced central governments in the preapocalyptic world conjured up in Snowman's memories.

One of the most surrealistic (or hyperrealistic) scenes in *Oryx and Crake* occurs at the Watson-Crick Institute. While visiting a laboratory named "NeoAgriculturals," Jimmy encounters a new life-form so "exotic" that he is unable to identify it: "a large bulblike object . . . covered with stippled whitish-yellow skin"; directly out of this object protrude "twenty thick fleshly tubes, and at the end of each tube another bulb was growing" (*Oryx* 202). In response to Jimmy's horrified inquiry—"What the hell is it?"—Crake matter-of-factly informs him that "[t]hose are chickens": "Chicken parts. Just the breasts on this one. They've got ones that specialize in drumsticks too, twelve to a growth unit." An advantage of such units, from their inventors' point of view, is that "the animal-welfare freaks won't be able to say a word, because this thing feels no pain." The corollary advantage, as Crake also clarifies, is the gross capital gain: "The students at Watson-Crick got half the royalties from anything they invented" (202–3).

Good Thing or Bad Thing? An Interlude

The literal salvation of an increasingly overpopulated world does require the availability of vast food supplies and therefore, perhaps, overcoming an impractical distaste for meat grown in vats and mother's milk extracted from genetically modified cows.[5] What's ethically wrong with hamburgers made in labs, for instance, if it staves off starvation in some parts of the world? What's wrong with implanting human genes in pigs if it produces organs capable of saving lives?

These issues are unlikely to be resolved in any foreseeable future. At this point, however, it is necessary to distinguish the value systems upheld by Wells's and Atwood's respective novels. In *The Island of Doctor Moreau* the vivisection and transmogrification of nonhuman animals into quasi-human monsters in the name of scientific knowledge is unequivocally condemned. It is denounced for the suffering caused to animals as well as for the sacrilege that accompanies Doctor Moreau's attempts at what he proudly terms "man-making" (*Island* 75). As Prendick writes in his retrospective firsthand account: "[Moreau] was so irresponsible, so utterly careless! His curiosity, his mad, aimless investigations, drove him on. . . . I must confess that I lost faith in the sanity of the world when I saw it suffering the painful disorder of this island" (95–96). *Oryx and Crake*, by contrast, presents a more nuanced response to such questions as, "What's ethically wrong with altering pigs, cows, chickens, etc.?" It is a response partly inflected by the shift from vivisection, the actual cutting of or operation on a living nonhuman animal, to the sophisticated technologies of present-day science and partly by the previously unforeseen, and well-nigh unimaginable, beneficial applications of these technologies.

Thus Jimmy's father is part of a research team at OrganInc Farms working on the "pigoon project," a project whose goal is to alter pigs so that they grow viable human organs. The pigoons are genetically upsized—that is, either enhanced or deformed, depending on the perspective—in the process, becoming "much bigger and fatter than ordinary pigs, to leave room for all of the extra organs" (*Oryx* 25). Once perfected, these custom-made organs would become available to those who have need of (and the means to pay for) a new heart, liver, kidney, or whatever. The profit motives that propel this science are publicly, unabashedly acknowledged in the conglomerate's triply punning name: it brandishes the word "organic" together with Organ Farms and Inc(orporated) Farms.

It is therefore unsurprising that Jimmy's father explains the advantages of the "pigoon procedure" to his young son in explicit economic terms: "It [is] much cheaper than getting yourself cloned for spare parts . . . or keeping a for-harvest child or two stashed away in some illegal baby orchard" (*Oryx* 23). On the one hand, as Atwood's collection of newspaper and science articles at the University of Toronto show, her fictive descriptions of the pigoon project draw on the actuality of xenotransplantation experiments aimed at enabling faulty human body parts to be replaced by pig parts.[6] On the other hand, the notion of children "for-harvest," as in "for-sale," also points to a world in which ethical values have broken down, a world in which "spare parts" are reserved for those with money to spare. Through the genetically spliced pigs, chickens, goats, dogs, and other creatures that proliferate in *Oryx and Crake*, Atwood expresses her concerns about the practice of heedless, profit-based bioengineering and experimentation with the human genome. The science leading to a cataclysmic end of human history and ushering in a posthuman future in this speculative fiction could also become the readers' (that is to say, our own) specific future.

A Poetics of Situation and Space

To recapitulate my argument thus far, as *Oryx and Crake* and the "Introduction" to *The Island of Doctor Moreau* demonstrate, Atwood looks back on her precursor's work with an appreciation untrammeled by the dual anxieties of influence and authorship. Tradition seems to be enabling for her individual talent. Playing with and against an earlier text or pre-text, such as Wells's 1896 novel, Atwood closely interweaves it into her posttext.

Several textual elements exhibit this difference-in-similarity. For example, there is the question of the participants in the communication situation represented in each novel. Edward Prendick disappears for eleven months when the *Lady Vain*, the ship on which he is traveling, collides with a "derelict," a ship abandoned at sea. The first-person retrospective account of his adventures after the collision posits the existence of a readership from its opening sentence: "I do not propose to add anything to what has already been written concerning the loss of the *Lady Vain*" (*Island* 7). The narrative that constitutes the published work is found among his papers by his nephew and heir who decides to put "this strange story before the public" (5). Clearly, then, Prendick's story has an audience within the fictional world, even though it remains a silent and inactive one. Recast in the terms of narratology, which studies the forms and conventions of literature, there is a narratee situated at the same narrative level as the narrator in Wells's text. In effect, "All narration . . . presupposes not only (at least) one narrator, but also (at least) one narratee, the narratee being someone whom the narrator addresses" (Prince 7).

In marked contrast to Prendick's narrative situation, in *Oryx and Crake* the one who experiences and recalls the events is his own narratee.[7] That is, Atwood's Snowman has, or believes he has, no potential audience, not now nor in the future. He is not just the survivor of a pandemic but also, insofar as he knows, the last man alive. As Snowman recognizes, for him there would be no point in filling in a logbook like the doomed captain of a ship as it founders in a storm, or in keeping a daily journal like a castaway on a desert island: "Even a castaway assumes a future reader, someone who'll come along later and find his bones and his ledger, and learn his fate. Snowman can make no such assumptions: he'll have no future reader, because the Crakers can't read. Any reader he can possibly imagine is in the past" (*Oryx* 41). So while Prendick's bleak portrayal of himself as "merely a bit of human flotsam, cut off from my resources" also aptly characterizes Snowman's existential situation, their communication situations are radically different (*Island* 17).[8] Moving beyond the tale of Wells's shipwrecked protagonist, in Atwood's postapocalyptic vision, the known world—not only one ship—has been lost.

Additional differences-in-similarity appear in what may be called the poetics of space in *The Island of Doctor Moreau* and *Oryx and Crake*. Specifically, just as Doctor Moreau conducts his gruesome experiments in man-making behind a walled-in enclosure on an island, so Crake fashions his hominid creatures within the "Paradice dome," a sealed-off area inside a self-contained corporative compound. Secrecy is another distinguishing feature of these two enclosures. In the chapter titled "The Locked Door," Doctor Moreau enigmatically refers to the spatial arrangements on his island as follows: "I'm sorry to make a mystery, Mr. Prendick. . . . Our little establishment here contains a secret or so, is a kind of Bluebeard's Chamber, in fact. Nothing very dreadful really—to a sane man" (32). As these secrets are gradually disclosed, it becomes evident that the allusion to "Bluebeard's Chamber" is not only a metaphor for mystery but also for murder and mayhem. Indeed, an intertextual "key" to *The Island of Doctor Moreau* is the gothic fairy tale about a serial killer known as Bluebeard who keeps the bodies of his victims behind the locked door of a bloody chamber.

Given Atwood's devotion to the Bluebeard motif in her writings,[9] I would now propose that a literary blueprint or model for Crake's

Paradice (spelled so that its last syllable rhymes with *vice*) is not only its biblical counterpart in the book of Genesis—a counterpart it reflects with inverted symmetry. Paradice is also modeled after the example of two chambers of horror: the one within the castle of the rapacious Bluebeard, and the other within the ironically named Noble's Island inhabited by the merciless Doctor Moreau. Once again, however, a difference is outstanding in the midst of these spatial-symbolic resemblances: Crake's "chamber," unlike Moreau's, is vast and able to hold all the formidable tools of modern genetic science. These considerably extend the range of his futuristic overreaching.

Recasting the Ancient Mariner

Another complexly resonant intertextual link between Well's romance-cum-morality tale and Atwood's is the figure of the Ancient Mariner. Whereas the legendary story of Bluebeard is expressly mentioned in *The Island of Doctor Moreau*, Samuel Taylor Coleridge's famous poem, "The Rime of the Ancient Mariner" (1798), remains unnamed and implicit. Nevertheless, I suggest that the poem provides a precedent for Prendick's story and, subsequently, for Snowman's on several counts: the events themselves, the act of telling or writing, and their verbal configurations. Moreover, if Atwood's "Introduction" of 2005 is taken into account, a fourth text adjoins this chain of narrative transmission, which extends from the late eighteenth to the early twenty-first centuries.

Beginning with the last or latest link, in section nine of her "Introduction" Atwood proposes a way of looking at *The Island of Doctor Moreau* titled "The Modern Ancient Mariner." After describing the dramatic finale in which Prendick escapes from the island in a sailboat whose arrival borders on the supernatural—as the boat carrying two corpses, one with "a shock of red hair," drifts toward shore, "a great white bird" flies out of it and then circles overhead (*Island* 127–28)— Atwood points to a parallel storyline:

In what other work of English literature do we find a lone man reduced to a pitiable state, a boat that sails without a wind, two death-figures, one with unusual hair, and a great white bird? The work is of course "The Rime of the Ancient Mariner," which revolves around man's proper relation to Nature, and concludes that this proper relation is one of love. ("Introduction" xxv)

In identifying the "Ancient-Mariner-like pattern" that structures the closure of *The Island of Doctor Moreau*, Atwood also notes the thematic relevance for Wells's modern mariner of the "lesson" understood by his precursor at the end of Coleridge's poem: "He prayeth well, who loveth well / Both man and bird and beast. / He prayeth best, who loveth best / All things both great and small" (lines 612–15; qtd. in Atwood, "Introduction" xxv). Although Atwood's essay contains no reference to her own writings and applies these well-known verses only to Wells's novel, they may be said equally to pertain to the *moralité* or moral "bottom line" of *Oryx and Crake*. Furthermore, the same verses arguably encapsulate the lesson to be learned from her other speculative fictions—*The Handmaid's Tale* (1986), *The Year of the Flood* (2009), and stories such as "Freeforall" (1987), "Hardball" (1992), and "Three Novels I Won't Write Soon" (2006)—which variously represent the dire consequences of man's improper relation to Nature.

Having drawn attention to the resemblances between "The Rime of the Ancient Mariner" and *The Island of Doctor Moreau*, Atwood concludes this section of her essay by remarking on a disparity between their protagonists' narrative positions: "the Ancient Mariner is doomed to tell his tale, and those who hear it are convinced by it. But Prendick chooses not to tell, because, when he tries, no one will believe him" ("Introduction" xxv–xxvi). It may be further remarked that the Ancient Mariner's audience is not just convinced but changed by his tale. The Wedding-Guest, at first a most reluctant listener, is left at the end "like one that hath been stunned, / And is of sense forlorn: / A sadder and a wiser man / He rose the morrow morn" (Coleridge

622–25). The prospect of effecting a change in those to whom the story is told—be they situated inside the fictional world (the narratee) or outside it (the real reader)—constitutes a strong motive for both the storyteller (the narrator) and the actual narrative agent (the real author). Even Prendick, who finds that "no one would believe me, I was almost as queer to men as I had been to the Beast People," does record his traumatic experiences in writing and leaves the document among his papers for his nephew to discover and publish (*Island* 130). Snowman alone is in a dead-end communication situation with no prospective audience other than himself.

These distinctive protagonists (who may be contrastively called "The Ancient Mariner," "The Modern Mariner," and "The Postmodern Mariner") are nonetheless closely related through their verbal patterning. To start with Snowman's idiom and then backshift to his antecedents, I want to recall the chapter simply titled "Voice" at the outset of *Oryx and Crake*. Standing on an empty beach beneath a blank sky, "except for the hole burnt in it by the sun," Snowman looks out on the silent metallic sea and feels the acute absence of other human voices like his own: "'Now I'm alone,' he says out loud. 'All, all alone. Alone on a wide, wide sea.' One more scrap from the burning scrapbook in his head. Revision: seashore" (*Oryx* 10–11). Snowman's poetic "scrapbook" of course reverberates with the Ancient Mariner's sad incantatory words: "Alone, alone, all, all alone, / Alone on a wide wide sea! / And never a saint took pity on / My soul in agony" (Coleridge 232–35). And here is Prendick in "The Man Alone," the final chapter of his adventure, drifting away from the island shore in a sailboat: "The sea was silent, the sky was silent; I was alone with the night and silence" (*Island* 128).

In this reiterative context, the Ancient Mariner's experience of the varieties of silence during his journey should be evoked as well: "We were the first that ever burst / Into that silent sea"; "The ocean hath no blast; / His great bright eye most silently / Up to the Moon is cast"; "The moonlight steeped in silentness / The steady weathercock / And the bay was white with silent light" (Coleridge 105–06,

415–17, 478–80). Rather than a chain of chronologically ordered narratives (1798→1896→2003), perhaps a chamber of echoes more accurately describes these intricate intertextual effects. Intersecting words, images, and storylines continually bounce off, resound, or play with/against each other.

Three Ways of Looking at *The Island of Doctor Moreau* and *Oryx and Crake*

Many other echo effects may be traced between *Oryx and Crake* and the varied intertexts considered in this chapter. The final part of my discussion, however, will focus on what is arguably the most fraught yet important factor that links Atwood's novel to *The Island of Doctor Moreau*—nonhuman, human, and posthuman relations—through three different representations of the issues involved.

1. Pigs and Pigoons

Bearing in mind the lesson at the close of Coleridge's poem, it is plain that Doctor Moreau is not a praying man. Noble's Island, as noted previously, is populated by hybrid creatures surgically "moulded" by his vivisectionist knife. Moreau's animal victims include the hyena-swine, the wolf-bear, horse-rhinoceros, and other strangely altered beasts. Most impressive of all, so to speak, is M'ling: "a complex trophy of Moreau's horrible skill, a bear tainted with dog and ox, and one of the most elaborately made of all" (83). Whereas some creatures are benign and tame (as is Jimmy's pet rakunk), others are extremely dangerous, grudge-bearing creatures. Correspondingly, like the Leopard Man who attacks Doctor Moreau, and like the puma who finally bashes in his brain—the source of her inhuman pain—the pigoons bioengineered for OrganInc Farms attack anything that smells of the human after the pandemic caused by Crake's lethal virus breaks out.

In effect, the pigoons of *Oryx and Crake* may be considered the "brain children" of Doctor Moreau. He thus edifies Prendick about his laboratory procedures: "it is a possible thing to transplant tissue from one part of an animal to another, to alter its chemical reactions and methods of growth . . . and indeed to change it in its most intimate structure" (*Island* 72). Moreover, he goes on to explain: "the possibilities of vivisection do not stop at a mere physical metamorphosis. A pig may be educated. The mental structure is even less determinate than the bodily" (72–73). To Prendick's expostulation, "the thing is an abomination—," he replies, "To this day I have never troubled about the ethics of the matter. . . . The study of Nature makes a man at last as remorseless as Nature" (75). One of the fascinations of Wells's fin-de-siècle novel for Atwood is quite possibly its uncanny anticipation of modern genetic technologies and the controversies surrounding them.

Be that as it may, the oppositional dialogue between Doctor Moreau and Prendick has its counterpart in a highly charged debate between Jimmy's parents. The occasion that sets off the dispute is his father's return from work one night with a bottle of champagne to celebrate a breakthrough at the lab: "We now have genuine human neocortex tissue growing in a pigoon. Finally, after all those duds! Think of the possibilities for stroke victims. . ." Jimmy, eavesdropping from his bedroom, hears his mother cut in: "More people with the brains of pigs. Don't we have enough of those already?" (*Oryx* 56). From there the argument escalates, and when his father asserts: "We can give people hope. Hope isn't ripping off!" his mother retorts: "You hype your wares and take all their money and then they run out of cash, and it's no more treatments for them" (56–57). In her adversarial view, "this pig brain thing" on which his lucrative job depends is "immoral" and "sacrilegious" because he is "interfering with the building blocks of life"; in his, "It's just proteins, you know that! There's nothing sacred about cells and tissue" (57). The battle continues to rage until doors slam and estrangement ensues. The bitter debate between Jimmy's parents in *Oryx and Crake*—like the intense arguments in my classroom when this scene is studied—remains unresolved. Simple answers are not forthcoming from the complex twenty-first-century world reflected in Atwood's novel.

2. Man-making and Myth-making

After Doctor Moreau's violent death, some of the Beast People demand to know: "Is there a Law now?" Grasping the danger of their impending loss of faith to the doctor's surviving assistants and himself, Prendick steps forward with an irrefutable reply:

> "Children of the Law," I said, "he is not dead. . . . He has changed his shape—he has changed his body," I went on. "For a time you will not see him. He is . . . [sic] there"—I pointed upward—"where he can watch you. You cannot see him. But he can see you. Fear the Law." (*Island* 103)

Because Doctor Moreau has defied the ways of nature (or Nature) and engaged in man-making, Prendick finds himself constrained to practice myth-making. In other words, as a direct result of Moreau's *imitatio dei*—his ungodly imitation of God—Prendick must reinvent and resurrect, as it were, the Father of the Law. Promising death to those who have broken the Law, Prendick commands: "Show us now where his old body lies. The body he cast away because he had no more need of it" (104). The creatures obey and guide him to the inert, bloody body of their tormentor-creator.

The brief scene of Prendick's invention of an afterlife for Doctor Moreau undergoes considerable expansion in *Oryx and Crake*. From Snowman's initial encounter with the Children of Crake and until his final encounters, he addresses their numerous questions ("Who are you? . . . Where have you come from, oh Snowman? . . . Why is your skin so loose?" et cetera) by spinning different tales. It is a side benefit, as he discovers, to the burden of Crake's injunction to look after them: "These people were like blank pages, he could write whatever he wanted on them" (*Oryx* 348–49). The narrative impulse here too, as in the case of Prendick, is generated by necessity—the responsibility Jimmy assumes for the Crakers after their maker's violent death—but also by the pleasures of creative invention. However, a problem emerges for Snowman (as it might for any flesh-and-blood author) in keeping his storylines coherent and continuous, for he is subject to the vicissitudes of his flawed human memory.

Thus, after Snowman returns from his harrowing expedition to the Paradice dome to seek provisions, the Crakers ply him with questions about his "journey into the sky" where, they suppose, he has met with Crake and received a message for them:

> "Why do you think I've been into the sky?" Snowman asks as neutrally as possible. He's clicking through the legend files in his head. When did he ever mention the sky? Did he relate some fable about where Crake had come from? Yes, now he remembers. He'd given Crake the attributes of thunder and lightning. (*Oryx* 361)

It follows, for the Children of Crake, that Crake now resides in "cloudland" (361)—and, as in "Our Father who art in heaven," his name is hallowed among them. So a central religious trope ironically returns "after the flood" or apocalypse designed expressly to eliminate all forms of worship and faith on earth. "God is a cluster of neurons" was Crake's secular dogma, and so it was possible, he believed, to eliminate "the G-spot in the brain" of his improved version of humanity (157). To heighten the irony, the resurgence of something akin to religious thinking among the Crakers occurs via the agency of Jimmy-Snowman, an unwitting (and unwilling) disciple of Crake, who made it his life's mission to wipe out all humankind and to create a new people in his own godless image.

3. Reversion and Inversion

Ultimately, if Doctor Moreau's less sweeping ambition to fashion human animals out of nonhuman ones is used as a measure of his success, it must be judged a failure or, at least, a lapse from the standards he has set for himself. The doctor admits as much in his long disquisition to Prendick about the mutilated creatures found throughout the island:

For twenty years altogether. . . . I have been going on, and there is still something in everything I do that defeats me . . . always I fall short of the things I dream . . . it is in the subtle grafting and reshaping one must do to the brain that my trouble lies. . . . And least satisfactory of all is something that I cannot touch, somewhere . . . in the seat of the emotions. (*Island* 77–78)

Time after time Doctor Moreau witnesses the reversion of the Beast People—"somehow the things drift back again," he says (77)—and this process, which entails the inversion of his great hopes and expectations, similarly takes place in *Oryx and Crake*. Only Crake is no longer around to witness the backsliding of his Crakers.

Furthermore, the regression (or, viewed otherwise, the progress) of the Children of Crake is not in the direction of what Moreau dubs the "stubborn beast flesh" (*Island* 77). On the contrary, by the novel's end they seem to be evolving in the direction of a distinctly humanlike civilization. During Snowman's prolonged absence from their dwelling place, they make something resembling an effigy or statue, create percussion instruments from found items (empty bottles, a hubcap, an oil drum, assorted sticks), and sit around the effigy chanting and emitting a sound that sounds alarmingly like "Amen" to Snowman's disbelieving ears: "Surely not! Not after Crake's precautions, his insistence on keeping these people pure, free of all contamination of that kind. . . . It can't have happened" (*Oryx* 360). The scene may be read as intended to recall the return of Moses after his long sojourn on Mount Sinai only to find the Children of Israel worshipping a golden calf, a demigod of their own making. But the evolution of the Crakers also represents a literary foil to the return of the nonhuman animal component in the Beast People. It would appear, then, that just as there is a resistant nonhuman strain that cannot be completely eradicated in Doctor Moreau's creatures, so there is something integral to the human animal, call it "soul" or "spirit," which cannot be taken out of the Crakers.

In the final analysis, this intertextual study of *Oryx and Crake* and one of its main pre-texts, *The Island of Doctor Moreau*, has not exhausted its subject. It has been primarily oriented by my developing interest in contemporary animal or animality studies and in environmental issues.[10] However, I have also taken a more traditional critical approach whenever it seemed necessary or relevant, analyzing the uses of verbal representation and narrative technique in these novels. The already double focus of this chapter and considerations of space have caused me not to take two "roads" that, I am aware, equally deserve close critical application. One of these roads or modes of access—literary feminist discourse—would involve exploring the implications of the absence of human female figures in Wells's plot (as in William Golding's island fiction, *Lord of the Flies*) and their prominent, even indispensable, roles in Atwood's. The other—literary postcolonial discourse—would look at the implied political positions in both texts concerning issues of power and imperialist conquest, be it of land in Wells's story (as in Shakespeare's island drama, *The Tempest*) or commodity markets in Atwood's. Each of these discourses well merits further study in comparing, contrasting, and generally appreciating the different yet similar achievements of *The Island of Doctor Moreau* and *Oryx and Crake*. Nevertheless, my discussion has provided, I hope, some insights into how literary tradition impacts on Atwood's writings without generating the anxious inhibitions of influence and authorship.

Notes

1. For a detailed analysis of *Oryx and Crake* in relation to another major precursor, Mary Shelley's *Frankenstein* (1818), see Stein.
2. It is fascinating to observe that Wells not only foresaw that English would become the world's lingua franca in this novel, but also predicted the creation of a system of knowledge storage and retrieval remarkably analogous to Wikipedia. In Wells's vision, this system would be a collective "Encyclopædia organization," with millions of dedicated "investigators, checkers and correspondents" worldwide, that "accumulates, sorts, keeps in order and renders available everything that is known" (*Shape of Things*, bk. 5, ch. 7).

3. See Parrinder xi. This section of my essay is indebted to Parrinder's "Biographical Note" for its succinctly informative account of Well's life and works.

4. See Atwood's research files for *Oryx and Crake* in Manuscript Collection 335 at the Fisher Rare Book Library of the University of Toronto.

5. On lab-grown meat, see especially Specter's "Test-Tube Burgers." On the production of human mother's milk from cows, see Webber's article in the technology section of *The Financial Times*: "Scientists in Argentina . . . have engineered a cow that they say will deliver the next best thing to mother's milk," and the science news article captioned: "China Genetically Modifies Cows To Make Human Breast Milk."

6. See the Atwood files located in Manuscript Collection 335, Box 111, Folder 9 (marked "Pigs"). Xenotransplantation (from the Greek *xenos-* denoting "foreign") involves the transplantation of living cells, tissues, or organs from one species to another. Throughout 2002–03, as Atwood was composing and completing her novel, many articles appeared (and some were filed) about organ replacement by xenotransplantation. See, e.g., Twyman's header in *The Human Genome*: "Pigs can be genetically modified to make organs tailored for transplantation to humans." During the same period, Atwood also wrote a highly engaged and favorable review of Bill McKibben's *Enough*: "a passionate, succinct, chilling, closely argued . . . and essential summary of the future proposed by 'science' for the human race" (294). Her review encapsulates the ethical and practical dilemmas of living in an engineered age that are thematically central to *Oryx and Crake*.

7. I am indebted for this formulation to Rimmon-Kenan: "A narratee . . . is always implied, even when the narrator becomes his own narratee" (89).

8. As this reading indicates, the major difference in technique does not consist in the use of a "first-person" narrator (Prendick) as opposed to a "third-person center of consciousness" (Jimmy-Snowman). In both novels the central protagonist is the focalizer of the story. However, in *The Island of Doctor Moreau* the focalizer and the narrator are coextensive (i.e., one and the same entity), whereas in *Oryx and Crake* they are separate constructs.

9. For detailed analyses of the Bluebeard tale in Atwood's writings up until the early 1990s, see Wilson. See also Bacchilega 104–19, Barzilai 107–54, Hermansson 171, 173–76, and Tatar 108–14.

10. See the Special Topic section of *PMLA* (March 2009) devoted to "Theories and Methodologies: Animal Studies" and especially DeKoven's guest column. For a brief but trenchant discussion of the crucial role played by genetically modified animals in *Oryx and Crake*, see Heise's article in this issue. For an analysis that takes human-animal studies in the direction of ecocriticism, see Bergthaller.

Works Cited

"Aesop's Fables." *Aesops-fables.org.uk*. Aesop's Fables, 1 Jan. 2005. Web. 18 July 2011.

Atwood, Margaret. Atwood Papers, Manuscript Collection 335. Thomas Fisher Rare Book Library, U of Toronto, Canada.

_____. "Freeforall." *Tesseracts2*. Ed. Phyllis Gotlieb and Douglas Barbour. Victoria, BC: Porcépic, 1987. 130–38.

_____. *The Handmaid's Tale*. New York: Fawcett, 1986.

_____. "Hardball." 1992. *Good Bones and Simple Murders*. Toronto: McClelland, 2001. 117–20.

_____. "Introduction: Ten Ways of Looking at *The Island of Doctor Moreau* by H. G. Wells." *Writing with Intent* 386–98.

_____. *Oryx and Crake*. London: Bloomsbury, 2003.

_____. *The Penelopiad*. New York: Canongate, 2005.

_____. "Review: *Enough: Staying Human in an Engineered Age* by Bill McKibben." *Writing with Intent* 294–304.

_____. "Three Novels I Won't Write Soon." *The Tent*. Toronto: McClelland, 2006. 85–92.

_____. "Writing *Oryx and Crake*." *Writing with Intent* 284–86.

_____. *Writing with Intent: Essays, Reviews, Personal Prose 1983–2005*. New York: Carroll, 2005. 284–86.

_____. *The Year of the Flood*. New York: Doubleday, 2009.

Bacchilega, Cristina. *Postmodern Fairy Tales: Gender and Narrative Strategies*. Philadelphia: U of Pennsylvania P, 1997.

Barzilai, Shuli. *Tales of Bluebeard and His Wives from Late Antiquity to Postmodern Times*. New York: Routledge, 2009.

Bergthaller, Hannes. "Housebreaking the Human Animal: Humanism and the Problem of Sustainability in Margaret Atwood's *Oryx and Crake* and *The Year of the Flood*." *English Studies* 91.7 (2010): 728–43.

Bloom, Harold. *The Anxiety of Influence: A Theory of Poetry*. 1973. 2nd ed. New York: Oxford UP, 1997.

Caine, Barbara. "Cobbe, Frances Power (1822–1904)." Oxford Dictionary of National Biography. May 2006. Web. Jan. 2012.

"China Genetically Modifies Cows To Make Human Breast Milk." *RedOrbit News*. RedOrbit.com, 10 June 2011. Web. 14 June 2011.

Coleridge, Samuel Taylor. "The Rime of the Ancient Mariner." 1798. *The Portable Coleridge*. Ed. I. A. Richards. New York: Penguin, 1977. 80–105.

DeKoven, Marianne. "Guest Column: Why Animals Now?" *PMLA* 124.2 (2009): 361–69.

Gilbert, Sandra M., and Susan Gubar. *The Madwoman in the Attic: The Woman Writer and the Nineteenth-Century Literary Imagination*. New Haven: Yale UP, 1979.

Golding, William. *Lord of the Flies*. 1954. London: Faber, 1958.

Heise, Ursula K. "The Android and the Animal." *PMLA* 124.2 (2009): 503–10.

Hermansson, Casie E. *Bluebeard: A Reader's Guide to the English Tradition*. Jackson: UP of Mississippi, 2009.

Parrinder, Patrick. Biographical Note. *The Island of Doctor Moreau*. By H. G. Wells. London: Penguin, 2005. vii–xii.

Prince, Gerald. "Introduction to the Study of the Narratee." *Reader-Response Criticism: From Formalism to Post-Structuralism*. Ed. Jane P. Tompkins. Baltimore: Johns Hopkins UP, 1980. 7–25.

Rimmon-Kenan, Shlomith. *Narrative Fiction: Contemporary Poetics*. London: Methuen, 1983.

Shakespeare, William. *The Tempest*. 1610–1611. Ed. Robert Langbaum. New York: New American Lib., 1964.

Specter, Michael. "Test-Tube Burgers: How long will it be before you can eat meat that was made in a lab?" *The New Yorker* 23 May 2011: 32–38.

Stein, Karen F. "Problematic Paradice in *Oryx and Crake*." *Margaret Atwood: The Robber Bride, The Blind Assassin, Oryx and Crake*. Ed. J. Brooks Bouson. London: Continuum, 2010. 141–55.

Tatar, Maria. *Secrets Beyond the Door: The Story of Bluebeard and His Wives*. Princeton: Princeton UP, 2004.

"Theories and Methodologies: Animal Studies." Special Topic. *PMLA* 124.2 (2009): 472–575.

Twyman, Richard. "Genetic Modification of Pigs for Xenotransplantation." *The Human Genome*. Wellcome Trust, 30 July 2003. Web. 28 July 2011.

Webber, Jude. "Scientists Engineer Mother's-Milk Cow." *The Financial Times*. 12 June 2011. Web. 14 June 2011.

Wells, H. G. *Anticipations of the Reaction of Mechanical and Scientific Progress upon Human Life and Thought*. 1901. London: Chapman, 1904.

_____. *The Island of Doctor Moreau*. 1896. Ed. Patrick Parrinder. London: Penguin, 2005.

_____. *A Modern Utopia*. 1905. Lincoln: U of Nebraska P, 1967.

_____. *The Outline of History: Being a Plain History of Life and Mankind*. 1920. New York: Garden City, 1931.

_____. *The Shape of Things to Come*. 1933. A Project Gutenberg of Australia eBook. n. pag. Oct. 2003. Web. 14 June 2011.

_____. *The War of the Worlds*. 1898. Ed. Patrick Parrinder. London: Penguin, 2005.

Wilson, Sharon Rose. *Margaret Atwood's Fairy-Tale Sexual Politics*. Jackson: UP of Mississippi, 1993.

CRITICAL
READINGS

Margaret Atwood's Poetry: Voice and Vision____

Kathryn VanSpanckeren

Atwood began as a poet, and her poetic voice infuses her novels with music even while she raises pressing issues of ecology, gender, and human rights. Many of these issues appear first in her poetry, and poems have always provided protected spaces for her to try out ideas and voices. Poetry was the genre in which she first gained recognition, and she has continued to write poems throughout her life.

Because Atwood began her writing career publishing primarily poetry, the early critical response to Atwood focused quite naturally on this genre. Davidson and Davidson's *The Art of Margaret Atwood* (1981) contains six essays dealing with her poetry and poetics, while Jerome Rosenberg's 1984 *Margaret Atwood* gives a thoughtful account of her poetry books up to *True Stories*. Frank Davey's *Margaret Atwood: A Feminist Poetics* (1984) offers an intriguing "Atwood Vocabulary" of categories: "Technological Skin," Mirrors," "The Gothic," "Refugees and Tourists," "Underground, Underwater," "The Maze," "Metamorphosis," and "Signs and Totems." *Margaret Atwood: Vision and Forms* (1988), which Jan Garden Castro and I coedited, contains four essays on the poetry. Later edited collections of essays organized primarily by genre, such as Lorraine York's *Various Atwoods* (1995), Reingard M. Nischik's *Margaret Atwood: Works & Impact* (2000), and Sharon Wilson's *Margaret Atwood: Textual Assassinations* (2003), include useful critical essays on the more recently published poetry. Since then, the sheer bulk of Atwood's work, and the fact that she has shifted into a new phase of science fiction and environmental themes, have made overviews difficult. Recent edited collections oriented to themes have appeared, such as Coral Ann Howells's *Cambridge Companion to Margaret Atwood* (2006) and Sarah Appleton's *Once Upon a Time* (2008); these stress the fiction (each contains one essay on poetry). With the publication of Atwood's newest book of poetry, *The Door* (2007), the time has arrived for a reappraisal of her poetry.

Naturally, each new volume of poetry by Atwood changes how we look at her oeuvre. *The Door*, though written in a plain style, is hauntingly beautiful—surprisingly so. The figure of Atwood in the public mind is no longer that of a pitiless Medusa as it once was, but her rapier wit, ferocious erudition, popular flair, and fearless social criticism are still daunting. There is another and opposite side to her work, though, a musical and even radiant dimension. This radiant side can be appreciated most directly in her poetry, especially in the original volumes. *Selected Poems* and *Selected Poems II*, though edited by Atwood, are constructs (anthologies) of constructs (volumes) of constructs (the poems). The *Selecteds* were made after the fact, and however well edited, they, like the author, were influenced by previous public reception, which had included vicious attacks provoked especially by *Power Politics*. The selections omit many of Atwood's personal, challenging, and meditative poems, in favor of bold and somewhat unassailable dramatic monologues in recognizable voices from history, myth, or popular culture, especially when they form sequences. On rereading, the poetry as a whole remains remarkable, not for its power to shock (though it can do that), so much as for its musical intermingling of voice and meaning, and—very secondarily—because to some extent it provides a key to her works in other genres including the novels.

Atwood has discussed her poetic practice in rich detail in her interviews. Though her poems typically work on many simultaneous levels of meaning and often contrast polarities (male/female, United States/Canada, nature/civilization), in her interviews Atwood identifies something beyond these "violent dualities" at work. She defines the poem as a musical event that is mysterious in origin and requires active listening on the part of the poet. Listening is always involved in poetry, but it is especially true of Atwood's poems, in which voice and vision are almost inseparable.

Atwood mentions sound as a mode of almost shamanic perception in her interviews. She says that her poetic inspiration wells up when she finds solitude or "empty space" and then engages in intense "listening," which she calls "a shamanistic technique. Well known to the prophets" (Meltzer 182). Atwood explains to Joyce Carol Oates that her poems are not "rational" but musical, and usually begin with words or phrases that appeal "more because of their sound than their meaning," and involve "movement and phrasing." While their music is subtle because she uses internal rhyme and avoids "immediate alliteration and assonance in favor of echoes," the overall "texture of sound" is as important as the poem's meaning (Oates 37). When she is writing poetry, Atwood experiences her personality as a poet as free and playful, and "almost totally different" from her novel-writing self (Oates 39). While as a novel writer Atwood says she is "better organized, more methodical," as a poet she is "in a state of free float" (Morris 143). In her view, a poem is something readers hear, and the primary focus of interest is "words," while a novel is something readers "see, and the primary focus of interest is people" (Sandler 29). Atwood considers oral performance and song to be primal for the human species: poetry "was oral first in human societies, and it's oral first when a child is learning language. Children learn to recite, chant, and make up their own verse long before they learn to read" (Hammond 60).

Crucial to the aural/oral experience is the embodied voice in poetry, for both poet and reader. Poetry is a speech act, an event, an experience. Atwood points out that, though one may speed read prose, "it's impossible to speed read poetry" because it demands "moving your lips when you read. You're sounding out the poem and anyone who just scans it visually is missing the whole point. If you can't get the aural quality right, then the poem will be wrong" (Hammond 60). In musical performance, patterns of particular sounds make up the music. Atwood says that the basic unit of the poem is the syllable (Hammond 62). Syllables, unlike morphemes or roots of words, lack intrinsic meaning, and perhaps for that reason they may be said to have an autonomous existence, like notes in a song whose melody can penetrate walls though the words may be muffled. Even without knowing what is being said or who is being addressed, the tone of a voice and its rise and fall can convey meaning. Intonation and gesture can telegraph urgent need, love, friendship, warning, danger, and many subtler things, even when two speakers are using mutually unintelligible languages.

Atwood envisions poetic sounds as moving not only between people, but traveling between worlds. As she remarks, "up to the romantic period poets cocked their ears to heaven, but since then the voice has tended to come from below: there's Milton saying 'Descend, O Dove!' . . . then it got reversed. With Blake it's definitely coming from below, and this sterile, controlling figure sits upstairs. Shelley has lots of caves, he's invoking dark powers. Keats has an early poem where the narrator goes under the sea and there he finds Proteus, the shape-changer" (Sandler 27). Atwood usually writes poetry "from below." One of her few early poems about her creative process is "Procedures for Underground," which she identifies as "a descent to the underworld" (Sandler 27–28). In her 2002 book *Negotiating with the Dead: A Writer on Writing*, Atwood expands on her vision of writing as contacting the "dead," as she calls the unconscious and archetypal realm of myth; her compelling sixth chapter traces descents to the underworld in poetry, from the great ancient oral epics of Gilgamesh, the Odyssey, and Beowulf to the written works of Virgil, Dante, Shakespeare, and modern poets including Rilke and D. H. Lawrence. She quotes Adrienne Rich's haunting poem "Diving Into the Wreck" as an example of a poetic descent by a "swimmer among the jeweled dead—double-gendered, like the seer Tiresias" (176). Atwood concludes by pointing to the ancient "shamanistic role of the writer" (179), and has discussed the poet as shaman elsewhere (Personal interview). Fittingly, *Negotiating with the Dead* gives the last word to Ovid's Sibyl of Cumae: "the fates will leave me my voice, / and by my voice I shall be known" (180). For Atwood, voice is the means, and the ultimate end, of the poetic quest for immortality: while other "art forms can last and last—painting, sculpture, music"— they "do not survive as *voice*" (158). Some of her most memorable poems emit cave-like echoes and amplified mysterious sounds; one can't always tell who is speaking, or to whom, and one shouldn't take the voices at face value. Like oracles, they are cunningly ambiguous, speak in a variety of tones, and convey branching meanings.

The recurring image she uses for her poetic inspiration involves "dipping a thread into a supersaturated solution to induce crystal formation" (Morris 143). Atwood explains that the crystals are the words of the poem: "from the language the poem condenses" (Hammond 61). For Atwood, the matrix is seen as a sort of language and also as a lake or sea, impregnated, as it were, with sounds like minerals and salts, out of which all creatures evolved. Water and ice are two forms of the same thing, and freezing—a function of the Canadian cold—involves crystals. As Atwood has commented, "poetry acts like a lens, or like a thread dipped in a supersaturated solution, causing a crystallization" and she also insists that creative work, specifically writing poetry, as in the case of Anne Sexton, is not a by-product of neurosis, but is done "in spite of" neurosis and thus is a "triumph over it" (Oates 42). Seeing creation as an underwater art, Atwood states that artistic activity cannot be neurotic because "if all art were pearls secreted by the miseries of the oysters, the totally healthy human" would be "the one without a creative or joyful bone in her body" while for her, writing poetry is the "most joyful form" of artistic creation (Oates 42). Atwood implies that poems are tiny, organic, luminous, and round, like pearls. A similar tiny image of happiness, that of a cold, crystalline lens, appears with great force in *You Are Happy*, and resolves the whole of *Selected Poems* with the clear simplicity of a small bell struck once only.

The crystallized language of poetry and its saturated meanings sometimes give Atwood an entry to her work in other genres; in fact she has called poems keys that open doors, and novels the corridors and rooms beyond the doors. "I don't think I solve problems in my poetry," she writes, "I think I uncover the problems. Then the [next] novel seems a process of working them out. I don't think of it that way at the time . . . [W]hen I'm writing poetry, I don't know I'm going to be led down the path to the next novel. Only after I've finished the novel can I say, Well, this poem was the key. This poem opened the door" (Morris 143). She thinks of these paths as "lines of descent" and gives two examples. "Progressive Insanities of a Pioneer" in *The Animals in That Country* led to the volume *The Journals of Susanna Moodie*, "and that in turn led into *Surfacing*," while in another line of descent, the poems in *True Stories* have "obvious affiliations with the novel *Bodily Harm*. It's almost as if the poems open something, like opening a room or a box, or a pathway" (Morris 144). According to Atwood, her novels usually begin with a scene that may appear to her years before the rest of the novel can be written. Two portions of *Surfacing* (1972), which Atwood says were "anchors for that novel," were written five years before the rest: the scene in which the mother's soul appears to the Surfacer-narrator as a bird, and the scene in which the Surfacer and her companions drive to the lake (Morris 147). It is beyond the scope of the present essay to explore the tantalizing links between Atwood's poetry and novels, but the careful reader of Atwood will notice many resonances.

Atwood has produced fourteen books of poetry to date, including the collections *Selected Poems I* and *II*, but not her early chapbook *Double Persephone*. Her first volume, *The Circle Game* (1966), won the Governor General's Award for Poetry, and by 1974 she had published five distinctive poetic works in rapid succession, selections from which appeared in *Selected Poems* in 1976. As her novels took off, Atwood increasingly turned to fiction, which unlike poetry could produce enough money to live on. While *The Edible Woman* (1969) gained a cult following, her novels reached a wider readership beginning with *Surfacing* (1972), and catapulted her to international celebrity with her dystopia *The Handmaid's Tale* (1985), which garnered the Governor General's Award for Fiction. After this, she published three volumes of poetry, represented in *Selected Poems II: Poems Selected and New 1976–1984* (1986). *Morning in the Burned House* (1995) appeared nine years later. *Eating Fire* (1998) reproduces *Selected Poems I* and *II*, dropping "New Poems" from *Selected II* while adding *Morning in the Burned House*. Twelve years after *Morning*, she published *The Door* (2007). This account makes it appear as if Atwood has not been much involved with poetry, but it could be argued, on the contrary, that her poetry has spawned an uncanny brood and has even invaded her novels. Other recent works include volumes of short fictions and other experimental hybrid forms, which have been examined at length by Atwood scholar Reingard Nischik (*Engendering* and "Murder"), along with Patricia Merivale, Sharon Wilson ("Fiction Flashes"), and others. Recent novels like *The Penelopiad* (2005) and *The Year of the Flood* (2009) contain extensive poetic intertexts, as well. Atwood has written libretti for opera since childhood, and is very comfortable in that blend of narrative and music. On the other hand, she has also included prose poems in books of poetry from *You Are Happy* (1974) through *True Stories* (1981), returning to the traditional layout of the lyric in *Interlunar* (1984) and subsequent volumes. After bending and testing the lyric, it seems she has found it to be of enduring value.

Suzanne Langer's *Philosopy in a New Key* (1942), which applies symbolic logic to ritual, myth, and art, offers a general way of understanding Atwood's poetry, since Langer sees symbol, along with ritual and myth, as constituting meaning. For Langer, humans differ from animals not due to our rational ability, but because of our innate gift of symbolizing. Langer warns against the danger of symbolizing, however, and explains that humans may persist in the same destructive rituals, such as human sacrifice, long after animals would have stopped. She defends intuition as the essence of thought. Influenced in her philosophy by studies in mathematics, Langer sheds light on music, which moves beyond symbolic meaning, in her chapter "On Significance in Music." Atwood parallels Langer's thinking both in her struggle to invoke the mythical without being used by it and in her movement away from myth in favor of a more textured, engaged, and humane vision.

An important woman philosopher during World War II, Langer is the unacknowledged spirit behind important poetry criticism, particularly that which deals with subtle musical effects. Her work influenced

M. L. Rosenthal and Sally Gall's seminal work *The Modern Poetic Sequence* (1983), in which the authors identify the poetic sequence form (which they trace to Whitman and Dickinson but not to Tennyson or, except briefly, to Browning), as the quintessential expression of the modern mind as seen in the work of Eliot, Pound, Williams, and more contemporary writers. Making an implicit claim that modern poetry in English is preeminently American, Rosenthal and Gill use a flexible terminology of voice, and warn explicitly against narrow, limiting "notions of 'voice' or 'persona'" in favor of Langer's "dynamic" and organic criticism "in a new key" (ix). Their attention to poetic sequences as the major modern poetic form is especially appropriate to Atwood because she has consistently employed such sequences. Though they do not mention Bakhtin, their practice is inherently dialogic; however, they focus on voices in poetry, whereas Bakhtin's great subject is the dialectic of changing narrative registers in fiction.

Rosenthal and Gall see the modern poetic sequence as a "grouping of mainly lyric poems, rarely uniform in pattern, which tend to interact as an organic whole" in a way that is "intimate, fragmented, self-analytical, open, emotionally volatile" (9). Rather than being strongly narrative, as in Browning's dramatic monologues, the modern sequence instead involves "a number of radiant centers, progressively liberated from a narrative or thematic framework" (11). Ultimately, the "object is neither to resolve a problem nor to conclude an action but to achieve the keenest, most open realization possible" of a psychic "pressure" that seeks a state of greater equilibrium (11). Atwood's sequences, and her volumes as wholes, fit this description. Atwood's voices animate individual short poems and employ the resources of contemporary lyrics, such as internal rhyme, rhythm, line breaks, repetition, contradiction, parallel construction, and colloquialism to reveal the ebb and flow of consciousness, revealing not only what the various speakers or personas think, but how they feel about what they think. The reader-listener, is, as it were, overhearing their thoughts, and their uncertainty and discomfort. The poems in any given book vary in subject, but the voice is distinctive; it is plangent—more viola than violin—and circles around its "radiant center," or preoccupation, like a crystal that is gradually built up from a solution over time, through more and more layers. The result is a multifaceted core of meaning that reveals itself in sequences like theme and variations, moving from dissonance and complication in the middle to harmonious equilibrium at the finish. In the following discussion page references are to the *Selected Poems* volumes (*SP* and *SP II*) for the ease of the reader, unless otherwise specified.

Selected Poems I: From *The Circle Game* to *You Are Happy*

The Circle Game (1966) has, as its radiant center, the problem of identity in a society trammeled by convention. The circular dance in the title connotes fixity, a trodden path, rather than original movement. The volume as a whole attempts various articulations of the speaker's identity, as announced in the frequently anthologized initial poem, "This Is a Photograph of Me." This haunting reflexive poem directs the reader to look intently at a photograph described as a page of "blurred lines and grey flecks"—i.e., the poems to come (*SP* 8).[1] Like music, this poetic sequence involves convention and invention, repetition and new ideas. The dancing children are transfixed in a repetition or continuing rhythm, a basic requirement for music (without continuity there cannot be variation, only chaos). Against this *basso continuo*, solos from the speaker (split again between her own voice and that of a lover) alternate with the dance sections.

In the original volume there are vulnerable poems as well as aggressive ones. One such poem, not included in *Selected Poems*, that reveals how Atwood can be both tender and tricky is "Letters, Towards and Away." This seven-poem love sequence begins with the female speaker fearing that her lover will disturb her life of writing—her "universe / mostly paper"—but eventually, though unsure what she will do with female conventions like "veils and silly feathers," she does seem to fall in love. It ends "quickly, / send me some more letters" (*CG* 85–86). Discussing the confessional element in another context, Nathalie Cooke warns that Atwood's poetry can use vulnerability to disarm and ensnare the reader. I do not see Atwood as confessional, but rather as playing with communication theory to trick readers in certain works (see "Atwood's Trickster Texts"). Cooke makes a crucial point, however: that it is possible to consider the roles played by author and reader as confessional in that they are performative. Cooke instances Elizabeth Bruss's well-known work on autobiography as a speech act. For Bruss, the "roles played by an author and a reader" lie "at the heart" of what we mean by autobiography (Bruss 5). Such performative roles are central to "Letters, Towards and Away" and a great many of Atwood's seemingly autobiographical poems. The speaker appears to be won over by love; the poem ends with her, vulnerable, in a roofless house without "wallpaper." However, the fact of the poems themselves deftly contradicts this "vulnerable" reading. Her writing is about not writing. The resonance between the two possible readings is in itself musical, like two overtones.

In *The Animals in That Country* (1968), the reader is brought into an uncanny northern wilderness. Themes of identity and creation continue, but now ecological issues appear; animals are bellwethers for the state of the human soul and society. Atwood depicts specific animals, for example, in "Elegy for the Giant Tortoises," rather than generic "pre-amphibian" creatures as in the earlier book. Atwood's lumbering line of tortoises—reminiscent of D. H. Lawrence's "doomed" male tortoise trudging doggedly through "Lui et Elle"—is headed for extinction along with the "passenger pigeon / the dodo / the whooping crane / the Eskimo" ("Elegy," *SP* 56). Nevertheless Atwood's tortoises speak to us via a kind of ponderous language: "their small heads pondering / from side to side, their useless armour / sadder than tanks and history" (*SP* 56).

In the title poem, the animals from "another country" are treated with dignity; their death has value. The fox is "run / politely to earth" and the bull is "given / an elegant death." In "this country," however, the animals and their deaths are drained of meaning: "their eyes / flash once in car headlights / and are gone" (*SP* 49). The voice of the poem registers the difference. The first half, about animals in "that" country (seemingly the past), uses evocative language; the bull is "embroidered / with blood" while the fox hunters stand around the fox in a "tapestry of manners." "This" country, in stark contrast, lacks adequate language. Even more interesting is the subtle ambiguity of "this" and "that" country. If both the reader and speaker live in "this" country (modern society), how can we know about "that" country, and how long until we, too, forget? Though it exists in the past, the medieval heraldic world is a lot more alive in this poem than the present world is. If we, like the animals in headlights, live in "this" world, our deaths—and lives—like theirs will also be meaningless (or worse, since we kill the animals heedlessly). Reading this poem, we've been turned into sleepwalking (or perhaps sleep-driving) ghosts of "this country," haunted by those we killed, like Lady Macbeth. "This country" is enough to send shivers up this reader's spine.

There is also the large territory of dangerous delusions associated, in Canada, with the haunted North. As Sherrill Grace has noted, an uncanny North animates two poems in *The Animals in That Country*, "Provisions" and "The Revenant." Perhaps because Atwood thought non-Canadians could not relate to them, both of these poems were omitted from the *Selected Poems*. In "Provisions," the poem that begins the original volume, the speaker and her companion find themselves totally unprepared, standing in "thin / raincoats and rubber boots" on "disastrous ice, the wind rising." Too late the speaker asks "What should we have taken / with us? We never could decide / on that, or what to wear, / or what time / of year to make this journey" (*AC* 1). One might interpret this as a vaguely existentialist poem, but Atwood's book *Strange Things: The Malevolent North in Canadian Literature*

(1995), opens new channels for understanding. Here she interprets the story of the doomed 1845 British imperial voyage of Sir John Franklin and 135 men who mysteriously disappeared in search of the fabled Northwest Passage from Europe to Asia. Franklin's two ships—the *Terror* and *Erebus*—boasted special fortified hulls, hot water and steam heating, a library of almost three thousand books, and scientific instruments, along with tinned provisions for three years. Atwood explains that these were the "most technologically advanced and luxurious ships ever sent on such an expedition" (14). Reports from the Inuit people indicated that Franklin's crazed sailors had died of starvation, but not before indulging in cannibalism; scientific analysis of corpses carried out in the 1980s demonstrated that the lead-fused tin cans that held their food—their "provisions"— had given the men lead-poisoning, helping incite them to cannibalism. Provisions that were meant to save the men instead maddened them and drove them to turn on each other in monstrous fashion when they ran out of food. Rereading the poem "Provisions" with Franklin in mind, the situation takes on new levels of meaning. What does "provisions" mean? Is Providence involved? What are the best kinds, and why? In the poem the people have nothing much, except each other. But isn't that the point? We are all mortal, all in need of companionship, all part of a common humanity. Their pockets yield "a pencil stub" and "a bundle / of small white filing-cards / printed with important facts." Are the "important facts" here an ironic reference to the futile scientific investigations performed by the Franklin expedition and perhaps, also, by the scientists in the 1980s, who missed the warning against hubris involved in what Atwood calls the "Franklin fiasco" (14)? Grace suggests this reading. Might the pencil stub and paper also be, in fact, important in themselves if repurposed by the writer, who may glean deeper human truths from such a disaster, and relate them to readers? Do the cards suggest the poems in the volume, or notes for them?

Another poem in *The Animals in That Country*, "The Revenant," makes reference to a Native American belief in Northern ghosts, particularly the ice-hearted Wendigo. In *Strange Things,* Atwood explains that this monstrous ghost is associated with cannibalism, winter, scarcity, and insanity. The two great fears of people who go into the Canadian bush are that they will be eaten by a Wendigo or will "go Wendigo"—that is, will turn into a Wendigo (81–83). Drawing on the idea that the Wendigo can represent "a split-off part" of the psyche (*Strange Things* 80), Atwood, in the poem "The Revenant," describes a maddened speaker's encounter with his or her split-off Wendigo-self: "Mirror addict, my sickness / how can I get rid of you." This poem identifies that which makes us go mad and turn on others: our own unfinished business. A whining vindictive child follows the speaker around like an evil twin that grows larger as it keeps writing its "own name / over and over in the snow." The speaker tries denying it: "you don't exist." However, the child, a poisonous split-off fragment of the speaker's Canadian psyche, goes alone into the North, "barefoot in thorny winter, / wrists bleeding, a frozen martyr." The frozen North, "vast as a hospital," is really "the skull's noplace" where "refusing to be buried, cured, / the trite dead walk" (*AC* 52). Identity is not, here, as simple as choosing roles; old ghosts, weaknesses, and wounds demand to "write their names."

In *The Journals of Susanna Moodie* (1970), the most popular of Atwood's volumes in Canada, voice and vision are tied to history. Moodie, who was an English immigrant woman in early nineteenth-century Canada, kept a journal of her pioneer experiences in the "bush," or Canadian wilderness. In the United States the frontier is often imagined as an Eden, but in Canada, for a host of reasons (closer ties to England, the freezing winters, and more) the bush has presented itself as an unforgiving, haunted space, as in the influential works of Northrop Frye, one of Atwood's mentors. The real Moodie never acculturated, but Atwood's Moodie is transformed by the land she tries to subdue. Atwood's chronological poetic sequence follows Moodie as she arrives with her husband in Quebec and they settle in the bush, through the burning of her cabin ("The Two Fires") and the deaths of her children, one by drowning and others by unnamed perils. In "Solipsism While Dying," at death Moodie acknowledges her responsibility for her Canadian life—"What I heard I / created." She finally becomes Canadian through a transformation of word and sound: the poem's layout, with failing senses or parts of the body on the left, and answering phrases on the right, echoes a dialogic liturgy for the dead; the poem's end is her last breath, an eerie exhalation of the talismanic name "tor oN T O" (*SP* 109–10). Rather than conclude on that spooky and highly performative note (the poem begs to be read aloud), Atwood tones down the book, bringing it to a quiet but satisfying resolution in the voice of Moodie's still-feisty spirit, imagined as the spirit of Canada. In "A Bus Along St. Clair: December," Moodie appears as a crone on the bus, embodying the immigrant past transformed into Canada's present identity; meanwhile, her body lies buried beneath modern Toronto's "concrete slabs" (*SP* 115–16).

Procedures for Underground (1970) continues previous concerns with the environment, animals, and identity. I have previously written of Atwood's poems as shamanistic, and it is important to distinguish the shaman's role from that of ghosts, both of which involve "negotiations with the dead." An important part of learning to read Atwood's poetry is learning to recognize the ghosts. The artist takes on shamanistic powers in the title poem, whose epigraph references Northwest Coast Native belief, as she enters "the country beneath / the earth" with its "green sun" and backward-flowing rivers, and encounters beings who "are always hungry." Gaining "wisdom and great power," like a shaman, she returns with the gift of being able to see the ghosts "when they prowl as winds, / as thin sounds in our village." Rather than haunting society as the ghosts do, the artist/shaman deals with the ghosts (neuroses or psychoses, or spiritual threats). In animist societies, disease is caused by imbalance; in poetry sequences, as Rosenthal and Gall state, after conflict, balance is restored. A shamanic author's cure involves putting words in the right order: "you will / tell us their [the ghosts'] names, what they want, who / has made them angry by forgetting them." Through appropriate mindfulness and rituals, balance will be restored and the unquiet ghost will be placated. "Few will seek your [the shaman's] help / with love, none without fear"—so ends the poem. The artist's special powers do inspire fear. However, this fear comes from association with death and the other world. The shamanic artist helps, rather than haunts; any harm that comes, comes to the poet, who "must suffer" for this gift and endure the ghosts "beckoning . . . back down" (*SP* 122).

Lothar Honnighausen clarifies that for Atwood, the underground is "the sphere in which epiphanies and metamorphoses take place" (104). Hades, as well as Native American myth, provides a setting for these moments (Honnighausen 105; Davey 109). In addition, a contemporary literary current is at work. In southern Ontario gothic, exemplified by the fiction of Alice Munro and Robertson Davies, the uncanny pervades the poor villages of the region, and the inhabitants' unpredictable acts often end in violence. In "Game After Supper," a "tall man" threatens playing children: "He will be an uncle, / if we are lucky" (*SP* 118). In "Girl and Horse, 1928," a viewer is haunted by a photo of a girl and horse that memory brings alive after 40 years (*SP* 119), and in "Cyclops," a flashlight terrifies night creatures: "where danger is not knowing, / . . . / you are the hugest monster" (*SP* 125). Even the writer's machines—typewriter, light, and clock—become vampires "drinking a sinister transfusion / from the other side of the wall" in "Three Desk Objects" (*SP* 126.)

Power Politics (1971) is a strikingly original antilove sequence. The title draws attention to one of the slogans of the counterculture: "the personal is the political." At the time the poems were written, Atwood's marriage to the American James Polk was heading towards divorce. As Reingard Nischik points out, 1970 was a turning point for feminism, and several crucial texts of the women's movement came out in that year, including Kate Millet's *Sexual Politics* (*Engendering* 20–21). The art on the cover of Atwood's original volume contributes to the meaning; Atwood often designed or consulted on the covers of the poetry volumes. This cover is a feminist version of the Hanged Man found in Tarot cards. In the bold woodcut style of a political poster, it depicts a helmeted armored knight who stands in the heroic pose of a statue, with outstretched metal-clad arm; from his wrist hangs a woman. Bound tightly as a mummy and entirely supported by the male, her hair dangling, she looks impassively at the reader. Nischik points out the painfulness of the strained posture for both parties, and the fact that the man's face is covered; the woman at least has eyes open, while the male suffers unseen (*Engendering* 23). The old myths of love must stop, but the man cannot see the need for change. The poems work to clear away these insupportable gender roles by exploiting the conventions of love poetry. Instead of the male undressing a female beloved, in the final poem the woman unpeels the many disguises—signaled by hypnotic, repeated prepositional phrases, varied phonemes or sounds, and charged language—from this "hinged bronze man, the fragile man / built of glass pebbles, / the fanged man with his opulent capes and boots" (*SP* 176).

Like a series of syllogisms, the poems in the book have the force of mathematical proof. The famous opening sets the tone: "you fit into me / like a hook into an eye // a fish hook / an open eye" (*SP* 141). The original volume lacks a table of contents and its poems—often left untitled—immerse the reader in the lovers' inchoate struggle. Titles use the third person, casting events as exemplary parables, or captions for an old clichéd silent film: "He reappears," "She considers evading him," "They eat out." Cumulatively, the poems build up hard evidence, delivered in a deadpan voice and flat monosyllabic diction, that the traditional patterns of heterosexual love harm both man and woman: "we are hard on each other / and call it honesty" (*SP* 152); "a truth should exist, / it should not be used / like this. If I love you // is that a fact or a weapon" (*SP* 152). For those who were anguished by the US war in Vietnam and do not condone later wars, the cartoon-like exaggeration, pop themes, and humor still carry powerful satirical meanings, as in "They eat out," where the male lover egoistically transforms himself into a quintessentially American Superman figure, while the demure (Canadian) woman continues dining. He rises over the table in "blue tights and a red cape" while Atwood's persona remarks with deflating understatement, "I liked you better the way you were, / but you were always ambitious" (*SP* 144–45).

Power Politics is the volume that gave Atwood the reputation of an anti-American man-hater, but in retrospect, she has always been a passionate defender of human rights regardless of gender or nationality. At the time *Power Politics* was published, female, multiethnic, and postcolonial voices remained muffled and New Historicism and Cultural Studies were in their infancy. It is small wonder, then, that the book was a bombshell. Political art, for many, remains an oxymoron, but Atwood has often maintained that literature must deal with social issues (Sandler 32). It is well to remember that Shelley and Poe, her first poetic models (Oates, "Dancing" 42), were philosophical and aesthetic idealists of the purest sort. Poe was deeply transgressive, and Shelley an outright revolutionary.

You Are Happy continues the political concerns in *Power Politics* in poems like "Newsreel: Man and Firing Squad" (*SP* 178–79), but the "radiant centers" of the central sequences see violence as a larger force growing out of deadening, unexamined social myths. The male lover in "Narcissus" stares into his fatal mirror, blind to the things of the world including the presence of his female lover. Impaired vision permeates "Songs of the Transformed," dramatic monologues spoken by animals. Like Narcissus, the animals see everything in terms of themselves. The dramatic monologues in the Circe/Mud Poems show Circe almost seduced into such abjectivity. As she tells it, she is a healer who uses her powers for good. Suppliants flock to her as clients would a psychotherapist for talk therapy; men with violent pasts, they seek relief from pain through words of absolution from those they have "assaulted daily." Circe collects these words with great difficulty, her "head pressed to the earth, to stone, to shrubs" (*SP* 204). There are not enough words to go around, however, so Circe cannot heal everyone who seeks her out; the men who turned into animals were just expressing their own proclivities. She is not responsible: "I sat and watched" (*SP* 203).

The varying moods of this sequence allow for a variety of interpretations. Branko Gorjup suggests that Circe is like the Siren who wants her words to be transformed into a "cry for help" (140); for me, Circe is the exact opposite and Ulysses is the one needing help. After all, the Siren's song is one of the "Songs of the Transformed" and the Siren has been transformed, presumably by Circe, into a singer doomed to sing the same fatal song forever. Circe has, and is, her own island. She can choose to perform healing or harmful actions. Most importantly, she can speak her mind. Confronted with sick, fragmented selves depicted as undifferentiated body parts (especially hearts and blood), Circe hungers for people with "real faces and hands" (*SP* 202). In Ulysses she believes she has found her soul mate, and she entrusts him with her magic words, forswearing her art like Shakespeare's Prospero. Ulysses, however, is a trickster; like a male Siren he lures her and then brutally half rapes her, betraying their emotional connection. In doing so, like her self-destructive clients, he cuts himself off from her healing power, which could have saved him from the wanderings that await him, as described in Tennyson's "Ulysses." In the end, Circe is the one who ends this stalemate by reclaiming her commanding words: "I don't have to take / anything you throw into me / . . . / Get out of here" *(SP* 216).

Selected Poems II: *Two-Headed Poems, True Stories,* and *Interlunar*

Atwood's choice to end *Selected Poems* with affirmative personal poems from *You Are Happy* suggested a rising emotional progression within her poetry as a whole to some early readers, such as Linda Wagner-Martin ("Making"). No such definitive linear movement is legible in the original volumes, however. With the exception of *Power Politics*, her earlier books all resolve with at least one final poem evoking tender shared moments and limpid sound. Nevertheless, happiness—defined as emotional vitality and clarity of vision—accurately predicts the emotional trajectory of the poems found in *Two-Headed Poems* (1978). Though Linda Wagner-Martin finds a "pervasive tone of despair" in *Two-Headed Poems* ("Giving Way" 87), in my view the book shows a venturesome vocabulary and delight in simple pleasures. With Graeme Gibson, Atwood had entered a period of family life on a farm in Alliston, Ontario, in 1973; their daughter Jess was born in 1976. Domestic ties find expression in "Five Poems for Grandmothers": "sons branch out, but / one woman leads to another" (*SP II* 14). In "All Bread" the poet's yeasty dough rises, a "live burial under a moist cloth," and "all bread must be broken / so it can be shared" (*SP II* 53). The two "Daybooks" sequences evoke the garden as the different plants flourish and decay with passing seasons. Poem 6 of "Daybooks I," subtitled "After Jaynes," provides an entry point to the "radiant centers" of doubled vision at the heart of the volume. Atwood read Julian Jaynes's book *The Origins of Consciousness in the Breakdown of the Bicameral Mind* in 1977, while working on these poems (Rosenberg 84). According to Jaynes, for most of history humans were at one with myth, guided by voices of ancestors, authorities, or gods—voices they had internalized, so that these voices were literally "heard" and perceived as real. With the rise of complex societies involving specialization and hence human choices, self-awareness and a fall into knowledge occurred, and the right hemisphere of the brain became autonomous from the left. Though Atwood rejects Jaynes as an explanation for poetry in poem 6, Jaynes's theory helps elucidate the violent polarities in "The Right Hand Fights the Left," "Four Small Elegies," "Footnote to the Amnesty Report on Torture" and in "Two-Headed Poems," the complex title sequence which dramatizes the Separatist movement sparked by the election in Quebec of Premier René Lévesque. Grumbling that "our fragments made us," the Siamese twin-headed voices shift shapes: divorcing parents, neighbors quarreling over barbeques, flags raised and slogans deployed, and arguments during immanent disaster. Ultimately this is "not a debate / but a duet / with two deaf singers" (*SP II* 24–35).

The next volume, *True Stories* (1981), begins with the title poem's punning admonition—"the true story lies / among the other stories" (*SP II* 58). Written in the same year as her novel *Bodily Harm*, this volume includes stories of torture and human rights abuse that also look forward to *The Handmaid's Tale* (1985). These were years of intense political activism for Atwood. In 1981 she became President of the Writers Union of Canada; she would be elected president of PEN International, Canadian Center (English speaking) from 1984–86. The most shocking of Atwood's poetry collections, this contains "Notes Towards a Poem That Can Never Be Written," a part of which is dedicated to her friend the poet Carolyn Forché. "A Conversation" recalls the "banality of evil" identified by Hanna Arendt in the person of a man "with sunglasses and a casual shirt / and two beautiful women" who manufactures "machines / for pulling out toenails, / sending electric shocks / through brains or genitals" (*SP II* 64). The ending glances at the thin line separating ordinary life from nightmare: "why was he at that party?" "Torture" begins with a question—"what goes on in the pauses / of this conversation / which is about free will"—and ends with a "flayed body hung / to the wall" (*SP II* 67). The most shocking poem is the ironically entitled "A Woman's Issue," in which forced sex in war, genital mutilation, and other often-ignored brutalities against women are shown to be crimes against humanity.

The molten anger at man's inhumanity powering the core of this book warms and illuminates its margins, however. In "Landcrab II" near the book's beginning, the crab, "no-one's metaphor," has its "own paths" (*SP II* 60). The book lingers on grotesque subjects, but its language luxuriates in the last section, in works such as "Blue Dwarfs," "Damside," "Blue Jays," "High Summer," and "Last Day," which envision growth from ripeness, decay, and detritus. In "Mushrooms," there is "leaf mold / starred with nipples, / with cool white fishgills, / leathery purple brains, / fist-sized suns. . . / poisonous moons, pale yellow" (*SP*

II 78). In "Damside," which is included in the complete version of *True Stories*, the messy brown river, with its "greasy rubbish" and "just-born flies," provides fragments of a particular shared moment—"a noon in early spring"—when the "stained river" offered the speaker and her companion two versions of the same story: "a prayer, a sewer, a prayer" (*True Stories* 98–99).

Although it begins with "Snake Poems," a short sequence about a creature linked with evil in Judaism, Christianity, and Islam, *Interlunar* (1984) offers a luminous and velvety vision, in which darkness itself shines with an inner light like that of consciousness without a sensory object. The "Snake Poems" sequence introduces the theme of the uncanny in simple terms. Atwood's speaker describes hunting for snakes so she could "carry them, / limp and terrorized, into the dining room, / something even men were afraid of" in "Snake Woman" (*SP II* 87). Atwood's snakes, like Louise Glück's flowers in *The Wild Iris* (1992), provide a vocabulary for speaking of spiritual things. "Eating Snake" explores blood sacrifice and incarnation, "Lesson on Snakes" probes taboo, and "Metempsychosis" mines the humorous potential in reincarnation. The most ambitious poem in the series is "Quattrocento," in which the "possibility of death" offered by the snake is described as "death upon death, squeezed together / a blood snowball." The wording recalls the snowball scene in *The Deptford Trilogy* (1988) by Robertson Davies that initiates a series of tragedies spanning decades, a masterful work that perhaps influenced Atwood's triple-layered novel *The Blind Assassin* (2000). In "Quattrocento," the snake offers the heart that can "see in darkness," since "it's the death you carry in you . . . that makes the world / shine for you / as it never did before" (*SP II* 93–94). This sonorous theme, which inspired the *Romantic* poets, reverberates throughout the rest of Atwood's works. Elsewhere in the volume, Atwood meditates on death in poems on violent men and demon lovers. "The Robber Bridegroom" regrets his "red compulsion," and in "No Name," a rapist haunts the speaker's dreams. "The Burned House" suggests nature's slow renewal; as Shannon Hengen notes, the image of the "ever burning cabin" with its "promise of renewal" is revisited in *Morning in the Burned House* (77). Death and rebirth merge, "trees rotting, earth returning," and finally death, imagined as a glowing interlunar "darkness visible," appears as a form of home, or at least a recognizable landscape (*SP II* 102–03).

Morning in the Burned House (1995) is Atwood's most achieved volume, offering stunning variety and compassion. She could well have published two volumes from these poems; her earlier books usually have three sections, but this book has five, each successful, and each distinct in tone and theme. The first section evokes personal life, moving seamlessly from sibling rivalry to old age. The speaker shows a new gentleness with her ordinary self here, as if accepting at last her own human failings. Memorable poems include "A Sad Child," in which the speaker remembers thinking, on the "day of the lawn party" that she was *"not the favorite child"* (4–5); "February," which humorously describes her cat as "the life principle, / more or less" in the midst of a cold Canadian winter, when it settles on her chest with his "breath / of burped-up meat and musty sofas, / purring like a washboard" (11–12); and "Asparagus," a funny and original comment on aging in springtime from the woman's point of view, as depicted over lunch (13–15).

The second section consists of dramatic monologues by a gallery of female pop stars and mythical figures. As ironic but moving portraits of women crammed into the straightjacket of 1950s Cold War convention, it is reminiscent of Elaine Risley's retrospective in *Cat's Eye*; there are parallels, too, with the male animals in "Songs of the Transformed." Yet these poems are more profound; perhaps Atwood is speaking from her personal experiences as a literary "star," even as she alludes to other recent female poets who have blazed trails. For instance, the end of "Helen of Troy Does Counter Dancing" echoes Plath's "Lady Lazarus" (33–36). Furthermore, these female figures are already public property: they exist as pinups, sphinxes, idealized Helens, or artist's models like Manet's Olympia; nothing is being objectified that hasn't been already. (Whether there are so many recognizable male figures ripe for satirizing is an interesting question.) The jest is that in these poems, the objects (women) talk back by exaggerating and exposing clichés about women. Where "Siren Song" lures readers, these boldly harpoon them. Some of the women deflect the male gaze back on itself, and tell the male viewer to "get stuffed" ("Manet's Olympia" 24–25), while others, like Sekhmet, prefer to sit and watch, catlike and impassive while humans rain down disasters on their own heads (39–41).

Part three is a fertile marsh whose "radiant centers" involve destruction of nature. Topics range from cancer ("Cell" 47–48) and environmental degradation ("Frogless" 56–57) to the unsuccessful hanging of Atwood's New England ancestress, Mary Webster, as a witch ("Half-hanged Mary" 58–69), which I discuss elsewhere (see "Margaret Atwood's Female Crucifixion"). The elegies for Atwood's father in part four are the most emotionally searching sequence she has written. Through characteristic techniques, such as entitling poems with names from literature ("King Lear in Respite Care"), she endows private suffering with archetypal dimensions. Part five blends childhood memories of the burned and still burning cabin with transcendent imagery. Elsewhere I discuss the volume as a contemporary reworking of ancient female descent and rebirth ritual (see "Atwood's Space Crone: Alchemical Vision and Revision in *Morning in the Burned House*").

The Door (2007) crowns Atwood's work in poetry by fusing the political, environmental, personal, and aesthetic. Atwood writes with simplicity of diction; sleight of hand has no room to hide in this plain style, which is not to say there is not rhetorical skill and unerring diction here, along with a supple colloquial voice that has become more playful than ever. In "The Poets Hang On" someone criticizes the impoverished poets' tattered black sweaters: "are they dead or what?" and impatiently demands they "spit it out" and "say it plain." "Cripes they're pretentious," the voice complains, though it admits in the end that these poets "do know something / . . . / we can't quite hear. / Is it about sex? / Is it about dust? / Is it about fear?" (35–37). Fear may open ears; even the most obtuse may be able to learn how to listen. The "radiant centers" of this book concern the environment and consumer society. Several poems, such as "Ten O'clock News," use irony to bestir the reader: "Oh hide your eyes," the writer says rhetorically, daring the reader to enjoy an old photograph of Niagara Falls while "trying not to see the weak swimmer, / or the two children in their yellow boat" (47). Depicted as "blind and deaf and stupendous," the weather has "no mind of its own," the speaker states in "The Weather" only to ask, "Or does it? What if it does? / Suppose you were to pray to it, / what would you say?" (48–49). In "Bear Lament" the polar bear—for Canadians a creature associated with magical protection, with its strong yet softly padding "big paw big paw big paw"—is starving and "thin as ribs" due to global warming and destruction of its food supply (2–3).

Atwood includes moving personal poems as well in *The Door*. Like *Morning in the Burned House*, *The Door* has five sections of unequal length, organized by theme. Section one contains personal poems, including the effective opening poem, "Gasoline," which obliquely introduces the theme of carbon usage (3). "Blackie in Antarctica" depicts Atwood's pet cat's body in the poet's freezer like an unlucky polar explorer; parts of this seriocomic elegy are probably already being read by grieving cat lovers over newly dug holes in back yards (9–10). "Butterfly," the most tender poem Atwood has written about her father, evokes his ascetic scientific expeditions into the Canadian bush as attempts to return to his roots in the Maritimes (14–15). "Crickets" shows an almost Buddhist concern for these small insects, often ignored, who have been "censored," but still, like whistle-blowing poets, sing choruses of warning (18–19). Section two is a tour de force on poetry as it is experienced; in "Heart" the poet's heart is a "huge glistening deep-red clot / of the still-alive past, whole on the plate," which is passed around to critics, "instant gourmets," who make disparaging comments while the poet stands ignored, hand to empty chest, in the corner (24). "Poetry Reading" depicts a well-known confessional poet "ransacking his innards." His art of despair seems futile, but in the end, like music, it works in ways his listeners cannot understand. Atwood's driving rhythms without caesuras or pauses dramatize the poet's frantic reading, his sheepish ending, and his stunned audience: "you feel your own intake of breath / like a fist of air slamming into you, / and you join the applause" (38–40). Section three—which contains the most poems—deals with the environment, especially global warming; section four returns to poetry writing, including gothic themes; the sequence "Another Visit to the Oracle" is a mock interview that ends "I tell dark stories / before and after they come true" (91–98). Section five presents the poet's failings, which she tries to overcome but to no avail. In "Boat Song" she is a member of the orchestra that plays on as the Titanic sinks; in "Dutiful" she decides to wear a "gold necklace adorned with the word NO" (101).

Atwood the poet is a latter-day romantic. She believes, with the romantics, that poetry is music, and that the poetic imagination is capable of transforming the world. Rereading her poems and experiencing her language in its most condensed form, one can enter into the essence of her philosophical and ethical vision. Undoubtedly the joy and freedom she finds in the process of writing poetry flow into her novels and other writings. Over the course of her career, her poetry has moved from personal concerns—identity and the tension between her desire for love and her commitment to art—to increasingly larger topics: Canada's national identity, women's struggle for equality, threats to citizens from repressive regimes and unjust wars, the need for artistic freedom of expression, and, most recently, the dangers of environmental decline in an era of global climate change. At the same time, she has grown ever more specific and compassionate in her choice of subjects. Throughout her poetry, she uses voice dramatically, in the manner of performance, carried out through the resources of musical language, to engage the reader in the making of meaning. By helping dismantle outworn and destructive mythologies, her poetry has opened up fresh paths. In an interview, Atwood offers us crucial insight into not only her meditative spirit but also her view of poetry: "mysticism is in the eye of the mystic—not necessarily in the stone or the tree or the egg. . . . If we had a sacred habit of mind, all kinds of things would be 'sacred.' Most are not at present. We would be able to see *into* things rather than merely to see things. We would see the universe as alive. But you're more likely to find such moments in my poetry than my prose" (Hancock 117).

Notes
The author thanks the University of Tampa for support of this research.
1. I use page, rather than line, numbers in citations when quoting from Atwood's poetry.

Works Cited
Appleton, Sarah A., ed. *Once Upon a Time: Myth, Fairy Tales, and Legends in Margaret Atwood's Writings*. Newcastle upon Tyne, UK: Cambridge Scholars, 2008.
Arendt, Hannah. *On Violence*. New York: Harcourt, 1969.
Atwood, Margaret. *The Animals in That Country*. Boston: Little, 1968.
_____. *The Circle Game*. Toronto: Anansi, 1966.
_____. *The Door*. Boston: Houghton, 2007.
_____. *Eating Fire: Selected Poetry 1965–1995*. London: Virago, 2005.
_____. *Interlunar*. Toronto: Oxford UP, 1984.
_____. *The Journals of Susanna Moodie*. Toronto: Oxford UP, 1970.
_____. *Morning in the Burned House*. Boston: Houghton, 1995.
_____. *Negotiating with the Dead: A Writer on Writing*. New York: Random, 2002.
_____. Personal interview. 4 Feb. 2005.
_____. *Power Politics*. New York: Harper, 1971.
_____. *Procedures for Underground*. Little, 1970.
_____. *Selected Poems*. Toronto: Oxford UP, 1976.
_____. *Selected Poems II: Poems Selected and New 1976–1986*. Boston: Houghton, 1987.
_____. *True Stories*. New York: Simon, 1981.
_____. *Two-Headed Poems*. New York: Simon, 1978.
_____. *You Are Happy*. New York: Harper, 1974.
Bakhtin, Mikhail. *The Dialogic Imagination: Four Essays*. 1930s. Ed. Michael Holquist. Trans. Caryl Emerson and Michael Holquist. Austin: U of Texas P, 1981.
Bruss, Elizabeth. *Autobiographical Acts: The Changing Situation of a Literary Genre*. Baltimore: Johns Hopkins UP, 1976.

Cooke, Nathalie. "The Politics of Ventriloquism: Margaret Atwood's Fictive Confessions." York 207–28.

Davey, Frank. *Margaret Atwood: A Feminist Poetics.* Vancouver: Talon, 1984.

Davidson, Arnold, and Cathy Davidson, eds. *The Art of Margaret Atwood.* Toronto: Anansi, 1981.

Davies, Robertson. *The Deptford Trilogy* [*Fifth Business*; *The Manticore*; *World of Wonders*]. Toronto: Macmillan, 1970, 1972, 1975.

Frye, Northrop. *The Bush Garden: Essays on the Canadian Imagination.* Toronto: Anansi, 1971.

Gluck, Louise. *The Wild Iris.* New York: Ecco, 1992.

Gorjup, Branko. "Margaret Atwood's Poetry and Poetics." *The Cambridge Companion to Margaret Atwood.* Ed. Coral Ann Howells. Cambridge, UK: Cambridge UP, 2006. 130–144.

Grace, Sherrill E. " 'Franklin Lives': Atwood's Northern Ghosts." York 146–66.

Hammond, Karla. "Defying Distinctions." Ingersoll 55–78.

Hancock, Geoff. "Tightrope Walking over Niagara Falls." Ingersoll 91–118.

Hengen, Shannon. Margaret Atwood and Environmentalism. *The Cambridge Companion to Margaret Atwood.* Ed. Coral Ann Howells. Cambridge UK: Cambridge UP, 2006. 72–85.

Honnighausen, Lothar "Margaret Atwood's Poetry 1966–1995." *Margaret Atwood, Works and Impact.* Ed. Reingard M. Nischik. Rochester, NY: Camden, 2000. 97–119.

Howells, Coral Ann, ed. *The Cambridge Companion to Margaret Atwood.* Cambridge, UK: Cambridge UP, 2006.

Ingersoll, Earl, ed. *Waltzing Again: New and Selected Conversations with Margaret Atwood.* Princeton, NJ: Ontario Rev., 2006.

Jaynes, Julian. *The Origin of Consciousness in the Breakdown of the Bicameral Mind.* Boston: Houghton, 1977.

Langer, Suzanne K. *Philosophy in a New Key.* Cambridge, MA: Harvard UP, 1942.

Lawrence, D. H. "Lui et Elle." *Norton Anthology of Modern Poetry.* 2nd ed. Eds. Richard Ellmann and Robert O'Clair. New York: Norton, 1988. 363–66.

Meltzer, Gabrielle. "Finding the Inner Silence to Listen." Ingersoll 177–85.

Merivale, Patricia. "From 'Bad News' to 'Good Bones': Margaret Atwood's Gendering of Art and Elegy." York 253–70.

Morris, Mary. "Opening a Door onto a Completely Unknown Space." Ingersoll 139–152.

Nischik, Reingard M. *Engendering Genre.* Ottawa: U of Ottawa P, 2009.

_____, ed. *Margaret Atwood: Works and Impact.* Rochester, NY: Camden, 2000.

_____. "Murder in the Dark: Margaret Atwood's Inverse Poetics of Intertextual Minuteness." Wilson, *Textual Assassinations* 1–17.

Oates, Joyce Carol. "My Mother Would Rather Skate than Scrub Floors." Ingersoll 37–42.

Ovid. *Metamorphosis.* Trans. Mary Innes. London: Penguin, 1955. 315.

Plath, Sylvia. "Lady Lazarus." In *Ariel* (1966). New York: Harper, 1999. 6–9.

Rich, Adrienne. "Diving Into the Wreck." *Adrienne Rich's Poetry*. Ed. Barbara Charlesworth and Albert Gelpi. New York: Norton, 1975. 65–68.

Rosenburg, Jerome H. *Margaret Atwood*. Boston: Twayne, 1984.

Rosenthal, M. L. and Sally Gall. *The Modern Poetic Sequence*. New York: Oxford UP, 1983.

Sandler, Linda. "A Question of Metamorphosis." Ingersoll 18–36.

VanSpanckeren, Kathryn. "Atwood's Space Crone: Alchemical Vision and Revision in *Morning in the Burned House*." *Adventures of the Spirit: The Older Woman in the Works of Doris Lessing, Margaret Atwood, and Other Contemporary Women Writers*. Ed. Phyllis Sternberg Perrakis. Columbus: Ohio State UP, 2007. 153–80.

_____. "Half-Hanged Mary: Atwood's Female Crucifixion." *Once Upon a Time* 151–78.

_____."The Trickster Text: Teaching Atwood's Works in Creative Writing Classes." *Approaches to Teaching Margaret Atwood's* The Handmaid's Tale *and Other Works*. Eds. Sharon Rose Wilson, Thomas Friedman, and Shannon Hengen. New York: MLA, 1996. 77–83.

_____ and Jan Castro, eds. *Margaret Atwood: Vision and Forms*. Carbondale: Southern Illinois UP, 1988.

Wagner-Martin, Linda. "Giving Way to Bedrock: Atwood's Later Poems." York 71–88.

_____ "The Making of *Selected Poems*: The Process of Surfacing." *The Art of Margaret Atwood*. Eds. Cathy Davidson and Arnold Davidson. Toronto: Anansi, 1981. 81–94.

Wilson, Sharon Rose. "Fiction Flashes: Genre and Intertexts in *Good Bones*." Wilson, *Textual Assassinations* 18–41.

_____, ed. *Margaret Atwood's Textual Assassinations*. Columbus: Ohio State UP, 2003.

York, Lorraine M., ed. *Various Atwoods: Essays on the Later Poems, Short Fiction, and Novels*. Concord, ON: Anansi, 1995.

"Consider the Body": Remaking the Myth of Female Sexuality in Margaret Atwood's Poems in *Morning in the Burned House*

Tomoko Kuribayashi

Margaret Atwood is a well-practiced hand at rewriting mythology in her poetry and fiction. Beginning with her first poetry collection, *Double Persephone* (1961), followed by the poems in *Procedures for Underground* (1970) and the Circe/Mud poems in *You Are Happy* (1974), and most recently in *Morning in the Burned House* (1995), Atwood has revisited classical mythology and given poetic voices, endowed with much wry humor and analytical power, to hitherto silenced females. She has also explored the mythmaking found in our recent and contemporary celebrity culture in *Morning in the Burned House,* most notably in poems such as "Manet's Olympia," "Ava Gardner Reincarnated as Magnolia," and "Miss July Grows Older." Sometimes, also, Atwood considers myths or narratives that are part of Canadian literary heritage in her poetry, as she does in *The Journals of Susanna Moodie* (1970) or in *Animals in That Country* (1968). In *Moral Disorder* (2006), her rare collection of more openly autobiographical stories, Atwood relates a family narrative, which can also be seen as a microcosm of the history or national mythology of twentieth-century Canada.

Atwood, who is often described as one of our leading feminist writers, has long been interested in women's sexual self-expression, an issue that she revisits in *Morning in the Burned House.* "Consider the body," Olympia, the speaker-character in "Manet's Olympia," states, giving voice to one of Atwood's long-standing preoccupations in her art. Atwood came of age as a writer during the second-wave feminist movement of the late 1960s and early 1970s and over the years she has openly criticized what she sees as the ideological constraints imposed on women writers by feminism. But she also has remained deeply interested in the kinds of questions about women's embodied experience addressed by feminism, particularly in a contemporary era in which the younger, third-wave generation of feminists has come to question what they see as the sexual puritanism of the second-wave movement, the generation of their mothers. Atwood, who has always been attuned to cultural trends, captures the generational conflict between second- and third-wave feminists in the kinds of questions she asks in her poetry. For example, if a woman publicly or privately presents herself in a sexually explicit manner, as happens in the poem "Helen of Troy Does Counter Dancing," or if a woman claims she enjoys being in the flesh, as does Ava Gardner in "Ava Gardner Reincarnated as Magnolia," is she demonstrating how liberated she is and how much autonomy she has? Or is she turning herself into an erotic object in order to gain the limited power and control available to her if she caters to the needs of men? In addition, how does her sexual self-expression or public display of her sexuality affect other women? Is she turning back the clock and thus threatening to undo the gains made by feminism by seemingly accepting the culturally damaging sexualization of women? Or is she empowering herself by taking control of and asserting her sexuality? Not surprisingly, questions surrounding female sexuality—how women view and express their sexuality, and whether they are in control of or are controlled by their sexuality—have been the subject of much debate in recent years among feminist thinkers and activists. Thus, the questions Atwood asks in her poetry are the same questions that many women, including self-proclaimed feminists, are continuing to grapple with in today's world.

Atwood, who says that she "first became aware of the constellation of attitudes or wave of energy loosely known as 'The Women's Movement' in 1969," recalls the early days of second-wave feminism as a time when there was "a willingness to explore new channels of thought and feeling" ("If You Can't" 19, 20). The women's movement,[1] she states, expanded "the territory available to writers" and also offered a "sharp-eyed examination of the way power works in gender relations" even as it revealed that much of this was "socially constructed" ("Spotty-Handed" 132). Arising in the late 1960s and early 1970s, the second-wave movement focused on raising women's awareness of the male oppression of women under patriarchy. But Atwood also came to find second-wave feminism confining, especially when it began to harden into orthodoxy and as feminists began to dictate to women writers the types of characters they should create in their art. Fascinated with female badness, Atwood came to argue against what she saw as the feminist insistence that the female character must be a victim who struggles against or is "done in by male oppression" ("Spotty-Handed" 132). Thus, Atwood's work can be mapped against both second-wave feminism, which focused on the power politics of male-female relations and the male oppression of women, and third-wave feminism, which began emerging in the 1980s and became popularized in the 1990s as authors like Katie Roiphe, Naomi Wolf, and Camille Paglia began to criticize the second-wave movement for being too focused on the view that all women are victims of men. For example, Roiphe, in her book *The Morning After: Sex, Fear, and Feminism on Campus* (1993), claimed that second-wave feminists exaggerated the reality of violence against women in American society while Wolf, in *Fire with Fire* (1993), and Paglia, in *Sex, Art, and American Culture* (1992), argued that women could choose to obtain and use power through their sexuality, as well as through financial and professional success. But Wolf and Paglia also advocated individualism and capitalism, which are antithetical to the egalitarian and communitarian orientation of the majority of both second-wave and third-wave feminists. As Carolyn Sorisio states:

It seems as if some white, middle-class women want to claim victory before the struggle is over. They want to race into the (not quite) top echelon of society, grab the booty, and bask in their newfound power. Yet we cannot seriously challenge sexual exploitation and race and class oppression until we also interrogate unchecked capitalism and American individualism. (146)

Despite the critique of egalitarian third-wave feminists like Sorisio, the ideas popularized by writers like Wolf and Paglia have heavily influenced the way that feminism has been viewed in recent years in the popular imagination, convincing some that all that second-wave feminists want to do is complain about women's oppression and victimization and ask for special treatment to compensate for past wrongs. Atwood herself, in a 1993 address that was later published in a collection of her essays, offered a pointed critique of this second-wave point of view, arguing not only that it "homogenized" women by making one "the same as another" but also that it deprived women of "free will" through its belief that "the patriarchy made her do it" ("Spotty-Handed" 134).

Even as Atwood has argued against what she sees as the ideological rigidity of second-wave feminism, she remains deeply invested in the issue of female embodiment. "I agree, it's a hot topic," she writes in "The Female Body" as she moves a "topic" of feminist discussion from the abstract to the concrete: "I get up in the morning. My topic feels like hell. I sprinkle it with water, brush parts of it, rub it with towels, powder it, add lubricant" (69–71). But she also makes pointed references to the sexualization and objectification of the female body in contemporary culture. "The Female Body has many uses. It's been used as a door-knocker, a bottle-opener. . . . It sells cars, beer. . . . It does not merely sell, it is sold" (74). In her continuing focus on the female body and women's sexuality, Atwood engages with yet another issue of deep concern to second- and third-wave feminists, who approach the question of women's sexuality in very different ways.

By and large, second-wave feminists have tended to downplay, or even dismiss, the centrality of a woman's sexuality to her sense of self, and this drive to "de-sex women" has grown out of the second wave's desire to liberate women from being objectified, turned solely into objects of male desire. In contrast, third-wave feminists allow and even openly encourage young women to freely express their sexuality. Not only do "third-wavers pit arguments about women controlling their own sexuality and using their sexuality to wield power over men against second-wave arguments about the inherently exploitative nature of sexual performance," but "many third-wavers believe in the use of female sexuality as a power tool" (Gilley 190). In her autobiographical essay titled "Lusting for Freedom," noted third-wave feminist Rebecca Walker asks a question that is pivotal to the new, younger generation of third-wave feminists: "What do young women need to make sex a dynamic, affirming, safe and pleasurable part of our lives?"(23). The third-wave's view of sexuality as a potential, or even likely or indispensable, source of power that can also provide a sense of fulfillment for women is in stark contrast to the second wave's view of women as sexually objectified by men and exploited by society. Indeed, the second-wave movement has been called "victim feminism" because feminists from the 1960s and 1970s primarily saw women as "victims, particularly of sexual violence" (Gilley 188). Second-wave feminism also describes contemporary culture as a "rape culture" that condones, justifies, and even encourages sexual violence against women. Third-wave feminism's "approach to sexuality," in contrast, places emphasis on women's sexual "pleasure and power" rather than their "victimization" (Henry 22). The kind of third-wave feminism advocated by Naomi Wolf in *Fire with Fire* is often called "power feminism" (Henry 28) in contrast to the "victim feminism" (Henry 28) of the second-wave generation of feminists.

Because Atwood began writing during the second-wave feminist movement, many critics have noted the relevance of second-wave feminism's view of women as victims to Atwood's work, both creative and critical. Her 1972 book of literary criticism, *Survival: A Thematic Guide to Canadian Literature*, examined what she called the "super-abundance of victims in Canadian literature" (*Survival* 39), and over the years, much of her fiction and poetry has also highlighted female (and sometimes male) victimhood. Of the numerous examples, the more recent include her novels *Cat's Eye* (1988), *Alias Grace* (1996), *The Blind Assassin* (2000), and the first two volumes of her speculative fiction trilogy, *Oryx and Crake* (2003) and *The Year of the Flood* (2009). But while Atwood has long focused on female victims in her works, she has also insisted, as the title of her 1972 book *Survival* suggests, that victims need to find a way to become survivors. Yet the pathway to survivorship can be full of pitfalls and traps. In particular, it is all too easy for the woman victim to become an abuser on her way out of victimhood as Atwood shows in her novels where female characters like *Cat's Eye's* Cordelia or *The Blind Assassin's* Iris Chase Griffen victimize or sacrifice other women in order to secure their own survival. The fact that these characters use whatever means available or necessary in order to escape victimhood and/or obtain power and control makes the kind of criticism often leveled against "power feminists" highly relevant. As Atwood, in her recent works of fiction and poetry, continues to explore the issues surrounding female victimhood and survival (or empowerment), she remains preoccupied with the subject of female sexuality—how it affects women, both negatively and positively, and how women may use it to their own advantage. Thus, as she investigates women's embodied experience, she reveals the inextricable links between women's victimization and empowerment and their sexuality.

Morning in the Burned House

Atwood's poems in *Morning in the Burned House* cover the entire spectrum of ways in which women view their sexual desires, experiences, and/or expectations. The poems offer a comprehensive range, from overt criticism of male sexist views of women, to a strategic transcendence of or escape from the body and bodily matters, to an insistence on the need to find pleasure in the body or use it to one's advantage. In many of these poems, Atwood employs female speakers who either belong to classical mythology or come to us from the realm of the recent popular or celebrity culture. From classical mythology, Atwood summons Helen of Troy, Cressida, and Daphne as her speakers; in "Miss July Grows Older," she features a former centerfold; in "Ava Gardner Reincarnated as Magnolia," she conjures up another sex symbol—a more famous and perhaps more individualized one—from the late-twentieth-century popular culture; and in "Manet's Olympia," she resurrects the courtesan-model of the nineteenth-century painter Manet in a poem that presents a fresh look at a famous nude painting.

In all of these poems, Atwood uses first-person speakers (or, in "Manet's Olympia," the woman being painted speaks in the last stanza) as she gives women their own voices with which to discuss sexual matters. Even when the female speakers focus on their less than pleasant sexual experiences or openly admit that they have little to no power in their sexual negotiations with men, they are given poetic space to question and critique the culture that deprives them of autonomy, sexual and otherwise. At the same time, Atwood leaves plenty of room for ambiguity even in poems in which the women speakers seem to boast of their sexual power. Thus, the reader often leaves a poem feeling that the author (and perhaps even the speaker) may have been tongue in cheek in her affirmation and celebration of what a woman may be able to achieve through the overt use of her sexuality.

Some poems, such as "Miss July Grows Older" and "Daphne and Laura and So Forth," address the problematic nature of the traditional view of women as sex objects, and the rape culture that such a view enables. In "Miss July Grows Older," a retired centerfold frankly discusses her past sexual escapades and presents her reflections on them as an aging woman. Other poems, like "Manet's Olympia," present speaker-characters who are able to maintain a cynical distance from women's sexual objectification, which allows them to form and voice candid criticism of male sexism and the sexual exploitation of women. On the other hand, Ava Gardner and Helen, both figures of mythological beauty and sex appeal, present a more affirmative view of the female body and female sexuality: Gardner proclaims that she would rather not give up her bodily pleasures while Helen proudly announces that she does not hesitate to use her sexual attractiveness in order to gain power and control.

The speaker of "Daphne and Laura and So Forth" (*Morning* 26–27)[2] describes being pursued by a man (or a male deity) and turning herself into a tree or a nonhuman creature to escape being raped—or even possibly murdered. In her poem, Atwood draws on the Greek myth of Daphne, a nymph who fatally attracted the love of the powerful Greek god Apollo. Despite his earnest admiration and passionate pursuit of her, Daphne preferred to remain unmarried and, seeing that there was no other way to escape the love-struck god, she asked her father, the river god Peneus, to change her into a tree. She turned into a laurel tree in front of Apollo's eyes, upon which Apollo promised that her leaves, woven into wreaths, should always adorn victors' brows (see Bulfinch 24–25). Atwood's poem places the incident in a more contemporary setting, even suggesting a rape (and possibly murder) trial—"or that's what gets said in the court." After her physical transformation, Atwood's speaker says, "It's ugly here, but safer," and adds, "I'm free to stay up all night. / I'm working on/ these ideas of my own." The poem indicts the rape culture in which a woman who shows "fear, / or so much leg" is accused of inciting male sexual aggression and in which male violence is blamed on male naïveté and is even forgiven: "His look of disbelief– / *I didn't mean to!*" The speaker calls men "gods [who] don't listen to reason / they need what they need," suggesting that in patriarchal society men are powerful and in control like gods and are not required to explain their actions or face any consequences. The only way a woman can escape male sexual violence, the poem posits, is to give up her human, female body, by becoming covered by "bark /fur /snow." Once she is free of lustful male pursuit, the speaker is able to nurture her mind, a privilege she gains only at the cost of having to give up her body.

Unlike Daphne, the first-person speaker in "Cressida to Troilus: A Gift" (*Morning* 28–29) does not escape being forced into sexual relations, but she puts herself in a position superior to Troilus by labeling him as "stupidly innocent" and claiming that the main emotion she has felt for him is "pity." In a mythological story set in the time of the

Trojan War, Cressida (or Criseyde) was a young widow in Troy, with whom a young Trojan prince, Troilus, fell madly in love. With the help of his cunning uncle Pandarus, Troilus managed to sneak into Cressida's chamber, giving her no choice but to become his lover. Upon the fall of Troy, however, Cressida was given to the Greeks in exchange for a Trojan prisoner of war, after which she was said to have become the lover of a powerful general of the Greek army that had defeated Troy. Stories about her vary somewhat in details and explanations for her choices, but it is obvious that she was a woman at the mercy of historical forces and most likely a pawn in men's struggles for power. To the contemporary audience familiar with British literature, Cressida is known through works such as Geoffrey Chaucer's long poem *Troilus and Criseyde* and William Shakespeare's play *Troilus and Cressida.* In Atwood's poem, Cressida is given an opportunity to present her views of the situation. She sees Troilus as a "beggar," who does not know that "greed and hunger / are not the same." The so-called gifts or sexual favors she has given him are actually poisonous to him, "like white bread to goldfish." He has invited the trouble upon himself by desiring her when she clearly did not want him. As she recalls, he basically forced himself on her, "by stealth, by creeping up the stairs": it was basically a rape, though nobody in their society would have called it that. "You forced me to give you poisonous gifts," she says, adding that "everything I gave you was to get rid of you." In concluding the poem with the words, "Well, take this then. Have some more body," Cressida detaches herself from her body, refusing to give Troilus what she sees as the essence of herself. Since she is unable to withhold her body from him, Cressida separates herself from her body and keeps the rest—her nonphysical self—out of his reach.

It is telling that Cressida identifies with the mind in Atwood's poem. For in Western culture's Cartesian mind-body binary, which splits mind and body apart, men are associated with the valued mind (and thus with reason and the spirit) and women with the devalued body (and thus with the irrational and the abject physical).[3] But Atwood's

Cressida, even as her body is being used and abused, identifies with the mind. Thus what Cressida does in Atwood's poem—she detaches herself from what is being done to her body in order to preserve what she can of herself or to survive (to survive both Troilus's imposition and the fall of Troy)—may be considered an ultimate expression of the Cartesian way of thinking because, in abandoning or transcending her body, she is in a way agreeing that the body is less important than the mind. Still, she at least manages to maintain some sense of control despite her horrible predicament.

Replicating the strategy used by Daphne and Cressida, the courtesan-model in Manet's Olympia" (*Morning* 24–25) who speaks in the last stanza of the poem maintains control by distancing herself from the body that is depicted in the painting. The poem begins with a third-person speaker who challenges traditional ideals of femininity through a blatant description of the famous painting: the speaker calls the model's body "unfragile, defiant, the pale nipples / staring you right in the bull's-eye," and then adds, "The body's on offer, / but the neck's as far as it goes." The speaker also mocks and belittles an unseen male viewer, saying, "As for that object of yours / she's seen those before, and better." Even more pointedly, the model herself takes over in the italicized last stanza, asserting that "*I . . . am the only subject.*" Édouard Manet (1832–83) was a French painter who was regarded as one of the major early Impressionists, and his painting "Olympia" (1863) is considered to be one of his masterpieces. A reworking of earlier, more traditional portraits of nude women, "Olympia" caused scandal when it was first exhibited because of the model's confrontational gaze and details suggestive of her occupation as a courtesan, such as the presence of a black cat, an animal closely associated with dangerous sexuality and prostitution (Krell 59–60). Unlike earlier nude women in paintings who cast their eyes softly elsewhere, "Olympia meets us eye to eye. It's an ingenious and unsettling device," as Mary Elizabeth Williams has remarked. "The image in the frame is the one doing the sizing up, and it is we who are left feeling appraised" (Williams). In contrast to the prevailing ideals of women as nurturing and comforting, or else as sexually arousing, "Olympia, for all her blatant accessibility, is tantalizingly self-sufficient" (Williams). In her poem, especially in the final stanza, Atwood further emphasizes Olympia's independence and her transcendence of the body. "*I, the head, am the only subject / of this picture,*" Atwood's Olympia declares and she refers to the male viewer as a passive object good only for sexual gratification: "*You, Sir, are furniture. / Get stuffed.*" Atwood deliberately gives the painter's model more control not only by providing a third-person speaker who highlights the aggressive defiance of Manet's model but also by concluding the poem with a stanza in which the model becomes the speaking "subject" of the poem rather than the "object" of the male gaze and male sexual desire.

Like Olympia, Cressida, and Daphne, Atwood's Miss July, in "Miss July Grows Older" (*Morning* 21–23), transcends the body, or sexual experience in general, even though she has not given up her flesh all together. As a former centerfold, Miss July is anonymous—even exchangeable—and she has had her share of female sexual objectification and male threats of violence. Still, after recounting her past experiences with men, most of which were unpleasant if not downright dangerous—as in the death threats she received— Miss July says, "You grow out / of sex like a shrunk dress / into your common senses," and she downplays the significance of sexual experience to her sense of self: "But after a while these flesh arpeggios get boring, / like Bach over and over; / too much of one kind of glory." Like Daphne and Olympia, Miss July has discovered she is more than her body:

> When I was all body I was lazy.
> I had an easy life, and was not grateful.
> Now there are more of me.
> Don't confuse me with my hen-leg elbows:
> what you get is no longer
> what you see. (23)

Miss July's frank feminist critique of the way young women are objectified and made into something they really are not—and made anonymous and replaceable—is one obvious outcome of her feminist consciousness raising, which seems to have occurred along with her physical aging. Atwood's Miss July is no longer "all body," nor is she "lazy." Her life is not as "easy" as it used to be, but she is busy thinking and is more than her physical appearance. She has substance of the nonphysical kind and her own ideas. For example, she contemplates her physical surroundings, noting the "way the sun / moves through the hours" and "the smeared raindrops / on the window." More importantly, her maturity enables her to realize that "Men were a skill, / . . . / It was something I did well," and that, even though she handled men well, "breath[ing] into / their nostrils, as for horses," she did not particularly want to do so; she was simply induced by society's expectations to have sex with men or to make herself sexually alluring to men.

Miss July's ability to see herself as more than the body is made possible or aided by the fact that she is growing older, which is another aspect of women's lives Atwood's poem highlights. Aging can and does liberate women from being sexually objectified. While the experience of old age may involve "inescapable corporeality" (Song 81) as the body undergoes inevitable decline, aging women may also feel a new sense of freedom as they are liberated from the social construction of a youthful and sexualized femininity. Moreover, many aging women, as researchers have shown, seem better able than men to accept the "contradictions of life and death" as they get older (Maierhofer 168). Just as the "greying of American feminists in the late 1980's and early 1990's" is reflected in recent works that show women characters learning to view aging as "an empowering experience" (Maierhofer 171), so Atwood reflects this trend in a poem like "Miss July Grows Older."

If in poems like "Daphne and Laura and So Forth," "Manet's Olympia," and " Miss July Grows Older," Atwood's speakers echo second-wave feminism's critique of the male use and abuse of women's sexuality, in poems like "Helen of Troy Does Counter Dancing" (*Morning*

33–36) and "Ava Gardner Reincarnated as a Magnolia" (*Morning* 30–32), Atwood openly gives voice to third-wave feminism's views of the female body and its sexual powers and of how women may make use of or take pleasure in them. Atwood's decision to write about the mythical Helen of Troy is telling, for in Greek mythology Helen was considered to be the most beautiful woman in the ancient world. Born of a rape committed by Zeus, the god of gods who took the form of a swan when he assaulted the human Leda, Helen was one of the female twins Leda bore along with twin boys. (Each set of twins came out of an egg that Leda had laid. The boys later became the constellation Gemini.) When Helen was already—and happily—married to Menelaus, king of Sparta, Venus (also known as Aphrodite), the goddess of love, promised her as a prize to Paris, a prince of Troy, if he would help the goddess in a contest against Minerva (Athena) and Juno (Hera). The contest was about which of the goddesses was the fairest, and Paris chose Venus because she had promised him the fairest woman for his wife while the other two had offered him glory and renown in the war or power and riches. After her victory, Venus helped Paris to become Menelaus's guest so that he could persuade Helen to elope with him to Troy. Helen did so under the influence of Venus, which led to the Trojan War as Menelaus summoned an army of Greek generals in order to take his wife back from Troy (Bulfinch 196–97). The story of Helen and the Trojan War has long been interpreted as offering a warning about the dangers of women's sexual powers by providing a vivid illustration of the destruction that can be caused by a beautiful woman and men's competition over the possession of her. But in Atwood's "Helen of Troy Does Counter Dancing," Helen insists on the value of what she "sells" to men—vision and desire, as well as men's own "worst suspicions"—even while she is well aware of the violence that men who find her kind of merchandise attractive can inflict on women: "Reduce me to components / as in a clock factory or abattoir. / Crush out the mystery. / Wall me up alive / in my own body." Helen knows that other women are critical of her: "The world is full of women / who'd tell me I should be ashamed of myself / if they had the chance." But hers is a conscious and practical choice. Offering a very contemporary explanation, Helen says she prefers to sell what her body symbolizes rather than to be exploited in minimum-wage jobs: "I've a choice / of how, and I'll take the money." Rather than passively accepting her sexual objectification, Helen insists on exploiting her sexuality for her own financial gain.

Unlike Atwood's Helen, who expresses a certain cynicism about her sexuality, Ava Gardner, the speaker in "Ava Gardner Reincarnated as Magnolia," points toward the possibility of women's more positive embrace of their sexuality if only they could escape society's misogynistic views. A major Hollywood actress whose career spanned from the early 1940s through the mid-80s, Ava Gardner (1922–1990) was considered one of the most beautiful women of the day ("Ava's Story"). In Atwood's poem, Gardner admits that she was "never . . . / . . . taken seriously" and that "when I was in / the flesh, to be beautiful and to be / a woman was a kind / of joke." Her preference would have been to "enjoy" herself: "a little careless / love, some laughs, a few drinks – / but that was not an option." Instead, she had to contend with men trying to "nail / me in the trophy room, on the pool- / table if possible, the women simply to poke / my eyes out." And yet, she would still choose to be a woman, rather than to enjoy men's "privileges." As she affirms, "I'd rather / be a flower," even a paper one to be trampled under the morning after the party, as that is preferable to "all their [men's] history," complete with slaughters and statues. She would rather have "the pleasures / of thoughtless botany"; she would "give anything / to have it back again, in / the flesh, the flesh, / which was all the time / I ever had for anything. The joy." Hers is the joy that Miss July seems to have never experienced or even imagined. Even though she has been the target of hatred and anger, both from men and women because of her beauty and sexual appeal, Atwood's Ava Gardner can still enjoy her life as a woman and take pleasure in her body. Indeed, she insists that women are superior to men, for they are less destructive and more life-giving—as evidenced in her comparison of herself, or of women in general, to flowers. "I'd rather / be a flower," she insists, and her comparison of the female body to flowers is reminiscent of the imagery used by such feminist artists as Georgia O'Keefe and Judy Chicago, in which flowers represent female genitalia.

In *Morning in the Burned House*, Atwood gives voice to an interesting array of women's contemporary views of female sexual experience, such as Helen, who claims that selling sexual fantasies to men who can pay good money for them is a better choice than working at jobs that are financially unrewarding but seemingly more dignified and respectable; or Ava Gardner, who insists that the joy women might find in the flesh is more important than being socially recognized or "taken seriously" by society; or Daphne, who describes herself as a sexual victim. The relevance of the body to a woman's sense of self is also questioned as speaker-characters like Miss July and Cressida choose to detach themselves from their bodies in order to survive the humiliating sexual experiences inflicted on them. One central issue that all the poems address is women's control over their bodies and sexualities: what determines the extent to which a woman feels that her body and sexuality is her own, and what changes in society and our ways of thinking about gender and sexuality might accord women a greater sense of autonomy? Atwood's poetic explorations of the question of female sexual autonomy are accompanied by a consideration of the extent to which men's historical dominance over and violence against women have deprived women of their autonomy and dignity as well as by tentative explorations of what future heterosexual relations may be possible.

While Atwood is deeply interested in the kinds of issues addressed by feminism, she refuses to write according to any kind of feminist formula. "Life [is] complex and mysterious, with ironies and loose ends" and is not "a tidy system of goodies and baddies usefully labeled," as Atwood remarks, and so writers "are called by inner voices that may not coincide with the strictures of prevailing policy formulators" ("If

You Can't" 21, 22). Because Atwood adamantly believes that as a woman writer she should not be limited by any specific ideology, her poems in *Morning in the Burned House* encompass second- and third-wave feminism's differing views of women's realities and choices. It is significant that Atwood has chosen to create poetic narratives featuring well-known female figures who have served as archetypes—as either society's ideals of femininity or warnings against undesirable behavior—for real-life women as she sets out to explore contemporary women's sexual problems and possibilities. Indeed, Atwood's revisions of long-familiar narratives invite readers to imagine new possibilities of self-actualization—possibilities made viable or at least visible by the second- and third-wave feminisms—as she gives poetic voice to both mythological women characters and to characters from our more recent celebrity culture. In the relationship between fictionalized women in Atwood's poems and contemporary readers, the kind of tension, distrust, and even hostility often found between older and younger women, or spokespersons for the second- and third-wave feminisms, is replaced by a longing and trust that are rooted in the reality of long-shared experiences of women's lives.

Notes

1. "The second wave, which arose in the 1960s and 1970s as women involved in the civil rights struggle began to recognize their own oppression, has, as yet, no official ending date," as Jennifer Gilley notes (188). Gilley also adds, "The defining characteristic of the third wave is coming of age in the 1980s and 1990s" (188). Leslie Heywood and Jennifer Drake, editors of one of the major "third wave" collections of articles, *Third Wave Agenda*, have a narrower definition of third-wave feminists as "coming of age . . . in the late 1970s through the late 1980s" (2). Quite likely, these different accounts can be explained by the fact that Heywood and Drake were writing in the mid-1990s (their book was published in 1997), while Gilley's article came out in 2005. Astrid Henry, in her 2004 book *Not My Mother's Sister*, also suggests the possibility that third-wave feminism can belong to youth rather than Generation X: "It would appear . . . that 'third wave' remains a signifier of youth rather than of a particular generation" (34). It also seems necessary to point out here that the "third wave" authors most popularized through mass media in the 1990s, such as Katie Roiphe, Nao-

mi Wolf, and Camille Paglia, are not necessarily representative of the third wave as a whole. I would also like to note that the three well-known authors are in disagreement over some issues: for example, Wolf believes that Paglia and Rophie underestimate the prevalence of sexual violence against women (Wolf 135–36).

2. I use inclusive page numbers rather than line numbers when quoting from Atwood's poems in *Morning in the Burned House*.

3. Traditionally, in the Judeo-Christian way of thinking, men are associated with the spirit while women are associated with the body and matter. This view is also shared and supported by the concept of the Cartesian split, the idea that the human mind is more important than the human body, established by the French philosopher René Descartes (1596–1650). Both Susan Bordo in *Unbearable Weight* (5) and Elizabeth Grosz in *Volatile Bodies* (4) discuss the dichotomous alignment of women with the body and men with the spirit or mind. Men are valued for what they can do with their minds while women are valued (or devalued) for what their bodies can do (or cannot help doing). The mind should control the body; therefore, men, who are more rational, should control women, who are less rational. The same need for control applies to nature, which is usually considered female as is obvious in the term "Mother Nature." Cressida's perceived betrayal of Troilus is in some ways expected because that is what women do: they seduce and then destroy men just by being female, if and when men do not take measures to keep women under control. Additionally, from the traditional male point of view, which Troilus and his co. may have shared, Cressida's giving her body to men and keeping the rest of herself for herself may not have mattered since to them a woman's mind would be nonexistent or of no value.

Works Cited

Atwood, Margaret. "The Female Body." *Good Bones and Simple Murders*. New York: Bantam, 1994. 69–77.

_____. "If You Can't Say Something Nice, Don't Say Anything at All." *Language in Her Eye: Views on Writing and Gender by Canadian Women Writing in English*. Ed. Libby Scheier, Sarah Sheard, and Eleanor Wachtel. Toronto: Coach, 1990. 15–25.

_____. *Morning in the Burned House*. New York: Houghton, 1995.

_____. "Spotty-Handed Villainesses: Problems of Female Bad Behavior in the Creation of Literature." *Writing with Intent: Essays, Reviews, Personal Prose, 1983–2005*. New York: Carroll, 2005. 125–38.

_____. *Survival: A Thematic Guide to Canadian Literature*. Toronto: Anansi, 1972.

"Ava's Story." *Ava Gardner Museum*. Ava Gardner Museum, 2010. Web. 1 June 2011.

Bordo, Susan. *Unbearable Weight: Feminism, Western Culture, and the Body*. Berkeley: U of California P, 1993.

Bulfinch, Thomas. *Bulfinch's Mythology*. New York: Modern Lib., 1998.

Gilley, Jennifer. "Writings of the Third Wave." *Reference and User Services Quarterly* 44.3 (Spring 2005): 187–98.

Grosz, Elizabeth. *Volatile Bodies: Toward a Corporeal Feminism*. Bloomington and Indianapolis: Indiana UP, 1994.

Henry, Astrid. *Not My Mother's Sister: Generational Conflict and Third Wave Feminism*. Bloomington and Indianapolis: Indiana UP, 2004.

Heywood, Leslie, and Jennifer Drake. Introduction. *Third Wave Agenda: Being Feminist, Doing Feminism*. Ed. Leslie Heywood and Jennifer Drake. Minneapolis: U of Minnesota P, 1997. 1–20.

Krell, Alan. *Manet and the Painters of Contemporary Life*. London: Thames, 1996.

Maierhofer, Roberta. "Third Pregnancy: Women, Ageing and Identity in American Culture. An Anocritical Approach." *Old Age and Ageing in British and American Culture and Literature*. Ed. Christa Jansohn. Munster, Germany: LIT, 2004. 155–71.

Paglia, Camille. *Sex, Art, and American Culture: Essays*. New York: Vintage, 1992.

Roiphe, Katie. *The Morning After: Sex, Fear, and Feminism on Campus*. Boston: Little, 1993.

Song, Ryan. "Comparative Figures of Ageing in the Memoirs of Colette and Beauvoir: Corporeality, Infirmity, Identity." *Corporeal Practices: (Re)figuring the Body in French Studies*. Ed. Julia Prest and Hannah Thompson. Oxford: Lang, 2000. 79–89.

Sorisio, Carolyn. "A Tale of Two Feminisms: Power and Victimization in Contemporary Feminist Debate." *Third Wave Agenda: Being Feminist, Doing Feminism*. Ed. Leslie Heywood and Jennifer Drake. Minneapolis: U of Minnesota P, 1997. 134–49.

Walker, Rebecca. "Lusting for Freedom." *Listen Up: Voices from the Next Feminist Generation*. 1995. Rev. ed. Ed. Barbara Findlen. Emeryville, CA: Seal, 2001. 19–24.

Williams, Mary Elizabeth. "Manet's 'Olympia.'" *Salon*. Salon Media Group, 13 May 2002. Web. 1 June 2011.

Wolf, Naomi. *Fire with Fire: The New Female Power and How It Will Change the Twenty-First Century*. New York: Random, 1993.

Gender and Genre in Atwood's Short Stories and Short Fictions_____

Reingard M. Nischik

Although Margaret Atwood is generally known for her novels, she belongs to the rare species of writers who have excelled in practically all literary genres. Thus my book, *Engendering Genre: The Works of Margaret Atwood* (2009), features comprehensive chapters on her poetry, her short fictions and prose poems, her short stories, her novels, her involvement with film, her works of literary and cultural criticism, and her comics. Focusing on the question of how Atwood has developed these genres to be gender-sensitive in content and also form,[1] I show that genre and gender in Atwood's oeuvre intertwine in a combination of complicity and critique. In her focus on gender issues in her works, Atwood often ends up revising the traditional design and demarcation lines of (sub)genres with respect to both content/theme and form. As I highlight this process—which I call "engendering genre"— I illuminate in Atwood's works not only the role gender plays in constituting genre and, conversely, the role genre plays in constituting gender, but also Atwood's self-conscious play with intersections of gender and genre (see *Engendering Genre* for more detail). In a less complex manner, "engendering genre" in Atwood's works also refers to the foregrounding of gender in specific textual formats, which will be my main focus in this chapter as I discuss the complexities of gender and genre in representative short stories and short fictions by Atwood.

The very versatility and variability of genre that characterizes Atwood's oeuvre as a whole may clearly be seen when focusing on her short prose. Indeed, Atwood is arguably at her most experimental in her short prose. In order to come to grips with the variability of these texts, we may roughly divide her short fiction, first of all, into short stories proper and, secondly, into so-called short fictions, prose poems, and "fictional essays." The second category, in particular, encompasses such a variety of different subgenres and formats of fictional short prose not easily classifiable that scholars and critics have resorted to a considerable number of different terms and generic labels—some of them rather inventive but not particularly useful, such as "short shorts" or "gems." Especially noteworthy for their formal and stylistic variability are Atwood's "short fictions"—the collective term most frequently used for these varied literary texts that are shorter than short stories proper. In her bending, twisting, crossing, and transcending of genre boundaries Atwood proves to be an experimental if not avant-garde practitioner of a genre that Brander Matthews, one of the earliest theorists of the short story, had already hyperbolically characterized as having "limitless possibilities" (77). Indeed, Atwood's genre-bending works are in line with what postmodern aesthetics and genre theory have diagnosed as "the arbitrariness and undecidability of generic boundaries" (Delville 57). As Atwood's short fictions combine genre and gender issues, they at the same time testify to the "arbitrariness and undecidability of gender boundaries" in line with, for instance, Judith Butler's research on the social constructedness of gender and the relativity if not arbitrariness of gender boundaries. As I will demonstrate in my chronologically structured assessment of Atwood's short fiction oeuvre, Atwood's works emphasize not only that genre and gender should not be taken for granted, but, more importantly, that they are subject to change since they are responsive to social, ideological, and cultural developments.

Not surprisingly, Atwood started out in this genre with the production of short stories proper—four of her seven collections of short prose belong to this first category: *Dancing Girls and Other Stories* (1977), *Bluebeard's Egg* (1983), *Wilderness Tips* (1991), and *Moral Disorder* (2006). The fifteen-year gap between her acclaimed third short-story collection, *Wilderness Tips,* and her latest short-story collection, *Moral Disorder*, may also be explained by her exploration of new generic territories during this period with her collections of short fictions as well as prose poems and fictional essays in *Murder in the Dark: Short Fictions and Prose Poems* (1983), *Good Bones* (1992), and *The Tent*

(2006). Even as Atwood returns to the short story proper in *Moral Disorder*, this collection also marks another generic debut in her oeuvre because *Moral Disorder* is her first short-story cycle.

The fourteen short stories collected in her first collection *Dancing Girls* had been first published individually between 1964 and 1977, thus indeed marking the early phase of Atwood's writing. When considering the character constellations and the themes of these stories, a statement from Atwood's poetry of the same period comes to mind: "This is not a debate / but a duet / with two deaf singers" ("Two-Headed Poems" 227), for these early short stories portray characters in unfitting, unfulfilling, or disintegrating relationships. A lack of self-confidence, the feeling of being trapped within the wrong body—such feelings of inadequacy lead many characters in *Dancing Girls* into dysfunctional relationships that confirm their negative opinions of themselves, whether through their partners' open lack of interest, their attitude of dominance, or their sexual betrayal. The stories demonstrate how the characters' failure to come to terms with themselves results in their inability to form meaningful relationships: the protagonists are ultimately defeated by themselves, not by their partners.

A case in point is the opening story of the collection, "The Man from Mars," which was first published in 1977, two years after the end of the Vietnam War. This is a typical Atwood story in that it combines intellectually challenging writing with high readability and many humorous twists, despite the seriousness of the topic and of the events rendered. The story's title, "The Man from Mars," suggests the perceived alien and thus "other" status of a male Vietnamese student, who is staying in Canada pretending to study. The appearance and especially the behavior of the nameless Asian man are so utterly different from what the female protagonist Christine has experienced in her shielded middle-class life that he appears as totally "other" in this story. In Christine's family, in which the multicultural aspects of Canadian society are kept at bay, foreigners and, one gathers, nonwhite Canadians are referred to as "person[s] from another culture." The seedy young man from

Vietnam, after Christine initially has been kind to him, starts to follow her around, persistently, mysteriously, and obsessively:

> She was aware of the ridiculous spectacle they must make, galloping across campus, something out of a cartoon short, a lumbering elephant stampeded by a smiling, emaciated mouse, both of them locked in the classic pattern of comic pursuit and flight (22).

Since Christine is quite an unattractive young woman, the stranger's motives remain utterly opaque. However, due to his unswerving persistence, his obsessive tracking of Christine on the university campus eventually "render[s] her equally mysterious" (23). Although he is even less attractive than Christine, the Vietnamese immigrant temporarily reinstates heavyweight, plain Christine as feminine in the eyes of the Canadian males around her. In the end, the story takes an ironic twist in that it is finally Christine—who for once had been the center of a man's attention—who ponders upon the deported Asian's motives and worries about him as she obsessively searches out news on his homeland in reports on the Vietnam War. As "The Man from Mars" blends questions of gender and ethnicity, it challenges conventional cultural constructions of both. By presenting the story from Christine's perspective and rendering the strange young man through her eyes, Atwood enables the reader to participate in the construction and deconstruction of prejudice and misconception. The story clearly demonstrates how fragile, painful, and sometimes irresolvable the relationships between the sexes may be, even more so when coupled with the attempt at transcultural understanding. "The Man from Mars," the Asian stranger, remains an enigmatic figure to the end, not only for Christine but also for the reader.

The twelve stories included in Atwood's second short-story collection, *Bluebeard's Egg*, were written in the 1970s and early 1980s. This collection no longer focuses on individual psychological problems as did the stories in her first collection, but instead place emphasis on sociopsychological themes. Individuals are increasingly seen as part of their social surroundings and as members of specific groups. Whereas in the first collection the characters are often presented in what for them would be exceptional surroundings and exceptional circumstances—indeed, they can be viewed as Atwood's early "tourist characters"—in *Bluebeard's Egg* the characters are usually shown at home or within their family circles. The volume, which Atwood dedicated to her parents, contains several "family stories"—such as "Significant Moments in the Life of My Mother," "Unearthing Suite," and "Loulou; or, The Domestic Life of the Language"—that are marked by a warmth quite unlike the dark mood surrounding the alienated, desperate characters of Atwood's first short-story collection. The family unit, of course, is usually the location of people's earliest significant experiences with gender and gender relations.

An especially compelling family story is the opening story of this collection, "Significant Moments in the Life of My Mother," which was first published in this collection. The story is rendered as a retrospective account by a nameless first-person narrator, who focuses mainly on the representation of her (nameless) mother. The mother's stories and remarks transmitted to her children are either vividly rendered in direct speech and embedded with comments by the narrator, or are summarized by the narrator. In either case, the narrator enters into a sort of indirect retrospective dialogue with her mother, whose apparently cheerful mentality colors the writing. By telling stories to her children and others, the mother is rendered as a highly communicative and expressive character, observant, mentally alert, caring, not taking herself too seriously, and with a pronounced sense of humor.

The thus doubly narrated episodes, which are added to each other apparently at random, seem at first to belie their classification by the title as "significant moments" in the life of the mother. The stories mainly belong to the narrator's "family and the traditionally female-dominated domestic sphere, such as the story about a cat that "wet itself copiously" (19) on the mother's lap. Nevertheless, these

domestic events are obviously worth a story, on different levels of reception: because of the manner in which the narrator's mother tells
these episodes, and how their telling characterizes her; because of her
daughter's interpretation of the stories, attaching further significance
to them; and because of the influence and effects this particular mother
must have had on her narrator-daughter, who is a budding writer, as
the story as a whole and particularly its ending suggests. Indeed, the
narrator's mother seems like a born storyteller in several respects. She
obviously loves telling stories, she is entertaining and witty, and she is
very conscious of her listeners. She tells her stories only to a female
audience, as the narrator stresses. By offering meaningful characterization as she contextualizes her mother's stories, the daughter-narrator
attaches a weightier cognitive significance to her mother's storytelling
and, in the writing process, transfers an aesthetic value to the stories,
thereby transforming the anecdotes and episodes indeed into "significant moments." In this step from oral to written storytelling, from the
mother as domestic storyteller to the daughter as conscious narrator
and writer, lies the metafictional gist of this short story and its Chinese
box-like setup.

The story is not only a daughter's homage to her mother as well as
a celebration of the art of storytelling, demonstrating Atwood's anti-
romantic, rather pragmatic view of artistic creativity; it is also a homage to the often neglected female tradition in literature. Asked once
whether her muse was male or female, Atwood replied: "Oh, she's a
woman" (Sullivan 37). What the daughter could (and, in a possible
autobiographical reading of the story apparently did) learn from her
mother is, among other things, that the art of storytelling partly consists of the right selection and arrangement of material and includes the
art of omission: "she never put in the long stretches of uneventful time
that must have made up much of her life" (16); that a good storyteller
is a good listener and perceptive observer: "In gatherings of unknown
people, she merely listens intently, her head tilted a little. . . . The secret
is to wait and see what she will say afterwards" (17); that storytell-

ing may (or perhaps should) be connected with fun and delight: "my mother's eyes shine with delight while she tells this story" (21); and, that being a good performer is conducive to effective storytelling: "She takes all the parts, adds the sound effects, waves her hands around in the air" (17). In fiction as in life, the narrator's mother—or Atwood's mother if we read the story as autobiographical—provides the model for her daughter's muse in that she supplies the first female voice.[2]

It is indeed the female connection that influences the daughter most in the story. The world in which the girl grows up is a gendered world, in her own as well as her parents' perception, with the female sphere appearing more exciting to her, definitely inspiring her to a greater extent, for while "the structure of the house was hierarchical, with my grandfather at the top . . . its secret life . . . was female" (13). The narrator learns from her mother that men "for some mysterious reason, find life more difficult than women do" and so they must not be told about painful things, for learning about "the secret depths of human nature, the sordid physicalities, might overwhelm or damage them" (22). Atwood is one of the few contemporary authors to occasionally set scenes of female bonding—as in the scene in which the mother and daughter share a collusive smile at the father's expense (15)—against an overwhelming (literary) tradition of male bonding. "Significant Moments in the Life of My Mother" demonstrates how high-quality literature may spring from the traditionally female sphere of the domestic and how well aware Atwood has been of the long-neglected female influences in life and art, of the female tradition of storytelling and writing in which she firmly places herself with this story.

Wilderness Tips (1991), Atwood's third collection of short stories, features ten stories written in the 1980s. These stories, moving away from the family orientation of the previous collection, tend to present characters in their work context. "Hairball" and "Uncles," for instance, focus on talented female characters who have succeeded professionally even in the face of resentment and nasty envy among their male colleagues. The story "Death by Landscape," following in the footsteps of

"Significant Moments," features an additional new thematic, gender-related aspect within Atwood's short prose. As she does in her novel *Cat's Eye* (1988), published three years earlier, in "Death by Landscape" Atwood places gender problems in a same-sex context that goes beyond the mother-daughter and father-son relationships that she had explored earlier. In this story, the tentative friendship that for several years links the Canadian schoolgirl Lois with the American girl Lucy turns out in retrospect to carry more emotional power than any of Lois's subsequent relationships, including that with her husband, Rob. The lasting bond between the girls is strengthened by Lucy's mysterious, unsolved disappearance into the Canadian wilderness during a summer camp excursion. After the death of her husband, the adult Lois reviews her life up to that point, recognizing that it has taken two paths: an "official" life that Lois has lived physically, and an "unofficial" inner life of the mind—a typical division among Atwood's characters. In this story, the "untold story" develops into the conscious, dominant path:

> she can hardly remember getting married, or what Rob looked like. Even at the time she never felt she was paying full attention. She was tired a lot, as if she was living not one life but two: her own, and another, shadowy life that hovered around her and would not let itself be realized—the life of what would have happened if Lucy had not stepped sideways, and disappeared from time. (127–28)

Here, as in the story "Weight" from the same collection, the male-female relationships and conflicts found in many early stories are reduced in importance because for the female protagonists their emotional and (in "Weight") intellectual friendships with other women turn out to be the deepest, most personal, and most formative relationships in their lives. Relationships between men and women, on the other hand, are marked too strongly by conventional gender patterns (not to say rituals) of behavior, and seem rather to get in the way of the female characters' individual development in this collection.

Since the 1980s, Atwood has employed new textual formats for her challenging rewritings and explorations, short texts that are altogether hard to classify and have few genuine forerunners in Canadian literature. Although the texts collected in *Murder in the Dark: Short Fictions and Prose Poems*, *Good Bones*, and *The Tent* do include pieces that operate within the generic parameters of the short story, it would be inaccurate to describe them simply as short-short-story or prose-poetry collections. Short dialogues, dramatic monologues, and "essay-fictions" are among the text formats featured in these collections.

Also representative of Atwood's contribution to the postmodern development of generic hybridization and intensified intertextuality is her involvement with the prose poem, especially in *Murder in the Dark* and in *Good Bones*. The prose poem had been mainly created by French author Charles Baudelaire, who was also known for his misogyny and his reification of women in his writing. In several of the pieces in *Good Bones* and *Murder in the Dark*, Atwood gets into an intertextual, revisionist dialogue with Baudelaire. For instance, her prose poems "Worship" and "Iconography" in *Murder in the Dark* can be read as critical cross-referencing of Baudelaire's prose poems, "Un hémisphère dans une chevelure" and "Un cheval de race," from his *Le spleen de Paris* (1864) and of his poems, "Le serpent qui danse" and "Le chat," from his *Les fleurs du mal* (1868). Atwood's "A Beggar" in *Murder in the Dark* refers back to Baudelaire's "Assommons les pauvres" from *Le spleen de Paris*; "Bad News," the opening work of *Good Bones*, recalls Baudelaire's "Au lecteur" from *Les fleurs du mal*; "Let Us Now Praise Stupid Women" in *Good Bones* includes a direct reference to the latter well-known text by Baudelaire; and, Atwood's prose poem, "Men at Sea," from *Good Bones* is an inversive writing back to Baudelaire's poem, "L'homme et la mer," from *Les fleurs du mal*.[3] In such texts, Atwood responds to Baudelaire in various ways: most fundamentally, in her elaboration of the hybrid genre of the prose poem, which did not really have a generic tradition in Canada when Atwood adapted the form in *Murder*; secondly, by way of specific intertextual references to Baudelaire's poems and prose poetry in her prose poems; and, thirdly and most importantly, by her revisionist handling of themes Baudelaire had dealt with, most notably in Atwood's very different treatment of gender. In fact, it is Baudelaire's self-serving and self-enhancing, reified and sexualized portrayals of women that most spur on Atwood's revisionist rewriting of Baudelaire, by means of a method that starts out by cleverly subverting Baudelaire's themes and evaluations and eventually using full-fledged inversion techniques.[4] As Atwood progresses from *Murder in the Dark* to *Good Bones*, she uses increasingly bold and drastic counterrepresentations hinging on gender, which are stirred and at the same time tempered by her injections of playful and comic elements.

This development in her technique of gender representation, largely from subversion to inversion, may be seen for instance by a comparison of "Liking Men" (from *Murder*) with "Making a Man" (from *Good Bones*). These two texts also demonstrate, of course, that Atwood is by no means only—or even mainly—concerned with the representation of female characters. In "Liking Men," there is a facetious irony right from the beginning—"It's time to like men again. Where shall we begin?" (53)—as Atwood subverts the traditional Baudelairean approach in which the male author's portrayals of women self-servingly reify them: that is, make them into dehumanized objects. In Atwood's text, an unusual reversal of roles takes place, with the woman author portrayed as reifying men. With Baudelairean symmetry, "Liking Men" is divided into two halves by the triggering phrase, "You don't want to go on but you can't stop yourself" (53). After dismissing a variety of male body parts as being too problematic to be liked, the speaker ironically singles out the seemingly harmless and utilitarian feet as pars pro toto objects for "liking men." But, alas, even in this context of male feet, a positive approach—"You think of kissing those feet. . . . You like to give pleasure" (53)—may hardly be kept up in the speaker's train of thought as she then remarks on less likable or even obnoxious styles of behavior connected with men: the associations evoked by footwear, though benign at first, inexorably lead from "dance shoes," "riding boots," "cowboy boots," and "jackboots," to scenes of war and rape in which man is the aggressor. Improving upon Baudelaire, who resorts to stereotypical representations of women, the first-person narrator in "Liking Men" attempts to differentiate between man as a category (which includes rapists and war mongers) and men as individuals: "just because all rapists are men it doesn't follow that all men are rapists. . . . You try desperately to retain the image of the man you love and also like" (54). This attempt at a circumspect, nonstereotypical view of men takes the first-person narrator back to the man's birth and his socialization, that is, to the social context and conditions that have influenced his life story. Despite the ironic undercurrents of "Liking Men," Atwood in this piece, quite in contrast to Baudelaire's very partial view of gender, thus grapples for a balanced, nonstereotypical acknowledgment of the individuality of men while remaining aware of the social and sociopsychological conditions that breed misogynistic behavior. Nevertheless, "Liking Men" in its rather unflattering and unimpressed view of men is a subversion of the Baudelairean intertexts with their heroification of man and reduction of woman (compare also Baudelaire's poem, "L'homme et la mer," from *Les fleurs du mal* with Atwood's subversive treatment of the text in her prose poem, "Men at Sea," from *Good Bones*). Both intra- and intertextually, "Liking Men" emphasizes the constructedness and thereby fluidity of gender images and roles. Atwood's unconventional, subversive portrayal of men, women, and gender relations has a fundamentally didactic as well as political intention, as can be seen even more clearly in her later collection, *Good Bones*.

"Making a Man" from *Good Bones* is a humorous attack on, and inversion of, women as commodities of popular culture. While Atwood in her intertextual method in these collections frequently gets into a dialogue with authors from world literature, as is the case with Baudelaire, or also Shakespeare (see Atwood's take on *Hamlet* in "Gertrude Talks Back"), "Making a Man" turns to intertexts of popular journalism and mocks its commodification of women. Mimicking the style of women's magazines as it gives readers tips on how to "make a man," the text takes the form of a recipe that presents various creative methods for baking, sewing, or even—ironically suggestive—inflating figures of men, thereby smugly parodying the stylistic conventions of cookbooks and other how-to books. The first, the "Traditional Method," of "making a man" irreverently parodies the biblical creation myth. The third, the "Clothes Method," too, is laced with word play and a critique of traditional gender roles: "Clothes make the man! How often have you heard it said! Well, we couldn't agree more! However, clothes may make the man, but women—by and large—make the clothes, so it follows that the responsibility for the finished model lies with the home seamstress" (55). The fifth and last method, "Folk Art Method," in its imagery stresses the reductive reification of man in this text, though nicely packaged in a kind of cute style: "You've seen these cuties in other folks' front yards, with little windmills attached to their heads. They hammer with their little hammers, saw with their little saws, or just whirl their arms around a lot when there's a stiff breeze" (57). Such stylized representations of men take the antiessentialist constructedness of gender images at face value and demonstrate Atwood's playful intertextual poetics of inversion at work in the smallest of places.

"The Little Red Hen Tells All," " similar to "Gertrude Talks Back," also from *Good Bones*, is an illuminative example of Atwood's gender revisionism concerning the representation of women. Again, as in "Death by Landscape," Atwood juxtaposes an "official," conventional story with an "unofficial" version. In this case, however, the differences between the two versions are directly explored and, so to speak, made "public." The parable-like tale by the hen telling "all" is also an example of Atwood's repeatedly "revising" received stories from popular culture, such as fairy tales and myths, with an eye to the gender models/stereotypes perpetuated by such influential tales. "The Little Red Hen Tells All" is based on a children's tale widely known in the English-speaking world. Atwood reproduces the basic structures of this fable but adds imaginative amplifications and ambivalent word play—for example, "A grain of wheat saved is a grain of wheat earned" (12)—as well as precisely integrated comments on the plot, which expose with apparent casualness the popular tale's intellectual implications by commenting, for instance, on the capitalist ideology supporting production and maximization of profits: "Sobriety and elbow-grease. Do it yourself. Then invest your capital. Then collect" (11). Atwood's most important reinterpretation in this story, however, concerns gender difference. By highlighting the gender of the female "narrator-hen," Atwood brings to light the ideological impact of the tale, both in its original and its new version.

The gender roles in the original folk tale (which is, ironically, often passed on orally from mothers to their children) are, on closer inspection, rather strangely conceived. The egocentric, hoarding, greedy behavior of the female "narrator," the hen—"I'll eat it myself, so kiss off," says the hen (13)—does not comply with the typical female behavior patterns of nourishment and generosity; it rather resembles the typical behavior of a "rooster." Atwood further parodies the original story by eventually supplanting this selfish demeanor with traditionally associated "feminine" qualities, such as freely putting oneself in second position and thinking of others first. The conflict is thus transferred from the external to the internal: because of her gender-specific socialization, the hard-working hen acts contrary to her own (economical) interests and needs in a way that is much in favor of the common good, but verges on her own self-denial. The capitalist ideology of the folktale is thus modified in Atwood's retelling through a foregrounding of gender difference. In her adaptation to a gender-conscious era, Atwood makes clear the pitfalls of gender differentiation, to which "hens"/women fall victim far more often than do "roosters"/men. Her story also makes clear that women's self-effacing behavior grows out of gender-specific socialization and is responsive to social context.

Atwood's most recent book of "short fictions," *The Tent* (2006), again includes a variety of textual formats: there are two works one can rightly call poems, mainly because they are printed with indentations;

two short dialogues, verging on minidramas; three fables; several episodic rewritings of previous literature and of mythology; as well as a hybrid textual format we may call "essay-fictions." The latter format tends to color this collection, with the predominant impression of the volume being a reflective rather than a narrative one.

The hybrid term "essay-fiction" tries to capture the fact that many of these works are written in the reflective "I" (or even "you") form and show us a mind at work, pondering some problem or state of affairs, rather than narrating a sequence of events. Yet these "musings" or "mini-musings" are not passed off as coming straightforwardly from the author's pondering mind, as in a traditional essay. Instead they are clothed in fictional, literary frameworks—such as the frame of a "narrated" event, as in "Winter's Tales," or a quasi-poetical use of language, as in "No More Photos"—which in fact brings some of these works close to, or makes them at times even indistinguishable from, prose poetry. The narrative impulse in these works is toned down in favor of metaphorical, symbolic, parabolic meaning rather than referential meaning (Stanzel 23), extending the range of significance towards the abstract and towards generalization, and sometimes even towards the archetypal. It is striking that these essay-fictions in *The Tent* are often concerned with an aging writer persona and with aspects of the writer's craft and profession, thus giving these texts an autobiographical as well as metapoetical twist, while at the same time using fictional/narrative elements to work against it. Gender issues are of less importance in this late collection.

A good example is "Encouraging the Young" (17–19), which begins straightforwardly, like an essay, about an older writer's stance towards the ambitious young (writers): "I have decided to encourage the young. Once I wouldn't have done this, but now I have nothing to lose. The young are not my rivals" (17). But even in the first paragraph, the poet raises her head by adding in metaphorical style: "Fish are not the rivals of stones" (17). The rather factual first paragraph is followed by a second paragraph that starts to twist the writer's self-expression in a weird, unreal direction by doing away with a reasonable, proportionate distribution of praise: "I will encourage them en masse. I'll fling encouragement over them like rice at a wedding. They are *the young*, a collective noun. . . . I'll encourage them indiscriminately, whether they deserve it or not. Anyway, I can't tell them apart" (17). This rather factual statement is immediately followed by a poetical version of it: "So I will stand cheering generally, like a blind person at a football game: noise is what is required, waves of it, invigorating yelps to inspire them to greater efforts" (17). The older author's persona writes from an apparently superior, cynical stance: "There you are, young! What is a big, stupid, clumsy mess like the one you just made—let me rephrase that—what is an understandable human error, but a learning experience? Try again! Follow your dream!" (18). The "I's" (ironically) self-congratulatory attitude—"What a fine and shining person I am. . . . now I'm generosity itself. Affably I smile and dole" (18)—is at the end of the text openly called into question by the writer herself: "my motives are less pure than they appear. They are murkier. They are lurkier. . . . and I see that I am dubious" (18–19). The writer persona then indirectly compares herself to an old fairytale witch who beckons with an "increasingly knobbly forefinger" as she lures the ambitious young to *"a lavish gingerbread house, decorated with your name in lights" (19)*. In other words, "Encouraging the Young" develops into a Hansel-and-Gretel story, in the writer's mind, with the writer as an ensnaring witch who knows that the ambitious young can hardly resist the glaring temptations of fame: *"Wouldn't you like to walk into it* [the lavish gingerbread house] *. . . stuff your face on sugary fame? Of course you would!"* (19).

Is "Encouraging the Young" Atwood's partly factual, partly fictional response to hoards of younger writers clamoring for her attention and support? Is cynicism an understandable reaction under the circumstances? Or is this work a warped reflection of envy on the aged writer's part towards "the young," who have everything still ahead of them? Is this essay fiction purely fictional or does it instead show us Atwood's/a writer's mind at work, analyzing her own attitudes and motives, as in an essay, but with fictional padding and twists? Significantly, the last sentence of the work is resoundingly ambivalent: "I won't fatten them in cages, though. . . . I won't drain out their life's blood. They can do all those things for themselves" (19). Does this mean that "the young" are destroying themselves and do not care about advice from the older, more experienced writer? Or might this ending cast, at second glance, also a new, more positive light on the text as a whole? For even though it is put in negative terms, this concluding sentence may suggest that the younger writers are not dependent on the older one, after all, but can strike out on their own. The narrator's superior, if not seemingly arrogant stance towards the young is thus relativized in the closure, which further complicates its meaning. The "actions" told by the narrator are self-reflective, showing us a writer's ponderings of, finally, her own situation, rather than telling a story.

With the generic extensions and experiments in *The Tent*, Atwood further inscribes her writing into the history of short prose. She playfully experiments with form and how to merge significant bits of reality with a fictional vision and presentation. In blending elements of the essay with that of (short short) fiction, Atwood probes the borderlines between factual and fictional narration as she had done already, though on the level of content rather than of form, with her earlier story "Significant Moments in the Life of My Mother." Because the works in *The Tent* are indeed essay-fictions and not straightforward essays, the "I" is still a persona and should not be fully equated with Atwood, the writer. Yet the writer's persona in these essay-fictions seems so quintessentially Atwoodian, at least for Atwood experts, giving us recognizable aspects of her personality, at least of her image, as well as of her writing strategies, that several reviewers have compared this late collection to a writerly notebook or sketch book. Indeed, some of these pieces are so condensed and quizzical that Atwood sometimes seems to speak more to herself than to her readers, presenting a writer's mind trying to come to terms with problematic issues, such as aging or creativity. In their self-referential, autobiographical foundations and their reflective, retrospective tendencies, the essay-fictions in *The Tent* signal a "late style"[5] of Atwood's short prose production.

Something similar may be said of *Moral Disorder*, published in the very same year as *The Tent*. With this short-story collection—the individual stories of which were first published between 1996 and 2006—Atwood formally returns to the short story proper, though linking the individual stories thematically in such an integrative way that we may speak of this work as Atwood's first short-story cycle. *Moral Disorder* is clearly also her most "autobiographical" book, with Atwood the writer and family person in her mid-sixties taking stock and looking back, step by step in the individual stories sketching the development of the protagonist Nell from childhood to adulthood and older age within her family context—two of the eleven stories deal with Nell's childhood, one with her youth, eight mainly with an adult Nell, who is present in all stories. The structure of the book is predominantly chronological, within a largely retrospective framework and a sometimes montage-like alternation between narrative past and narrative present, a technique used in "The Headless Horseman," "The Labrador Fiasco," The Boys at the Lab." Yet the introductory story, "The Bad News"—presented in the present tense—shows an aged Nell with her long-time husband Tig, thus opening the book with the latest chronological story, to signal an essential aspect and tone of the collection as a whole: "The Bad News" exudes a sense of loss—loss of reckless optimism, of vitality—and a sense of fear and anxiety. In a way closing the circle with Atwood's first short-story collection, *Dancing Girls*, danger seems to lurk everywhere, although in this later collection danger also exists on a larger, political scale. Afraid of old age, illness, and a potential loss of mental capacity, Nell is in a precarious, gloomy mental state, with gender in this later existential situation—and later time period—apparently no longer a pressing issue for her.

It is significant that the two stories in which gender does figure prominently come in the first third of the book, which deals mainly with a young/er Nell in her childhood and youth. These periods, of course, are crucial for gender socialization, especially given the stories' setting in the 1950s and 1960s, when gender was a particularly defining and restrictive issue, especially for women. "The Art of Cooking and Serving" and "My Last Duchess" in *Moral Disorder* thus belong to the relatively few stories in Atwood's short-story oeuvre similar to "Betty" in *Dancing Girls*, "Hurricane Hazel" in *Bluebeard's Egg*, "Uncles," and "Death by Landscape" in *Wilderness Tips*—that show gender at work in the crucial younger, formative stages of life and that emphasize that gender is not in-born but is transmitted, constructed, and performed.

The story with the telling title, "The Art of Cooking and Serving," the second story in *Moral Disorder*, is a female initiation story telling of the daughter Nell's initiation into domestic life and mothering, and her eventual distancing from her family as she comes to reject her mother's influence. The story reveals that conventional gender expectations and restrictions are part of Nell's upbringing, for instance, by the fact that knitting is one of Nell's prime pastimes, not least because her mother is expecting a "late" child. Lillie is an unplanned baby and turns out to be "one of those" (22), as the doctor puts it, a nervous and nerve-racking child who hardly ever sleeps and who exhausts her family, especially her mother. Before the baby's sex is known, Nell reflects on the gendered color system for babies, blue for boys and pink for girls (11–12). She is praised by others for knitting diligently for the baby and is called "a good little worker" (20), thus reinforcing gendered socialization patterns that train little girls in the direction of motherhood. Whereas Nell, "with single-minded concentration" (14), is fully integrated into the family preparations for the birth of the third child, Nell's brother is hardly mentioned and his task under the new circumstances is not exactly taxing: "We would all have to pitch in, said my father, and do extra tasks. It would be my brother's job to mow the lawn, from now until June" (13).

When Nell is not knitting the layette for the baby or cleaning the house, another pastime of hers is to read a how-to book, Sarah Field

Splint's *The Art of Cooking and Serving* (1931), published about ten years before Nell was born (just like Atwood herself, incidentally). Splint's book sets Nell's thoughts into motion: "Did I want to transform, or to be transformed? Was I to be the kind homemaker, or the . . . untidy maid? I hardly knew" (19). In her insecure, transgressive state of development, she is on the one hand thankful for guidance from role models, but, on the other hand, cannot decide on one or the other— probably because both of them are heavily engendered and she is looking for other options. Yet when Nell openly rebels against her mother and the nurturing role her mother is steering her toward in a gender-essentialist manner, she is punished. To act against ingrained gender roles in an open manner may entail pain, in more than one sense: "My mother stood up and whirled around, all in one movement, and slapped me hard across the face" (23). Nevertheless, the end of the story sees young Nell drifting away from the domestic, nurturing role supposedly cut out for her, mentally drifting into a new kind of outside world of peer groups, "to all sorts of . . . seductive and tawdry and frightening pleasures I could not yet begin to imagine" (23).

Whereas this distancing between mother and daughter in puberty is a common developmental step, the mother's pregnancy is rendered in rather unusual problematic terms in this story, thereby also working against any kind of euphemistic motherhood myth. For one thing, Lillie is a late, unplanned baby. Due to the advanced age of Nell's mother, her pregnancy is viewed with trepidation. Second, the newborn baby totally disarranges the family with her constant wailing. Third, Nell's mother becomes exhausted physically and mentally after giving birth to Lillie. Perhaps no wonder, then, that Nell eventually and explicitly opts against this kind of female familial restriction by rejecting responsibility for her younger sister. Again, the men in the family seem to have little to do with the baby; they are not shown to support the mother in her caring for the child and do not seem to particularly care. Atwood's "The Art of Cooking and Serving" thus renders traditional gender roles in problematic terms, showing these roles to work against women's independence and freedom of choice. Giving birth to a child and nurturing it are shown to be the concerns of women who must either accept the prescribed role or, painfully, opt out of it, as Nell does at the end of the story, leaving her overtaxed mother in the lurch.

As Atwood deals with the girlhood and youth of her protagonist Nell in her largely chronological short-story cycle in *Moral Disorder*, she emphasizes the social constructedness of gender and the performance status of femininities and masculinities in Nell's troubled coming of age. And she also, in this work, moves to other concerns as Nell comes to realize the reality of her aging: "These are the tenses that define us now: past tense, *back then*; future tense, *not yet*. We live in the small window between them" (4). Interestingly, over the course of some four decades Atwood's treatment of gender issues in her short stories and short fictions has developed largely according to the various stages of "victim positions" she differentiated early on in her 1972 work *Survival*: "Position One: To deny the fact that you are a victim"; "Position Two: To acknowledge the fact that you are a victim, but to explain this as an act of Fate . . . the dictates of Biology (in the case of women, for instance)"; "*Position Three: To acknowledge the fact that you are a victim but to refuse to accept the assumption that the role is inevitable*"; and finally "*Position Four: To be a creative non-victim*" (36–38). Especially in *Murder in the Dark* and in *Good Bones*, Atwood's subversive and inverse views on gender conceptions become even more incisive and outspoken, though not without a lighthearted, humorous treatment of a complex issue.

Atwood's treatment of gender relations in her short stories and short fictions may be read as "Instructions for the Third Eye," to take up the title of the resonant rounding-off text in *Murder in the Dark*. Atwood admonishes us, female and male readers alike, to transcend the dualistic thought pattern of either/or, which chains us to fixed identity positions and gender roles, and to be open to liberating, nonessentialist views of gender relations. In her recent short-story cycle *Moral Disorder*—although its protagonist in her younger years repeatedly feels subjected to gender clichés—an altogether nonessentialist view of gender relations seems achieved eventually, so much so that over larger parts of this collection gender is seldom foregrounded. As Nell reflects at the end of "The Entities" in *Moral Disorder*, "All that anxiety and anger, those dubious good intentions, those tangled lives, that blood. I can tell about it or I can bury it. In the end, we'll all become stories" (188).[6]

Notes

1. See my "Introduction" to *Engendering Genre* 1–15.
2. For an autobiographical reading of the story see Nischik, "Translation" 337–39.
3. For further details see chapter 2 in my book, *Engendering Genre*.
4. I earlier called this technique Atwood's "inverse poetics of intertextual minuteness"; see chapter 2 in my book, *Engendering Genre*.
5. The term "late style," as most prominently introduced by Theodor W. Adorno in 1937 and recently elaborated upon by Edward Said in his 2006 book, *On Late Style*, describes the work, or one single piece, of an aging author, which refers back to her or his previous work or earlier creative periods and which is possibly also marked by reflections on old age and death.
6. The framework for this chapter was provided by my earlier publications on Atwood's short prose, most notably my article, "Translation," and chapters 2 and 3 of my book, *Engendering Genre*.

Works Cited

Atwood, Margaret. *Bluebeard's Egg*. Toronto: McClelland, 1983.
_____. *Dancing Girls and Other Stories*. Toronto: McClelland, 1977.
_____. *Good Bones*. Toronto: Coach, 1992.
_____. *Moral Disorder and Other Stories*. Toronto: McClelland, 2006.
_____. *Murder in the Dark: Short Fictions and Prose Poems*. Toronto: Coach, 1983.
_____. *Survival: A Thematic Guide to Canadian Literature*. Toronto: Anansi, 1972.
_____. *The Tent*. Toronto: McClelland, 2006.
_____. "Two-Headed Poems, xi." 1978. *Eating Fire: Selected Poetry, 1965–1995*. London: Virago, 1998.
_____. *Wilderness Tips*. Toronto: McClelland, 1991.
Delville, Michel. "Murdering the Text: Genre and Gender Issues in Margaret Atwood's Short Short Fiction." *The Content and the Culmination*. Eds. Marc Delrez and Bénédicte Ledent. U of Liège: L³, 1997. 57–67.

Matthews, Brander. "The Philosophy of the Short Story." 1885. *The New Short Story Theories*. Ed. Charles E. May. Athens: Ohio UP, 1994. 73–80.

Nischik, Reingard M. *Engendering Genre: The Works of Margaret Atwood*. Ottawa: U of Ottawa P, 2009.

_____. " 'The Translation of the World into Words' and the Female Tradition: Margaret Atwood, 'Significant Moments in the Life of My Mother'" (1983). *The Canadian Short Story: Interpretations*. Rochester, NY: Camden, 2007. 331–40.

Said, Edward W. *On Late Style: Music and Literature Against the Grain*. New York: Pantheon, 2006.

Stanzel, Franz K. "Textual Power in (Short) Short Story and Poem." *Modes of Narrative: Approaches to American, Canadian and British Fiction*. Eds. Reingard M. Nischik and Barbara Korte. Würzburg: Königshausen, 1990. 20–30.

Sullivan, Rosemary. *The Red Shoes: Margaret Atwood Starting Out*. Toronto: Harper, 1998.

Atwood and the Gothic_____

Carol Margaret Davison

In both her critical and creative work, Margaret Atwood, one of Canada's most distinguished and prolific contemporary writers, has long exhibited a fascination with gothic literature. On at least two occasions in the mid-1980s, she taught a course on the subject of southern Ontario gothic and, in an interview with Joyce Carol Oates in 1978, she made reference to her long-standing interest in supernatural fantasy and the gothic, and to the doctoral dissertation she started at Harvard relating to the subject. Tentatively titled "The English Metaphysical Romance," Atwood's doctoral project, a copy of which is now housed in the Thomas Fisher Rare Book and Manuscript Library at the University of Toronto, focused on works by H. Rider Haggard, the author of the popular gothic work, *She* (1887), and several other late-Victorian writers. Taking their cue from critic Eli Mandel in his 1977 article, "Atwood Gothic," various scholars have argued that Atwood's graduate work was not ultimately abandoned but, rather, was distilled into her creative productions (169–70). While this cross-fertilization remains in evidence in some of Atwood's more recent publications, such as *The Blind Assassin* (2000) and *Oryx and Crake* (2003), its roots are readily apparent in her early productions, which constitute the focus of the present chapter. Thus Atwood's works may truly be said, as Karen F. Stein has recently claimed, to be marked by accretion, some being "especially rich in Gothic plots, stories, and narrative techniques" (32–33). Indeed, Margaret Atwood's seemingly disparate experiments in a variety of gothic forms, ranging from female gothic and gothic parody to postcolonial gothic and what Coral Ann Howells has categorized as "wilderness Gothic" (Howells, "Canadian" 106), has been vital in adapting an Old World gothic mode to address New World gothic issues and concerns within a Canadian context. Thus, Atwood may be credited with laying some crucial groundwork for the serious study of Canadian gothic literature in three works of critical

---

scholarship published over the thirty-year period between 1972 and 2002—*Survival: A Thematic Guide to Canadian Literature* (1972); *Strange Things: The Malevolent North in Canadian Literature* (1995); and *Negotiating with the Dead: A Writer on Writing* (2002). Curiously and notably, despite her occasional blind spots and erroneous claims about the gothic, Atwood's critical commentary occasionally serves as a key for interpreting her creative productions.

A Brief History of Gothic Literature

A brief overview of the anatomy and history of gothic literature, with an eye to its particular relevance and peculiar manifestation within a Canadian context, serves as a necessary launching-off point for considering the gothic's various reconfigurations—technical, thematic, and ideological—in Atwood's works. While the nature of this symbolic cultural form continues to be debated, certain key features have been recognized and theorized. Historically, the gothic elicited its greatest terror by threatening or transgressing symbolic boundaries relating to the self, the family, and the nation—identities that were being developed and contested in the eighteenth century with the rise of the middle classes and modernity. In its earliest manifestation in the mid-eighteenth-century British novel, the gothic registered these sociocultural developments. A battle ensued in gothic literature between pre-Enlightenment and Enlightenment belief systems, values, and ideas, the former being generally regarded as traditional and aristocratic, and the latter as progressive, capitalist, and middle-class. In text after text, modernity and what was conceived of as moderate/balanced rationalism was often placed in opposition to a religious worldview associated with superstition, the supernatural, and excess/fanaticism. The gothic, which soon spread as a mode/aesthetic to other forms such as poetry and short fiction, evinced multiple and sometimes contradictory standpoints vis-à-vis the Enlightenment. While in some instances it cast aspersions on the pre-Enlightenment worldview and its cautionary tales featuring various spectacular monsters, it also pointed up the Enlightenment's inadequacies, disabusing it of its smug certainties. The gothic offered up the timely reminder, to revise Hamlet's words in the face of his father's uncanny specter, that "there are more things in heaven and earth . . . than are dreamt of in . . . [Enlightenment] philosophy" (Shakespeare, *Hamlet* I.v.166–67). In doing so, it also, ironically and fittingly, shed light on the Enlightenment's dark propensities and blind spots.

Dark propensities and blind spots are writ large in the pages of the gothic. Indeed, obscurity is the gothic's calling card, darkness and repression being the order of the day. Gothic literature often features a central character who is (dis-/re-)located in a series of obscure, unknown settings, and in search of certainties in the way of a clearer sense of self, direction, and worldview. At its best, the gothic offers up a trenchant exposé of the dark side of institutions and of identity in its various forms—individual, familial, cultural, national, religious, etc. In some of the most terrifying gothic narratives, the boundary between self and other is blurred, thus threatening the protagonist's sense of self-identity and autonomy. The theme of transformation, a common gothic motif where, as Eugenia C. DeLamotte describes it, "what was x becomes y, the line dividing them dissolving" (21), is a principal dynamic: the self is threatened by the other or, as the tradition develops into the Victorian period and beyond, the other is revealed to be a repressed/secret/closeted aspect of the self. This terrifying self-other dynamic assumes additional significance in the subgenre of the gothic known as the female gothic, an adaptable form that Margaret Atwood has frequently employed in her writing. These narratives focus on a young woman's rite of passage into womanhood and her ambivalent relationship to contemporary gender roles and domestic ideology, especially the joint institutions of marriage and motherhood. In these works where, as one critic wittily notes, women "just can't seem to get out of the house" (DeLamotte 10), constraints abound and *real* identities are revealed, often at an emotional cost. The dark side of the home/domestic sphere, along with the gender roles that subtend the public/

private sphere division, is exposed as being, in certain respects, potentially imprisoning and the husband a potential prison master.

The "return of the repressed"-style scenario involving dreaded revelations about the self in relation to the obscure other is also extended into the role of history, both personal and political, and is brought to bear on the question of progress. In the eighteenth century, an era obsessed with the past, the gothic staged various dreams and nightmarish fears in which the past, whether it was regarded with longing or dread, was shown to cast a specter over the present. The gothic, therefore, sometimes served as a cautionary tale that registered the fallout of progress should the lessons of the past not be heeded. The primary Biblically derived message articulated in the gothic's grandfather text, Horace Walpole's *The Castle of Otranto* (1764)—"the sins of the fathers are visited on the sons to the third and fourth generations" (7)—is repeatedly taken up and considered. Past ordeals and sins are shown often to plague the potential for personal or social progress and yet, in the face of such traumas and transgressions, the gothic suggests that we can expose, confront, and even redress, to some degree, the terrors of history. The process of civilization and progress, therefore, is neither straightforward nor steady. Those who call themselves enlightened remain figuratively haunted by the ghost of Hamlet's father and the joint issues of paternal authority and inheritance in its spiritual, ethical, and material dimensions.

The Canadian Gothic and Atwood's Critical Work

At the height of the gothic's popularity in the eighteenth century, its transference from the Old (British) World to the New (North American) World involved its naturalization from what some considered to be the gothic's highly unrealistic and stylized conventions. The gothic's American grandfather, Charles Brockden Brown, a Quaker novelist, historian, and editor from Pennsylvania, consciously worked to bring the gothic to bear on specifically American concerns. In the introduction to his novel, *Edgar Huntly: Or, Memoirs of a Sleep-Walker* (1799),

Brown bluntly rejected what he described as the "puerile superstition and exploded manners, Gothic castles and chimeras" frequently used in late eighteenth-century British literature to call forth the passions of his readers and engage their sympathies. In their stead, Brown deemed "the incidents of Indian hostility, and the perils of the Western wilderness" to be "far more suitable" toward realizing the same ends in an American context (3).

Similar terrors in the form of what Coral Ann Howells has called "wilderness Gothic" (Howells, "Canadian" 106), were tapped a few decades later in Canada in John Richardson's 1832 publication, *Wacousta*. While this novel has been erroneously identified as the first Canadian novel, it arguably marked the inauguration of the gothic into the Canadian literary canon. *Wacousta* has been deemed a primary influence on Susanna Moodie's *Roughing It in the Bush* (1852), an occasionally gothic account according to Gerry Turcotte (289) rife with gothic projections onto the Canadian landscape. Ironically, despite its assertion that Canada was a country "too new for ghosts" (Moodie 267), this stark and powerful account of Moodie's early years as a pioneer in Canada served as the springboard for Margaret Atwood's 1970 poetry sequence *The Journals of Susanna Moodie*. Although the exact role of the gothic in Canadian literature continues to be debated, some critics argue that no such "tradition" actually exists. While gothic elements have been identified in Canadian literature by an ideologically varied assortment of critics, including feminist, postcolonial, and cultural critics, the general consensus has been that the gothic never assumed the major role in Canadian literature that it played in British, American, and European culture.

Much of Margaret Atwood's critical work considers the presence and relevance of the gothic within Canadian literature while some of her early creative work distills and adapts that mode/aesthetic into a Canadian context. Despite its occasional misperceptions of the gothic, Atwood's 1972 book *Survival: A Thematic Guide to Canadian Literature* takes its cue from Northrop Frye's description of Canadian poetry as marked by "incubus and *cauchemar* [nightmare]" (Frye 143) and helps to shed light on the "darker side" of Canadian literature. According to Atwood, the single unifying symbol at the core of Canadian literature is survival, for physical survival dominates the early literature of Canada while spiritual survival dominates more contemporary works. Death in its varied but connected forms—by nature, by Indian, and by bushing (where "a character isolated in Nature goes crazy")—is the preeminent Canadian experience, an ever-present threat that happens, she claims, "with startling frequency" (*Survival* 54). Atwood fails to mention the term *gothic* in *Survival* and, in her second chapter "Nature the Monster," she may misunderstand the nature of the Burkean sublime—the idea fundamental to gothic literature that aesthetic terror may elicit a pleasurable reaction. She nevertheless emphasizes the way Canadian writers draw a connection between physical landscapes and psychic states, something that is found (as she also, curiously, fails to note) at the forefront of the established European gothic tradition.

It took Margot Northey, another Canadian literary critic in the 1970s, to tease out the implications of Atwood's observations in *Survival* and, thus, to better establish the nature, parameters, and development of the gothic tradition in Canadian literature. In her insightful book *The Haunted Wilderness: The Gothic and Grotesque in Canadian Fiction* (1976), Northey advances a corrective both to the bias she perceives toward realist fiction in Canadian literary criticism and to the common misperception that the gothic is a rarity in Canadian literature, although she does this in a somewhat sketchy and elementary manner, due in part to the then prevalent view of the gothic as an illegitimate form in combination with the dearth of specialized studies devoted to it. In *The Haunted Wilderness*, Northey illustrates, in works ranging from John Richardson's *Wacousta; Or, A Tale of the Canadas* (1832) and William Kirby's *The Golden Dog* (1877) to Leonard Cohen's *Beautiful Losers* (1966) and Mordecai Richler's *Cocksure* (1968), that "there is a dark band of gothicism which stretches from earliest to recent times" (3). Northey rightly takes Atwood the critic to task for "repeatedly head[ing] towards the subject [of gothic] only to veer off" (3). But Northey also includes in her study an examination of Atwood's 1972 novel *Surfacing,* which she describes as a didactic and prescriptive fictional counterpart to Atwood's critical work and also as a prime example of "sociological Gothic" (62), a category Northey coins to describe gothic fiction whose principal agenda is social critique.

Atwood's 1977 essay, "Canadian Monsters: Some Aspects of the Supernatural in Canadian Fiction," essentially extends *Survival's* central thesis. Describing herself as a "mere collector of Canadian monsters" whose job is not necessarily to interpret their significance (121), Atwood counters Earle Birney's assertion in the last lines of his famous poem "Can. Lit"—lines that seem, on one hand, to speak back to Moodie's *Roughing It in the Bush*—that Canada is haunted only by its lack of ghosts. Given the role of the North in Canadian literature as "a symbol for the unexplored, the unconscious, the romantic, the mysterious, and the magical" (Atwood, "Canadian" 100), Atwood declares that it is "not surprising that a large number of Canadian monsters have their origin in native Indian and Eskimo myths" (Atwood, "Canadian" 101). She cites the legendary figures of the cannibalistic Wendigo and the trickster Coyote as supportive examples. By way of an examination of recurrent "image-clusters" in the available literature, Atwood returns to a more detailed examination of the ambivalent role of the North in the Canadian cultural imagination in her 1991 Clarendon Lectures in English Literature, which were subsequently published as the volume *Strange Things: The Malevolent North in Canadian Literature.* Although not considered in the light of the established gothic tradition and its conventions, Atwood's discussion about the allure and terror of becoming the other by "going native" in her chapter "The Grey Owl Syndrome" provides some interesting raw material for a reassessment of the gothic literary tradition in Canada.

Atwood's ongoing fascination with things gothic in more recent years is in evidence in her 2002 work *Negotiating with the Dead: A Writer on Writing,* a book that commenced life as the prestigious

Empson Lectures delivered by Atwood at the University of Cambridge in 2000. Designed to address topics of broad literary and cultural interest, Atwood's lectures take the sociocultural role of the writer as their point of focus. Grounded in the claim that all writing is motivated by "a fear of and a fascination with mortality" (156), *Negotiating with the Dead* is notably and fittingly rife with the gothic-inflected language found in much of Atwood's creative work. In its pages the writer emerges as a type of intrepid hierophant whose mysterious enterprise involves a mythic descent into a figurative underworld to recover lost truths. The writer's obsession with the figure of the double is rendered comprehensible, Atwood illustrates, when one considers the writer's possession of a secret identity and powers that enable his or her quest for immortality beyond the history-bound pages of the book.

Atwoodian Gothic: Atwood's Poetry in Fiction

Turning to an examination of Atwood's creative writing, it may be argued that while most of her productions invoke a gothic mood or incorporate gothic conventions—such as an ambivalent hero-villain or the figure of the double—few may be described as being sustained or cohesively gothic in nature. Although some critics, especially in recent years, regularly yoke the terms *Atwood* and *gothic*, they generally fail to identify and illuminate how any of Atwood's works are truly gothic in a comprehensive sense. While many contemporary works of literature employ gothic conventions and possess gothic elements, few consciously and conscientiously work solely within this tradition. Literary critics would do well to tread with greater caution onto gothic terrain. Nevertheless, if Atwood may be said to have a gothic period, it falls between the late 1960s and the mid-1970s. Included in her 1968 poetry collection *The Animals in That Country*, "Speeches for Dr. Frankenstein" attests to Atwood's early interest in the genre. While she exploits Mary Shelley's use of the double motif in her rendition of the relationship between Victor Frankenstein and his creature, and her monster also gets the last word, "Speeches" diverges from its parent text as Atwood's monster ultimately deserts its maker.

Atwood's earliest experiment in sustained gothic occurs in *The Journals of Susanna Moodie*, a series of unsettling poems arranged into three sections inspired by the life and writings of the nineteenth-century author of *Roughing It in the Bush*. (Notably, Moodie's 1852 novel is one of the texts Atwood cites in *Survival* as best exemplifying the ambivalent attitude toward nature in early Canadian literature.) Like classic gothic works, *Journals* is an oneiric production featuring dream sequences: "Journal II," for example, uses a dream sequence to explore the permeable boundary between conscious reality and unconscious dream. As Atwood relates in the afterword, this volume took a year and a half to complete and was itself engendered by a strange dream in which she sat watching a solitary white figure singing in an opera she had written about Susanna Moodie. According to Atwood, Moodie is the prototypical Canadian as she exhibits a "violent duality" (Afterword, *Journals* 62). In Atwood's words, Moodie "claims to be an ardent Canadian patriot while all the time she is standing back from the country and criticizing it as though she were a detached observer, a stranger" (Afterword, *Journals* 62). Intriguingly, Moodie's double voices in *Journals* are more complex and work on more levels than Atwood's brief description suggests. Indeed, *Journals* serves as a template for Atwood's later manipulation of the gothic (particularly in *Surfacing*) to probe various connected and complex aspects of identity, especially those relating to gender and the nation.

Journals is arranged into three sections: "Journal I," 1832–40, chronicles the seven years Moodie spent in the Canadian bush; "Journal II," 1840–71, recounts Moodie's reflections about that time; "Journal III," 1871–1969, relays her later years in Belleville, her death, and her "resurrection" in the twentieth century when Atwood transforms her into the irrepressible voice of the Canadian wilderness. The popular female gothic image of a woman traveling into unknown territory, which represents both her unconscious self and her heretofore repressed desires and fears about the institution of marriage, opens the first journal. Atwood transfers the traditional motif of terra incognita (which usually applies to the tenebrous, labyrinthine Gothic castle in a foreign, generally Roman Catholic setting) to the Canadian bush, which Moodie enters, fittingly, via Quebec. Here, Moodie is a representative Canadian immigrant, an invading alien who believes, mistakenly, that order may be created out of chaos. As Atwood suggests in "The Planters" and its sister poem, "The Immigrants" ("Journal II"), immigrants to Canada are necessarily delusional: the past—represented by the old country in the appropriately gothic form of "perfect, thumbnail castles preserved / like gallstones in a glass bottle" (32)[1]—feeds their vision of a future civilization. To embrace the possibility of order, Moodie intimates, the settlers must deny their present-day reality and the true nature of the bush.

As Moodie especially discovers in "Journal II," the dark wilderness calls out the darker forces within the human psyche. In the poem "Charivari," for example, a black man who marries a white woman is brutally murdered by several European settlers. As Atwood also suggests later in *Surfacing*, the Canadian bush elicits the heart of darkness that exists at the core of the so-called civilized or cultured individual and Western civilization. A fascinating counterdynamic is also at work along gender lines, however, as Moodie not only enters her "own ignorance" (12) as do other immigrants when she arrives in the bush, but eventually comes face to face with her own repressed female nature as reflected within it. "Looking in the Mirror," a poem set just before Moodie's departure from the bush, best conveys this association. During her seven years there, Moodie has been irreversibly altered. A physical interfacing even seems to have occurred as her skin has become "thickened / with bark and the white hairs of roots" (24). The poem's concluding lines, however, confirm her awareness that she has not developed in any way alien to her nature. As she articulates it, "(you find only / the shape you already are / but what / if you have forgotten that / or discover you / have never known)" (25). Intriguingly, Atwood's invocation of the classic female gothic anxiety regarding the husband's or the prospective husband's potentially terrifying secret identity (as a violent criminal or even murderer), is more consciously brought to bear on Moodie's own lack of self-awareness. The predominant focus in the poem "The Wereman," for example, may be on her "shadowy husband" (13) who is perceived as "an X, a concept / defined against a blank" (19), but Moodie concludes by suggesting that as she serves as his mirror, she is equally impenetrable to both him and herself. Toward the poem's end, the tables are turned as she wonders what he sees when he looks at her.

In "Journal II," Moodie's connection to the bush assumes a deeper, more macabre tone. In her repeated suggestions that the wilderness is a type of cannibal that ritualistically devours its victims (like Moodie's son who, in his act of drowning, is figuratively consumed by a lake), Moodie's voice assumes a calmer, more matter-of-fact tone. Without a trace of hysteria, and increasingly like a prophetess who articulates a series of truths about the wilderness, Moodie dispels the illusions of the settlers with definitive claims. The immigrants, she says, ride in railway cars "across an ocean of unknown / land to an unknown land" (33). There is no safe or known place. In the third dream poem, "Night Bear Which Frightened Cattle," it is Moodie's voice of reason, in keeping with the gothic tradition, that articulates the most chilling truth—she reminds the settlers that while they may laugh at their fears from within their houses, real terrors actually lurk without. Attempts to repress this knowledge, to shelter themselves from the wilderness and the associated wild side of their nature, are entirely in vain. The bush will, in the final analysis, overcome everything. Life is, Moodie calmly asserts in "The Deaths of the Other Children," a slow-but-sure process of disintegration. This new insight radically alters her assessment of her seven years in the bush. Reconsidering them, she wonders, "Did I spend all those years / building up this edifice / my composite / self, this crumbling hovel?" (41). Ultimately, all so-called order, civilization, and individuality will be consumed by the void. The final poem in the section, "The Double Voice," delineates how Moodie develops

---

two voices as a result of her Canadian experience: she is simultaneously possessed of a genteel, mannered voice that focuses on the picturesque aspects of the bush (associated with the stereotyped notions of femininity), and of a more brutally realistic voice that underscores the grotesque aspects of the bush (associated with a traditionally masculine sensibility).

The third and final set of journal poems covers Moodie's postbush life in Belleville, Ontario, when, among other things, she becomes fascinated with criminals and the insane. As she deteriorates physically, the question of her own mental health is raised. Although this issue is never fully resolved, Atwood seems to suggest that Moodie is, in the eyes of her society, slightly mentally unbalanced. A better understanding of Moodie's psychic division vis-à-vis Canada is, however, granted more coherence in "Thoughts from Underground," in which Moodie relates her deep hatred of this new country after her bush experience. She cannot, she says, simply begin to love it once her husband has become successful. While this piece seems to be conveyed from the perspective of Moodie's ostensibly genteel and civilized self, "Alternate Thoughts from Underground" taps into her more nature-affiliated voice. In fact, the belief system embraced in "Alternate Thoughts" is indisputably pagan. In this poem, Moodie becomes one with the land. Speaking from beyond the grave to the surrounding "babylons" populated by their "glib superstructures" (57), Moodie is now fervently anticivilization. She decisively subverts the Christian sense of apocalypse when she declares at the conclusion of "The Resurrection" that "at the last / judgement we will all be trees" (59). In the volume's final poem, "A Bus Along St. Clair: December," not only is the boundary between Moodie and the wilderness eradicated, so is that between past and present. Portraying herself as an old woman seated opposite a complete stranger on a Toronto bus in 1969, Moodie enunciates her most gothic message, namely, that repressed truths will invariably return to plague those who attempt to deny them. Moodie's becomes the prophetic and resonant voice of a repressed and abused natural world that will, in the course of time, consume the purportedly civilized city. She reminds the delusional and smug city dweller that "though they buried me in monuments / of concrete slabs, of cables . . . I have my ways of getting through" (60). She saves her most dramatic and unsettling revelation for last, however, when she declares that "there is no city; / this is the centre of a forest / your place is empty" (61).

In terms of its focus on a female protagonist whose repressed nature and emotions are released and healed by a profound experience in the wilderness, Atwood's 1972 novel *Surfacing* is a modern prose version of *The Journals of Susanna Moodie*. Relayed from the perspective of an unnamed female narrator, *Surfacing* chronicles a trip she, her lover, and another couple take into the forests of Quebec after her father has been reported missing from his cabin there. While initially regarded as casual, the trip soon becomes an intense exploration of the narrator's long repressed feelings regarding her family (particularly her father), and of her emotionally wrenching experiences in various love relationships. An abortion she had during a relationship with a married man is a particularly burdensome and painful memory that has left her both emotionally dead and haunted. Confronting and allaying such irrepressible memories constitutes the novel's focus.

As in *Journals*, the Canadian replaces the European castle as the site of the protagonist's exploration of her psychic closets. In its role as a foreign, Roman Catholic, and "uncanny" locale where the foreign and the familiar, the conscious and the unconscious, intermingle, Quebec is the equivalent of Italy in Ann Radcliffe's classic female gothic works. Atwood puts a more feminist spin on this, however, as Quebec functions as a patriarchal space where women are socially repressed. As the narrator relates in the early chapters, the Roman Catholic Church plays a special role in this regard. Women have no access to birth control or divorce and even their attire is regulated—"many of them lived all their lives beside the lake without learning to swim because they were ashamed to put on bathing suits" (*Surfacing* 25). Given these associations, Quebec functions as a particularly appropriate locale in which the narrator grapples with her earlier, generally negative experiences with men. Her healing/purification process is ritualistic in nature and involves a type of shamanistic merging with the landscape. Notably, it also involves swimming naked in the lake, an especially significant act given the traditional constraints placed upon Québéçois women.

In keeping with gothic conventions, the narrator must unearth, examine, and resolve fundamental questions of inheritance before this final cleansing ritual occurs (in her case, however, spiritual/emotional inheritance is key while material inheritance is virtually neglected). She considers and ultimately rejects her rationalist father's unbalanced worldview as it denies the emotions. Only then does she reconcile the two halves of what she describes as her divided self and feel as if she is more than just "a head." She also considers her failed relationship with a married man who coerced her into having an abortion before making a decision regarding her current lover, Joe. Although she gives no definitive response to Joe's marriage proposal, the narrator ultimately chooses to remain with him and move into a new stage of their relationship. Her suggestion that she is pregnant at the novel's end signals both the fertility of their union and her regeneration on the heels of a traumatic abortion.

The gothic is manipulated in *Surfacing* to address pressing gender and nationalist issues. Here again, the ambivalent wilderness is key. While it may be the site of healing and reconciliation, it also engenders violent regression and discord. In that it may annihilate barriers and hierarchies and return people to an earlier state of equality, it is positive. The lake water, for example, is described as "multilingual" (178), a site where the English-French language barrier is eradicated. The narrator intimates, however, that so-called Western "civilization" has a darker side that may emerge after prolonged contact with the wilderness. We all, she suggests, possess the innate ability to return to a barbarian state. Her representation of Americans—who serve to some degree, as Margot Northey has noted, as a synecdoche for contemporary technological society (66)—is inextricably bound up with this threat and provides what is, perhaps, this novel's most gothic image. Drawing on the genre of American horror cinema, the narrator proffers a disturbing futuristic vision of Americans as machine-like body snatchers who are steadily moving north where they threaten to control Canadians. A resolution is advanced, however, in the final two chapters regarding the narrator's views on Canada's relationship to the United States. Although this "pervasive menace" may be advancing (189), she assuages her fears with the thought that one can police them and/or resist their influence.

In terms of Atwood's early literary works, *Lady Oracle* (1976) has garnered the most critical attention as an explicitly gothic production. In fact, one critic (Sybil Korff Vincent) has, in a problematically exaggerated statement, deemed it "the most gothic of gothic novels, a gothic novel about gothic novels" (153). Originally subtitled "A Gothic Romance," *Lady Oracle* is clearly Atwood's most self-consciously gothic production. In several interviews about this work, she labels the gothic a distinctively female form; this novel, as Atwood and others have pointed out, stands in the parodic tradition of Jane Austen's *Northanger Abbey* (1818). Although the power of Atwood's gothic parody, especially as a daughter-text to Austen's, has been greatly misrepresented, *Lady Oracle* works within this tradition as it also foregrounds and plays on the disjunction between "the real world" and the romantic expectations generated by such genres as gothic/romance literature.

Atwood's novel relates the story of Joan Foster, an author of costume gothics who stages her own death and flees to Italy when her "past lives" and various identities begin to catch up with her. Joan is a mistress of escape, a female Houdini whose life is bound up in denial, specifically the denial of complex gender identities. In embracing a simplistic idea of men as dominant persecutors and women as passive victims—a vision reflected in her gothic novel-in-progress—Joan is portrayed as a truly Frankensteinian product of her monstrous society. *Lady Oracle* should be classified as a "feminist Gothic" novel as

Atwood exposes how established late twentieth-century sexual norms and feminine ideals are truly gothic in nature. In advancing this message, Joan anticipates Angela Carter's claim in the afterword to her collected short stories, *Burning Your Boats* (1996), that "we live in Gothic times" (460).

Drawing on *Frankenstein* (1818), Joan's principal bogey is her monstrous mother, an obsessive-compulsive housewife who upholds, at the cost of her own happiness, her society's ideals regarding femininity. Tyrannized by her triple-mirrored vanity table, Joan's triple-headed monster mother (66–67) is extremely ashamed of her young, overweight daughter. Significantly, this mother's emotional distance persists even after Joan successfully loses weight and, for all intents and purposes, conforms to feminine ideals. In keeping with such traditionally gothic works as Radcliffe's *The Mysteries of Udolpho* (1794), Atwood portrays Joan as plagued by the question of her true parentage and "the sins of the fathers" (although, in this instance, the emphasis is on the sins of the mothers). In her unsuccessful attempts to resist and deny her society's damaging gender ideology, Joan eventually evolves, at tremendous emotional cost, into "a duplicitous monster" (95). Her escape into and production of costume gothics set in an earlier era, where gender roles seemed unproblematic, exhibits a concerted effort to uphold a dangerously romantic worldview that necessitates female victims. In the final analysis, Joan's efforts fail.

Writing in retrospect from the vantage point of Italy, Joan recounts her life's highlights, interspersing them with highly melodramatic segments from her latest escapist novel. The climax of the novel, which relates Joan's revelation regarding her essentially schizophrenic society, involves a subversion of the costume gothic's gender conventions, which dictate that women are potential victims of men, and a blurring of the boundary between her life-story and that of her novel's two principal female characters, Charlotte and Felicia. It is implied that the reconciliation of the disparate fragments of Joan's identity will follow. Convinced that the future will be, in general, better for people, Joan decides at novel's end to abandon costume gothics and turn her hand to science fiction.

Margaret Atwood's creative experiments with the gothic mode in the early stages of her literary career tend toward a type of generic hodgepodge in the service of her poststructural aesthetics and themes. They may all be said to be, to one degree or another, marked by what Atwood identifies as the key characteristic of the gothic, namely, "the lure of the unmentionable—the mysterious, the buried, the forgotten, the discarded, the taboo" (*Curious* 218). Atwood's more recent work attests to this ongoing fascination.

Notes

1. I use inclusive page numbers rather than line numbers when quoting from Atwood's poems in *The Journals of Susanna Moodie*.

Works Cited

Atwood, Margaret. "Canadian Monsters: Some Aspects of the Supernatural in Cana-
    dian Fiction." *The Canadian Imagination: Dimensions of a Literary Culture*. Ed.
    David Staines. Cambridge, MA: Harvard UP, 1977. 97–122.
_____. *Curious Pursuits: Occasional Writing, 1970–2005*. London: Virago, 2005.
_____. *The Journals of Susanna Moodie*. Toronto: Oxford UP, 1970.
_____. *Lady Oracle*. Toronto: McClelland, 1976.
_____. *Negotiating with the Dead: A Writer on Writing*. Toronto: Anchor, 2002.
_____. "Speeches for Dr. Frankenstein." *The Animals in That Country*. Toronto:
    Little, 1968. 42–47.
_____. *Strange Things: The Malevolent North in Canadian Literature*. Oxford and
    New York: Oxford UP, 1995.
_____. *Surfacing*. 1972. Markham, ON: PaperJacks, 1978.
_____. *Survival: A Thematic Guide to Canadian Literature*. Toronto: Anansi, 1972.
Becker, Susanne. *Gothic Forms of Feminine Fictions*. Manchester and New York:
    Manchester UP, 1999.
Brown, Charles Brockden. *Edgar Huntly, Or, Memoirs of a Sleepwalker*. 1799. Har-
    mondsworth, Middlesex: Penguin, 1988.
Carter, Angela. "Afterword." *Burning Your Boats: Collected Short Stories*. New York:
    Vintage, 1996. 459–60.
Davison, Carol Margaret. *History of the Gothic: Gothic Literature, 1764–1824*. Car-
    diff: U of Wales P, 2009.

_____. "Margaret Atwood." *Gothic Writers: A Critical and Bibliographical Guide.* Eds. Douglass H. Thomson, Jack G. Voller, and Frederick S. Frank. Westport, CT, and London: Greenwood, 2002. 24–32.

DeLamotte, Eugenia C. *Perils of the Night: A Feminist Study of Nineteenth-Century Gothic.* New York: Oxford UP, 1990.

Edwards, Justin D. *Gothic Canada: Reading the Spectre of a National Literature.* Edmonton: U of Alberta P, 2005.

Frye, Northrop. *The Bush Garden: Essays on the Canadian Imagination.* 1971. Concord, ON: Anansi, 1995.

Gillespie, Tracey. "Elements of the Gothic in the Novels of Margaret Atwood." MA thesis. University of Alberta, 1990.

Grace, Sherrill. *Violent Duality: A Study of Margaret Atwood.* Montreal: Véhicule, 1980.

Howells, Coral Ann, ed. *The Cambridge Companion to Margaret Atwood.* Cambridge, UK: Cambridge UP, 2006.

_____. "Canadian Gothic." *The Routledge Companion to Gothic.* Eds. Catherine Spooner and Emma McEvoy. London: Routledge, 2007. 105–14.

_____. *Margaret Atwood.* London: Macmillan, 1996.

Ingersoll, Earl G., ed. *Margaret Atwood Conversations.* Princeton, New Jersey: Ontario Rev., 1990.

Mandel, Eli. "Atwood Gothic." *Malahat Review* 41(1977): 165–74.

McCombs, Judith. "Atwood's Haunted Sequences: *The Circle Game, The Journals of Susanna Moodie,* and *Power Politics.*" *The Art of Margaret Atwood: Essays in Criticism.* Eds. Arnold E. Davidson and Cathy N. Davidson. Toronto: Anansi, 1981. 35–54.

McMillan, Ann. "The Transforming Eye: *Lady Oracle* and Gothic Tradition." *Margaret Atwood: Vision and Forms.* Eds. Kathryn VanSpanckeren and Jan Garden Castro. Carbondale and Edwardsville, IL: Southern Illinois UP, 1988. 48–64.

Moodie, Susanna. *Roughing It in the Bush.* 1852. Toronto: McClelland, 1989.

Northey, Margot. "Sociological Gothic: *Wild Geese* and *Surfacing.*" *The Haunted Wilderness: The Gothic and Grotesque in Canadian Fiction.* Toronto and Buffalo: U of Toronto P, 1976. 62–69.

Rao, Eleonora. *Strategies for Identity: The Fiction of Margaret Atwood.* New York: Lang, 1993.

Rosowski, Susan J. "Margaret Atwood's *Lady Oracle*: Fantasy and the Modern Gothic Novel." *Critical Essays on Margaret Atwood.* Ed. Judith McCombs. Boston: Hall, 1988. 197–208.

Stein, Karen F. "*The Blind Assassin* by Margaret Atwood as a Modern 'Bluebeard.'" *Twenty-First-Century Gothic: Great Gothic Novels Since 2000.* Ed. Danel Olson. Lanham, MD: Scarecrow, 2011. 32–41.

Turcotte, Gerry. "English-Canadian Gothic." *The Handbook of the Gothic.* 1998. Ed. Marie Mulvey-Roberts. 2nd ed. New York: New York UP, 2009. 288–92.

Vincent, Sybil Korff. "The Mirror and the Cameo: Margaret Atwood's Comic/Gothic Novel, *Lady Oracle.*" *The Female Gothic.* Ed. Juliann E. Fleenor. Montreal: Eden, 1983. 153–63.

Walpole, Horace. *The Castle of Otranto.* 1764. Oxford: Oxford UP, 1996.

"This Is Border Country": Atwood's *Surfacing* and Postcolonial Identity_____

Laura Wright

I.

The field of postcolonial theory constitutes a set of tools for looking at and analyzing literary texts by and about the peoples of formerly colonized locales. Since its codification as a field of scholarly inquiry in the late 1970s, it has generally been associated and concerned with former, predominantly British, colonies in Africa, in the Caribbean, and in South Asia, locations where colonization resulted in the violent takeover of peoples and exploitation of natural resources. But situating the beginnings of the field—like ascribing its applicability to a specific work of literature—is a point of debate. According to Leela Gandhi, "while the publication of [Edward] Said's *Orientalism* in 1978 is commonly regarded as the principal catalyst and reference point for postcolonial theory . . . this ur-text . . . evolved within a distinctly post-structuralist climate" (25), which was, in fact, dominated by the French philosophers Jacques Derrida and Michel Foucault. Furthermore, in *Postcolonial Criticism*, Nicholas Harrison situates another originary moment in the formation of postcolonial studies as occurring "when Chinua Achebe, lecturing at the University of Massachusetts in 1975, declared that 'Joseph Conrad was a bloody racist'" (2).[1] And while it is possible to read postcolonial studies as a field of critical inquiry informed by Said's early work that traces its beginnings to the Subaltern Studies Group of the early 1980s, a collective of South Asian scholars—of which Said was a member—Donna Bennett asserts that "use of a postcolonial perspective as a way of looking at literary studies began in the late 1970s among Australian critics" like Bill Ashcroft, Gareth Griffiths, and Helen Tiffin whose *The Empire Writes Back: Theory and Practice in Post-Colonial Literatures* (1989) is considered a foundational work in the field. These various interpretations of postcolonial studies' starting point—South Asian, French, or Australian—indicate the difficulty of situating the genesis of the field and challenge the idea that the field of postcolonial studies constitutes a singular theoretical perspective.

In the introduction to her 2003 edited collection *Is Canada Postcolonial? Unsettling Canadian Literature*, Laura Moss poses two interrelated questions: is Canada postcolonial, and can Canadian literature be read through the lens of postcolonial theory? Only recently have scholars begun to question whether it is appropriate to examine the so-called "settler" colonies of New Zealand, Australia, and Canada through a postcolonial lens, as these colonies, at least theoretically, have been more "peacefully" colonized than those that such a perspective more commonly critiques. But Moss does find a similarity between Canada and countries like India or Nigeria, for all of these countries are "in the process of trying to build nations on a common model that is predominantly British" (Moss 1). Not only is postcolonialism concerned with "cultural imperialism" and "emergent nationalisms," according to Moss, but it also focuses on related issues such as "the process of decolonization" and the critique of "hierarchies of power, violence, and oppression," which are concerns found in Margaret Atwood's 1972 novel *Surfacing* (Moss 4).

Indeed, Atwood's second novel *Surfacing* can be read as a work that posits Canadian identity as postcolonial by situating that identity within an enmeshed matrix of colonial dominance (of native peoples by British and French colonists and later, of the French by the British) and cultural subjection (by the United States, a pervasive and homogenous ideological construct negatively depicted by Atwood's female unnamed narrator as "American"). But *Surfacing* also complicates postcolonial identity by situating its protagonist in "border country" (30), the liminal space both between and outside categorization and language. It is from within this space that boundaries, binary classifications, and language break down and out of which a narrative of continually shifting colonial power dynamics emerges.

Atwood's novel follows the physical journey and subsequent mental breakdown and reconstitution of an unnamed female narrator as she travels with her lover and another couple to her family's cabin on an island in Quebec's wilderness. She makes this journey in search of her father, who has gone missing. In its examination of the relationships between these four characters, the novel explores the binary of man/woman and implicates that power dynamic as part and parcel of the colonial framework that it critiques. Contrary to the claim that the equation of "women's victimization with Canada's colonial status" in *Surfacing* marks a somewhat immature vision as compared to the "more complex postcolonial and postfeminist awareness" in Atwood's later novels (Fiamengo 144), *Surfacing* is, in fact, an extremely complicated work. For in order for the Surfacer-narrator to break through to a liminal border country, she must experience the breakdown of all of the oppositions in which she initially believes. Over the course of the several days that she spends on the island, the narrator confronts her previous and unacknowledged abortion and the immediate loss of her father, but she is also forced to recognize and then renounce the self-proclaimed victimization she feels to be caused, primarily, by an American ideology inherently linked to the technology and development that intrudes upon the Canadian wilderness, and, secondarily, by her previous lover and Joe, the men with whom she has been involved. She is forced to "surface" into a different national and gendered consciousness, one that requires that she view victimization as a shifting process established in the contact zones between cultures and peoples. Ultimately, she realizes that she "is just as much an alien invader [of Canada] as the Americans" (Wilkins 209). According to the *OED*, a "surface" is the "outermost boundary of any material body, immediately adjacent to the air or empty space, or another body." "Surfacing" can mean to cover over or to emerge from beneath—to surface from sleep (in terms of consciousness) or water—as Atwood's narrator does when she dives into the lake in search of Native American cave paintings only to encounter, when she sees the body of her drowned father, her unconscious, the baby she aborted: "My hand came out of the water and gripped the gunwale, then my head; water ran from my nose, I gulped breath . . . the lake was horrible, it was filled with death" (167). This initial breaking of the surface ultimately allows the narrator access to the space of the liminal, the space of the boundary, and so, as she experiences a kind of breakdown, she also breaks through into a new kind of dynamic awareness as she moves beyond the static and fixed world of binary oppositions.

II.

In order to fully understand how it is possible to read Canada and, by extension, *Surfacing* as postcolonial, it is necessary first to examine Canada's history and second to define two theoretical terms that will prove essential to understanding my argument. These terms are "binary oppositions" and "liminal space." In terms of Canada's history, Mark Shackleton notes, "inhabited originally by Aboriginal peoples, the first permanent European settlements in Canada were established . . . by the French at Port Royal in 1605 and Quebec City in 1608, and by the English in Newfoundland around 1610" (83). The company of New France, the entity that oversaw France's North American colonies, was founded in 1627. The fur trade of the 1600s took place in Canada between the English, French, and Dutch, and in 1701, thirty-eight Native American nations signed a peace agreement with the French. During the Seven Years War, which began in 1756, Quebec fell to the English; at the war's end in 1763, England obtained all French colonies east of the Mississippi. The British North America Act, which took place in 1867, officially united Ontario, Quebec, Nova Scotia, and New Brunswick in the Dominion of Canada, but according to Donna Bennett, while "officially Canada ceased to be a British colony in 1867 . . . its complete independence has only been achieved since that time and by increments." For example, despite the apparent unification of the nation, so-called rebellions by native peoples continued; two of the most famous were the Red River Rebellion of 1869–70, and the

North-West Rebellion of 1885, which resulted in the imprisonment of two Cree chiefs and claimed the lives of eight other native leaders (Shackleton 84). Furthermore, the Quebec Act of 1774 established French as the official language of that province, and so linguistic and cultural tensions still exist between the French- and English-speaking provinces of Canada.

As various groups have vied for power and for the financial benefits to be gained through the exploitation of natural resources (fur, in particular), Canada's history has been fraught by the oppositional relationships between those groups: English and French, European and indigenous. These "binary" relationships, as they are called, are dependent upon one side of the binary being perceived to be superior to the other; in that way, domination of the one by the other can be justified. In *The Location of Culture,* postcolonial theorist Homi K. Bhabha discusses his concept of the liminal space that exists between such binaries:

> It is in the emergence of the interstices—the overlap and displacement of domains of difference—that the intersubjective and collective experiences of nationness, community interest, or cultural value are negotiated. How are subjects formed 'in-between', or in excess of, the sum of the 'parts' of difference (usually intoned as race/class/gender, etc.)? (2)

Bhabha contends that the story of the nation is a performative process rather than a static narrative, continually formed and reformed at linguistic and spatial thresholds, borders, and boundaries defined by national identity, and in the interstitial spaces between the false binary constructions of colonizer and colonized, oppressor and oppressed. In other words the story of the nation is shaped by the spaces in between, or what Atwood's narrator calls "on the border," which in the case of *Surfacing* is the literal space between Ontario and Quebec—a location, according to Peter Wilkins, "that destabilizes the notion of Canada as a seamless, innocent whole threatened only by outside antagonism from the United States" (209). If we construct an understanding of the world out of the binary opposition of self and other, an opposition that always holds "self" to be superior to "other," then articulating the space between is difficult at best and, perhaps, impossible at worst. Indeed, the spaces between such black and white oppositions are taboo and *un*speakable, for this is the inarticulate gray area, the space of the border.

Consider the following case: how do we articulate the space between animal and human, if we can assume that such a space exists? Atwood engages with this concept in *Surfacing*, and what exists in this in-between space is a werewolf. Early in the novel, we learn that the narrator is an illustrator who wants to include a "*loup-garou*" or werewolf story in the collection of *Quebec Folk Tales* that she is illustrating, but she realizes that her editor would refuse to include such a story since it would be "too rough for him" (65). Yet when the narrator confronts the ghost of her dead father, he is a wolf-man:

I say Father.

He turns toward me and it's not my father. It is what my father saw, the thing you meet when you've stayed here too long alone.

I'm not frightened . . . it gazes at me for a time with its yellow eyes, wolf's eyes (218).

The wolf-man, who considers paths and fences to be "violations," wants "the borders abolished" and he wants "reparation" (218) as he patrols the spaces between not only animal and human, but also between self and other. When the narrator goes to trace the wolf-man's tracks the next morning, "the footprints are there . . . . But the prints are too small, they have toes; I place my own feet in them and find that they are my own" (219). The borders are abolished, and the narrator herself is the wolf[2] and the human is the animal, at least for a moment of "reparation."

In addition to its destabilization of the ghostly/material, father/ daughter and human/animal binaries, *Surfacing* engages with various other oppositions as well—"American"/Canadian, English/French, settler/indigene, and civilization/wilderness—that underlie Canada's history of colonial oppression. As the wolf-man desires, "reparation" is what the text seeks for the damage done via the establishment of colonial and national boundaries, as well as the hierarchical binary opposition between male and female. As the narrator recognizes, "there had to be a good kind and a bad kind of everything" (44), and this dualism establishes, she notes, the need for the "good" to save the world from the "bad": "men think they can do it with guns, women with their bodies, love conquers all, conquerors love all, mirages raised by words" (193). The realization that "words" raise the "mirages" or untruths of such categories and are responsible for the narrative histories that justify colonial oppression is countered by the narrator's rejection of words, names, and language. "I no longer have a name," as she states after her "vision quest"/breakdown at the end of the novel (198). But such a rejection is unsustainable. Thus, the narrator knows that she must at some point return from the border country, that she "can't stay here forever," that there is "no total salvation," and that even within her unborn child, "word furrows potential already" (220, 221, 223). Language—words—it seems, will always force us to take a side, to narrate, assign names, and categorize.

Even though "no aboriginal people appear in the novel's present tense" (Fiamengo 156), for Peter Wilkins, "the 'Indian' world represents the antithesis to the 'American' symbolic" (215) in *Surfacing*. The text is haunted by Canada's colonial history with regards to first peoples. The narrator's father, as she remembers him, read the works of the "eighteenth-century rationalists," British writers who, in his view, "avoided the corruptions of the Industrial Revolution" (44)—men who wrote during the height of British imperialism. But then the narrator discovers that, prior to his disappearance, her missing father had developed a new interest in Native American cave paintings. Initially, when the narrator finds her father's drawings of human figures "faceless and minus the hands and feet" alongside his indecipherable notations, she assumes that her father had gone crazy and perhaps wandered off. But when she finds an academic article on Indian rock paintings among her father's papers and discovers that her father had become "hooked on" the Native American pictographs, she realizes that his drawings are "not originals then, only copies," which to her provides "indisputable" proof of his "sanity" and thus his "death" (123). The moment that the narrator dives down into the lake in search of these paintings is the moment that she comes into contact with her unconscious, but it is also a moment of postcolonial encounter predicated on her search for lost peoples: Native Americans, her father, and her unborn child. She has followed her father's map to the spot, knowing that her father "would not have marked and numbered the map so methodically for nothing" (166). She dives down three times before she sees "it":

> But it wasn't a painting, it wasn't on the rock. It was below me, drifting towards me from the furthest level where there was no life, a dark oval trailing limbs. It was blurred but it had eyes, they were open, it was something I knew about, a dead thing, it was dead. (167)

The three instances of diving down mark the narrator's encounter with three losses, one national (Native Americans), one familial (her father), and one personal (her unborn child).

After she surfaces, the narrator hides from her companions and then burns the contents of her parents' cabin—"the map torn from the wall, the rock paintings . . . and the album, the sequence of my mother's life, the confining photographs" (207)—materials that attempt to codify, via language and image, national narratives of various kinds. She takes off her clothes and ventures into the wilderness for five days, staying hidden from her companions, who return to the mainland in frustration. Over the course of the five-day period, the narrator comes to accept that Canadians are just as responsible for the destruction of their wilderness as Americans are. According to Eleonora Rao, this realization "indicates the pointlessness of splitting the world into discriminatory categories and opposites" (8). While the narrator comes to recognize that "American" is a state of mind that can transcend national borders, initially, however, "American" is the identity that the narrator ascribes to anyone or any behavior that she views as antithetical to a Canadian identity, which is associated with the wilderness. In *Surfacing*, "the illustration *par excellence* of the psychology of the Canadian position" (Wilkins 207), the narrator states that she "used to think that [Americans] were harmless and funny and inept and faintly lovable, like President Eisenhower" (77), but she comes to think of them as encroachers and polluters, wantonly destroying the Canadian landscape and its creatures. When she discovers a mutilated heron, she concludes that "it must have been the Americans" who killed the bird, simply "to prove they could do it, they had the power to kill" (138). When she discovers that the killers are Canadian, she thinks that "it doesn't matter what country they're from . . . they're still Americans, they're what's in store for us, what we are turning into. They spread themselves like a virus . . . and the ones that have the disease can't tell the difference" (152).

Atwood has engaged this oppositional image, Canada as *not* America, not only in *Surfacing* but elsewhere in her writing. In the short story "Death by Landscape" from her 1991 collection *Wilderness Tips*, two girls, one from Canada and one from the United States, become friends at a Canadian summer camp. The relationship between the two is characterized by the extroversion of Lucy, the American, and the introversion of Lois, the Canadian. The narrator notes that Lucy's mother "had been a Canadian once, but had married her father" (134). For Lois, the United States is exotic and powerful, the place "where the comic books came from, and the movies" (133). To Lucy, Canada is a backwater, boring, a place that does not "measure up" (134). Likewise, in her "Letter to America," written in 2003 as the United States set out to invade Iraq (another colonial endeavor), Atwood expresses similar sentiment with regard to Canada's status as cultural subaltern, the imitation (or colonial mimic) to the United States' dominating might:

> We've always been close, you and we. History, that old entangler, has twisted us together since the early seventeenth century. Some of us used to be you; some of us want to be you; some of you used to be us. . . . We're like the Romanized Gauls—look like Romans, dress like Romans, but aren't Romans—peering over the wall at the *real* Romans. (Atwood, "Letter to America" 281, my emphasis)

"Mimicry," another of Bhabha's terms, is important to Atwood's various depictions of Canada's relationship to the United States. According to Bhabha, "mimicry emerges as the representation of a difference that is itself a process of disavowal" ("Of Mimicry" 126). To mimic, in the context of a binary relationship such as the American/Canadian relationship, is to imitate—which is, of course, what one does if one wants access to power. Imitating those more powerful allows one the ability to achieve the same kinds of things (although probably not the exact same things) as those obtained by the one being imitated. But mimicry also implies a level of heightened awareness on the part of the imitator; in order to imitate, one must have an intimate knowledge of that which is being imitated. So mimicry, while implying imitation, also allows the imitator/Canadian a degree of power that is not available to the imitated/American. Thus to mimic "Americanism" disavows—or denies—the authority of that which is mimicked.

In 1972, Atwood published not only *Surfacing* but also *Survival: A Thematic Guide to Canadian Literature*, a work that dealt very explicitly with Canadian literature's relationship with and comparison to its counterpart, American literature. Atwood's project in *Survival*, as she asserts, was to consider Canadian literature as something other than "British literature imported or American literature with something missing" (281)—the colonial mimic to the dominant ideology. Her project, in essence, was to establish the existence of a Canadian literature, or "Canlit," that imagines the Canadian nation in ways that are distinctly Canadian in order to help the reader "distinguish this species from all others, Canadian literature from the other literatures with which is often compared or confused" (19),[3] like those of the United States or Britain. She does this by establishing a primary trope of survival that she then traces throughout a body of Canadian fiction that spans Canada's national beginnings to the 1970s present of the work's first publication. The trope of survival, Atwood claims, functions in Canadian literature as the trope of the frontier functions in American literature or the trope of the island functions in the literature of England, as the primary metaphor or symbol for the nation itself. She begins with a preliminary explanation of what *Survival* is *not*—it is not exhaustive, evaluative, biographical, or even, as she states, original since "many of the ideas that inform [*Survival*] have been floating around, diffused in scholarly journals and private conversations, for a number of years" (19)—and then she explains that she will treat the works that she examines "as though they were written by Canada," (18–19) by the nation, a project that allows the Canadian authors she discusses to function collectively as "transmitters of their culture" (19). Atwood's act of literary and cultural articulation in *Survival*, then, can be understood as an act of Canadian nationalism: as an attempt to articulate a national identity in a country that had historically viewed nationalism with suspicion and that had attempted to establish its identity in opposition to its imposing neighbor, the United States. And in taking on the Canadian nationalist role in writing *Survival*, Atwood, who became part of the literary scene in Canada "at a peculiarly charged historical moment," ended up "playing a major role in forging the means by which she could write with confidence as a Canadian woman writer" (McWilliams 48).

Atwood wrote *Surfacing* and *Survival* during a Canadian historical period exemplified by an unclear national self-concept. Seemingly complicit assimilation to British rule has made Canada's national and postcolonial position complex and unclear; as Frank Birbalsingh notes, "unlike most former colonies which established nationality by resisting imperial rule, Canada steered a middle course that generally avoided resistance" (vii). While it is possible to view Canada, initially, as a colonial or provincial outpost of empire and, later, as a colonial nation, currently, there is "scarcely any consistent image" of Canada (Birbalsingh 5). Part of the reason for this current ambiguity is Canada's "unavoidable proximity to the United States whose size and power make the emergence and ultimate survival of a truly independent Canadian nation . . . perhaps unworkable" (Birbalsingh 5). As Peter Wilkins notes, "from Canada's beginnings, English-Canadian nationalism has consisted of contrasting Canada with the United States," and "over time, however, loyalty to Britain has given way to economic and cultural dependence on the United States, which has eroded Anglo-Canadian 'difference'" (205). Before 1965, according to Wayne Fraser, Canada sought a cooperative relationship with the United States, and Canadian policy, in many ways, emulated that of its neighboring country. With the escalation of the Vietnamese War, however, Canadians sought political and ideological distance from the United States, and "began to think of themselves as a 'nicer' people" (126). Canada's earlier sense of inferiority was replaced in the 1970s by a sense of ethical superiority, but both of these identities relied on a position of opposition: Canada was what Canada was because it was *not* the United States. *Survival* provided an alternative national narrative, one that was distinctly Canadian.

As Atwood offers a response to the lack of consistent image Canada projected by the mid-twentieth century, the national narrative that she provides in *Survival* is prescient, enacting and codifying an articulation of Benedict Anderson's now famous later argument in *Imagined Communities* (1983) that nations are recent entities that constitute communities only via the shared imaginary belief in their communal affiliations—and that these affiliations are primarily established through the fictions of a nation's literature. According to Anderson, the nation "is an imagined political community—and imagined as both inherently limited and sovereign" (6). Anderson claims that during the increasingly secular eighteenth-century, nationalism, as a way of ordering one's place in the world, filled the space left by a decline in religious thought (11). Because he credits the novel and the newspaper as "two forms of imagining which first flowered in Europe in the eighteenth century" (25), the shared experience of reading—and of reading specific texts, particularly novels—helps establish a national collective consciousness and shapes the individual's understanding that she or he is part of the imagined community of the nation. In writing *Survival*, Atwood in many ways articulates and, more importantly, authorizes, via a thematic analysis of Canadian literature (based on the inclusion of certain works and the exclusion of others),[4] Canada's national narrative. In this work, Atwood states that the central theme in Canadian literature is survival and she locates in Canadian literature four "victim positions"—ranging from denying that one is a victim, to becoming a creative nonvictim. These victim positions, according to Atwood, are universal, "whether you are a victimized country, a victimized minority group, or a victimized individual" (46). It is, therefore, not only through the trope of survival that Atwood reads Canadian literature and interprets Canadian national identity, but also through the trope of victimization. Indeed, in order to survive, one must first be a victim of something else.

III.

It is at this point that I would like to put forth one of Atwood's key points in *Survival* because I feel that it is largely *because* of *Survival* and because of Atwood's project in *Surfacing* that we can read and teach Canadian literature as postcolonial. In *Survival*, Atwood says

> Let us suppose, for the sake of argument, that Canada as a whole is a victim, or an "oppressed minority," or "exploited." Let us suppose in short that Canada is a colony. A partial definition of a colony is that it is a place from which a profit is made, but *not by the people who live there*: the major profit from a colony is made in the centre of the empire. (45)

To suppose for the sake of argument that Canada constitutes a colonized entity is not a difficult stretch, but it is not my primary point in this chapter to prove that point nor to take up the debate as to whether Canadian literature should be considered postcolonial; such arguments exist elsewhere,[5] and there appears to be no firm consensus in response to such a designation. And as Atwood herself has said, "genres may look hard and fast from a distance, but up close it's nailing jelly to a wall" (*"The Handmaid's Tale"* 513). Instead, I tend to agree with Donna Bennett's assertion that, as a term, "postcolonialism" has evolved so that "more than a way of specifying time and place, [it] has become a loose conceptual field, or an attitude" and "a point of view that contains within it a basic binarism: it divides our ways of thinking about people into two parts, as colonial opposed to postcolonial. Colonial denotes a way of seeing the world that accepts the imperial point of view, while postcolonial is a viewpoint that resists imperialism." What interests me more, and what I hope this essay demonstrates, is the way that Atwood *writes* Canada as a postcolonial location and the way that reading *Surfacing* through a postcolonial lens enables engagement with shifting power dynamics that have allowed Canada to function both as an oppressor of indigenous peoples and as an oppressed entity—in terms of its relationship to England and France and especially in terms of its relationship to the United States. Over the years, Atwood has become notorious for her public remarks on the US domination of Canada, for example, her assertion that if there were a marriage between the two countries, "the States would proclaim, 'with all my worldly goods I thee endow' in exchange for Canada's adopting the missionary position" ("Canadian-American Relations" 389). As Peter Wilkins notes, "Atwood has always been a vocal nationalist, arguing against what she sees as a version of American colonialism," and "the Canadian anxiety of being swallowed up by the United States is a central theme" (206) in *Surfacing.* This is especially evident in the narrator's fear of the spread of the "virus" of Americanism (*Surfacing* 152) into the Canadian culture and people.

If Atwood's project in *Survival* was revolutionary in its articulation of a specific national literary narrative, one dependent on the acceptance of her postcolonial victim premise, it was also incendiary in the affront that it posed to previous conceptions of Canadian literature, both as it was taught and as it was understood, and, indeed, *Survival* continues to be influential, for even while Atwood's brand of nationalism may seem outdated in today's multiethnic Canada, "it sometimes still holds say abroad," as Laura Moss observes, and, moreover, Atwood is sometimes read as a "writer who touches on 'global' concerns that transcend national borders" ("Margaret Atwood" 28). In her introduction to the 2003 edition of *Survival*,[6] Atwood marvels at both the popularity and power of her thematic study of Canadian literature, noting that in its first year, the book sold ten times the three thousand copies it was predicted to sell, a feat that turned her into an "instant sacred monster"—and turned Canlit into "everybody's business" (3–4). Atwood's work not only established Canadian literature as the articulation of a colonial survivalist mentality, but it also established Canadian literature as a legitimate entity. As Atwood remarks:

The few dedicated academic souls who had cultivated this neglected pumpkin patch over the meagre years were affronted because a mere chit of a girl had appropriated a pumpkin they regarded as theirs, and those who had taken a firm stand on the non-existence of Canadian literature were affronted because I had pointed out that there was in fact a pumpkin *to* appropriate. (4)

As Atwood notes, teaching Canadian literature "is a political act" (21), and *Survival* conceives of such literature not only as a mirror for Canadian identity but also as a map, "a geography of the mind" (26). Into the newly established "pumpkin patch" of Canlit sprung *Surfacing*, a work that situates its protagonist in *Survival*'s established victim positions, which she is able to overcome to various degrees.

Initially, the narrator feels like a victim because her lover "made" her have an abortion, telling her that the fetus "wasn't a person, [but was] only an animal" (170). Because she succumbed to his pressure and had an abortion, she has become "one of them too, a killer" (170)—like the Americans of whom she has been so critical. While at the cabin, she feels pursued by the American developers who want to buy her land and, later, by the men who come to the island to search for her. Running away, she becomes like an animal as she sleeps "in relays like a cat" in a hollow lair "near the woodpile" (209). When the men come to search for her, she feels like a terrified animal. "Behind me they crash, their boots crash. . . . They clank, heavy with weapons and iron plating." After the men leave, she wonders if they have set traps. "Caught animals gnaw off their arms and legs to get free, could I do that" she wonders (217). Later, when she looks in the mirror, she sees herself as "a creature neither animal nor human" (222). And yet her near breakdown leads to a breakthrough. Ultimately, she asserts, "this above all, to refuse to be a victim. Unless I can do that, I can do nothing" (222). Through its careful deconstruction of power politics—imperial, gendered, national—*Surfacing* furthers Atwood's supposition, which is stated and codified in *Survival*, that Canada is a victim, that Canada is a colony, and that it is possible to imagine Canada as, therefore, a postcolonial survivor, a country, like Atwood's narrator in *Surfacing*, seeking to articulate and map the unspeakable and liminal space of the border. Late in the novel, Atwood's narrator, in essence, becomes that space. She says, "I no longer have a name," and "why talk when you are a word," and she also states, "I am not an animal or a tree, I am the thing in which the trees and animals move and grow. I am a place" (198, 212, 213).

Near the end of *Surfacing*, the protagonist discards both gendered and national identity as she comes to occupy the liminal space of the border. As she says early in the narrative when she describes a linguistically complicated exchange that takes place in a grocery located between Ontario and Quebec, "this is border country" (30). This encounter at the border occurs when the English-speaking narrator asks a question in French to a woman in a grocery store in Quebec: *"Avez-vous du viande haché?"* (30). Her accent gives her away; it is not important for the survival of the narrator, as an English-speaking Canadian, a representative of the dominant culture, to speak French with a flawless accent. The narrator does not have to correctly mimic the Québécois, for the inhabitants of this province "are not civilized" (30) since they are considered inferior to the Anglo-Canadians. The shopkeeper, however, speaks both English and French, and demonstrates her prowess in an affront to the narrator: "'Amburger, oh yes, we have lots. *H*ow much?' she asks, adding the *H* carelessly to show she can if she feels like it." (30) She then cuts the meat and charges the narrator "'doo leevers,' . . . *mimicking* [her] school accent" (30, my emphasis). During this encounter, the narrator wishes she "had pretended to be an American" (30), as this is a form of mimicry in which *she* could engage. This scene illustrates the shifting power dynamics of the border. The narrator is culturally superior, an English speaker in Quebec, but, because she is mimicked, and thus her position disavowed, she wishes she had pretended to be American, a citizen of the culture that she resents for its colonial encroachment on Canada's environment and cultural psyche.

At the end of the novel, the narrator returns from the border spaces—the constantly shifting spaces where language and identity break down—that define her five-day period of self-imposed isolation. But her temporary occupation of "border country" gives her the ability to be more nuanced and discerning and less absolute in the designations—the words—that she ascribes to aspects of both her national and personal identity. She realizes ultimately that Joe, who returns to the island to find her, "isn't American . . . he isn't anything, he is only half formed, and for that reason [she] can trust him," even though she does not respond as he calls her name, at least not "yet" (224). While the Americans still exist and "must be dealt with," it is possible that "they can be watched and predicted and stopped without being copied" (221). This possibility marks a moment of hope, both for the narrator with regard to Canada's national position and for Atwood with regard to the state of

Canadian literature that she defines in *Survival*. To know the dominant force and predict its behavior are the goals of the colonized individual; these mechanisms allow for the survival of the dominated entity. And while mimicry may allow for access to some kinds of power, the imitator will never achieve the status of the original, the "real" Romans, as Atwood says in her "Letter to America." But to establish a third space of signification—as Atwood does for Canadian literature in *Survival* and as her narrator hopes to do at the end of *Surfacing*—allows for independence and reparation by allowing for a refusal of the colonized space and thus the refusal of victimhood.

Notes

1. Harrison is, of course, speaking about Achebe's lecture entitled "An Image of Africa," a text that is now widely anthologized.

2. For more on this, see my article, "National Photographic: Images of Sensibility and the Nation in Margaret Atwood's *Surfacing* and Nadine Gordimer's *July's People*."

3. Tellingly, Atwood states that her project in *Survival*—her determination to outline a number of key patterns that are apparent in Canlit—should "function like the field markings in bird-books" (19) in that these patterns help differentiate "species."

4. Atwood is careful to explain that her work is not exhaustive, that she is not a scholar, and that she hopes that "a reader who finds this approach worthwhile won't stop with the examples [she gives]; they are merely a starting-point" (18). Nonetheless, her choices for inclusion in *Survival* generate a particular national narrative, one for which she is the author.

5. See, for example, Laura Moss's *Is Canada Postcolonial?* and Donna Bennett's "English Canada's Postcolonial Complexities."

6. It is worth noting that *Survival*'s reissue was in 2003, the same year that Moss's postcolonial analysis of Canadian literature was published.

Works Cited

Achebe, Chinua. "An Image of Africa: Racism in Conrad's *Heart of Darkness*." *Hopes and Impediments*. New York: Doubleday, 1989. 1–18.

Anderson, Benedict. *Imagined Communities: Reflections on the Origins and Spread of Nationalism*. London and New York: Verso, 1983.

Atwood, Margaret. "Canadian-American Relations: Surviving the Eighties." *Second Words: Selected Critical Prose.* 1982. Boston: Beacon, 1984. 371–92.

———. "Death by Landscape." *Wilderness Tips.* New York: Bantam, 1991. 127–53.

———. "*The Handmaid's Tale* and *Oryx and Crake* in Context." *PMLA* 119.3 (2004): 513–17.

———. "Letter to America." *Writing with Intent: Essays, Reviews, Personal Prose, 1983–2005.* New York: Carroll, 2005. 280–83.

———. *Surfacing.* New York: Simon, 1972.

———. *Survival: A Thematic Guide to Canadian Literature.* Toronto: McClelland, 2004.

Bennett, Donna. "English Canada's Postcolonial Complexities." *Essays on Canadian Writing* 51–52 (1993/1994): 164–210.

Bhabah, Homi K. *The Location of Culture.* New York and London: Routledge, 1994.

———. "Of Mimicry and Man: The Ambivalence of Colonial Discourse." *Discipleship* 28 (1984): 125–33.

Birbalsingh, Frank. *Novels and the Nation: Essays in Canadian Literature.* Toronto: TSAR, 1995.

Fiamengo, Janice. "Postcolonial Guilt in Margaret Atwood's *Surfacing.*" *The American Review of Canadian Studies* 29.1 (1999): 141–63.

Fraser, Wayne. *The Dominion of Women: The Personal and the Political in Canadian Women's Literature.* New York: Greenwood, 1991.

Ghandi, Leela. *Postcolonial Theory: A Critical Introduction.* New York: Columbia UP, 1998.

Harrison, Nicholas. *Postcolonial Criticism: History, Theory, and the Work of Fiction.* Cambridge, UK: Blackwell, 2003.

McWilliams, Ellen. *Margaret Atwood and the Female Bildungsroman.* Farnham, Eng.: Ashgate, 2009.

Moss, Laura. *Is Canada Postcolonial? Unsettling Canadian Literature.* Waterloo: Wilfrid Laurier UP, 2003.

———. "Margaret Atwood: Branding an Icon Abroad." *Margaret Atwood: The Open Eye.* Ed. John Moss and Tobi Kozakewich. Ottawa: U of Ottawa P, 2006. 19–33.

Rao, Eleonora. *Strategies for Identification: The Fiction of Margaret Atwood.* New York: Lang, 1993.

Said, Edward. *Orientalism.* New York: Vintage, 1978.

Shackleton, Mark. "Canada." *Routledge Companion to Postcolonial Studies.* Ed. John McLeod. New York: Routledge, 2007. 83–94.

Wilkins, Peter. "Defense of the Realm: Canada's Relationship to the United States in Margaret Atwood's *Surfacing.*" *REALB* 14 (1998): 205–22.

Wright, Laura. "National Photographic: Images of Sensibility and the Nation in Margaret Atwood's *Surfacing* and Nadine Gordimer's *July's People.*" *Mosaic* 38.1 (2005): 75–92.

Hanging (onto) Words: Language, Religion, and Spirituality in Atwood's *The Handmaid's Tale*_____

Michael P. Murphy

Only a Word, Embroidered

"He has something we don't have, he has the word. How we squandered it, once." (88)

Many aspects of Margaret Atwood's 1985 literary speculations about a future world ruled by the firm hand of a religious theocracy have come to fruition and have thus situated her not only as an imaginative writer of fiction, but an insightful cultural critic as well. As ever, there are fundamentalisms afoot and text-fixated devotees of the world's religions exert as much influence as they did in 1985. Similarly, the popularity of fundamentalist atheism and pseudoscientism is increasing at a fevered clip, which clues readers into the fact that fundamentalism cuts two ways. Atwood's *The Handmaid's Tale* (1985) contemplates and indicts the human inclination towards religious fundamentalism;[1] and, while she is clearly critical of disordered religiosity, she is also a champion of the mystery of the "living spirit" (Interview) promulgated by the humanism embedded in religious traditions. One of the best ways to track this interesting ambivalence is by examining Atwood's unrestrained logophilia, her religious love of words—what they mean, and what they can and cannot do.

Readers interested in the critical relationship that exists among theology, religion, and literature will not be surprised to learn that the current debates in the field (and related fields) are both ever-ancient and ever-new, focusing on the limits of what language can mean (on the ground) and the possibility that language can bind itself to a transcendent reality. The word *religion* finds its root in the Latin *religio*, "to bind," and this is vital in Atwood. The Handmaids in the novel are spiritually assailed by the regime of Gilead because communication is acutely regulated, reading is illegal, and speech is "amputated" (201). As chief among all the human signs, language surpasses all other signs at not only binding the species together and disclosing shared values, but revealing what the theologian Hans Urs von Balthasar calls the "mysterious more" that attends human existence.[2] Regina Schwartz reminds us in her recent book, *Sacramental Poetics at the Dawn of Secularism: When God Left the World* (2008), that the "art of language is to point beyond itself," (6) that it works "by evoking something beyond itself, something that transcends the sign," and because it does, it points to the "realm of mystery" (4). Schwartz builds upon the vast tradition of sacramental aesthetics and seeks to situate this tradition in a late modern context in ways that are both intellectually credible and critically valuable. The promise of language is in its transcendent quality, in "its intent to create a community that coheres, not from blood or territorial boundaries, not from history or from political allegiance, but through sharing divinity" (141). It is in this sense that we find in Atwood, an avowed agnostic, the roots of her relational spirituality. In *Oryx and Crake* (2003), Jimmy/Snowman, from the dust of the apocalypse, utters an insight that illuminates the spiritual power of language: "Hang onto the words" for when they're gone "they'll be gone, everywhere, forever" (68). Jimmy's insight, however opaque, points to the major thesis of Schwartz's important work and to the mystery of sacramentality in general: the word is a "gift" (136). If the gift is squandered so, too, is the possibility for human relationship. To the reader with Christian sensibilities, there is vital consonance here, particularly with theologies that envision Christ as cosmic *Logos*, as transcendent Word who binds the universe together. In any case, through this lens we can glean a retroactive clue from Atwood and interpret *The Handmaid's Tale* as a kind of sacramental text, an exodus narrative that delivers the true word about humanity (in this case the hard tale of human bondage and captivity) as a cautionary tale for future generations.

In *The Handmaid's Tale*, the founders of Gilead love the "word" both too much and too narrowly, and Atwood's artful presentation of language in the novel admonishes readers to be mindful of the political power of speech. Language is a mediator of not only power and agency but of human community and anthropological intelligibility. By means of hanging myopically onto a small series of biblical words, Gilead has, ironically, lost the plot—lost the word—and has become literalist to an inordinate and destructive end. On the surface, Atwood's grievance appears to be with Christianity, especially the evangelical iterations of Christianity that held sway in the 1980s. However, on closer consideration, the religiosity she indicts is more a condemnation of fear-based and misguided interpretations of scripture than it is a denial of the theological mystery of faith that these scriptures—with their contradictions, mixed literary modes, and idiosyncrasies of context—are meant to convey. As a hodge-podge of conflated texts, Gileadean religion lacks any shred of theological intelligibility. In the morning, Offred must listen to a reading from the Gileadean guide-text—Genesis 30:1–3—used to justify the sexual enslavement of the Handmaids: the story of the barren Rachel and her handmaid Bilhah in which Rachel tells her husband Jacob to impregnate her handmaid "and she shall bear upon my knees, that I may also have children by her." Offred, who was forcibly reeducated at the Rachel and Leah Center by the Aunts, resists the morning reading of the Genesis story, thinking of it as "the moldy old Rachel and Leah stuff." In the afternoon, Offred must listen to a heavily redacted version of the Beatitudes piped through a cassette player that includes a made-up blessing—*"Blessed are the silent"*—that acts as a horrible reminder of the use of force to silence the Handmaids in the Gilead regime. "I knew they made that up, I knew it was wrong," muses Offred, "and they left things out, too, but there was no way of checking" (88–89). In this sense, Atwood is not indicting religion so much as she is revealing the dark anthropology at the heart of humankind. Rather than exposing the shortcomings of spirituality, she is, instead, intent on warning against the subtle advent of totalitarian rule. According to

Atwood, "the most potent forms of dictatorship have always been those that have imposed tyranny in the name of religion; and even folk such as the French Revolutionaries and Hitler have striven to give a religious force and sanction to their ideas" ("Writing Utopia" 97). As this dynamic is central to the novel, we will examine it in detail in short order.

Dystopian fiction has long been a prime venue for exploring and demonstrating the power of language. The palpable tension introduced to a culture by neologisms (new terms and concepts that signify and sustain new social realities) and transignifications (terms and concepts whose traditional meanings have been dramatically reassigned) are key structural elements in dystopian novels that reveal the profound conflicts between liberation and servility, speech and silence, and justice and oppression.[3] As in novels by Huxley and Orwell (and so many others), *The Handmaid's Tale* is brimming with inverted grammar and troubling neologisms. The "Prayvaganzas," "compuchecks," "econowives," and "unwomen," to name only a few, have become normative aspects of Gileadean society and sustain the new regime. For Atwood, writing in a postmodern context, these invented terms are not exercises in innocuous literary games. To the contrary, while Atwood, in her language play, is postmodernist in every way, she does not, like Roland Barthes—and other critics from the more liberal wing of the postmodern school—seem to support the utterly free play of language and signs. Instead, her purpose in lampooning neologisms is to provoke her readers into serious reflection about the connections among language, community, and political meaning. Postmodern critics justly critique the imperialism of language—whether in religion, politics, gender relations, or commerce—and the tradition of dystopian literature demonstrates how adherence to the overarching metanarratives provided by language is not without its problems. However, the alternatives are certainly more frightening and Atwood meticulously demonstrates how the annihilation of the language of metanarrative results in fragmentation, personal trauma, and social disintegration—spiritual wounds of the highest order.[4]

One can be a postmodernist who values the diversity and abundance of meaning and still believe that language is not fundamentally subjective. In *The Handmaid's Tale* (and more fully in the companion novels, *Oryx and Crake* and *The Year of the Flood*), Atwood clearly takes an explicit position: our social systems fail if language fails to mean. The theological critique of late modern thought runs along the same lines: because post-Christian and posthuman secularists have foreclosed upon and/or extinguished the fundamental link among language, the transcendent and the human person, theological readings have lost validity. As an agnostic, Atwood is likewise suspicious of the transcendent and holds tight to the necessity of empirical data to validate truth claims. However, in her love of and regard for language, she belies her position by showing us the cost of such a denial. When she was asked, "Could you eliminate the hunger for God?" Atwood responded with what amounts to the core premise of sacramental theology: "I could not eliminate the hunger for God without eliminating language" (Interview). Her dystopian novels outline the social cost exacted when language disincarnates and fragments and, as a result, signs begin to erode and mean nothing in relation to one another. The Gilead regime gains control over women, in part, by making use of the disconnection between language and meaning. In the novel, the takeover of the finances of women, for example, was all too simple because money became digitized and banking was utterly abstracted to the clouds. As Offred recalls, "I must have used that kind of money myself, a little, before everything went on the Compubank" (173). The abstractions are refined to a fevered pitch in *Oryx and Crake* and *The Year of the Flood* (2009), where Atwood depicts a futuristic, dystopian world that has eerie resemblances to our own: one in which gated communities, corporate ghettoes, and the filtered enclaves of digital life have annihilated true mutuality while breeding, in turn, cultures of narcissism and social atomization. Thus, as Atwood is intent on showing in her futuristic novels, impediments to communication paralyze culture in a comprehensive way. They occlude the fluidity of "living spirit" and, by establishing a landscape of vast loneliness, impeded speech stifles the cultivation of genuine religious community. Let us now turn our focus more acutely to the religious quality of words and examine how, with a careful eye on grammar and diction, Atwood reveals the power of words to describe and dictate culture.

Meet the New Boss; Same as the Old Boss

> "'So now that we don't have different clothes,' I say, 'you merely have different women.' This is irony, but he doesn't acknowledge it." (237)

If we examine the annals of history, we can find a profusion of examples of nation-states making use of transignification as they reassign meanings to traditional terms for particular political ends. There are, of course, positive examples of the phenomenon—countries that have been transformed from places of suffering and destruction to healing spaces;[5] however, as *The Handmaid's Tale* is a dystopian novel, it is more instructive to focus on examples on the negative side of the ledger. In particular, Nazi Germany, as one large study of transignification, provides readers of Atwood with a useful (and unsavory) historical referent. The architects of the Nazi regime, knowing full well of the power of German folk tradition and the structural allure of Christian liturgy, evacuated these traditions of their essence and focus and then "rebranded" them with the image of and devotion to a new god: Adolf Hitler. First by the cup and then by the barrel, the new wine of Nazism was poured from the old skins of German culture and religion. The familiar melody of a campfire song about the beauty of the German countryside was given a new lyric: "kill the Jew, spill his blood";[6] the familiar liturgies of Christian devotion were subtly supplanted and then replaced by state-run rallies that exalted (and then demanded) the body and blood of the German *volk*, not to mention the millions of other innocent victims of the Holocaust. Atwood, all too mindful of these insidious usurpations, invokes the Nazi phenomenon in *The Handmaid's Tale*.

In a documentary film Offred remembers viewing in her youth, an old woman in heavy makeup recounts her lover from "one of those wars," a death camp commandant. The commandant in question was notoriously "cruel and brutal," but to her "he was not a monster," and, even if he was, she offers the typical apologia of a relativist in denial: "the times were abnormal" (145). Offred, thinking of Commander Fred in this light and musing her way back to the Gileadean setting decides "how easy it is to invent a humanity" and how, in order to survive, one must tread the muddy waters of relativism for "context is all" (146, 144). The woman in the documentary, however, has one more lesson to teach. As she tells her "war story," something brutal—and fundamentally ethical—is awakened in her. The unreconciled narrative of her life, told for all to hear, ignites in her a sense of guilt and dread. She commits suicide several days after the interview. For Offred, the woman's experience, with all of its analogical immediacy and painful relevance to her own situation, is instructive. "What could she have been thinking about?" Offred wonders, realizing that the woman "was thinking about how not to think" (145). Unlike the woman, Offred is determined to think about her situation and to hold tight to the right to be her own signifier. This is the path Atwood writes for Offred—that she may survive to give birth to her own exodus narrative instead of birthing in her soul a would-be doppelganger, a repugnant "signified" and Nazi-esque concubine that the Commanders would have her become. Offred signifies her resolve to resist this outcome by offering a kind of prayer: *Nolite te bastardes carborundorum*—Don't let the bastards grind you down (146). As she utters this botched Latin phrase, she touches the letters etched into the closet wall by the previous Handmaid so that it becomes a kind of sacramental act, a devotional mantra of resistance passed down from one Handmaid to another. In this fragment, the allusion to Mary "Goody" Glover, however oblique, is not lost on the astute reader. An accused witch, Glover was executed on pre-Gileadean grounds (i.e., on Boston Common) in 1688 because she could only recite the Lord's Prayer in Latin. *Nolite te bastardes carborundorum*, indeed.

The Nazis' systematic upheaval of German culture is an example of their dark genius. For her part, Atwood also knows the power of totalitarianism as an instrument of wielding social power and the repetitious nature of such power structures in history, for, as she has remarked, "Stalinist Russia would have been unthinkable without Czarist Russia to precede it, and so forth" ("Writing Utopia" 97). The Dominican reformer, Savanarola, was burned to death in the same piazza in Florence where he made his popular (if puritanical) bonfire of the vanities a year or so before; Solzhenitsyn's *The Gulag Archipelago* (1973–75; Eng. trans. 1974–78) is layered upon the older pages of Dostoevsky's *The Demons* (1871–72) and Lenin's "The April Theses" (published in *Pravda* 26 April 7, 1917) ; the Rachel and Leah Reeducation Center, the "Red Center," in Gilead where the Handmaids are trained—where they are written into a transvalued existence—is a repurposed Bostonian prep school "where the washroom used to be for boys" (72). Atwood invokes the voice of Kurt Vonnegut as she illuminates the absurd instability of social agreements and the symbolic ambivalence of physical place: "And so it goes," Offred ruminates and, like Vonnegut's Billy Pilgrim, nobody knows why (262).[7] As a fellow critic of the recurrent manifestations of human error and fallibility, Atwood's allusion to Vonnegut is meaningful. "It was in the light of history," Atwood reports, "that the American constitutionalists in the eighteenth century separated church from state. It is also in the light of history that my leaders in *The Handmaid's Tale* recombine them" ("Writing Utopia" 97). The one sure pattern of history is this: while it appears to be whimsical and random, it always rhymes. And so it goes.

The field of semiotics is devoted to finding meaning in these various rhymes, repurposings, and reconstructions and suggesting the ways "signs" (language, physical places, objects) signify psychological and spiritual realities. As a method that describes the context-driven meanings of religious expression, semiotics is also important to theology.

Because Atwood is likewise enthusiastic about semiotics—and about the idea that humans are "symbol making creatures who reside in symbolical systems" (Interview)—she provides readers with a rationale for digging deeper. For his part, Ferdinand de Saussure, a major figure in modern linguistics, was quite clear that linguistic signs, "though basically psychological, are not abstractions" (Saussure 15). *Signifiers*, because Saussure ties them to symbols, are the more concrete aspects of linguistic signs and are thus usually physical in nature; the *signified*, on the other hand, because it has to do with psychological meaning and the more fluid associations that attend a sign, fluctuates and is less fixed (67). In *The Handmaid's Tale*, Harvard University provides a representative example of the interpretive plasticity encoded in a place.[8] Harvard is itself a kind of text that keeps being rewritten, a signifier that, as a physical place, has signified a host of conflicting concepts with vastly different psychological associations. In Atwood's novel, which is set in Boston, Harvard is part of the fundamentalist Gileadean regime. But Harvard has a most interesting history when it comes to signifier and signified. Founded by Puritans as a college for missionaries in 1636, recast as a mecca for Enlightenment thought by the mid-nineteenth century, evolving into a schizophrenic incubator for both Marxism and the mandates of noblesse oblige in the twentieth century, and morphing into a laboratory for technological innovation and new atheism by the twenty-first century, Harvard has run the gamut when it comes to signification. That Harvard has become what it is in the novel is, to say the least, pulsating with psychological meaning.

There are many other cultural signifiers in *The Handmaid's Tale* that undergo similarly significant value changes to their traditional (and more or less stable) trajectories of signification. These reassignments, in fidelity to the tradition of dystopian fiction, are almost always for the worse. The "Jezebel's" scene in the novel is exemplary in this sense and a brief foray into it will help clarify the relationship between signifier and signified. Late in the novel, Commander Fred takes Offred on "a date," an evening of food, drink, and dancing at a hotel, now referred to as Jezebel's. Offred knows the place well as she remembers spending happier days there with her husband: "I've been here before: with Luke, in the afternoons, a long time ago. It was a hotel, then. Now it's full of women" (234). For all the reader knows the hotel is the Boston Marriott, blocks away from the Boston Common where "witches" like Mary Glover were executed in the days of the Puritans. "It's like walking into the past," says Fred as he leads Offred to the room and unlocks the door. When Offred enters the room, she thinks:

> Everything is the same, the very same as it was once upon a time. The drapes are the same, the heavy flowered ones that match the bedspread, orange poppies on royal blue, and the thin white ones to draw against the sun; the bureau and bedside tables, square-cornered, impersonal; the lamps; the pictures on the walls; fruit in a bowl, stylized apples, flowers in a vase, buttercups and devil's paintbrushes keyed to the drapes. All is the same. (251)

But appearances deceive, for it is not the "same" at all. The hotel is no longer a site for commerce and business meetings, no longer a place for weddings and receptions, and no longer a place of noontime trysts for consenting adults. To the contrary, now the hotel is a state-sanctioned brothel, pimped by the Aunts in order to provide sexual "services" for the Commanders and other power elites. Offred pines over this revelation, approaching the "fallow state" that Atwood will develop as an important theme in *The Year of the Flood* (2009): "I sit on the edge of the bathtub, gazing at the blank towels. Once they would have excited me. They would have meant the aftermath, of love" (252). The aftermath that Offred experiences instead is not love but abuse, and the juxtaposition of her remembered hotel visit with Luke and her present visit with the Commander elicits in her a further, if incommunicable, sense of trauma and mourning.

"Just another crummy power trip," remarks Moira when she discovers Offred and her Commander Fred at Jezebel's. "They get a kick out of it. It's like screwing on the altar or something: your gang are supposed to be such chaste vessels" (243). But theologically speaking, the Jezebel's visit is more than "just another crummy power trip." Instead, it becomes a case study in evil. Too often, we imagine that evil, if we still believe in it at all, announces itself on the scene in dramatic fashion. This, of course, is almost never the case. As Hannah Arendt observed, evil is quotidian and mundane and is unleashed upon the world in subtle fashion. When we quietly assent to the normalization of immoral and unjust schemes, when we buy into illusions of entitlement (in the novel the Commanders project the lie that they are "beyond reproach"), we—quite literally—realize the "banality of evil."[9] In this sense, Jezebel's is not only a revelatory cultural marker in the novel, but also an icon that communicates a spiritual phenomenon that is beyond what is conventionally "sayable." As such, Jezebel's is a mundane avenue for a dark spirituality to be made manifest in the world.

Human See, Human Do

> *"But also I'm hungry. This is monstrous, but nevertheless it's true. . . . I think of the word relish . . . I could eat a horse." (278)*

A deeper level of transignification in *The Handmaid's Tale* is one that is more systematic and structural and one that reveals the darker modulations of religious anthropology. In Gilead, the culture of hotel going has been rendered topsy-turvy; and, while this development illustrates more finely the world that Gilead has become, such a transignification is by no means new in the history of human culture and linguistics. Words can have several meanings—something Hamlet knows well when he exhorts Ophelia to "Get thee to a nunnery"—and places, as we have observed, can be and often are repurposed. History is a terrain, a palimpsest upon which cultures rise and fall, upon which victors are written in and the vanquished are marginalized, subjugated, and/or erased. Similarly, literature and language credibly represent the dynamics of social experience and the state of human anthropology in any given historical or fictive context; and, in the novel, it is clear that Gilead, under the guise of religion, has transignified important social experiences for totalitarian ends. However, the more significant matter is that, with regard to religion, Gilead has not transignified as much as it has regressively reiterated primitive modes of religious liturgy. This is a central signal and one that illuminates the theological misuse of religion in a decidedly powerful way. René Girard's work is indispensable here and will enrich our reading of the novel significantly.

René Girard is an original and sui generis thinker. Born in 1923, his fundamental training is in historical anthropology and his analysis of the *pharmakos* (ritual scapegoat mechanism) in the tradition of world mythologies, along with his observations about mimetic desire as a key component of human development, have proven to be valuable resources for critical and cultural theory. Girard converted to Christianity in 1959 and gained notoriety for his work as a literary critic soon after. Readers interested in the intersection of religion, literature, and cultural anthropology and will benefit by Girard's expansive work in these related fields. Indeed, Atwood has declared that "human nature has not changed in thousands of years" (Interview) and Girard's work is a historical accounting and a literary analysis of why this might be. Unlike the majority of postmodernist thinkers, who tend to be concerned with the transmission of phenomena more than phenomena itself, Girard has refused to jettison critical emphasis on the anthropological dimensions of language and sign or on the importance of history and the relationship among violence, religion, and the sacred. A postmodernist in his own right, he nevertheless critiques the postmodern tendency to retreat from these dimensions in preference for more closed (i.e., nontranscendental) systems of meaning. For Girard, the reduction of meaning to the confines of language, text, and intertextuality is a tenuous move. Instead, he articulates a persuasive rationale for the religious nature of language and provides a vital interpretive optic for readers of Atwood, especially those considering the anachronistic theology that undergirds the Gileadean rituals of "Salvaging" and "Particicution."

As outlined in so many myths, the victimage (i.e., scapegoat) mechanism is both a foundational act of human culture(s) and a repeating ritual that maintains those cultures. Girard observes that our notion of culture originates from the release of violence (or potential violence) in repeated acts of mimesis—acts of imitation as humans imitate each other in the process of hominization (the process by which hominids become human). This violence—unleashed upon a scapegoat who is almost always innocent—relieves cultural tension by supplying a physical focal point upon which a culture can fix its blame for cultural and environmental ills and unleash its inherent lust for blood. According to Girard, the scapegoat transaction is not ethically neutral; it is explicitly a "disorder" (*Things Hidden* 366). However, with a nod to Freud, Girard holds that the disorder is also "hidden" and "non-conscious" and is ingrained in human anthropology, no matter how technologically or philosophically "advanced" the culture might appear to be. Girard supplies vast examples in the development of his theory— scapegoats from the Bible (Leviticus, the Joseph cycle in Genesis), scapegoats from literary and cultural history (in *The Bacchae* and *Oedipus Rex,* in Shakespeare and Dostoevsky), and scapegoats in modern history (the famous Dreyfus affair). We may now add Atwood's *The Handmaid's Tale* to the list. The hinge that initiates and sustains the scapegoat mechanism is found in mimesis, the key component in the psychological, behavioral and cognitive development of humans. Humans are constantly in a state of imitation, of each other, of the past, of the things they see, read, witness, and experience.

That mimesis is a normative "operating system" is obvious enough, and, unlike the scapegoat mechanism, Girard views it as an absolutely neutral component in human "development." However, it is with the issue of models—the objects, rituals, and persons imitated—that things begin to get interesting, especially when we read Girard as a resource for meaning against the Judeo-Christian backdrop of *The Handmaid's Tale.*

For Girard, the models we imitate are "contagions"; humanity has been locked in a fixation on violent and destructive contagions and the only possibility for restoration is a fixation on a "good contagion," one that is altruistic, compassionate, and nonviolent. Girard, again a convert, saw something in the Jesus event (the passion, the crucifixion, and the subsequent literature and liturgy that attend these occurrences) from the classic *pharmakos* (that is, scapegoat) model. As incarnated Logos, Christ is anthropologically unique. Christ is the Word that is the transcendental referent in all significations and the model on which we should base our "conversionary imitation." In short, Christ alone salvages humanity; Christ destroys the scapegoat mechanism and provides rescue from human abandonment to the destructive repetitions of the mimetic loop.

In this sense, the Gileadean Salvaging and Particicution rituals described in *The Handmaid's Tale,* rituals that in the novel function as religious liturgy, strike the reader as nothing new in the history of socially sanctioned violence. However, that Gilead enacts and sanctions these rituals in the name of God is the precise point in the novel when astute readers will realize that a regressive and not-so-subtle transignification is taking place, one that reveals the spuriousness of Gileadean religion once and for all. Atwood describes the setting of the Salvaging that Offred attends: "The sun comes out, and the stage and its occupants light up like a Christmas crèche," a burlesque manger not for birth but bloodlust (274). Offred decides, "Obscene, I think, let's get this over with," and her intuitions are correct again (275). According to Girard, "A non-violent deity can signal his existence to mankind by having himself driven out by violence—by demonstrating that he is not able to establish himself in the Kingdom of Violence" (*Things Hidden* 219). The premise is this: it is precisely because Jesus is divine (that is, God incarnate moving through the finite, but who is not of this world) that violence in religious liturgy is to be done away with once and for all.[10] Through his salvaging—his unreserved self-donation and historical revelation—Christ acts as an "*arch*-scapegoat in order to liberate mankind," as Girard explains ("Anthropology" 263). Christ, who always sides with the victims, can be the *only* scapegoat, and, indeed, Christ capitulates to violence in order to declare the cycle repugnant. The sacrifice of the Christian liturgy does the liturgical work of salvaging and recapitulates, over and over again, the divine gift of bloodless sacrifice. Thus a close reading of the Gileadean liturgy discloses the ways that the Gileadean religion, which makes bloody sacrifices out of those deemed to be enemies of the state, is really no religion at all.

Gilead is infected by the bad contagion that leads inevitably to violence against others, and Atwood does strikingly well to illuminate how mimesis has run amok in ways that harmonize with Girardian insight. Illustrating that bloodlust is both mimetically transmitted and that it transcends gender, Atwood describes how Offred participates first in a Salvaging and then in a Particicution. "Today's Salvaging is now concluded. . . . But you may stand up and form a circle," the Handmaids are told as the second ceremony begins (277). The feminine circle is perverted—"the Wives and daughters leaning forward in their chairs, the Aunts on the platform gazing down with interest" (280)—and the Handmaids are set free to execute the last shred of upside-down freedom they possess as they attack a male prisoner who has been convicted of rape. The requisite *pharmakos* supplied, the Handmaids exhibit all the typical symptoms of negative contagion as they prepare to Particicute:

> There's an energy building here, a murmur, a tremor of readiness and anger. The bodies tense, the eyes are brighter, as if aiming. . . . I don't want to see, yet I don't pull back either. . . . It's true, there is a bloodlust; I want to tear, gouge, rend. We jostle forward . . . our nostrils flare, sniffing death, we look at one another, seeing the hatred (278–79).

As the Handmaids unleash their mob-fed violence, there is "a surge forward like a rock concert in the former time. . . . The air is bright with adrenaline, we are permitted anything and this is freedom, in my body also, I'm reeling, red spreads everywhere" (279). The drugged victim—clearly an innocent political prisoner (perhaps a "Femaleroad" operator?)—is consumed by "arms, fists, feet," a sea of red (280). The Particicution provides a social catharsis, and by the afternoon, "things are back to normal" (282). But, as Girard has demonstrated, the downside is that the relief is temporary and the cycle will begin again once the scapegoat has been sacrificed.

That these murders take place at all under the guise of a cleansing ritual is unsavory enough; but the fact that they are legitimized and executed by women is another layer of criticism through which Atwood inserts an even voice. In *The Handmaid's Tale*, Gilead is a totalitarian regime with a decidedly male version of hierarchy; however, it is virtually impossible for the patriarchy to gain any long-lasting legitimacy or executive power without the support and participation of women. It is interesting, then, that the mimetic apparatus used in Gilead exposes an all-too-common way that women do violence to one another. In particular, the Aunts engage in the brutal reeducation of the Handmaids at the Rachel and Leah Center where Offred is trained in her breeder role. They also preside over Gileadean liturgies for women. At the Salvaging Aunt Lydia, as high priestess, states: "I am certain we would all rather be doing something else, at least I speak for myself, but duty is a hard taskmaster, or may I say on this occasion taskmistress, and it is in the name of duty that we are here today" (274). As Atwood establishes, the Aunts are involved in a willing conspiracy, and this is evident in their mindful use of language. One cannot blame patriarchal hegemony here alone as Aunt Lydia, consciously and systematically, moves from "taskmaster" to "taskmistress," from imitator (of patriarchal power structures) to model (for other women to imitate). On one hand, the Wives and Aunts, who are able to retain some social capital because they comply with the regime, can be interpreted as trading true liberty for social safety, as Atwood suggests (Interview). But their behavior is also dastardly and corrupt, for they are more than willing to enact their roles as coconspirators because, as a core component of human anthropology, it is only natural to seek one's own safety even if it means being required to jettison the nobler aspects of one's humanity: empathy, compassion, and love.

Clearly, male power is the main contagion in Gilead. But woman-on-woman violence has its own rich tradition and, when coupled with male versions of violent repression, the dystopia begotten is formidable and implacable. As J. Brooks Bouson has done well to point out, "women uphold the male supremist power structure of Gilead with its hierarchical arrangement of the sexes, and they play an active role in the state's sexual enslavement of the Handmaids" (141). The Wives supervise serial rape, the Aunts terrorize in the Red Center by using cattle prods to keep the Handmaids in line as they reeducate them; all women of power encircle and entrap the Handmaids and their sister victims at the Salvagings who are offered up "like birds with their wings clipped, like flightless birds, wrecked angels" (277). The deepest level of Particicution is here revealed; and the unconscionable conspiracy perpetrated by women against women originates as a sad example of the mimetic contagion set loose in Gilead. The scapegoat sacrifices the scapegoat in a circuit of destruction, something Offred bears witness to and offers, as a kind of corporate confession, to future generations: "I've leaned forward to touch the rope in front of me, in time with the others, . . . then placed my hand on my heart to show my unity with the Salvagers and my consent, and my complicity in the death of this woman" (276).

The I-Thou Encounter: Living Spirit Embedded in Language

"We were waiting, always for the incarnation. That word, made flesh."
(226)

For Offred, the violent experience of Gileadean liturgy has a revelatory effect and it is at this point in the novel where Atwood's notion of spirituality shines brightly. In the middle of the chaotic drubbing of the male prisoner, Offred is led to an epiphany—what Flannery O'Connor would call the "advent of a gracious catastrophe"—and, out of the violence, she begins to retaliate. She observes Ofglen's expert performance in the Particicution —"She pushes him down . . . sharp painful jabs with the foot, well aimed" (280)—and realizes in a flash the central depravity of the regime: the state-sponsored theft of human dignity. Offred's insight is provoked by a physical blow—"Something hits me from behind. I stagger" (280)—and suddenly she recognizes the absurdity of Gilead in a way that is deeply felt, embodied, and totally understood. Offred declares that "He has become an *it*" (280); and she begins to see how, like the political prisoner, she and the Handmaids have been dehumanized to "it-ness" by the state so abjectly and completely. In this sense, Offred understands the prisoner fully as "one of ours," and, by doing so, she is restored to her senses: "Now I am beginning to feel again: shock, outrage, nausea. Barbarism" (280). In a speech act that vibrates with religious significance, Offred then proclaims aloud the moral error of Gilead and rises up with a prophetic accusation: "I saw what you did. . . . Why did you do that?" (280).

Even though Offred subsequently learns that Ofglen's intention was to end the suffering of the political prisoner, her vociferous objection to the violence marks a breakthrough for Offred. The living spirit at work, Offred begins to identify deeply with the innocent victim, not as objectified "Other," but as human person. To reach this spiritual threshold—to see one's self inscribed in the face of another—is to encounter a relational mystery that resonates with a vast theological tradition and one that reveals the deep spirituality enfleshed by human solidarity. "One can only affirm one's Being before another's right to be," observes Schwartz in her reading of the contemporary philosopher Emmanuel Levinas, because "the irruption of the mystery of another person bears the overwhelming ethical responsibility that the irruption of the divine does"; indeed "the face of the Other" is Levinas's "understanding of divinity" (27). For Levinas, the divine exists in the very fabric of human community and is made fully known when we recognize and assent to the dignity and freedom of "the Other." Along these lines, then, when Offred sees the reality of her own victimage inscribed in the experience of the male prisoner (and in her sister Handmaids who were Salvaged), she protests vehemently and, by doing so, affirms and reclaims her own right to be. More significantly, this "irruption" provides the spark that awakens Offred's spirit and pushes her to decisive action. She will trust Nick and give herself "over into the hands of strangers"; she will make her May Day escape and "step up"—both in hope and of her own volition—into "the light" (295). That the spiritual revelation received by Offred moves through the finite is not only an insight of postmodern spirituality, but is also a cornerstone of sacramental theology. The infinite moves through the finite; grace builds on nature. Indeed, this is what spirituality is: the transcendent is revealed in the mundane, not in cryptic prophecy and platitudes transmitted from the airy nowhere of "Planet God."

Jewish personalistic theologian Martin Buber would diagnose the spiritually wounded Gilead as an exemplary case of what he calls the "I-it" relationship. In the I-it state, our view of God is eclipsed, and the objects that keep us from the spiritual are, tragically, of our own making. When we are unable to relate with one another by the cultural machinery we impose or because we prefer our own devices, we eclipse the living God. The challenge, of course, is to be in relationship with God; and in Buber, this phenomenon is accomplished and represented by authentic persons relating with one another in true community, what he calls the "I-Thou" encounter: "Egos appear by setting themselves apart from other egos. Persons appear by entering into relation with other persons" (*I and Thou* 123). Buber's I-Thou personalism is a spirituality that Atwood seems to advocate. When Offred prays, as best she can, she prays to the "Thou," to the "*You*": "My God. Who art in the Kingdom of Heaven, which is within. I wish you would tell me Your Name, the real one I mean. But *You* will do as well as anything" (194). The desire to call each other by name is revealed as a major theme in the novel and Offred makes the leap of faith in final preparation for her liberation by giving more to Nick than her body: "I tell him my real name," she reports, "and feel that therefore I am known" (270).

The representation of Offred's prayer life reveals the link among language, liberty/liberation, and community. Moreover, this dynamic relationship reveals the heart of the novel's spirituality: Offred's hunger for linguistic intimacy—for the I-Thou encounter—illuminates the connection between speaking and being. Offred's entire narrative then serves as a kind of spiritual handbook, a diary that accounts for the dramatic development of one's interior life. As a postmodern exodus narrative that describes the captivity and liberation of a community, it can rightly be considered a text with religious concerns. Moreover, the pattern of the reception of Offred's tale recalls the way that the biblical book of Exodus was orally rendered, redacted by "scribes," analyzed by clerics and scholars, and then appropriated as seminal by disparate communities. The disconcertingly dim reception of Offred's important text by Dr. Pieixoto and colleagues notwithstanding (and Atwood's satire is delicious and refreshing in this regard), the wisdom of *The Handmaid's Tale* continues to instruct. Still, a less referenced Handmaid may lend additional wisdom here and make way for one final language play: "Behold, I am the handmaid of the Lord" (Luke 1:38). A young woman, Mary of Nazareth, agrees to carry in her womb the story of truth—the divine Logos—to a world too consumed by its own desires and devices to truly hear or understand. In a grammar of faith and assent, she continues, "let it be done to me according to your word," responding, in true liberty, to the divine invitation—not as a conscript enslaved by totalitarian thugs, but as a free person who enters into a vital relationship of her own accord. So too does Offred deliver in her "womb" a living truth of liberation to share with the world and in this way she transforms like Mary: she is no longer "Offred," but "offered." Atwood's implicit pun is not only clever, but is also a deeply meaningful linguistic signal of emancipation and recovery.

In *The Handmaid's Tale*, the causeway of language, cleared of its muck and debris, enables the "living spirit" to reveal itself as enrooted organically and physiologically in matter. "I believe you into being," Offred tells those she loves—Moira, Luke, and her daughter. "Because

I'm telling you this story I will your existence. I tell therefore you are" (268). The spiritual solipsism of the Cartesian motto undone by this literary apostrophe, Offred offers, as much as her situation will allow, the binding words of genuine human encounter. It "is not much," she allows, "but it includes the truth" (268). This is a spirituality for agnostics and theists alike.

Notes

1. Atwood's futuristic postapocalyptic companion novels *Oryx and Crake* (2003) and *The Year of the Flood* (2009) likewise provide a cautionary tale to an atomized world ruled by a "corpacracy" and devoted to the religion of materialist scientism.

2. The "mysterious more" posited by Balthasar is critical to objective knowing: "It is this never-failing 'something more' than what we already know, without which there would be neither knowing nor anything to be known" (112.) Of course, Balthasar's "mysterious more" is a metaphysical proposition and one that points to the ineffable and inexhaustible nature of God. In postmodern parlance, the term has been transmuted into "excess," "remainder," and "surplus."

3. Transignification is an element of semiotics (or "semiology")—the study of human sign making. As it seeks to understand the structure, content, and significance of all human communication, semiotics is a vital component to literary criticism. It is particularly relevant in Atwood studies as Atwood is a writer uniquely and explicitly concerned with linguistic sign. However, any thoroughgoing discussion of semiotic theory is quite outside the scope of this chapter.

4. Atwood begins this project in *The Handmaid's Tale* but really perfects it in *Oryx and Crake*. In this 2003 novel, Atwood illustrates how society implodes when it loses the sense of language as unifier of culture and community. Unintelligible organizations and businesses such as "AnooYoo," "RejoovenEsense," and "HelthWyzer" anticipate the fragmented feeling, born of language, of current culture—especially digital culture. What kind of communal/social sense are we to make of "Hulu," "Kazaa," "Mozilla," or "Flickr," not to mention the googolplex of airborne neologisms that constitute internet jargon? Atwood is dead critical of these abuses of language and consistently critiques them in her work. Far from being a benign element, the language play in *Oryx and Crake* (ridiculously spelled homophones, bastardizations, and the like) signal the apocalypse. Likewise, the devolving quality of Scrabble-playing in *The Handmaid's Tale* (and the fact that it is illegal at all) can be read as a symbolic barometer of Gileadean "health"—the lush diction of "valence" and "quince" (139) descends into the gibberish of "smurt" and "crup" (209). Commander Fred cheats at Scrabble and

"encourages" Offred to do the same, giggling all the while at words that "don't exist" (209). The disintegration of language in this regard, especially for a logophile like Atwood, symbolizes the spiritual and political atrophy of the state. To blaspheme the rules of Scrabble is to impede the opportunity for language to perform its vital mission: to mean. Atwood, wary of such disintegrations, cautions her readers: "Just scratch the surface and there's a utopia/dystopia there" (Interview).

5. As The Truth and Reconciliation Commission in South Africa showed the world in the 1990s and its counterpart in Rwanda demonstrated in the early 2000s, states that use violence, abuse, and murder against their citizens can also be places that initiate and host the process of forgiveness and reconciliation.

6. For a complete discussion of the Hitler Youth and institutionalized child abuse, read H. W. Koch, *The Hitler Youth: Origins and Development 1922 –1945* (New York: Cooper Square Press, 2000).

7. Atwood and Vonnegut have complementary literary imaginations. Both are expert satirists who, because they are fundamentally constructive, wield their craft for humanitarian ends. Still, they both are very clear about the repetition of human folly in history. Vonnegut's *Slaughterhouse Five* (or *The Children's Crusade: A Duty Dance with Death*) is a memoir/novel about the absurdity of war and the immorality of sending ill-prepared adolescents to die as soldiers. While the novel is experimental, the theme—"war again?"—is ancient. In chapter one of the novel, Vonnegut's narrator (who is Vonnegut himself at this stage) speaks with a "movie-maker," Harrison Starr:

> "You know what I say to people when I hear they're writing anti-war books?"
>
> "No. What *do* you say, Harrison Starr?"
>
> "I say, 'Why don't you write an anti-*glacier* book instead?'"
>
> What he meant, of course, was that there would always be wars, that they were as easy to stop as glaciers. I believe that too. (4)

Atwood's invocation of "And so it goes" is an allusion that initiates an important and enriching intertextuality.

8. Atwood knows Harvard well and the setting of the novel is of vital importance to her. In a capstone of transmutation, the lawn in front of Widener Library is no longer a site for the exchange of ideas, but the place in the novel where prisoners are executed. In an interview for a Reader's Companion on the novel, Atwood offers additional remarks about why she chose to set *The Handmaid's Tale* on the former grounds of the Massachusetts Bay Colony: "The society in The Handmaid's Tale is a throwback to the early Puritans whom I studied extensively at Harvard under Perry Miller, to whom the book is dedicated. The early Puritans came to America not for religious freedom, as we were taught in grade school, but to set up a society that would be a theocracy (like Iran) ruled by religious

leaders, and monolithic, that is, a society that would not tolerate dissent within itself. They were being persecuted in England for being Puritans, but then they went to the United States and promptly began persecuting anyone who wasn't a Puritan. My book reflects the form and style of the early Puritan society and addresses the dynamics that bring about such a situation."

9. Hannah Arendt's *The Origins of Totalitarianism* (1951) is a must read for any reader of dystopian fiction and/or Atwood. The "banality of evil" is a term Arendt first coined in her 1963 reportage on the trial of Adolf Eichmann.

10. In these passages, Girard adds his own emphasis to the Gospel text:

> In him (the Logos) was life;
> And the life was the light of men.
> And the light shineth in darkness,
> *And the darkness comprehended it not* (John 1:4–5)

> He was in the world
> And the world was made through him,
> *yet the world knew him not.*

> He came to his own home,
> *And his own people received him not* (John 1:10–11)

Girard's interpretation underscores a genetic distinction that is often missed. According to Girard, "Christ is God, born of God," and of the same substance of God. "He is completely alien to the world of violence into which he was born— the world of violence within which humankind has been imprisoned ever since the foundation of the world" (*Things Hidden* 223). For the Christian (in Gilead or elsewhere), the whole of the bible leads to this axial mystery. The Commandments from Exodus declare "Do not kill"; the Gospel message of Jesus is largely about forgiveness and reconciliation. Girard's insight shows how the misreading of scripture, especially by people of faith, imprisons us in the ancient circuit of violence. Christ, as part of the Godhead, offers a different path. Furthermore, because he is radically unique, Christ is the only one who can authentically "salvage" (i.e., absolutely "save"), a premise ignored by Gileadean leadership. In Atwood's novel, then, Gileadean theology is revealed a sham based on the same scriptural grounds that it would otherwise claim its legitimacy.

Works Cited

Atwood, Margaret. *The Handmaid's Tale*. 1985. New York: Anchor, 1998.

_____. "Interview with Bill Moyers. *Bill Moyers on Faith and Reason*. PBS. New York. 28 July 2006. Television.

_____. *Oryx and Crake*. 2003. New York: Anchor, 2004.

_____. "Reader's Companion Interview with Anchor/Doubleday Reader's Circle." *Reader's Companion to* The Handmaid's Tale. Doubleday, 1998. Web. 23 Jan. 2012.

_____. "Writing Utopia." *Writing with Intent: Essays, Reviews, Personal Prose: 1983–2005*. New York: Carroll, 2005. 92–100.

_____. *The Year of the Flood*. Toronto: McClelland, 2009.

Balthasar, Hans Urs von. *Theo-Logic: Theological Logical Theory—Truth of the World*. Trans. Adrian J. Walker. Vol. 1. San Francisco: Ignatius, 2002.

Bouson, J. Brooks. *Brutal Choreographies: Oppositional Strategies and Narrative Design in the Novels of Margaret Atwood*. Amherst: U of Massachusetts P, 1993.

Buber, Martin. *I and Thou*. Trans. W. Kaufman. New York: Scribner, 1970.

Girard, René. "Anthropology of the Cross: A Conversation with René Girard." *The Girard Reader*. Ed. James G. Williams. By Williams. New York: Crossroad, 1996.

_____ *Things Hidden Since the Foundation of the World*. Stanford: Stanford UP, 1978.

The Holy Bible. Rev. Standard Version. New York: New American Lib., 1962.

Saussure, Ferdinand de, *Course in General Linguistics*. Eds. C. Bally, A. Sechehaye, A. Riedlinger. Trans. R. Harris. London: Duckworth, 1983.

Schwartz, Regina Mara. *Sacramental Poetics at the Dawn of Secularism: When God Left the World*. Stanford: Stanford UP, 2008.

Vonnegut, Kurt. *Slaughterhouse Five* (or *The Children's Crusade: A Duty Dance with Death*). 1969. New York: Dial, 1999.

Sexual Trauma, Ethics, and the Reader in the Works of Margaret Atwood _____

Laurie Vickroy

Despite the varied contexts of her novels, persistent themes surrounding women and traumatic circumstances reoccur in various guises throughout Margaret Atwood's career as a novelist as she addresses the particularly gendered effects of the oppression of women. Whether presented within the realities of contemporary society, as in *Surfacing* (1972) or *Bodily Harm* (1981), or placed in a historical context, as in *The Blind Assassin* (2000), or projected into an imagined future, as in her convincing speculative fictions *The Handmaid's Tale* (1985) and *The Year of the Flood* (2009), Atwood examines the traumatic effects of women's vulnerability to physical, sexual, and psychological violence in situations of male domination. As victims of trauma, her female protagonists often begin in the throes of suffering and use psychological defenses—repression, emotional withdrawal, or rationalization—against punishing environments and then go through the painful process of working through trauma. Atwood's female characters, like the Surfacer-narrator in *Surfacing*, Rennie in *Bodily Harm*, Offred in *The Handmaid's Tale*, and Iris in *The Blind Assassin*, are victim-survivors who are ethically or emotionally compromised by their fears of male violence and exploitation. However, they are also inspired by the actions of brave women who resist their tormentors though they pay heavily for it, such as Moira in *The Handmaid's Tale* and Laura in *The Blind Assassin*. Characters like Moira and Laura also serve an important function by provoking awareness in Atwood's protagonists so they can discover ways of rejecting and resisting forces of domination, primarily by trying to redefine and reclaim their own value and agency against those forces.

Believing that as a Canadian she should not use her "privileged position . . . as a shelter from the world's realities but as a platform from which to speak" against oppression ("Amnesty International" 396),

Atwood has long been interested in the power politics of gender—and human—relationships. In Atwood's works, trauma is often socially induced in contexts of domination and power. She says:

> Power is our environment. We live surrounded by it: it pervades everything we are and do. . . . We would all like to have a private life that is sealed off from the public life and different from it, where there are no rulers and no ruled, no hierarchies, no politicians, only equals, free people. But because any culture is a closed system and our culture is one based and fed on power, this is impossible, or at least very difficult. . . . So many of the things we do in what we sadly think of as our personal lives are simply duplications of the external world of power games, power struggles. ("Notes on *Power Politics*" 7).

Atwood particularly examines how her women characters are psychologically overwhelmed by personal relations that reinscribe dominance and submission in particularly gendered behavior codes. She explores the personal ramifications of the political in the broad sense: "Politics for me is everything that involves who gets to do what to whom. . . . Politics really has to do with how people order their societies, to whom power is ascribed, who is considered to have power. A lot of power is ascription. People have power because we think they have power, and that's all politics is" ("Using" 149). Atwood's characters learn that they have been socialized to give others power, but that the power others have over them is not absolute. Seeing the chinks in power structures helps her protagonists face their fears enough to loosen psychological defenses and patterns so that they can reconsider their lives as trauma victims and act in their own behalf.

The complex plight of Atwood's victim-survivors is illuminated by the work of contemporary trauma specialists like Judith Herman, who has worked with many female trauma survivors. As Herman explains, trauma is a psychological wound resulting from events that are so overwhelmingly intense that they impair normal emotional or cognitive functioning. Such events are often violent, involving war, rape, or physical brutalities, and the bodily humiliations or violations that result from such events can have devastating effects on individuals' self-regard and ability to achieve intimacy (Herman, *Trauma* 108–10). Trauma victims, who may suffer from a tainted or diminished sense of self, or feel unsafe in their daily lives, may unconsciously deploy defense mechanisms that help protect them from reexperiencing pain, including suppressing memory or dissociating, that is, distancing themselves physically or emotionally from the sources of their fears (51–56). But while these defenses may protect against further trauma, they can also jeopardize human relations, making victim-survivors skeptical or distrustful of others, or alienated (42–47). At its worst, trauma can create feelings of helplessness and guilt, and destroy in victim-survivors the belief that they can act independently or meaningfully in the world (Janoff-Bulman 19–22). If it is normal for people to try to overcome their fears and acquire a sense of relief by both approaching and avoiding what causes anxiety, those who have been traumatized experience an extreme version of this: suffering from intrusive or repressed memories, they are at once driven to and fearful of remembering (Laub and Auerhahn 288). While trauma often involves a single horrific event, such as rape, trauma, as Kai Erickson points out, can also be part of daily life and result from a "pattern" of emotional or physical abuse (Erikson 457). Because Atwood's victim characters daily confront such patterns of abuse in situations that threaten and diminish them particularly because they are women, my focus is on the sexual trauma that results when physical or mental violations are coupled with social demands to conform. Atwood's victim protagonists also often experience emotional neglect early in life that makes them more vulnerable to subsequent traumas.

Because victims of trauma typically engage in self-defeating, defensive, and repetitive behaviors, Atwood's trauma-survivor characters may seem overly passive and emotionally paralyzed, unreliable and overly defensive, unheroic and even unethical—failures that are manifestations of trauma. If Atwood's victim characters, like the Surfacer-narrator or Rennie Wilford or Offred or Iris Chase Griffen, seem at first glance unreliable or overly defensive as they justify their behavior, Atwood reveals that the obvious flaws of her characters—their helplessness, their faulty cognition or memory, their need to repress or hide from the past, their avoidance of the suffering of others—are symptomatic of trauma. Rendered helpless and passive and thus deprived of agency, these characters may seem utterly unheroic and may seem unethical in their wish to avoid further trauma. And they may seem unreliable,[1] not because they are dishonest, but because they are defensive and unaware of the fears that drive them. As Atwood reveals that the passive helplessness of her female victims results from trauma and the wish to survive, she also asks us to consider to what degree the lurking fears that grip her victim characters prevent them from bearing responsibility for others or themselves or from treating others fairly and compassionately. Just as classic trauma narratives may be structured to mimic the actual symptoms of trauma—such as the victim's experience of intrusive thoughts or memories or her need to defensively split off the memories of and emotions associated with traumatic experiences[2]—so Atwood, in her novelistic investigations of trauma, depicts her victim characters reliving trauma and beginning the process of recovery from trauma by encountering intrusive memories of the past through their dreams and nightmares, as suppressed emotions connected with traumatic fears emerge before they can reach consciousness. Not only do dreams offer clues to readers about the characters' subconscious conflicts and fears, but they also reveal that repressed thoughts of the trauma are surfacing, which if acknowledged and processed emotionally, can lead to recovery.

Sexual and Political Trauma in *Bodily Harm*

The central character of *Bodily Harm*, Rennie Wilford, grows up in an emotionally barren family with a mother who hides the shameful secret that Rennie's absent father is living with another woman. Rennie's grandfather, who is known for having a violent temper, sets a tone of fear in the house, establishing that men's control constrains and silences the women, compromising their ability to nurture. Her mother's life of drudgery and self-sacrifice convinces Rennie to reject this kind of life, and so she determines that she does not want to be "anyone's mother, ever" (50). Rennie inherits her mother's defensive denial of feelings, and since her mother discourages intimacy, Rennie never learns to trust others and consequently lacks the emotional fortitude to face subsequent traumas.

Rennie's upbringing explains her choice of partner, Jake, who likes to dominate her, but does not offer or demand anything of her emotionally. Rebelling from the moralistic inhibitions of her family, she seems to enjoy Jake's sexual objectification of her, not considering why she accepts this. Despite the fact that Jake likes to play sadistic sexual games with her, postfeminist Rennie insists that she does not feel threatened in her relationship with him. "Pretend you're being raped," Jake says to Rennie, and even though he sometimes hurts her, she tells herself he is just playing a game (109). Similarly, when she agrees to write a piece on pornographic art, she, at first, thinks that there is no harm in it until she sees the Metro Police collection of seized pornographic objects, the "raw material" for such art. While Rennie watches "with detachment" the "sex-and-death" films depicting women being "strangled and bludgeoned or having their nipples cut off by men dressed up as Nazis," she is shocked into awareness by the film showing a rat emerging from a woman's vagina (200). Afterward, Rennie has trouble dismissing Jake's sadistic sexual games, feeling that he is using her as "raw material" (202). And Jake is unable to give her the assurance she seeks from him: "She didn't want to be afraid of men, she wanted Jake to tell her why she didn't have to be" (201).

"Massive involvement. . . . It's never been my thing," Rennie comments to her surgeon when she learns that she has breast cancer and must have a partial mastectomy (26). Terrified at the thought of her surgery, Rennie has a "horror of someone, anyone, putting a knife into her and cutting some of her off," which she compares to the horrific fate of women victims of sex crimes who are found "strewn about ravines or scattered here or there in green garbage bags" (14). Aware that her mother will see her cancer as her "fault" (73), and finding Jake's discomfort after her surgery intolerable, Rennie initially defends herself by distancing herself from her fears. Rennie, who is a Toronto lifestyles reporter, imagines herself writing a trendy piece on cancer: "*This is a fact, it's happened to you, and right now you can't believe it*, she would begin. . . . Dying was in bad taste, no doubt of that. But at some point it would be a trend, among the people she knew. Maybe she was way out ahead on that one too" (19). After her mastectomy, the deeply traumatized Rennie feels dissociated from her mutilated body, which is a "sinister twin"; in her "resurrected" body, she feels that she is "not all that well glued together" and that she will "vaporize" (73, 134). No longer feeling secure with Jake, she does not want him to touch her or to see her "damaged, amputated" body (187). Instead, she latches on to her surgeon, Daniel, hoping that he will save her. "I want you to save my life. . . . You've done it once, you can do it again," she thinks of Daniel (135). Yet even as Rennie's interest in Daniel, who is married and emotionally unavailable, points to her need for male protection, she also sees Daniel, with his surgeon's knife, as a potential persecutor. Traumatized by her cancer diagnosis and her surgery, Rennie must come to terms with her fears of bodily harm and death.

When Rennie, soon after her surgery and after Jake leaves her, comes home to find a coiled rope on her bed left by an unknown sadistic stranger, she defends herself from her fears of male persecution— from the faceless stranger with the rope—by going to a Caribbean island to write a travel piece. Instead of escaping her fears in the Caribbean, Rennie is forced to confront them, head-on. "There's only people with power and people without power," Rennie learns in the Caribbean as she witnesses the brutality unleashed by political turmoil (230). Rennie, who, as a tourist, has felt like a "spectator, a voyeur" as she has witnessed the suffering of others (117), is forced to open her eyes and awaken to the reality of male violence against women when she ends up in prison with the lower-class Lora. Just as Lora was abused while she was growing up, so she ends up being horrifically abused in prison, and Rennie's experience as she shares a prison cell with Lora lead her to a series of revelations about the pervasive threats of power politics as Atwood links individual trauma to more widespread social and political dangers. Indeed Rennie's first words in the novel—"This is how I got here" (3)—refer to her awakening as she shares a prison cell with Lora.

Having long protected herself through her spectator's vision and her detachment from the suffering of others, Rennie is forced, finally, to become involved with the plight of Lora, a woman that Rennie initially dislikes. When the two first meet in the Caribbean, Rennie is hypercritical and defensive about Lora's open exhibition of the emotional distress in her life, which is evident in her chewed nails. "She can't stand the self-righteousness of people like Lora, who think because they've had deprived childhoods or not as much money as everybody else they are in some way superior" (81). Lora sells drugs, which is a typical means of survival on the island, but she is also idealistic, helping provide firearms for the dictator's opponents. When Rennie and Lora are imprisoned together, both under suspicion of aiding the opposition, Lora confides in an unsympathetic Rennie that she has been raped in the past. Rennie still wants distance from Lora, blaming her for their arrest, and, at first she is disgusted when she realizes that Lora is trading sex with the prison guards for some minor comforts. But through this trade-off, Lora is also protecting Rennie from being abused, and thus Lora models a sense of obligation toward others that Rennie will later embrace. Indeed, Rennie must learn to care about others to be a fully functioning and useful human being, and her relationship with Lora, which evolves from antagonism to empathy, makes this possible.

When Rennie finds herself trapped with Lora in the traumatic environment of the prison, where, she realizes, the two may die, she puts her earlier traumas into perspective. "Once she would have thought about her illness: her scar, her disability. . . . Now this seems of minor interest, even to her. . . . She may be dying, true, but if so she's doing it slowly, relatively speaking. Other people are doing it faster: at night there are screams" (273–74). This terrifying environment evokes nightmares in which the faceless man who left a coiled rope on her bed becomes "a shadow, anonymous, familiar" (277), suggesting that she now recognizes a more generalized male threat. After witnessing the shearing and beating of other prisoners through the window of her prison cell, Rennie recalls the pornographic vagina with rats and anticipates that the prison guards will eventually come up with similarly horrible tortures. "She's afraid of men and it's simple, it's rational, she's afraid of men because men are frightening. . . . Rennie understands for the first time that this is not necessarily a place she will get out of, ever. She is not exempt. Nobody is exempt from anything" (279–80). The prison delivers many forms of "bodily harm": the humiliation of no sanitation, sleep deprivation, and possible violence. Lora is apparently beaten to death after she threatens the guards, and Rennie is too frightened to ask the guards to stop beating Lora. Afterward, Rennie feels guilty and complicit and wants to save Lora: "How can she bring her back to life?" (287). Readers may question why Lora must be sacrificed so that Rennie can be transformed, but Lora is also a realistic example of the way that those with power can victimize with impunity those who do direct battle with them. Survivors initially lay low, as Offred does in *The Handmaid's Tale*. Rennie's attempt to comfort Lora is evidence of internal growth, a new recognition of her connection to the suffering of victimized others and of the ethical imperative to recognize others' (and her own) suffering and to act to alleviate it.

Rennie's experiences have awakened her to her ethical responsibilities as a writer. At the end, she determines that if she gets out of prison she will write about the political situation, embracing Lora's request to "Tell someone what happened" (272). The end of the novel redirects us back to the beginning, indicating that it is possible but not certain that Rennie will live to tell the tale. Her time may be running short, but she becomes aware that "she will never be rescued. She has already been rescued. She is not exempt. Instead she is lucky" (291). In other words, if she is not rescued from her prison cell, she nevertheless has been saved from her trauma-induced patterns of callousness toward others and herself. She recognizes abuses of power and resolves to no longer be complicit in them as a victim or a passive onlooker.

Political and Sexual Repression in
The Handmaid's Tale

The contexts for trauma in Atwood's futuristic dystopian novel *The Handmaid's Tale* are primarily political and sexual repression. In Atwood's imagined future, the United States is taken over by a violently enforced totalitarian, Christian theocracy in which the male patriarchs—called the Commanders—enforce a range of gender-implicated traumas as they assert complete control over women. Nuclear and environmental disasters have limited the pool of fertile women, so women are forcibly conscripted to perform breeder roles as Handmaids, or support roles, such as the Marthas, who are domestic servants in the homes of the Commanders, or the Aunts, who serve the regime by forcibly reeducating the Handmaids. The patriarchal regime of Gilead enforces control of these functions by breaking up families and assigning sole reproductive rights to the Commanders, older men from the highest echelons who are often, ironically enough, not fertile themselves, and it is the role of the Commanders' Wives to raise the children born to the Handmaids. The Gilead regime uses surveillance, secrecy, and propaganda to maintain power and to prevent opposition, and they target women in particular, utilizing them to indoctrinate other women, or punishing them for activism, or using them sexually. Attempts to resist the regime are met with arrests, executions, and Gulag-type imprisonment or exile. These threats terrorize the population and turn people against one other as they attempt to survive under totalitarianism.

By focusing on the plight of one Handmaid, Offred, in *The Handmaid's Tale*, Atwood draws connections between the personal and the political as she exposes the working of power politics in the Gilead regime. Assigned as a breeder woman to the Commander Fred, she is "of-Fred," and having suffered the loss of her family and her citizenship, the deeply traumatized Offred is forced to procreate for the survival of Gileadean society. Her husband's fate is unknown, but she learns her daughter is being raised in a Commander's family. These circumstances for a time strip her of her identity and will, and Offred is torn between wanting to remember the life she once had and thinking it best to avoid what is painful and unrecoverable if she wants to survive. Yet Offred cannot totally forget her losses, and simple associations like smells evoke involuntary, painful memories of her daughter. And Offred also has recurring nightmares of her family's attempted escape and capture, which bring back anguished memories and anxious speculations about the survival of her husband Luke. She maintains the slim hope that she might be allowed to see her daughter again. Though painful, these emergent shreds of her past life become crucial in reclaiming her individuality, and the comparisons between past and present also help her become more actively analytical of the regime's instabilities and inadequacies.

Offred, who is part of the "transitional" generation of Handmaids (15), recalls the freedoms she once enjoyed and how she acted unethically toward other women—in particular her feminist mother—in her embrace of postfeminism. A "refugee from the past," Offred recalls how young women from her generation enjoyed the benefits of feminism, feeling as if they were "free to shape and reshape forever the ever-expanding perimeters" of their lives (294). "You're just a backlash. Flash in the pan. History will absolve me," Offred's feminist mother once told her (156). But Offred did not want to "vindicate" her mother's life or be the "incarnation" of her mother's feminist ideas or the "justification" of her mother's "existence" (157). Years later, in her prisonlike existence as a Handmaid, Offred understands her mother's principled stance against patriarchy and is heartbroken over the fate of her mother, who has been condemned by the regime to a shortened life by being forced to clean up toxic waste.

Being treated as sexual slaves traumatizes the Handmaids, though the Aunts tell them to be grateful: "In the days of anarchy, it was freedom to. Now you are being given freedom from. Don't underrate it" (33). Signs of Offred's trauma—that she feels helpless and indistinct as an individual—are associated with the total supervision of her body in the Gileadean regime. Offred considers how her body, once powerfully physical and pleasure-seeking, is now reduced to a reproductive function. The metaphors she uses emphasize her feelings of personal indistinctness in contrast to the power of her body's potential fertility: "I'm a cloud, congealed around a central object, the shape of a pear, which is hard and more real than I am and glows red within its translucent wrapping" (95). She must dissociate to escape the harsh realities of being merely a birth vessel: "I avoid looking down at my body . . . because . . . I do not want to look at something which determines me so completely" (82). And she must also distance herself from the sexual trauma she must endure during the monthly insemination ceremony. In describing the Ceremony, Atwood highlights how oppressors create bizarre realities that deny individuals agency or principles by offering only fatal or humiliating choices. Offred tries to defend herself mentally from the very personal assault of this ceremonial rape. During the ritual she rationalizes her situation by recalling that she chose to become a Handmaid over other worse, and even deadly, options, and she also distances herself from her body and feelings by noting the absurdity of what is happening to her as the commander's Wife sits behind her, holding Offred's hands, while the Commander has sex with her in a grotesque parody of a biblical scene (see Bouson, *Brutal* 145). Yet even as Offred tries for a measure of control, she is being repeatedly victimized as she is subjected to the horrors of state-sanctioned rape.

"Maybe the life I think I'm living is a paranoid delusion," Offred thinks (139). As the deeply traumatized Offred struggles to retain her sanity, she employs the defense mechanism of intellectualizing: for example, she plays word games and keeps her mind active by considering the possibilities of her situation and those of others. Even as she tries to remain emotionally distant, she stretches herself to see all points of view, including her enemies', at times feeling that she risks empathizing with them. These strategies help her rediscover her own ethics by building identifications with other victims. Because the regime keeps the public ignorant, uncertain, and fearful, Offred needs to speculate about possible signs of rebellion because she "needs perspective" or she will be reduced to "[living] in the moment. Which is not where I want to be" (185). During her secret affairs with Commander Fred and with Nick, she discovers that the regime is not an implacable force but a constellation of shifting alliances and rule breakers (both within and against the regime). For instance, despite the fact that the Commander is a powerful man within the regime, he wants to escape the sexual limitations imposed by his official position and he also feels the sting of his wife's resentment.

Even as Offred feels utterly traumatized and defeated, she comforts herself by telling "a different story, a better one," as she recalls Moira, her "irreverent, resourceful" friend from the past who openly rebelled against the Gilead regime and who, when she first arrived at the regime's indoctrination center, called it a "loony bin" (69, 92). While Moira, who managed to escape the indoctrination center, ended up getting caught and then forced into prostitution, she nevertheless inspires Offred. Memories of Moira's resistance and heroism and her persistent attempts to escape despite torture inspire Offred to question the regime's lies and legitimacy. Moira acts as her conscience, leading Offred to risk contacting the resistance, and to reclaim her desire by pursuing an affair with Nick. And while Offred does not openly defy the regime as her mother and Moira did, she does rebel by telling her story. "*Blessed are the silent*," according to the Gileadean Bible (115). But Offred refuses to remain the silenced trauma victim. Her account highlights an ethical, empathetic, and psychological view of history in stark contrast to the pseudo-objective, intellectual distance of the participants at the historical conference at the end of the novel. In denying the suffering Offred reports, these intellectuals display defenses that create complicity with power and withhold empathy for those affected. Offred demonstrates for future readers the traumatizing effects of oppression, particularly how fears diminish people, make them unwilling participants, and adaptable to horrors. In describing Offred's situation, Atwood urges readers not to condemn victims but to understand how power can shatter lives, and subsequently how those lives can be reclaimed if traumatized individuals refuse to believe that the powerful have the authority to define them. When Offred finds the "taboo message" left by a former Handmaid—"Don't let the bastards grind you down"—she is inspired that this message has "made it through" (69). Offred, too, resists the Gilead regime, and much like Rennie in *Bodily Harm*, she awakens to her ethical responsibility as she tells her trauma story—her own taboo message—and thus offers vital testimony to those who come after her.

The Repression of Sexual Trauma in *Surfacing*

Although *Surfacing* is set in the sexually liberated and feminist 1970s, it focuses on sexual trauma in describing the Surfacer-narrator's response to an abortion she had at the behest of her married lover. Left emotionally devastated, the Surfacer must confront her sexual trauma and break through the repression and fantasy that she has used to shield herself. The Surfacer's defenses are tested and broken when she goes on a quest to the Canadian north woods with her travel companions Anna, David, and Joe to find her missing father, whom she has not seen in years. While ultimately she is able to reconnect the unmoored strands of her past life, she must also, in confronting her fears of male persecution and sexual trauma, eventually recognize her ethical responsibility to stop passively obeying others and acting contrary to her own interests and well being. Her perspective is confusing, even off-putting, through much of the narrative; readers are drawn along into the narrator's own uncertainties and irrationality. She appears unreliable and untrustworthy: she will not report to others important information, such as her discovery of her father's body, because it is so traumatizing that she cannot process this information consciously. Also, her extreme reactions express an unexplained rage, but as she gets closer to understanding her traumas readers can attribute her behavior to repressed memory and to fantasies she has employed to avoid confronting her losses.

At the outset of her journey, the deeply traumatized Surfacer is unable to trust or bond with others. Wary, she refuses to give away too much and she does not reveal to her travel companions, Anna, David and Joe, who all reject their parents, her need to rediscover hers, or that she is suffering from intense emotional conflicts. She is suspicious rather than sympathetic when Anna confides in her about her husband David's cruelty. When Anna asks her if she feels bad about rejecting Joe's marriage proposal, she acknowledges (to herself) that she doesn't feel much: "I hadn't for a long time. . . . At some time my neck must have closed over, pond freezing or a wound, shutting me into my head" (105). This is a key metaphor for the narrowness of her emotional range, which will expand and even explode over the course of the novel.

As her repression weakens, the Surfacer responds to the physical environment and the people around her in intensely emotional ways because of her traumatic history. Her descriptions of land and nature focus on death, disease, and the decline of the natural world, reflecting her own tainted sense of life. As she approaches these changed but familiar places, her simultaneous need to find her missing father and fearful attempts to avoid the painful possibility of his death create inner turmoil. Her fear of discovering him seems to relate to a fear of knowing things about herself. The process through which she remembers her traumas begins when she finds a mutilated heron strung up in a tree "like a lynch victim." The intense rage she feels toward the "Americans"—men who destroyed the heron to "prove they could do it, they had the power to kill" (116)—is symptomatic, and, in a traumatic context, such feelings of uncontrollable rage indicate a connection to forgotten horrors, which for the protagonist are associated with male domination. Indeed, the Surfacer's anger toward men is generalized and overdetermined: that is, it often exceeds the context and thus indicates some unresolved trauma. Throughout much of the novel she says "he," not identifying clearly which man she means. The reader must guess from the context. "He" can refer to any of the men who have been close to her (her lovers and her father), creating similarities between them, and, in fact, conflating them all as objects of her love and anger. Her confusion is transferred to readers through a mindset patterned on emotions and not on a rational or ethically fair attempt to distinguish among the various men in her life.

"Straight power, they mainlined it," the Surfacer thinks of the men she assumes are Americans but who turn out to be Canadians. "The innocents get slaughtered because they exist . . . there is nothing inside the happy killers to restrain them" (127–28). When the Surfacer and her friends are fishing, she reflects on the violence of the sport: "Anything we could do to the animals we could do to each other: we practiced on them first" (120–21). As she remembers how her brother threw leeches into the campfire when the two were children, she concludes: "To become like a little child again, a barbarian, a vandal: it was in us too; it was innate" (132). She believes this is a clue to what underlies her own thinking and behavior and begins a process of struggling with her memories, which she simultaneously wants to access but fears. Yet she begins to realize that the idea that violence is "innate" will not solve her issues. "A thing closed in my head, hand, synapse, cutting off my escape: that was the wrong way, the entrance, redemption was elsewhere, I must have overlooked it" (132).

In the dramatic scene in which the Surfacer dives underwater and sees the body of her dead father, she begins the process of confronting her trauma. "It was below me, drifting towards me . . . a dark oval trailing limbs." When she finds the body of her missing father, she begins to uncover the sources of her trauma through association: "it was something I knew about, a dead thing, it was dead." She panics and rushes out of the water and emotionally screens or camouflages the trauma of finding her father's body with the idea that she had witnessed her brother's near drowning, which happened before she was born. "It wasn't ever my brother I had been remembering, that had been a disguise. I knew when it was, it was in a bottle curled up, staring out at me like a cat pickled. . . . It wasn't a child but it could have been one, I didn't allow it" (143). She realizes that, yet again, she is "wrong," for she "never saw" the fetus after the abortion. The abortionist "scraped it into a bucket and threw it wherever they throw them" (143). Unable to accept the "mutilation" and "ruin" she had made, she defended against her traumatic affair and abortion by creating associative memories of her brother's collection of animals in bottles. "The bottle had been logical . . . [a] remnant of the trapped and decaying animals, secreted by my head . . . something to keep the death away from me" (143). As she finally confronts her deep sexual trauma, she recalls that her married lover pressed her to have an abortion. "He said I should do it, he made me do it; he talked about it as though it was . . . simple, like getting a wart removed." Because she complied with his wishes, she, too, is "a killer." Since then, as she realizes, she has "carried that death" inside her, "layering it over, a cyst, a tumor, a black pearl" (144–45).

As the Surfacer confronts her trauma and her rage, she enters, temporarily, a terrifying world. Identifying with the animals, she becomes a "natural woman" and when men come to search for her, she imagines that they are predators—male killers—hunting her down. The Surfacer, who has deliberately tried to get impregnated by Joe, imagines giving birth by herself, without the medical "death machine" associated with the abortionist and with men (162). Wanting to protect the life she may have within her—"it must be born," she insists—she begins to recover and comes to a new determination. "This above all, to refuse to be a victim. Unless I can do that I can do nothing. I have to recant, give up the old belief that I am powerless and because of it nothing I can do will ever hurt anyone" (191). She sees a potential future life with Joe, who cares for her and who seems relatively uncorrupted by civilization. Driven to undo her earlier mistake by trying to become pregnant with Joe, she continues an unfinished process of trying to refashion an identity that rejects the gender indoctrination and female submissiveness that left her vulnerable to exploitation and trauma.

Traumatic Splitting and Sexual Self-Sacrifice in *The Blind Assassin*

As Iris Chase Griffen, the protagonist/narrator of *The Blind Assassin*, tells the story of her compelling and suppressed life history in her memoir, she presents a challenge to readers and tests their sympathies because, although wounded herself, she in turn has injured others, but at times seems only dimly aware of her motives. Like the Surfacer, Iris reveals a belated recognition of painful details, or they intrude on her in involuntary memories. Though she may not want to face painful details of her past, she is driven to write about her life and to be understood, which leads her down paths of uncomfortable memory and devastating realizations of her complicity in her sister's death.

As the elderly and dying Iris writes her memoir near the end of the twentieth century, she chronicles the many contexts of trauma in her and her sister Laura's lives. Their father, Norval Chase, returned from World War I emotionally destroyed by battle and the deaths of his two brothers. A prominent and wealthy factory owner, he expressed his grief in angry alcoholic rages. Their emotionally unavailable mother died after a difficult miscarriage, and her philosophy of self-sacrifice endures in both girls. Iris and Laura are only nine and six when their mother dies but are not allowed to grieve. Suppression of anything painful or embarrassing is a Chase family trait, and even their loving caretaker Reenie feels that "least said, soonest mended" (142). In the 1930s during the Depression, their father's business falters, and he sells it to an ambitious industrialist, Richard Griffen. Iris marries Richard to save her father's business, but Richard breaks his promises to keep the Chase factories going. "I'd married Richard for nothing then. I hadn't saved the factories, and I certainly hadn't saved Father. But there was Laura, still; she wasn't out on the street. I had to think of that" (314).

Tragically, while Iris thinks she is protecting Laura through her marriage to the wealthy Richard, instead she is putting her sister at risk by placing her under the potential control of Richard, who views the two sisters as his sexual possessions.

As the elderly Iris writes her memoir, she tries to understand her past actions and recognize how split off from herself she was when younger. Looking at her wedding picture she refers to herself in third person: "I say 'her,' because I don't recall having been present, not in any meaningful sense of the word. I and the girl in the picture have ceased to be the same person. I am her outcome, the result of the life she once lived headlong" (239). Recognizing the consequences of her past heedlessness, she reaches some insight only belatedly. Such belatedness takes on tragic proportions for Iris as she becomes aware of the extent of her guilt long after she can do anything about it, or apologize to long-dead loved ones. Her grief emerges compulsively: "But some people can't tell where it hurts. They can't calm down. They can't ever stop howling" (2).

As Iris probes her symptoms and concealed motivations, she reveals how they are related to the hidden actions and effects of Richard Griffen. When she married Richard, she scarcely knew him, and she has long repressed memories of her wedding and the sexual traumas she endured as the wife of a sadistic and controlling man. As a sign of her traumatic splitting, Iris separates her life as a married woman into "two lives, a daytime one and a nighttime one." As a society bride, she lives a respectable life but she is also a battered woman. Her life is one of "[p]lacidity and order. And everything in its place, with a decorous and sanctioned violence going on underneath everything" (371). Even as Iris shields herself from Richard through what he sees as her "willful and even aggressive lack of attention," she feels estranged from herself: "How lost to myself I have become," she thinks (297, 298).

The stronger emotions Iris has long repressed emerge years later in her dreams. Nightmares about Richard wake her up regularly decades after his death, and though she does not talk about them in detail, she acknowledges that past horrors relentlessly surface. "When you're young, you think everything you do is disposable. . . . You think you can get rid of things, and people too—leave them behind. You don't yet know about the habit they have, of coming back. . . . Time in dreams is frozen. You can never get away from where you've been" (396). Her dreams return her to the fear and violence that she fought to distance herself from during her marriage to Richard. "I dreamt that Richard was back. I could hear him breathing in the bed beside me. . . . My heart was hammering painfully, as if I'd been running. It's true, what they used to say, I thought. A nightmare can kill you" (222). These dreams bring back the strong sense memories typical of unprocessed traumatic memories, which are suspended in time and remain overwhelming because the traumatic experiences have not been integrated into normal memory and thus are re-experienced in repetitive, unconscious patterns (Van der Kolk and Van der Hart 441–42).

Though much of Iris's story is located in a prefeminist past in which women had much less power, Iris's passivity is nevertheless meant to be disturbing to contemporary readers. The ethical crux of the novel is how this affects Iris's relationship to Laura and how Iris fails to protect Laura from Richard's sexual pursuit of her. Preoccupied with her own problems and trapped in her own self-insulating mindset, Iris does not investigate why Laura had been committed to an institution where she was forced to abort Richard's baby. Laura always had the capacity to see the truth and confront Iris with the dreadfulness of her life with Richard, which Iris wanted to evade. J. Brooks Bouson has analyzed the many ways Iris bought into the culture's sexism and patriarchal diminishment of women, limiting them to social and reproductive roles ("Commemoration" 262). Significantly, Laura rejects the high society trappings that seduce Iris, and she tries to convince Iris not to sell herself in marriage. Iris's emptiness, her disconnection from loved ones, and regrets are the costs of her sacrifice in marrying Richard. Finally, Iris and Laura are rivals for Alex's love. Iris wins Alex's love, but fears the power he would have over her should she choose him, and she also fears leaving her affluent life with Richard to be with Alex. When during their final conversation, Laura tells Iris that she has sexually sacrificed herself to Richard to save Alex, Iris misunderstands Laura and thinks that Alex is the father of Laura's child. In one awful moment, Iris destroys Laura's hope that she might reunite with Alex after World War II, callously revealing his death in the war and the fact Iris and Alex were lovers, provoking Laura's suicide. Only after Laura's death does Iris realize the truth of Laura's forced sexual relationship with Richard, who had a "yen for young girls" and who got "a bargain— two for the price of one"—when he married Iris (505).

As the elderly Iris writes her memoir, she breaks the code of silence surrounding the sexual sacrifice—and traumas—that she and Laura endured. As readers follow Iris's slow and resistant path toward admitting her own culpability for Laura's suicide, we also witness her movement from a silenced victim to someone who takes responsibility. Iris, who was reduced to a society lady caricature as Richard's wife, is a victim-survivor, and her greatest wish at the end of life is to be seen as a complete and flawed human being who exists most fully in the manuscript she leaves behind. Iris feels enormous guilt over Laura, but also for failing to nurture her own daughter Aimee. Thus, there is an ethical imperative in Iris's wish to communicate to her granddaughter Sabrina, to whom she wills her manuscript. What little Iris knows of Sabrina's life bodes well for the future; Sabrina does humanitarian work and does not chase status or safety. Iris seeks understanding but also expects to have her life evaluated by Sabrina as an example of future generations of young women: "I leave myself in your hands. What choice do I have?" (521). Finally, Iris offers a self-conscious and ethical inquiry into the ways power hides itself in social norms and notions of stability, and how these became deeply absorbed into her sense of self.

In telling these trauma stories, Atwood warns her women readers that they must be vigilant about the ways power works and must not invest themselves in systems of belief that split individuals off from an ethical sense of self, and caring and compassion for others. Atwood's long-term interest in the power politics of gender relations continues in her postapocalyptic work, *The Year of the Flood* (2009), which offers gruesome descriptions of male violence against women in an environmentally devastated and posthuman future. In *Year of the Flood*, as in her other works, Atwood depicts trauma as a kind of living death that deprives us of memory, identity, and vitality. Power feeds on fear and complicity. While sexual trauma can break down the human spirit, through her novelistic portrayals of Iris, the Surfacer, Rennie, and Offred, Atwood suggests recovery is possible. Though it can be a slow and painful process, with help, Atwood's victim characters are able to contend with overwhelming forces and begin to reclaim themselves from tainted identities and from ascriptions of power.

Notes

1. Unreliability, as narrative theory explains, can involve failures to inform, but more significantly failures of judgment or ethics (Abbott 75–77) that in the case of trauma narratives can be tied to symptoms such as helplessness, faulty cognition or memory, shame, repression, or dissociation. Often more principled (or less traumatized) characters are offered to provide as an implicit value structure with or against which a protagonist's behavior can be measured. Readers' cognitive responses to texts involve the ability to attribute mental states to characters (see Alan Palmer 245 and David Herman "Cognition" 253). Thus, texts must offer clear signals to readers that the faulty behavior of characters results from their traumatic circumstances.

2. For further discussion of this, see Vickroy 24.

Works Cited

Abbott, H. Porter. *The Cambridge Introduction to Narrative*. New York: Cambridge UP, 2008.

Atwood, Margaret. "Amnesty International: An Address." *Second Words: Selected Critical Prose*. Toronto: Anansi, 1982, 393–97.

_____. *The Blind Assassin*. New York: Doubleday, 2000.

_____. *Bodily Harm*. New York: Anchor, 1998.

_____. *The Handmaid's Tale*. New York: Fawcett, 1985.

_____. "Notes on Power Politics." *Acta Victoriana* 97.2 (1973): 7.

_____. *Surfacing*. Don Mills, ON: PaperJacks, 1972.

_____. "Using What You're Given." By Jo Brans. *Margaret Atwood: Conversations*. Ed. Earl G. Ingersoll. London: Virago 1992. 140–51.

Bouson, J. Brooks. *Brutal Choreographies: Oppositional Strategies and Narrative Design in the Novels of Margaret Atwood*. Amherst: U of Massachusetts P, 1993.

_____. "A Commemoration of Wounds Endured and Resented: Margaret Atwood's *The Blind Assassin* as Feminist Memoir." *Critique* 44.3 (Spring 2003): 251–69.

Erikson, Kai. "Notes on Trauma and Community." *American Imago* 48.4 (1991): 455–71.

Herman, David. "Cognition, Emotion and Consciousness." *Cambridge Companion to Narrative*. Ed. David Herman. Cambridge, UK: Cambridge UP, 2007. 245–59.

Herman, Judith. *Trauma and Recovery*. New York: Basic, 1992.

Janoff-Bulman, Ronnie. *Shattered Assumptions: Toward New Psychology of Trauma*. New York: Free, 1992.

Laub, Dori, and Nanette C. Auerhahn. "Knowing and Not Knowing Massive Psychic Trauma: Forms of Traumatic Memory." *International Journal of Psychoanalysis* 74.2 (1993): 287–302.

Palmer, Alan. *Fictional Minds*. Lincoln, NB: U of Nebraska P, 2004.

Van der Kolk, Bessel A., and Onno Van der Hart. "The Intrusive Past: The Flexibility of Memory and the Engraving of Trauma." *American Imago* 48.4 (1991): 425–54.

Vickroy, Laurie. *Trauma and Survival in Contemporary Fiction*. Charlottesville, VA: U of Virginia P, 2002.

Freed from the Salt Mines of Virtue: Wicked Women in Margaret Atwood's Novels _____

Sarah Appleton

> [In literature,] were women to be condemned to virtue for life, slaves in the salt-mines of goodness? How intolerable. (Margaret Atwood)

In her well-known essay entitled "Spotty-Handed Villainesses: Problems of Female Bad Behaviour in the Creation of Literature," Margaret Atwood asks, "But is it not, today—well, somehow *unfeminist* to depict a woman behaving badly?" She continues: "When bad women get into literature, what are they doing there? Are they permissible? And what, if anything, do we need them for?" (126). Atwood, who insists that literature cannot do without bad behavior, clearly shows the worth of less-than-virtuous women in her works. Villainesses are important not only in fictional plots in Atwood's view, but also in helping readers understand that women are multidimensional individuals who should never be condemned, even by feminists, to stereotypical roles.

"Create a flawless character and you create an insufferable one," Atwood insists ("Spotty" 125). Her interest in female badness, she explains, started at an early age when she was "exposed to the complete, unexpurgated Grimms' fairy tales," which were originally "told and retold by women" ("Spotty" 134). While she was delighted by the "Cinderellas and "Snow Whites found in fairy tales, she also knew that there were "spellbinding evil parts for women" in such stories ("Spotty" 134). For while fairy tales feature passive and adventuresome girls and resourceful and wise women, they also contain "a variety of evil witches, both in disguise and not, and bad stepmothers and wicked, ugly sisters and false brides as well" ("Spotty" 134–35). In her novels, Atwood delights in portraying contemporary versions of these maybe evil, but maybe—more importantly—powerful women who must develop survival strategies of their own: in particular, in *The Handmaid's Tale* (1985), Serena Joy is a wicked stepmother" type; in *Cat's Eye*

(1988), the child Cordelia is tormentor of another girl; in *The Blind Assassin* (2000), Iris is the treacherous sister; and in *The Robber Bride* (1993), Zenia is the false friend who betrays her female friends and steals their men.

Atwood, who began writing during the second-wave feminist movement, is often called a feminist writer. While she feels indebted to the movement, she also has been troubled by the restrictions placed on writers like her by feminist orthodoxy. Second-wave feminism, as she remarks, has offered real benefits to women writers by expanding the "territory available to writers" and by providing a "sharp-eyed examination of the way power works in gender relations" ("Spotty" 132) But she also has objected to the "tendency to cookie-cut" found in the second-wave's polarizing model of men as oppressors and women as victims, making "women intrinsically good and men bad." Such "oversimplifications," she asserts, are "problematical for novelists unless the novelist has a secret desire to be in billboard advertising" ("Spotty" 132).

To Atwood, such a model, as it dictates that heroines must be "spotless of soul" as they struggle against male oppression, confines women "yet again to that alabaster pedestal so beloved of the Victorian age" and it condemns them "to virtue for life, [as] slaves in the salt mines of goodness" ("Spotty" 132–33). Although feminism has made certain kinds of formerly "bad" behavior available to the woman author—who can depict her heroine leaving her husband and deserting her children—it is still not acceptable to "talk about women's will to power" since women are supposedly "communal egalitarians" ("Spotty" 133). Can the woman writer, asks Atwood, "examine the Seven Deadly Sins in their female versions— . . . Pride, Anger, Lust, Envy, Avarice, Greed, and Sloth—without being considered antifeminist?" Or will woman authors who write about such things be accused of "aiding and abetting the enemy, namely the male power structure" since men have been "giving women a bad reputation for centuries?" ("Spotty" 133). Just as prefeminist images of women tended toward stereotypes of the totally good or bad woman but never a combination of the two—such as the innocent Dorothy from *The Wizard of Oz* or the Wicked Witch of the West, the good Cinderella or her evil stepmother, the licentious Scarlett O'Hara or the dutiful Melanie—so second-wave feminist images of women have ended up emphasizing a new set of stereotypes by depicting women as victims of men. To Atwood, this development has been distressing. As she states, "[Are] women to be homogenized— one woman the same as another—and deprived of free will—as in, *The patriarchy made her do it?*" ("Spotty" 134).

"Writing and *isms* are two different things," Atwood has long asserted, and people who are loyal to isms "often hate and fear artists and their perverse loyalty to their art, because art is uncontrollable and has a habit of exploring the shadow side, the unspoken, the unthought" ("If You Can't" 21). Atwood strongly supports "women's efforts to improve their shoddy lot in this world which is, globally, dangerous for women, biased against them, and at the moment, in a state of reaction against their efforts." ("If You Can't" 21) But she also views "with some alarm the attempts being made to dictate to women writers, on ideological grounds, various 'acceptable' modes of approach, style, form, language, subject, and voice" ("If You Can't" 22). Indeed, "if the women's movement is not an open door but a closed book, reserved for some right-thinking elite, then I've been misled," she states ("If You Can't" 24). Thus Atwood insists on her right to depict women as villains in her art. As she argues: "Evil women are necessary in story traditions for . . . obvious reasons, of course. First, they exist in life, so why shouldn't they exist in literature? Second—which may be another way of saying the same thing—women have more to them than virtue" ("Spotty" 133). Atwood, in her contemporary revival of the villainess, creates a cast of female characters that are most certainly wicked and have questionable morality. Her works contain stories of female treachery, betrayal, deceit, lies, vindictiveness, and a whole host of similar evils. In her cultural re-visioning of the bad female character, Atwood is intent on going beyond stereotypes, for her female villains are never wholly evil and, in fact, often we end up seeing them as individuals who have made mistakes, or who have maintained a wicked facade as a means of protection, or who have found that the lives they have chosen have not allowed for generosity of spirit. While readers might want to disidentify with the villainess character—saying that she is "not-me"—Atwood insists that we take a second look. For as she remarks, such characters can "act as keys to doors we need to open, and as mirrors in which we can see more than just a pretty face" ("Spotty" 135). Thus, as we shall see, Atwood's wicked women, like *Cat's Eye*'s Cordelia and *The Robber Bride*'s Zenia, do act as mirrors even as they allow other characters—and readers—to explore the necessity of sometimes acting badly.

The Handmaid's Tale: Serena Joy as the Wicked Stepmother

The Handmaid's Tale, published in 1985, relates a possible future United States that has been taken over by a fundamentalist religious regime intent on repopulating the white race, many of whom are now sterile due to pollutants and toxic waste. A Handmaid in the Gilead Republic, Offred recalls her pre-Gilead past in a society much like our own—one in which second-wave feminism had succeeded in gaining new freedoms for women—even as she describes her present in a repressive society in which women have been relegated to roles such as Wives, Marthas (domestic servants), and Handmaids (surrogate mothers). In Gilead, women are forbidden to read and write, own property, or live in any independent circumstances. The thirty-three-year-old Offred is a Handmaid to Commander Fred and his unhappy Wife, Serena Joy. As a breeder woman, Offred must bear a child to the Commander and relinquish her child to Serena Joy, who, as a Wife, is expected the inculcate Gileadean values in the children she raises.

A witch-like woman who uses a cane and has knobby hands, Serena Joy is past child-bearing age and so she is forced to rely upon her Handmaid to become a mother herself, the only "occupation" that will

---

Wicked Women in Margaret Atwood's Novels   **279** validate her status as a Wife in the new regime as well as ensure her safety. But, of course, she does not like having in her home a strange woman who, during monthly ceremonies, is to be impregnated by Serena Joy's husband. "I want to see you as little as possible," she tells Offred when they meet (20). Like Offred, Serena Joy is imprisoned in her role as she spends her days knitting, gardening, feigning illness so she can receive other Wives as guests, and watching videos of her former self as a famous gospel singer.

"I wanted," Offred says of Serena Joy, "to turn her into an older sister, a motherly figure, someone who would understand and protect me" (21). Instead, because Serena Joy is full of cold and angry contempt, Offred reacts with her own countercontempt, seeing Serena Joy as "withered" (105). Later, when the Commander secretly entertains Offred in his private study with games of Scrabble and forbidden fashion magazines, Offred initially feels little sense of betrayal in deceiving Serena Joy, and she does not understand that Serena Joy is also living a precarious life; each woman's potential fate is the mirror of the other woman's. While Offred will be sent to clean up toxic wastes if she fails to conceive a child—a certain death sentence—Serena Joy, as a disempowered female in the new regime, is also at the mercy of her powerful Commander husband; without his protection Serena Joy, too, could be sent to clean up toxic wastes.

In her training to become a Handmaid, Offred is instructed that life will become easier for the Handmaids in the future. "The women will live in harmony together, all in one family; you will be like daughters to [the wives]," she is told" (209). Although Offred contends that she hates Serena Joy, she nevertheless begins to feel guilty because she is "an intruder, in a territory that ought to have been" Serena Joy's: "I was taking something away from her, although she didn't know it" (208). Offred starts to understand that Serena Joy's coldness and rage is born of her awareness that her own position as a Wife is precarious. Serena Joy does not have the luxury of being a benign "stepmother"; she must use all of her strength for self-preservation.

At the novel's end, Serena Joy discovers that Offred has been secretly seeing the Commander. Offred awaits punishment, but Serena Joy only says, "You could have left me something" (369). When the van arrives to arrest Offred—or save her—Serena Joy is the one who reacts with the most fear; without a Handmaid to provide her with a child, Serena Joy has no value. If in her portrayal of Serena Joy, Atwood invokes the wicked stepmother stereotype, she also insists that her villainess character acts as a mirror in which we can see how female oppressors like Serena Joy may be acting out of fear. That is, the reader, instead of dismissing Serena Joy as a mere stereotype, a simple evil stepmother, must see herself in the mirror of Serena Joy, who is wary of other women because she is aware of the precariousness of her own position as a Wife. Thus, the cause of Serena Joy's ostensibly villainous nature can be explained: her very survival is at risk.

Cat's Eye: The Villainess Cordelia as the Victimizer/Victim

When the middle-aged Elaine Risley returns to Toronto for a retrospective exhibition of her artwork, she undergoes a troubling journey into her past as she recalls her girlhood torment at the hands of her so-called girlfriends. Even as *Cat's Eye* reveals the depths of the treachery that girls (and women) will engage in against each other and offers some insight into female bullying, it also draws connections between the victim Elaine and her chief tormentor Cordelia, who ends up acting as the dark double and mirror image of Elaine.

Elaine spends her early childhood up until age eight in the Canadian bush with her family. Because her chief playmate during those years is her brother, when her family moves to Toronto, the school-aged Elaine enters the utterly foreign world of girls: "real girls at last in the flesh. But I'm not used to girls, or familiar with their customs. I feel awkward around them, I don't know what to say" (50). Carol Campbell and Grace Smeath, the two girls Elaine initially befriends, introduce her to a strange world ruled by absent, but somewhat menacing, fathers and bib-aproned mothers who are apparently unaware of their daughters' cruel behavior to others. As she learns about the rules governing the feminine world of girls, Elaine at first feels "strange" and "self-conscious" as if she is "doing an imitation of a girl" (55). But over time she begins to identify with the feminine world represented in the "hope chest" scrapbooks she makes with her friends, which include cut-out pictures of women and household items from the Eaton's catalogue. As Elaine notes, "I begin to want things I've never wanted before: braids, a dressing gown, a purse of my own. Something is unfolding, being revealed to me" (57). She begins to realize that her parents are considered strange because they do not fill their home with decorations, appliances, and other possessions.

"She creates a circle of two, takes me in," Elaine remarks of her first encounter with Cordelia (75). Becoming the group leader of the girls, Cordelia begins to bully Elaine. "Look at yourself! Just look!" Cordelia says as she holds a mirror up to Elaine's face. "Her voice is disgusted, fed up, as if my face, all by itself, has been up to something, has gone too far" (168). As Cordelia victimizes Elaine, her tactics escalate from acts of taunting and shunning to more dangerous forms of bullying. When Elaine is buried in a hole in the ground, she is terrified: "I have no image of myself in the hole; only a black square filled with nothing, a square like a door," which marks the point at which she loses "power" (112–13). Another time Cordelia punishes Elaine by throwing her hat into the ravine and then ordering her to navigate the ravine and its icy creek to retrieve it. When Elaine falls through the ice, she thinks: "If I don't move soon I will be frozen in the creek. I will be a dead person" (199). Elaine almost freezes to death before she sees or imagines a protective and all-good female figure—like the Virgin Mary or a fairy godmother—who walks on the air toward her and leads her to safety. Taking on the sacrificial role of the scapegoat, Elaine, as Molly Hite has observed, "is the surrogate victim . . . for the others who use her . . . in order to displace their own suffering as members of a patriarchy" (137). Indeed, Cordelia torments Elaine to avoid becoming the victim herself. "Wipe that smirk off your face," as Cordelia's bullying father said to her when she was growing up, and later Cordelia uses the very same words when she bullies Elaine (268, 183). Thus, as Stephen Ahern explains, "Cordelia uses Elaine in this classic pattern of projecting what one is trying to escape/reject within oneself onto an 'Other.' Elaine rapidly internalizes Cordelia's insecurity, and the malice it generates" (13). If Cordelia is the chief female villainess in *Cat's Eye*, Grace, the silent leader of the group, represents the patriarchal ideal of the complicit female. She participates in the brutalization of Elaine, as does her mother, the "perfect" housewife and mother. While Elaine originally believes that the mothers are unaware of their daughters' sadistic behavior, she overhears Mrs. Smeath defending Grace. When asked if the girls are being "too hard" on Elaine, Mrs. Smeath responds, "It's God's punishment. . . . It serves her right" (190–91). Shamed, Elaine harbors a lasting hatred of Mrs. Smeath.

Over time, Elaine begins to suffer from severe anxiety and starts to mutilate herself in an attempt to control her pain and fear: "In the endless time when Cordelia had such power over me, I peeled the skin from my feet. . . . I would go down as far as the blood" (120). She is torn between being afraid of the girls and her fear of rejection. She would rather be tormented by Cordelia than be ostracized from the world of girls. But if, when Elaine is buried in the hole by Cordelia she feels "sadness, a sense of betrayal" and then "terror" after she falls through the ice in the ravine, she chooses to free herself by walking away from her friends: "Nothing binds me to them. I am free" (205). Even though Elaine suppresses her memories of her childhood torment at the hands of Cordelia, she acts suspiciously like someone who is enjoying a belated revenge when she becomes friends once again with Cordelia in high school. Cordelia now demonstrates all of the vulnerability Elaine once had, and Elaine, who has developed a "mean mouth," uses it mostly on Cordelia: "I use her as target practice" (248). Yet Elaine's newfound toughness cannot be equated with gaining strength. In fact, it is during this period of her life that Elaine has her deepest feelings of social inadequacy. What Elaine has learned from Cordelia is not how to be powerful, but how to cover up feelings of powerlessness.

Elaine's last encounter with Cordelia takes place at an asylum following Cordelia's suicide attempt. Alternating between feelings of anger and pity, Elaine thinks, "It's as if Cordelia has placed herself beyond me, out of my reach, where I can't get at her" (376).What infuriates and terrifies Elaine is her own likeness to Cordelia: "There's a frantic child in there, behind that locked, sagging face," she thinks of Cordelia (377). As the middle-aged Elaine reflects on her life, she sees the villainess Cordelia as part of her own identity. In one of her paintings, *Half a Face*, Elaine attempts to depict Cordelia as cruel and aggressive. But Cordelia's frightened eyes "sabotage" her. "Cordelia is afraid of me, in this picture. I am afraid of Cordelia. I'm not afraid of seeing Cordelia. I'm afraid of being Cordelia. Because in some way we changed places, and I've forgotten when" (239).

During an introspective walk back into her old neighborhood, re-endowed with the memories of her lost childhood, the adult Elaine "prays" to Cordelia: "Get me out of this, Cordelia. I'm locked in. I don't want to be nine years old forever" (421). And Cordelia, it appears, responds. In her mind, Elaine replays the scene at the ravine. This time, Elaine first thinks she imagines herself as a child, but then she recognizes that the child is Cordelia with her "face closed and defiant" (443). Elaine recognizes that they share "the same shame, the sick feeling in my body, the same knowledge of my own wrongness, awkwardness, weakness; the same wish to be loved; the same loneliness; the same fear" (443). In her vision, Elaine opens her arms to save Cordelia from being "left behind, in the wrong time" and tells her, "*It's all right. . . You can go home now*" (443). Because, as Atwood insists, the villainous Cordelia and her victim Elaine are mirror reflections, Elaine, through her relationship with Cordelia, not only comes to a deepened understanding of her own capacity for the cruelty that grows out of feelings of powerlessness but she also, by forgiving Cordelia, comes to forgive herself.

The Blind Assassin: Iris as the Treacherous Sister

Like *The Handmaid's Tale*'s Serena Joy and *Cat's Eye*'s Cordelia, who wield a limited but vicious power against other women, *The Blind Assassin*'s Iris Chase Griffen is a woman whose rage at her powerlessness in a patriarchal world is used—with disastrous results—against another woman: her own sister. As the eighty-two-year-old Iris writes her memoir, she attempts to justify her past. Even though she insists she has no ill will toward her dead sister Laura, the novel reads like an elaborate excuse for her utter betrayal of the younger Laura. As Sharon Wilson notes, because Iris is "so blind, lacking insight into history, current events, mythology, her father, husband, sister Laura, and her own motivations, she threatens the survival of others as well as of herself" (185). While Iris is not a deliberately villainous woman, she has created havoc for her family and, as she writes her memoir, she confesses her role in her sister Laura's suicide.

As Iris looks to the past to reconstruct what has happened to Laura, she depicts the power of patriarchy in the lives of women from her generation, who come of age early in the twentieth century. The Chase sisters, living in an old Victorian house, are sheltered from the lower-class citizens of the town; both sisters are alienated and have difficulty communicating with others. The daughter of an industrialist who faces economic problems and a mother who died as a consequence of childbirth, Iris describes herself as she recounts her past as both a victim and a victimizer. Iris is four years old when her sister Laura is born. Understanding that the birth has deteriorated her mother's health, Iris resents Laura. She does not understand her more naive sister and becomes irritated by what she considers to be Laura's eccentricities: "Laura was *different. Different* meant *strange*" (89). And when her dying Mother asks her to take care of Laura, Iris resentfully thinks, "why was it always me who was supposed to be a good sister to Laura, instead of the other way around? Surely my mother loved Laura more than she loved me" (93). When Iris, on the day after the funeral, pushes Laura off the ledge of the lily pond, she enjoys hearing Laura's cry: "I wanted her to suffer too—as much as me. I was tired of her getting away with being so young" (97). Making a pact with God that she will sacrifice herself in order to bring her mother back to life, Laura jumps in the river. Although Iris pulls her out, she also thinks about how "close" she had come to "letting go" of Laura before she was out of the water (151).

As the elderly Iris reflects on her past, she sees herself as the sacrificial daughter and thus as a victim. Iris's father marries her to the wealthy Richard Griffen in return for the false promise of capital infusion for the failing Chase factories. Thus, "Iris's identity," as Coral Ann Howells remarks, "is defined by her gender, her class and her role as 'good sister to Laura,' and her feminine destiny is already laid out for her: as the eldest daughter of an old Anglo-Canadian family it is her duty to marry well in order to restore the family fortunes and to safeguard Laura's interests" (159). Unlike the industrialist and "sweatshop tycoon" Richard, labor activist and socialist Alex—the man Iris ends up having an affair with—is, in Richard's view, "an armchair pinko" (*Blind Assassin* 177, 188). When Alex is accused of burning down the Chase factory, Iris and Laura hide him until he can escape, and each of the sisters falls in love with him. Laura is fascinated with Alex's political doctrine, and Iris is sexually attracted to him. Whereas he calls the fourteen-year-old Laura "a saint in training" (212) while he is hiding at Avilion, he is sexually provocative toward Iris, kissing her and unbuttoning her blouse. After Alex leaves, both sisters continue to have a secret relationship with him, and it is their sisterly rivalry over Alex that later leads to Iris's betrayal of Laura and Laura's subsequent suicide.

When Richard reneges on his promise to Iris's father, Iris realizes that she has sacrificed herself by marrying him "for nothing" (314). A ruthless businessman, Richard has "too much money, too much presence" in the world so that "what was average in him seemed like deficiency" (480). Dominated by Richard and his sinister sister, Winifred, Iris protects herself by appearing to sleepwalk through her life, turning a blind eye toward most, including Laura. Richard, though he claims to be "besotted" by Iris, is sadistic, bruising her and causing her pain, and he claims ownership rights over both Iris and Laura. Laura, with her heightened sense of perception, her ability to see beyond facades, recognizes that Richard is "very evil" (485). Yet, publicly, Richard is well regarded and his political success is practically ensured.

Trapped in a loveless and abusive marriage, Iris begins a clandestine affair with the fugitive Alex even though she is aware of Laura's feelings for him. For Laura, the allure of Alex is her conviction that she can "save" him, both from police capture and from his loss of faith in God. If she has any sexual attraction toward Alex, she does not acknowledge it. In contrast, Iris has a passionate sexual affair with Alex. Experiencing an "extreme pleasure" that is "also a humiliation," Iris is unable to "resist" Alex and so she "renders herself up, is blotted out" (261). Ultimately Iris views her clandestine encounters with Alex as an antidote to powerlessness; she possesses a truth that is unknown to others.

"Should I have behaved differently?" the elderly and dying Iris asks as she writes her memoir. "Should I have been able to read Laura's mind? Should I have known what was going on? . . . Was I my sister's keeper?" (428). When Laura, in yet another pact with God, sexually sacrifices herself to Richard to save Alex, she gets pregnant and Richard sends her to a clinic to have an abortion. Years later, in their final conversation, when Laura confirms that she was pregnant and sacrificed herself to save Alex, Iris misunderstands and thinks that Alex fathered Laura's child. In a moment of "spite," Iris pushes Laura "over the edge" by telling her that she had had an affair with Alex. By destroying the "words" Laura has relied on to sustain her life—"*God. Trust. Sacrifice. Justice. Faith. Hope. Love.* Not to mention *sister*" (490)—Iris drives her to suicide (488, 490). Just as Iris acts spitefully toward Laura, so she also gets revenge against Richard by publishing under Laura's name a romance novel called *The Blind Assassin*, which offers a lurid account of her affair with Alex. As Iris says to Richard after he reads the book, "You can't face the possibility that all the time you were having your squalid little fling with her, she must have been in and out of bed with another man—one she loved, unlike you. Or I assume that's what the book means—doesn't it?" (510). Afterward Richard is found dead, with a copy of *The Blind Assassin* at his elbow.

An Atwoodian villainess, Iris, who learned as a girl "that revenge is a dish best eaten cold" (167), ends up acting as an agent of revenge as she destroys Richard for Laura's sake. And as she writes her memoir, she thinks of it as a "memorial" to the past injustices she and her sister Laura suffered: "But what is a memorial, when you get right down to it, but a commemoration of wounds endured? Endured, and resented. Without memory, there can be no revenge" (508). Iris and Laura, as mirror images, both offer models of negative female sacrifice. While Laura deliberately attempts several sacrificial actions such as drowning herself and submitting to Richard, Iris feels as if her sacrifices have been imposed upon her. Yet as she writes to justify herself, she ends up confessing the truth, and she writes, ultimately, to leave a message for her granddaughter Sabrina, seeking in her "a listener" and "someone who will see" her. But she also insists, "Don't prettify me, though, whatever else you do" (521).

The Robber Bride: Zenia as the Betrayer of Friendship

For most readers, *The Robber Bride*'s Zenia is Atwood's most vile villainess and yet she ends up acting as a kind of mirror to Tony, Charis, and Roz, the middle-aged women she has befriended and betrayed. Tony, Charis, and Roz, who first meet in college, come from different backgrounds and have different personalities, yet they become close friends, bound together by their mutual fear of Zenia. When at the beginning of the novel, the three women are having lunch at the Toxique restaurant on the eve on the Gulf War in the early 1990s, they believe that Zenia is dead only to have her magically reappear "on this side of the mirror" (34). When Zenia comes back from the dead, the three women are forced into a necessary mirror confrontation with Zenia, who comes to embody the shadow side of their identities. Thus even while Zenia has an uncanny knack of leading the three friends into betraying their most precious convictions, she also, in true Atwoodian fashion, ends up having an important and even a positive effect upon her weaker friends.

The child of a father who committed suicide and a mother who abandoned her, Antonia, known as Tony, compensates by living an imaginary life during her girlhood as a female warrior; as an adult, she becomes a history professor who specializes in war. Yet outwardly, Tony seems anything but a warrior. In the 1960s, Zenia befriends Tony, who is a quiet and dedicated college student. Tony becomes fascinated with Zenia's irreverence and daring, and her admiration of Zenia is so compelling, she even forgives Zenia for dating West, the man Tony secretly loves. In the course of their friendship, Zenia talks Tony into writing a term paper for her, dumps West, and leaves town with the money she has gotten by blackmailing Tony by threatening to expose the fact that Tony has ghostwritten Zenia's term paper. Zenia returns later after Tony and West are married and takes West away again only to dump him again a year later. Believing that West is "frangible" and "subject to breakage," Tony spends her time protecting him, for she feels he has been "damaged enough" by Zenia. "For kindly and susceptible souls like West's, the real world, especially the real world of women, is far too harsh a place" (110). Tony sees Zenia as an utterly destructive villainess, yet there is still a part of her that secretly identifies with Zenia and wants to "participate in her daring, her contempt for almost everything, her rapacity and lawlessness" (184). But even as Tony secretly admires Zenia's power, she does not realize that she can have the same power herself.

Charis, originally named Karen, has also had a difficult childhood. Physically abused by her mother and then, after her mother died, sexually abused by the uncle who helped raise her, Charis ends up deeply traumatized. When her uncle begins to rape her, she splits in two as the victimized Karen is taken over by Charis, who watches the "flailing and sobbing" Karen from a safe distance (260) "Charis is more serene than Karen, because the bad things have stayed behind, with small Karen" (261). When Zenia enters her life in the 1970s, Charis is a yoga teacher living in a virtual shack on an island. An idealist who has adopted some of the era's hippie philosophy, Charis is living with an American draft dodger, Billy. Blind to Billy's faults—he is a freeloader, an uncaring lover, and he abuses her—Charis imagines him to be much better than he really is. Claiming that she has cancer, Zenia induces Charis to tend to her so she can get access to Billy and turn him in to the authorities. Charis is able to be betrayed by Zenia because she is gullible: "she realizes she has no weapons, no weapons that will work against Zenia. All Charis has on her side is a wish to be good, and goodness is an absence, it's the absence of evil; whereas Zenia has the real story" (473). Yet Charis also has a secret attraction to Zenia; in particular, Charis seems to admire Zenia for her easy sexuality. In fact, Charis believes her daughter Augusta was conceived during the one occasion she had felt sexual pleasure with Billy and wonders if both she and Zenia are Augusta's mother.

The daughter of a bitter woman and a war-profiteering father, Roz grows up conflicted about her mixed Jewish-Catholic heritage and harbors the idea that she is not good enough. Like Tony and Charis, Roz carries her childhood traumas with her as an adult, hiding behind a mask of cheer and humor. Even though she is a wealthy and highly successful businesswoman and the owner of a feminist magazine, Roz puts up with the constant womanizing of her husband Mitch and constantly forgives him for cheating on her. Zenia enters Roz's life in the 1980s when Roz hires her to work as the editor of her women's magazine, which Zenia revamps into a successful and glossy fashion magazine. When Zenia has an affair with Mitch and then dumps him, he kills himself, leaving Roz as a widowed mother of three. Even though Zenia victimizes Roz by feeding into her inability to assert herself with her husband, Roz is still secretly attracted to Zenia. For while Roz tries to be worthy, "to be nice, to be ethical, to behave well," there are times when she would like "to cast off her muffling Lady Bountiful cloak, stop tiptoeing through the scruples, cut loose" and commit a "great whopping thoroughly despicable sin." Thus, as Roz comes to realize, there are times that "she would like to be Zenia" (389).

"What is she doing here, on this side of the mirror?" (37), Tony wonders at the beginning of the novel when Zenia returns from the dead. Zenia is the villainess robber bride who betrays her friends and steals their men. But it is telling that the name "Zenia" is a combination of the last letters of the women's real names—Roz, Karen, Antonia—for each woman secretly identifies with Zenia. Thus, while Zenia has victimized each woman, Tony, Charis, and Roz find it difficult to let her go because she is a part of each one of them. As Lynn Bloom and Veronica Makowsky observe, Zenia is important to Tony, Charis, and Roz because she represents "power" to them, "the power within each woman" and yet they are "ambivalent toward her since they are confused about the power within themselves" (172).

Because the three women want to be perceived as "good" women, they, in essence, "allow" Zenia to do their dirty work. Roz needs to get rid of her philandering husband; Charis needs to save herself from Billy's brutality and needs to stop saving every person she meets; and Tony needs a reason to find West interesting. If Zenia performs the necessary but perhaps not "good" tasks, she can be blamed for their hidden badness, even as she "menaces the carefully constructed shells" that permit the three women to remain "good" (Bloom and Makowsky 167). By embracing Zenia, as Shannon Hengen aptly comments, the three women "find relief from thralldom to the men in their lives" and because she brings the three women together as friends, she also has a positive effect on them by helping them overcome their "negative views of other women" (279). When Zenia returns from the dead, she forces the women to confront the truth and also to take ownership of their own hidden badness. "Zenia may be a shadow cast by men, but she's a shadow cast by women, as well," as Atwood insists ("If You Can't"). By confronting Zenia—the bad woman and the shadow self—the women recover the power hidden in the shadows that comes from the recognition of attributes that "good girls" should not have: anger, indignation, resentment, aggression, ambition, self-centeredness, artifice, and egoism. Zenia returns to force each woman to reclaim all of those "bad girl" qualities, essential qualities not just for success but for survival as well.

In "Spotty-Handed Villainesses," Atwood notes that important "bad" female characters "act as keys to doors we need to open, and as mirrors in which we can see more than just a pretty face. They can be explorations of moral freedom—because everyone's choices are limited, and women's choices have been more limited than men's, but that doesn't mean women can't make choices." She explains, "Such characters can pose the question of responsibility, because if you want power you have to accept responsibility, and actions produce consequences" ("Spotty" 135). Her vivid portrayals of evil women allow other characters—and readers—to explore the necessity of sometimes acting badly. Thus, Serena Joy, Cordelia, Iris, and Zenia, as well-known Atwoodian villainous characters, serve to open up possibilities to their readers. These characters are not monstrously evil women; in fact, as each is metaphorically suggested as a mirror image to another character, these characters then represent the presence of wickedness in all women. By using the "evil" characters as doubles for the "virtuous" characters such as Offred, Laura, Elaine, Tony, Charis, and Roz, Atwood clearly demonstrates the ineffectual nature of women attempting to maintain only the commonly accepted attitudes of "good girls." Because each "bad" girl operates as a source of strength to her ostensible victims, each then becomes the triumphant face in the mirror.

Works Cited

Ahearn, Stephen. "'Meat Like You Like It': The Production of Identity in Atwood's *Cat's Eye*." *Canadian Literature* 137 (Summer 1993): 8–17.

Atwood, Margaret. *The Blind Assassin*. New York: Doubleday, 2000.

_____. *Cat's Eye*. New York: Doubleday, 1988.

_____. *The Handmaid's Tale*. New York: Ballantine, 1985.

_____. "If You Can't Say Something Nice, Don't Say Anything at All." *Language in Her Eye: Views on Writing and Gender by Canadian Women Writing in English*. Ed. Libby Scheier, Sarah Sheard, and Eleanor Wachtel. Toronto: Coach, 1990. 15–25.

_____. Introduction. *The Robber Bride*. By Atwood. Franklin Center, PA: Franklin Lib., 1993.

_____. *The Robber Bride*. New York: Doubleday. 1993.

_____. "Spotty-Handed Villainesses: Problems of Female Bad Behavior in the Creation of Literature." *Writing with Intent: Essays, Reviews, Personal Prose, 1982–2005*. By Atwood. New York: Carroll, 2005. 125–38.

Bloom, Lynn Z., and Veronica Makowsky. "Zenia's Paradoxes." *LIT* 6 (1995): 167–79.

Hengen, Shannon. "Zenia's Forgiveness." *Various Atwoods: Essays on the Later Poems, Short Fiction, and Novels*. Ed. Lorraine M. York. Concord, ON: Anansi, 1995. 271–86.

Hite, Molly. "Optics and Autobiography in Margaret Atwood's *Cat's Eye*." *Twentieth-Century Literature: A Scholarly and Critical Journal* 41.2 (Summer 1995): 135–59.

Howells, Coral Ann. *Margaret Atwood*. 2nd ed. 2005. Hampshire: Palgrave.

Wilson, Sharon. *Margaret Atwood's Fairy-Tale Sexual Politics*. Jackson: UP of Mississippi, 1993.

The "Historical Turn" in Margaret Atwood's *The Blind Assassin* and *Alias Grace*

Alice Ridout

Introduction

Margaret Atwood's fin-de-siècle novels, *The Blind Assassin* (2000) and *Alias Grace* (1996), demonstrate an interesting "historical turn" before her twenty-first-century turn to science fiction set in the frighteningly near future in *Oryx and Crake* (2003) and *The Year of the Flood* (2009). Based on a sensational nineteenth-century murder case, *Alias Grace* tells the story of the historical figure, Grace Marks, an Irish immigrant who worked as a domestic servant and was accused of being an accomplice in a double murder. While *Alias Grace* focuses on the lower-class immigrant experience, *The Blind Assassin*, which is set in the twentieth century, particularly in the years between World War I and World War II, tells the story of the upper-class Chase sisters. We can gain some crucial insights into Atwood's "turn" to history in these two novels in her critical writing on the Canadian historical novel. Just as Atwood, after writing *Oryx and Crake* and *The Year of the Flood*, published a critical consideration of the genre of science fiction, so after writing *Alias Grace,* she published a critical essay on historical fiction, "In Search of *Alias Grace*: On Writing Canadian Historical Fiction," which was first presented as a lecture in 1996.[1] Offering interesting evidence of Atwood's critical awareness and self-consciousness of the genre she is working in, Atwood's meditation "on writing Canadian historical fiction" is a very helpful place to start when thinking through what it means to label and read *The Blind Assassin* and *Alias Grace* as "historical fiction."

At the start of "In Search of *Alias Grace*," Atwood reflects on the popularity of historical novels as she "meditate[s] on why so many of this kind of novel have been written by English-speaking Canadian authors lately" (3). In doing so, she recognizes a trend for historical fiction that other authors and critics have already identified. For example, Dennis Duffy published *Sounding the Iceberg: An Essay on Canadian Historical Novels* (1986), in which he argues that the historical novel has long been a popular and important genre in Canadian literature. In the first half of the twentieth century, however, he argues that "writers and readers of Canadian historical novels were not taken seriously by critics" but that "by the 1970s, a number of works appeared that placed historical fiction squarely in our literary mainstream" (i, ii). His long essay, or short book, offers "a story of how the historical novel in Canada moved from a popular and revered form, to a merely popular one, and then finally to its position among the serious fiction of our time" (iii).

It would be wrong to imply that the "serious" contemporary historical novel is only a Canadian phenomenon. Mariadele Boccardi, for example, opens her study of *The Contemporary British Historical Novel* (2009) by quoting A. S. Byatt's *On Histories and Stories* (2000) in which Byatt talks of a "sudden flowering of the historical novel in Britain" after World War II (1). It is helpful, however, to consider how Margaret Atwood as a Canadian author of historical fiction offers us two novels in *The Blind Assassin* and *Alias Grace* that demonstrate the intersection of nation and historical fiction. Andrea Cabajsky and Brett Josef Grubisic explain that their coedited book, *National Plots: Historical Fiction and Changing Ideas of Canada* (2010), "is organized around the following question: What happens to the 'Canadian' when it intersects with the 'historical' in fictional writing?" (vii). This is a question that Atwood poses in her lecture, "In Search of *Alias Grace*: On Writing Canadian Historical Fiction," (1997) and that she addresses in her two historical novels, *Alias Grace* and *The Blind Assassin.*

Critics such as Diana Wallace and Jerome de Groot have also argued for the important intersection of genre and gender in the case of the historical novel. Wallace's gender focus is immediately evident from the title of her influential study of the genre—*The Woman's Historical*

Novel: British Women Writers, 1900–2000 (2005).[2] In *The Historical Novel* (2010), de Groot explains that historical novels for women tend to be historical popular romances, whereas "historical fiction for men tends to be more based in adventure and concerned in the main with warfare" (78).

Atwood's *The Blind Assassin* and *Alias Grace* are interesting examples of how genre and gender are intertwined in the historical novel. In *Alias Grace*, Atwood skillfully combines historical material, some of it included in direct quotations from newspaper articles and first-hand accounts like Susanna Moodie's in *Life in the Clearings* (1853), with a fictional account of Grace Marks's psychoanalysis by Dr. Simon Jordan, who becomes sexually attracted to Grace as he treats her and tries to recover her "repressed" memories of the murder scene. When the hypnotized Grace acts as if she is possessed by the spirit of Mary Whitney, readers are left uncertain whether her account of the murders under hypnosis is a staged performance set up between Grace and the hypnotist or if it reveals what actually happened. Indeed, one of the key aspects of Atwood's treatment of this case is that her novel never resolves the central mystery of whether Grace is guilty of murder or not. In *The Blind Assassin*, the elder sister, Iris, is married off by her father to the wealthy industrialist Richard Griffen in an attempt to save the Chase family business. Trapped in an unhappy marriage, Iris has an affair with Alex Thomas, a man that she and her sister Laura both fall in love with as adolescents. While married to Iris, Richard manipulates Laura into having an affair with him by pretending he has control over Alex's future. As the elderly Iris writes her memoir, she slowly comes to confess her own feelings of culpability for Laura's suicide a half century earlier, which followed Iris's revelation to Laura of her long affair with Alex and the news of his death. Like *Alias Grace*, *The Blind Assassin* focuses on Canadian history and it, too, is made up of several different texts: contemporary newspaper articles, an earlier novel published under Laura Chase's name, and an autobiography written by Iris late in her life.

But while *Alias Grace* and *The Blind Assassin* both focus particularly on how women are positioned in history, neither conforms to the plotline of the popular; instead, the common plot of the popular historical romance novel is playfully alluded to in both novels, in particular in telling of Dr. Jordan's sexual obsession with Grace in *Alias Grace* and in describing the clandestine love affair between Iris and Alex in *The Blind Assassin*. Both novels also consciously explore a variety of popular genres. *The Blind Assassin* explores gender and popular genre writing through the examples of Iris's confessional romance novel, which Iris publishes under Laura's name and which includes Alex's science fiction stories. Drawing on firsthand accounts of a nineteenth-century double murder case, *Alias Grace* plays with the ways in which Grace Marks's guilt or innocence regarding the double murder she is accused of participating in remains unknown despite how much she speaks throughout the novel. It calls attention to popular writing through its references not only to sensational newspaper reports of the double murder and trial but also to Susanna Moodie's nineteenth-century account of meeting the imprisoned Grace Marks in *Life in the Clearings Versus the Bush* (1853).

The inclusion of other texts, such as newspaper articles and other accounts of the same events, functions metafictionally in both novels to draw attention to the processes of historiography. Thus both novels demonstrate what Linda Hutcheon famously termed "historiographic metafiction" in her book, *A Poetics of Postmodernism* (1988). Speaking particularly of Canadian historical fiction in *The Canadian Postmodern* (1988), Hutcheon describes these works of "historiographic metafiction":

> These works are not quite historical novels in the traditional sense, for they are also very metafictional in their attention to the processes of writing, reading, and interpreting. They are both self-consciously fictional but also overtly concerned with the acts (and consequences) of the reading and writing of history as well as fiction. (13–14)

Mariadele Boccardi argues that the contemporary historical novel is "inherently metafictional and as such [is] not only ideally receptive to postmodernism's positions on narrative, representation and knowledge but also supremely equipped to probe their validity." She sees the historical novel as the genre where postmodernism both "manifests itself most clearly" and "proves theoretically inadequate" (6). Given these claims about the historical novel's relationship to postmodernism and Hutcheon's famous thesis that Canada has a particular sympathy and aptitude for postmodernism, it is helpful to ask in what ways Atwood's historical novels are examples of postmodern "historiographic metafiction."

Nicola Renger also raises the interesting question of postcolonialism in relation to historiographic metafiction. In contrast to Hutcheon's desire to read this genre as "part of Canada's move toward postmodernism," Renger "would rather place it within the context of postcolonialism" (21). Both Atwood's *The Blind Assassin* and *Alias Grace* demonstrate an acute awareness of Canada's position as a British settler colony. In *The Blind Assassin*, Iris and Laura's grandfather's button business booms during World War I servicing the British wartime requirements for buttons while her soldier-father is wounded at the Somme, at Vimy Ridge and, even more seriously, at Bourlon Wood (75). Set in the nineteenth century, *Alias Grace* describes Grace's family's emigration from Ireland and the death of her mother on the perilous journey across the Atlantic Ocean. Atwood also addresses the Rebellion of 1837, which, as she explains, "influenced both Grace's life before the murders and her treatment at the hands of the press" ("In Search" 34). The rebellion resulted in a shortage of servants, which enabled Grace to move from one position to another as she does in the novel. Atwood also notes, "In 1843—the year of the murder—editorials were still being written about the badness or worthiness of William Lyon Mackenzie; and as a rule, the Tory newspapers that vilified him also vilified Grace—she had, after all, been involved in the murder of her Tory employer, an act of grave insubordination; but the Reform newspapers that praised Mackenzie were also inclined to clemency towards Grace" ("In Search" 34–35). Thus both novels present characters whose lives are directly impacted by Canada's colonial relationship to England and the historical events that grew out of that relationship.

As I consider *The Blind Assassin* and *Alias Grace* within the framework that I've outlined in the introduction—the historical novel's relationship to the nation, to gender, to postmodernism, and to postcolonialism—I will show how Atwood, in her "historical turn," is intent not only on presenting Canada as a location for historical fiction but also on using postmodern strategies of historiographic metafiction to re-vision Canadian history as she tells the stories of two women: *Alias Grace*'s Grace Marks and *The Blind Assassin*'s Iris Chase Griffen.

Canadian Historical Fiction

In her 1996 lecture, "In Search of *Alias Grace*," Atwood is keen to position herself within a Canadian national tradition of the historical novel. This national tradition is directly related to Canada's postcolonial situation, a topic I will return to at the end of this chapter but which cannot be wholly separated from the issue of nation with regards to Canada. Atwood suggests that contemporary Canadian authors have turned to historical novels because they are "more confident" about themselves as Canadians and are now permitted to find themselves "more interesting" than they "once did" (23–24). She links this to "a worldwide movement that has found writers and readers, especially in ex-colonies, turning back towards their own roots, while not rejecting developments at the imperial centres" (24). Thus it is significant that *Alias Grace* offers a particularly Canadian version of the neo-Victorian novel, which Boccardi rightly argues John Fowles brought to critical attention with *The French Lieutenant's Woman* in 1969 and which authors like Sarah Waters (see, for example, *Affinity,* 1999) have continued to make both highly popular and critically well regarded. Just as Atwood draws on historical material in her careful depiction in *Alias Grace* of Canadian cities like Toronto and Kingston in the latter half of the nineteenth century, so she draws on the historical archive as she revisits the sensational double murder case involving Grace Marks.[3] As Hilde Staels has noted, "Atwood supplies abundant historical data about social reality and scientific life in nineteenth-century Canada, and indeed, in her afterword, she gives a survey of the text's documentary apparatus, the extratextual sources that provided some of the material for her novel" (429–30). Atwood's focus on the particularities of the Canadian setting for this novel highlights the fact that the history this novel tells is a Canadian one. For example, the trauma Grace experiences of losing her mother at sea is a trauma particular to the emigrant's life and, as we have seen, Atwood, in her essay "In Search of *Alias Grace*," comments on the ways in which Grace's life as a domestic servant was impacted by the 1837 Rebellion.

Even as Atwood renders the neo-Victorian novel in Canadian form in *Alias Grace,* she also, as Staels argues, "imitates conventions of the historical novel" in *Alias Grace* (430). In considering Atwood's imitation or parody of the neo-Victorian novel, it is helpful to recall Martin Kuester's argument that parody is "of special importance in the context of the new literatures in English that have to define their own stances in opposition to a strong literary tradition stemming from the British Isles" (22). This cultural imperialism is echoed within the novel itself when Dr. Simon Jordan, the young American doctor who tries to use the methods of psychoanalysis to retrieve Grace's repressed memories of the murders, travels to Europe in order to research the latest theories and scientific knowledge in the field of mental disorders. Yet the novel implies that Dr. Jordan could learn a great deal more by facing his own growing obsession with Grace and admitting that his medical interest in her covers his secret sexual attraction to her, which he acts out by having a sordid affair with his landlady. In an echo of Joseph Conrad's *Heart of Darkness*, Atwood tells us what Dr. Jordan plans to do as he flees from Kingston:

Once in Europe, he'll continue his researches. He will study the many prevailing schools of thought, but he will not add to them; not yet. He has gone to the threshold of the unconscious, and has looked across; or rather he has looked down. He could have fallen. He could have fallen in. He could have drowned. (494)

Dr. Jordan's escape to Europe is presented as just that—an *escape from* dark and troubling knowledge of himself. He could have gained true self-knowledge, the novel implies, had he dared to confront his growing obsession with, and sexual attraction to, Grace.

As Atwood depicts the relationship between Dr. Jordan and his patient, she is intent on subverting or leveling out male authority. In providing us with an absorbing Canadian version of the neo-Victorian novel, replete with an uncanny hypnotism scene in which Grace behaves as if possessed by the spirit of Mary Whitney, Atwood consciously writes back to the "strong literary tradition stemming from the British Isles" in just the way Kuester suggests parody often functions in the contemporary English-Canadian historical novel. What her novel seems to be saying is exactly what she suggests the Canadian historical novel is out to prove: "You want squalor, lies, and corruption? Hell, we've got 'em homegrown, and not only that, we always have had, and there's where the past comes in" ("In Search" 24). Thus, *Alias Grace* can be read as Atwood's demonstration that Canadian history has always been as fascinating as British history.

Similarly, in *The Blind Assassin*, Atwood carefully draws on historical accounts in her depiction of Toronto in the early- to mid-twentieth century.[4] The opening sentence of the novel draws attention to the relationship between the historical and the personal: "Ten days after the war ended, my sister Laura drove a car off a bridge" (1). The disassociation of Laura's life from the celebration of the end of World War II is exemplary of Canada's tangential relationship to European events. Like her father, who suffered shell shock and injury fighting for the British in World War I, Laura suffers as a result of World War II, losing the man she loves; her tragedy, like her father's, is invisible in British history. Canadian lives are depicted as tragically impacted by European events but in ways that are invisible or forgotten by Europe and Britain. This is also true, of course, of women's lives in relation to the authorized, official versions of national public history. For many women, the end of the war was a tragic period of time as they struggled to return to everyday life without loved ones. The official public history of celebration and victory silences their stories.

Women's Historical Fiction

Like other contemporary women authors, Atwood is attracted to and makes interesting use of the genre of historical fiction in her women-centered works. Both *Alias Grace* and *The Blind Assassin* are concerned with how women's histories are erased from official, public history. In *Alias Grace* this is particularly ironic. Atwood draws on historical texts as she tells Grace's story and the novel presents long sections of Grace's fictionalized first-person narrative voice, yet readers never learn with any certainty whether Grace was a willing accomplice to murder and thus Grace's true story never gets told. Just like the epilogue of *The Handmaid's Tale* (1985) in which Professor Pieixoto presents his paper examining Offred's tapes at an academic symposium in 2195, Dr. Simon Jordan attempts to exert male control over Grace and come to know her story in order to present it as research findings to the emerging global scholarly community of psychoanalysts. And just as with Professor Pieixoto, the reader is left feeling that Dr. Jordan has entirely missed the point: that the social and cultural conditions of Grace's existence as a woman are the engaging and crucial aspects of her life-story rather than the fact of her guilt or innocence.

Magali Cornier Michael offers invaluable insight into Atwood's presentation of Grace Marks's history by pointing to its patchwork quilt-like qualities. Disrupting linear patriarchal history, Grace's story is made up of many stories placed alongside each other. As Michael argues, "Through its juxtaposition of a gradation of official and authorized texts—published histories, newspaper clippings, interviews, confessions, letters, poems—with the more overtly fictionalized first-person narration of Grace Marks and third-person narration, Atwood's novel engages in a curious leveling out of the authority of all the texts it presents" (421). The patchwork quilt image that Atwood uses throughout her novel, as Michael shows, is inherently feminine. By constructing her novel like a quilt made up of many different voices and texts, Atwood offers a "spatialized version of history," which, even as it approaches a successful representation of "historical events and persons," serves to undermine official, linear, patriarchal history and disrupt the detective impulse of Dr. Simon Jordan (Michael 426).

Alias Grace not only approaches historiographic issues regarding women's history—or what has been termed "her-story"—but Atwood also plays with the gendered genre expectations of the woman's historical novel. The woman's historical novel, as Diana Wallace and Jerome de Groot both outline, is so often a historical romance. Both Dr. Jordan and Grace are described at different moments in the text as fantasizing a romantic life together. Grace sees Dr. Jordan as her savior, and after she is pardoned, she thinks that he has kept his promise to write to the government on her behalf: "you must have sent the letter to the Government after all, because it got the results in the end, along with all the petitions; although I must say they took a good long time about it, and said nothing about your letter, but only that it was a general amnesty" (527). Of course, the reader knows that Dr. Jordan did not write a letter to the government, partly because he himself is suffering from posttraumatic amnesia. And when Grace is told that a gentleman friend of hers wants her to come to him upon her release, she admits to her romantic fantasy about Dr. Jordan, thinking that he is the man who is waiting for her: "The only other one I could think of, Sir, was you yourself. I must admit that the idea did cross my mind" (538). Instead, the gentleman who is waiting to see Grace and who ends up marrying her is Jamie Walsh, who played a damaging role in her court case but has since decided she was entirely innocent and thus is guilt stricken over his role in her incarceration. As her husband, Jamie enjoys hearing stories about her imprisonment: "The more watery I make the soup and the more rancid the cheese, and the worse I make the coarse talk and proddings of the keepers, the better he likes it" (547). Much like the hero of a historical novel, Jamie sees himself as Grace's rescuer, but the need to be blamed and then forgiven for Grace's imprisonment is also part of his sexual ritual and he gains erotic pleasure from perceiving himself as both the source of Grace's ruin and rescue: "after I have told him a few stories of torment and misery he clasps me in his arms and strokes my hair, and begins to unbutton my nightgown, as these scenes often take place at night; and he says, Will you ever forgive me?" (548). Dr. Jordan also has erotic fantasies about Grace. Wondering what it would be like to live in Thomas Kinnear's house and have Grace as his housekeeper, he thinks: "Not only his housekeeper: his locked and secret mistress. . . . But why only mistress? It comes to him that Grace Marks is the only woman he's ever met that he would wish to marry" (466). Even as he rejects the idea of marrying Grace as "madness, of course; a perverse fantasy, to marry a suspected murderess," he admits to his sexual attraction to her:

> *Murderess, murderess*, he whispers to himself. It has an allure, a scent almost. Hothouse gardenias. Lurid, but also furtive. He imagines himself breathing it as he draws Grace towards him, pressing his mouth against her. *Murderess*. He applies it to her throat like a brand. (467).

In describing Dr. Jordan's secret sexual attraction to Grace, Atwood offers a contemporary rendering of the popular "bodice-ripper" historical romance usually written by and for women.

The Blind Assassin similarly draws on gendered expectations of genre as it evokes women's confessional fiction side by side with the science fiction stories of Iris's lover, Alex, in the embedded *The Blind Assassin* romance novel authored by Iris and published under Laura's name. Like *Alias Grace*, *The Blind Assassin* includes a patchwork-quilt collection of texts—the elderly Iris's memoir, *The Blind Assassin* romance novel, and newspaper articles and other materials that Iris has left in her steamer trunk for her granddaughter Sabrina. As the elderly Iris writes her memoir, she sets out to tell the "real" and personal story behind the death of her sister Laura, who died in 1945 at the age of twenty-five by driving Iris's car over a bridge. While two witnesses said that they saw Laura turn the car "sharply and deliberately," Laura's death is, nevertheless, ruled as accidental in the coroner's report, as readers learn from the "official" newspaper account of the coroner's inquest, which is included in the opening sequences of the novel. Even though the "official" verdict is that Laura's death was "accidental," the elderly Iris privately knows it was a deliberate act of suicide because Laura "had her reasons" (3, 1).

The "real story" behind Laura's suicide is encrypted in Laura's private notebooks, which Iris finds hidden in her bedroom drawer immediately after she learns of Laura's death from a policeman. The opening section of Iris's memoir ends with the elderly Iris confessing of her continuing despair: "But some people can't tell where it hurts. They can't calm down. They can't ever stop howling" (2). This implies that what follows as the elderly Iris writes her memoir and recounts the story of her relationship with Laura will be Iris's "howling," and, indeed, Atwood's novel is a self-conscious rendering of feminist confessional autobiography (for detailed discussion of this, see Bouson and Ridout). The ways in which Iris and Laura can and cannot tell their stories and articulate their pain very much enact and demonstrate feminist accounts of autobiographical acts by previously silenced women. "Without memory, there can be no revenge," the elderly Iris states near the end of her account (508). As she reveals in her memoir how Laura's sexual exploitation by Richard led to her suicide—for Laura sexually sacrificed herself to Richard in an attempt to save Alex—Iris tells the "real" story behind the "official" and public account of Laura's death.

Postmodern Historical Fiction

A key term in relation to Atwood's historical novels is "historiographic," a term coined by the Canadian literary and cultural critic Linda Hutcheon in *A Poetics of Postmodernism* to label what she perceives to be a new approach to writing history in contemporary literature.[5] Hutcheon's term can be helpfully broken down into its parts: *historio-* means "relating to history" and *graphic* refers to writing, while *metafiction* is fiction that is self-conscious about its own processes as fiction. Thus *historiographic metafiction* is fiction that reminds the reader of its own workings as fiction while also drawing attention to the processes of writing history or, as Hutcheon herself puts it, "fiction that is intensely, self-reflexively art, but is also grounded in historical, social, and political realities" (*Canadian Postmodern* 13).

Countering the long tradition of placing history and fiction in opposition by claiming that history is a carefully researched, true, and verifiable version of *what really happened*, Hayden White has drawn attention to the ways in which the processes of storytelling are at work in both fiction and history. The belief that history stands in opposition to fiction has been thoroughly questioned, undermined, and deconstructed by White, who has explored the ways in which authorized versions of history have undergone the same processes of omission, emphasis, bias, limitations of point of view, and imposition of causal patterns as fictional stories have undergone. Historiographic metafiction raises similar questions about who tells history and how we come to "know" history. One of its central assumptions is that "language in a sense constitutes reality, rather than merely reflecting it" (65), as Linda Hutcheon remarks in her discussion of historiographic metafiction in *The Canadian Postmodern*. We can only access the past via its textual traces and we can only tell the story of what happened in the past by using language. Because language therefore constructs history and reality rather than simply mirroring past events, this raises questions about ideology and authority. As Hutcheon states: "Historiographic metafiction . . . in a very real sense is ideological fiction, taking ideology as meaning 'those modes of feeling, valuing, perceiving and believing which have some kind of relation to the maintenance and reproduction of social power.' To write either history or historical fiction is equally to raise the question of power and control: it is the story of the victors that usually gets told" (*Canadian Postmodern* 72).

It is noteworthy that both *Alias Grace* and *The Blind Assassin* are fragmentary texts, that both novels offer us multiple voices—although in *The Blind Assassin* we come to realize that several of the other voices in the text are actually Iris masquerading as her younger sister, Laura, and her lover, Alex—and that both novels juxtapose different texts and, importantly, different types of texts. As critics have often observed, Atwood's inclusion in *Alias Grace* of poetry, newspaper accounts, Susanna Moodie's dramatic account of visiting Grace, Grace's hypnotism and subsequent apparent possession by Mary Whitney, and fictional first- and third-person accounts by Grace and Dr. Jordan function to contradict and undermine narrative authority or claims to truth (see, for example, Michael and Staels). At the end of the novel we do not know if Grace was a willing accomplice to murder or whether she was "possessed" by Mary Whitney at the time of the murders, and thus we come away with the central mystery unsolved and without one authoritative version of the truth. In its fragmentation and deconstruction of authority, *Alias Grace* can most certainly be read as a postmodern historiographic metafiction.

The Blind Assassin is equally concerned with which versions of history get authorized as Iris, at the beginning of the novel, promises to tell the "real story" about Laura's death, which was officially rendered as an accident but which, as Iris shows, was actually suicide. Indeed, Iris plots her way into public discourse through writing and rewriting history (see Ridout for a detailed discussion of this). In *The Blind Assassin* romance novel, written by Iris to provide a memorial to Alex, the unnamed male love (Alex) makes a promise to his upper-class lover (Iris): "I'll take it back. I'll change it. I'll rewrite history for you. How's that?" Alex says, to which Iris replies, "You can't" (30). *The*

Blind Assassin explores to what extent the insights offered by theorists like Hayden White open up opportunities for women to "change" the past and "rewrite history." The novel certainly ends ambivalently on this issue. After writing her memoir, Iris dies and leaves her papers to her granddaughter, Sabrina. Thus the novel is framed by the deaths of the two Chase sisters. This history cannot be rewritten. Throughout the contemporary autobiography she is writing, the elderly Iris mourns the loss of her sister as she "commemorates" the "wounds" the two sisters "endured" and that she resents (508). However, Iris has managed a textual revenge of sorts on Richard Griffen, her husband and Laura's abuser. Furthermore, she has managed to pass on her historiographic metafiction to Sabrina, and by confessing that Alex, not Richard, is Sabrina's grandfather, she wants to free Sabrina from the Chase family burden and thus leave her "free to reinvent" herself "at will" (513). This revisionist approach to history and also the novel's emphasis on the ways in which we can only know history via textual traces, such as Laura's encoded notebooks or Iris's grandfather's self-publication, *The Chase Industries: A History*, are two of the most evident ways in which *The Blind Assassin* adheres to Hutcheon's concept of postmodern historiographic metafiction. As Atwood puts it: "The past is made of paper" ("In Search" 31).

Postcolonial Historical Fiction

In wanting to place historiographic metafiction in the context of postcolonialism rather than postmodernism, Nicola Renger is not so much contradicting Hutcheon as expanding on one possibility of the form that Hutcheon herself explores in *The Canadian Postmodern*. Equally, however, we can read Adrienne Rich's feminist theory of "re-vision" as a precursor to the kind of self-conscious, revisionist texts that Hutcheon labels historiographic metafiction, and thus we can claim the form for feminism rather than postmodernism. Moreover, by placing historiographic metafiction in the postcolonial context, we can draw attention to its antiauthoritarian potential and to the fact that, as Hutcheon argues, historiographic metafiction, is "ideological fiction" (*Canadian Postmodern* 72).

While scholars such as Laura Moss in her book, *Is Canada Postcolonial?* (2003), question the applicability of theories of postcolonialism to Canada, it is clear from one of Atwood's earliest works—*Survival* (1972)—that Atwood herself views Canada as postcolonial. In *Survival*, Atwood argues that Canada needs to work its way through a series of what she terms "victim positions" generated by its colonial relationship with Britain, and thus Atwood sees Canada's colonial history as central to its identity. Both *The Blind Assassin* and *Alias Grace,* as we have seen, draw on Canadian history, and Atwood's comment in "In Search of *Alias Grace*" that the contemporary interest of Canadian writers in historical fiction points to their growing confidence in themselves as Canadians reveals that Atwood sees the Canadian historical novel functioning in support of Canadian cultural nationalism. She does, however, also see the contemporary Canadian historical novel as functioning as a literary repository for things the nation has forgotten or suppressed. As she remarks, "The lure of the Canadian past, for the writers of my generation, has been partly the lure of the unmentionable—the mysterious, the buried, the forgotten, the discarded, the taboo" ("In Search" 19).

In describing different historical periods in Canada's colonial relationship to Britain, Atwood's two novels reveal the many ways in which individual Canadians have been affected by Canada's colonial relationship with Britain. *Alias Grace* explores how Grace's life and treatment in the press was affected by the 1837 Rebellion lead by William Lyon Mackenzie despite her having played no direct role in the uprising. A hundred years later, the battalion of volunteer soldiers that Alex joined to fight in the Spanish Civil War was called the Mackenzie-Papineau Battalion (or "the Mac-Paps"), thereby linking the two historical periods Atwood explores via a shared set of left-wing politics. Politics cuts across Iris's life in *The Blind Assassin* repeatedly and often in careless and violent ways, such as when she loses Alex in

World War II or when her father is badly injured in World War I. What Atwood also anticipates in *The Blind Assassin* is the new challenge to Canadian nationalism that has emerged in the move towards a global economy. While Iris's grandfather does well selling buttons through Canada's colonial relationship to Britain, her industrialist husband, Richard Griffen, in contrast, trades with Germany right up until World War II. As Iris explains, "At the outbreak of the war, Richard was in a tight spot. He'd been too cozy with the Germans in his business dealings, too admiring of them in his speeches," and so he has to scramble in order not to lose money (480). Even as Atwood's use of historiographic metafiction allows us to imagine how the everyday lives of Canadians have been affected by historical and political events, both novels enact a leveling out between Britain and Canada as Atwood presents Canada as a location for historical fiction.

Conclusion

Having separated out the different aspects and contexts of Atwood's historical fiction—nationalism, gender, postmodernism, and postcolonialism—I want to conclude by acknowledging how intersecting these aspects and contexts are. In her essay, "On Being a Woman Writer," Atwood discusses directly her competing identities:

> Time after time, I've had interviewers talk to me about my writing for a while, then ask me, "As a woman, what do you think about—for instance—the Women's Movement," as if I could think two sets of thoughts about the same thing, one set as a writer or person, the other as a woman. But no one comes apart this easily; categories like Woman, White, Canadian, Writer are only ways of looking at a thing, and the thing itself is whole, entire and indivisible. *Paradox*: Woman and Writer are separate categories; but in any individual woman writer, they are inseparable. (*Second Words* 195)

Similarly, as she remarks, "We have to write out of who and where and when we are, whether we like it or not, and disguise it how we may" ("In Search" 5). As a "Woman, White, Canadian, Writer" of the contemporary period, Atwood has produced two historical novels that use the postmodern strategies of historiographic metafiction to revise Canadian history as she tells the compelling stories of two women who lived in Ontario: the Irish immigrant and domestic servant, Grace Marks, and the upper-class society bride, Iris Chase Griffen.

Notes

1. Atwood's Charles R. Bronfman Lecture in Canadian Studies, which she presented on November 21, 1996, was published by the University of Ottawa Press in 1997 under the title, "In Search of *Alias Grace*: On Writing Canadian Historical Fiction." *In Other Worlds: SF and the Human Imagination* was published in 2011.

2. Diana Wallace has a helpful short clip on YouTube in which she summarizes her view of the relationship between women and the historical novel.

3. Atwood's Acknowledgements for *Alias Grace*, which includes a long list of thanks to a number of librarians and archivists, confirm that her novel is very much based on the historical archive.

4. See Atwood's Acknowledgements for *The Blind Assassin*, which list a number of researchers and archivists who have assisted her with the details of depicting Toronto in the early to mid-twentieth century.

5. Patricia Waugh's 1984 publication, *Metafiction*, paved the way for Hutcheon's work on historiographic metafiction and is very helpful on the topic of self-conscious fiction.

Works Cited

Atwood, Margaret. *Alias Grace*. Toronto: Seal, 1996.

_____. *The Blind Assassin*. Toronto: McClelland, 2000.

_____. *The Handmaid's Tale*. Toronto: McClelland, 1999.

_____. *In Other Worlds: SF and the Human Imagination*. Toronto: McClelland, 2011.

_____. "*In Search of Alias Grace*: On Writing Historical Fiction." Charles R. Bronfman Lecture in Canadian Studies. Ottawa: University of Ottawa Press, 1997. (Rpt. *Writing with Intent: Essays, Reviews, Personal Prose, 1983–2005*. New York: Carroll, 2005. 158–76.

_____. *Second Words: Selected Critical Prose*. Toronto: Anansi, 1982.

_____. *Survival: A Thematic Guide to Canadian Literature*. 1972. Toronto: McClelland, 2004.

Boccardi, Mariadele. *The Contemporary British Historical Novel: Representation, Nation, Empire*. Basingstoke: Palgrave, 2009.

Bouson, J. Brooks. "'A Commemoration of Wounds Endured and Resented': Margaret Atwood's *The Blind Assassin* as Feminist Memoir." *Critique* 44.3; Mar. 2003: 251–70.

Cabajsky, Andrea, and Brett Josef Grubisic, eds. *National Plots: Historical Fiction and Changing Ideas of Canada*. Waterloo, ON: Wilfrid Laurier UP, 2010.

De Groot, Jerome. *The Historical Novel*. The New Critical Idiom. Abingdon: Routledge, 2010.

Duffy, Dennis. *Sounding the Iceberg: An Essay on Canadian Historical Novels*. Toronto: ECW, 1986.

Eagleton, Terry. *Literary Theory: An Introduction*. Oxford: Blackwell, 1983.

Hutcheon, Linda. *The Canadian Postmodern: A Study of Contemporary English-Canadian Fiction*. Oxford: Oxford UP, 1988.

_____. *A Poetics of Postmodernism: History, Theory, Fiction*. New York: Routledge, 1988.

Kuester, Martin. *Framing Truths: Parodic Structures in Contemporary English-Canadian Historical Novels*. Toronto: U of Toronto P, 1992.

Michael, Magali Cornier. "Rethinking History as Patchwork: The Case of Atwood's *Alias Grace*." *Modern Fiction Studies* 47.2 (Summer 2001): 421–447. *Project Muse*. Web. 4 Aug. 2011.

Moss, Laura. *Is Canada Postcolonial? Unsettling Canadian Literature*. Waterloo: Wilfrid Laurier UP, 2003.

Renger, Nicola. *Mapping and Historiography in Contemporary Canadian Literature in English*. European University Studies. Frankfurt am Main: Lang, 2005.

Rich, Adrienne. "When We Dead Awaken: Writing as Re-Vision." 1971. *On Lies, Secrets and Silence: Selected Prose 1966–1978*. London: Virago, 1980. 33–49.

Ridout, Alice. "'In Paradise there are no stories': Iris Chase Griffen's Textual Revenge in Margaret Atwood's *The Blind Assassin*." *Margaret Atwood Studies* 2.2 (December 2008): 14–25.

Staels, Hilde. "Intertexts in Margaret Atwood's *Alias Grace*." *Modern Fiction Studies* 46.2 (Summer 2000): 427–450. *Project Muse*. Web. 4 Aug. 2011.

Wallace, Diana. "English degree: Women and the historical novel." *YouTube*. YouTube, 7 Mar 2011. Web. 23 Jan. 2012.

_____. *The Woman's Historical Novel: British Women Writers, 1900–2000*. London: Palgrave, 2005.

Waugh, Patricia. *Metafiction: The Theory and Practice of Self-Conscious Fiction*. 1984. London: Routledge, 1988.

White, Hayden. *Metahistory: The Historical Imagination in Nineteenth-Century Europe*. Baltimore: John Hopkins UP, 1973.

Surviving the Waterless Flood: Feminism and Ecofeminism in Margaret Atwood's *The Handmaid's Tale, Oryx and Crake,* and *The Year of the Flood*_____

Karen Stein

Adam One, the leader of the God's Gardeners in Margaret Atwood's novel *The Year of the Flood* (2009), predicts an apocalyptic Waterless Flood. When this apocalypse does occur, apparently few members of the privileged social classes live through the catastrophe, while some of the poorer, more egalitarian and environmentally conscious Gardeners survive. In *The Year of the Flood* and in her feminist dystopian novel *The Handmaid's Tale* (1985) and her postapocalyptic novel *Oryx and Crake* (2003), Atwood warns us that our disrespect for the environment and for our fellow beings may be pushing us toward catastrophic political and environmental upheavals. But in *The Year of the Flood* and in her nonfiction work *Payback: Debt and the Shadow Side of Wealth* (2008), Atwood also points to alternative behavioral codes that may help to promote the health of our planet and its inhabitants. Even as Atwood's voice in these texts is admonitory, it is also satirical, as she utilizes feminist and ecofeminist ethics to critique the wastefulness, arrogance, and greed of contemporary society. In these works, Atwood warns that we may be heedlessly destroying the planet and heading toward a posthuman future, but she also holds out hope that apocalyptic fictions such as hers may lead readers to imagine more favorable future scenarios and therefore to practice more egalitarian and ecofriendly behaviors that will avert ecological disasters and insure the survival of our planet and the human race.

Feminism and Ecofeminism

Feminist theorists across a wide ideological spectrum address relationships of women and men to each other and to social, economic, and political institutions, focusing in particular on structures of power and how they operate in society. Feminists assert that a masculinist ethic perpetuates hierarchies of domination derived from a dualistic world-view that divides the perceived universe into polar opposites: human and nonhuman, reason and emotion, mind and body, culture and nature. According to this system, men are equated with the first, more highly valued terms in each of these pairs, and women with the second, less valued terms. In contrast, feminism posits a nonhierarchal, nondualistic vision. Atwood's novels, essays, and poetry expose and critique such hierarchical and dualistic thinking through a variety of representational strategies such as humor inversion, irony, parody, and satire.

Ecofeminism, a relatively new branch of feminist theory,[1] adds another dimension to the feminist analytical system by combining the perspectives of social ecology and feminism. According to Ynestra King, ecofeminism "finds misogyny at the root of the opposition" between nature and culture. King explains that among the tenets of ecofeminism are the beliefs that "life on earth is an interconnected web, not a hierarchy. . . . A healthy, balanced ecosystem, including human and nonhuman inhabitants must maintain diversity. . . . The survival of the species necessitates . . . a challenging of the nature-culture dualism" (408). Some theorists, such as Riane Eisler, argue that there is a principle of partnership and nurturance associated with the feminine and a contrasting principle of domination and violence associated with the masculine (Korten, 19). Greta Gaard writes: "At the root of ecofeminism is the understanding that the many systems of oppression are mutually reinforcing" (21–22). Another theorist, Glynis Carr, explains:

> social eco-feminism . . . questions the value of social hierarchies, especially those arising in the modern nation-state as consequences of the capitalist mode of production, and provides a powerful critique of capitalism's waste, violence, unsustainability (in its requirement for constant growth), and faulty assumption that nature is an inexhaustible resource deriving its value solely from human needs (17–18).

Carr points out that ecofeminists not only criticize existing social structures but they also "envision alternatives" as they seek to transform daily life and to create "political and social structures that liberate oppressed groups (not only women) as well as nature." Insisting that "their utopian visions are not mere pipe dreams," ecofeminists maintain a "guarded optimism," according to Carr (17). Consequently, ecofeminists seek to analyze structures of domination and to promote corrective approaches to achieve both environmental justice and social equality.

Although Atwood's early poems (such as "A Place: Fragments" and "The City Planners" in *The Circle Game*, 1966) suggest that nature may resist human attempts to control and modify it, her recent work recognizes that humans can inflict serious damage on the environment. Her futuristic dystopian novels *The Handmaid's Tale*, *Oryx and Crake*, and *The Year of the Flood*, like her nonfiction work *Payback: Debt and the Shadow Side of Wealth* (2008), depict social hierarchies that, having lost imaginative contact with and respect for nature, abuse women and the environment. In *Oryx and Crake* and *The Year of the Flood* technological manipulation of the natural world is ratcheted up to catastrophic levels, as scientists unleash a menagerie of bioengineered life forms—such as the liobam, a lion/lamb mixture, or the wolvog, a wolf/dog combination—for fun and profit. Using narrators from different social strata, Atwood represents the viewpoints of both the victims and the perpetrators of sexism and classism in these works, and she also points to the strategies that help some of her victims to survive. The female narrators of *The Handmaid's Tale* and *The Year of the Flood* are outsiders in misogynistic societies. In contrast, *Oryx and Crake* is told by an insider, Jimmy, who provides insight into the arrogant pride and lack of empathy of the dominant (mostly male) social caste. Each of these novels uses a range of narrative strategies, such as parody, irony and satire, to depict the objectification and mistreatment of women, especially in the graphic and violent porn films, TV shows, and video games that provided popular entertainment in "the time before."

Atwood begins each novel after a violent event has undermined the previous social order and damaged the environment in some way, and then she focuses on the struggles of her characters to come to terms with what has happened as they recall "the time before," even as they struggle to survive in the postapocalypse world they inhabit.

The Handmaid's Tale: Threats to Women and the Environment

A dystopian narrative set in the near future, *The Handmaid's Tale* examines the deleterious impact of a totalitarian, male-dominated government on both women and the environment. The book focuses on gendered hierarchies, although environmental degradation is an important factor. Unspecified destructive events have produced toxic pollution that causes a decline in the birth rate. This decline provides one rationale for the sexual enslavement of fertile women by the misogynistic regime that has wiped out the government of the United States and instituted the totalitarian, theocratic Republic of Gilead. The government ousts women from their jobs, denies them access to their money, and then assigns them to limited, subservient roles. Fertile women are defined by their bodies. They are offered a choice between cleaning up toxic waste or providing sexual service to the ruling clique of Commanders so as to produce children and replenish the dwindling population.

The novel's narrator, Offred, has accepted the role of sexual Handmaid. Her name is a patronymic indicating that she is temporarily the property "Of Fred," the high-ranking Commander she must serve. In Gilead, the social identity of the Handmaids is based on their role as breeder women and is centered on their bodies. Reduced to their breeder function, they have been stripped of their individuality and, as Offred remarks, are little more than "walking wombs":

> Now the flesh arranges itself differently. I'm a cloud, congealed around a central object, the shape of a pear, which is hard and more real than I am

---

and glows red within its translucent wrapping. Inside it is a space, huge as the sky at night and dark and curved like that, though black-red rather than black (73–74).

She explains: "I avoid looking down at my body, not so much because it's shameful or immodest but because I don't want to see it. I don't want to look at something that determines me so completely" (63).

As a Handmaid, Offred's sole function is to procreate. The men are assumed to be fertile; therefore failure to procreate is presumed to be the Handmaid's fault. Should Offred fail, she will be assigned to toxic waste cleanup. She worries that environmental pollution may already have damaged her body and could prevent her from producing the child she desperately needs to remain relatively safe in Gilead. Well might she worry, for in Gilead the chances of having a defective baby are one in four. In an anticipation of the environmental concerns that become central in Atwood's later works, Offred describes the high human costs of environmental pollution:

The air got too full, once, of chemicals, rays, radiation, the water swarmed with toxic molecules, all of that takes years to clean up, and meanwhile they creep into your body, camp out in your fatty cells. Who knows, your very flesh may be polluted, dirty as an oily beach, sure death to shore birds and unborn babies (112).

In *The Handmaid's Tale* the toxic colonies are elsewhere, offstage, and the novel's focus is on the exploitation of women rather than on the damaged environment—although pollution is curtailing reproduction and thus providing a justification for the subjugation of women. In *Payback*, *Oryx and Crake*, and *The Year of the Flood*, environmental issues are central, while misogyny remains a constant theme.

Payback and the Spirits of Earth Day Past, Present, Future

In 2008, Atwood delivered a series of five Massey Lectures on the topic of debt, published as *Payback: Debt and the Shadow Side of Wealth*. After reviewing the relationships between debtors and creditors in Western cultures and literatures, Atwood devotes the concluding chapter, "Payback," to a different form of debt and payback, the system of human exchanges with nature. She imagines a new character, Scrooge Nouveau, who has accumulated wealth, property, and a series of wives. Unlike Charles Dickens's miserly and self-denying Scrooge, Atwood's character indulges himself in the luxuries his wealth can purchase, and thus utilizes many scarce natural resources. He owns several lavishly appointed homes and eats Chilean sea bass, "an almost extinct fish" (177). Like the original Scrooge in *A Christmas Carol* (1843), Atwood's twenty-first-century Scrooge is visited by three spirits, but these are the spirits of Earth Day Past, Present, and Future. They show him the history and consequences of overexploitation of natural resources. The Spirit of Earth Day Past explains, "The primary wealth is food, not money. Therefore anything that concerns the handling of the land also concerns me" (182). The Spirit of Earth Day Present shows Scrooge various examples of unsustainable resource extraction such as a fishing trawler that is dragging a net across the floor of the sea and "destroying everything in its path" to extract a small amount of useable fish catch. He explains: "This is like taking a front-end loader and scraping up your entire front garden and shredding it, keeping a few pebbles, and dumping the rest of it down the drain" (191). The Spirit of Earth Day Future depicts several alternative futures. In the positive one, people have replaced their lawns with small vegetable gardens and wear natural-fiber clothing. Energy is derived from "wave-generation machines and from solar installations on the tops and sides of their buildings" (198). In a more negative possible future, food and other natural resources have become scarce and money has lost its value. Scrooge's ex-wives must sell their bodies in exchange for a meager supply of food. Scrooge himself finds that wheelbarrows of money are useless, and so he is forced to join a population of scavengers, who fight over dead cats for food. After his excursions with the three spirits, a redeemed Scrooge decides "to pay back what I owe," now living more consciously and donating money to protect the environment (203).

Atwood's Ecofeminist Novels: Two Views of the Apocalypse in *Oryx and Crake* and *The Year of the Flood*

Just as *Payback* can be read as "a companion text" to *Oryx and Crake* (Hengen 133), so *Oryx and Crake* and *The Year of the Flood* are "companion" novels, the first two works in a proposed trilogy of speculative, apocalyptic fiction in which Atwood, as she does in *Payback*, expresses her environmental concerns as she warns her readers that the very future of the planet may be at risk if we continue on our current course. In Atwood's near future preapocalyptic world, humans have inflicted disasters on the environment through their irresponsible consumerism and greed and their failure to regulate technological innovation. Global climate change has already occurred, unleashing a weather pattern of recurring storms and causing extinctions of many plant and animal species. Elite scientists have produced new species that run wild on a planet where most of the human population has been wiped out by a bioengineered hemorrhagic virus.

Both works are set on the East Coast of the United States in a postapocalyptic future and in both works the focalizing characters—*Oryx and Crake*'s Jimmy and *The Year of the Flood*'s Toby and Ren—recall "the time before" the apocalypse, which is depicted as a world rather like our own, one in which powerful and largely unregulated corporations prey on people's anxieties in order to sell products while women are objectified and abused. Both novels address issues highlighted by ecofeminist Glynis Carr, who critiques our contemporary ethos of individualistic capitalism and widespread consumerism with its related "waste, violence, [and] unsustainability," and who also questions our mistaken belief in the anthropocentric assumption "that nature is an inexhaustible resource deriving its value solely from human needs" (16–18). In *Oryx and Crake*, Atwood focuses on an elite and masculine world as she tells the story of Crake and Jimmy, Crake's friend who is left alive to act as the guide of the Crakers, while in *The Year of the Flood*, she focuses on the life of the nonaffluent masses as she tells the story of Toby and Ren, who, like Jimmy, are survivors of Crake's viral plague. In both works, Atwood's "time before" world is a satirically exaggerated depiction of contemporary society, and she also incorporates into her works, as Shannon Hengen has observed, a prophetic "language of spiritual guilt and retribution concerning . . . worldwide economic and environmental failures" (131). Thus these novels exhort us to respect other beings and the earth itself, while they satirize the excesses of our contemporary corporation-controlled and technologically driven world where we have become subjected to the dangers of scientific imperialism. Indeed, both speculative novels ask the same urgent questions: What if we continue on our current path? Have we put our very humanity at risk in a contemporary era of biotechnology and genetic engineering? How can we live in harmony with other beings and with nature? What effects are we producing on the spaces and places we inhabit? The two novels together investigate the dangers of a flawed social order that values profits above people and that accords the most prestigious caste unlimited power to use technology to change the world.

"Sitting in Judgment on the World": Scientific Imperialism in *Oryx and Crake*

In *Oryx and Crake*, a cadre of powerful (mostly male) scientists hired by pharmaceutical companies experiments freely with bioengineering, and even develops new diseases in order to market cures at exorbitant cost. Crake, the mastermind of global destruction, is a genius scientist whose plan is to kill off humanity with a genetically engineered virus and then replace humanity with his genetically engineered creatures, the Crakers, who are perfectly adapted to the globally warmed environment of the near future. Thus, ironically enough, Crake appears to be motivated by a desire to counteract the environmental destruction caused by overpopulation and by the human domination of nature.

Oryx and Crake describes the world both before and after Crake's pandemic plague wipes out most of humankind. The society before the apocalypse is deeply stratified, consisting of the higher caste of prestigious scientists and businessmen, who live in luxurious gated communities called Compounds, and the mass of the lower caste population, who live in the cities, known as pleeblands, turbulent ghettos of poverty and disease. Life in the Compounds is comfortable on the surface, and provides luxuries and amenities: there are spas, shopping centers with entertainment, and fine dining (with real as well as ersatz foods). But as Jimmy describes life in the Compounds, his tone is pessimistic. The corporations that control the Compounds have taken over the security functions usually performed by governments and wield power over the residents. The house cleaners are probably spies, and the security guards at the gates watch both inside and outside the Compounds: "The lid was screwed down tight. Night patrols, curfews for growing minds, sniffer dogs after hard drugs" (73).

Women, like nature, are manipulated and consumed. Student Services at Crake's college, the Watson-Crick Institute, arranges for carefully screened temporary sexual partners. People from the Compounds go to the pleeblands to visit brothels, such as Scales and Tails, which is where *The Year of the Flood*'s Ren ends up working as a trapeze dancer. Young Oryx, who grows up in Southeast Asia, is sold by her desperately poor mother into sexual service to help ensure the survival of the family. She is cast in child porn films, and, by a circuitous route through trading sexual favors, she ends up in the United States where she eventually becomes the consort of two friends, Jimmy and Crake, who utilize her for sexual purposes and as a medium of exchange between them.

Jimmy, the humanist and the "word-man" narrator, ranks himself on the status scale below his brilliant scientist friend Crake. However, although he is slightly lower in the social hierarchy, he belongs to the privileged class and grows up in the Compounds. Highly paid scientists like Jimmy's parents work for pharmaceutical companies, researching genetic modification, and developing such life forms as the pigoons, pigs that are engineered to grow multiple organs for transplanting into humans. Although the scientists develop cures for diseases, they also produce new ailments disseminated in random samples of vitamin pills sold in the pleeblands so that they can profit from selling the cures. When Jimmy's mother learns that scientists have introduced human neocortex cells into the pigoons, she accuses Jimmy's father, who is working on the project, of "interfering with the building blocks of life." She argues "It's immoral. It's . . . sacrilegious" and she points out that the corporations promise treatments that will prolong life in order to exploit desperate people who pay exorbitantly for the supposedly wonder-working elixirs (57).

Years later when Jimmy visits Crake at the Watson-Crick Institute, what he sees there—"the labs, the peculiar bioforms, the socially spastic scientists" (205)—reminds him of the Compound world he grew up in. At the prestigious Watson-Crick Institute, a science-focused university known colloquially as Asperger's U, student-scientists like Crake are encouraged to produce new life forms. "Wave of the future," Crake says to Jimmy (201), as he shows him student projects at Watson-Crick, such as the shocking-pink butterflies with wings the size of pancakes, or the modified headless chicken that has become a protein factory producing chicken parts. To Jimmy, the headless chicken is "a nightmare," for it is "like an animal-protein tuber" (202). And Jimmy is similarly dismayed when Crake shows him the wolvogs, vicious doglike creatures: "Reach out to pat them, they'll take your hand off. There's a large pit-bull component," Crake explains (205). Jimmy, who is appalled by this manipulation of nature, feels that "some line has been crossed, some boundary transgressed," and he wonders "how much is too much, how far is too far" (206). But to Crake, once a new organism is produced it becomes part of nature, and "the process is no longer important" (200). Moreover, he asserts that he doesn't believe in Nature with a capital *N*, and postulates that "Nature is to zoos as God is to churches. . . . Mankind needs barriers in both cases" (206).

When Crake becomes a top scientist at the RejoovenEsense Compound, he carries his genetic engineering to extremes, implementing a secret plan to replace humans with a quasi-human life form. He calls the new race of beings the Paradice Project floor models, but others call them the Crakers. They are raised in the Paradice dome, a fallen Eden, an artificial construction that provides them with their simple physical needs. Crake has designed them as much as possible to avoid the negative traits that mar the "ancient primate brain" (305). He tries to eliminate the qualities he deplores—such as prejudice, jealousy, spirituality, abstract thinking, and greed—because they lead to strife and warfare. Bioengineered to live in the posthuman, posttechnology world, the Crakers have limited vocabularies and no written language. Designed with genetically built-in sunscreen and bug repellant, they need neither clothing nor shelter, and they subsist on grass and leaves. Atwood's ironic humor comes into play here: the Crakers are the perfect "low environmental impact" creatures. They respect nature and other life forms; they are vegetarians; their consumption of resources is close to zero; they recycle materials. Crake has even designed them to recycle their own excrement because "for animals with a diet consisting largely of unrefined plant materials . . . such a mechanism was necessary to break down the cellulose" (159).

Left alone in a posthuman, corpse-littered world by Crake so he can lead the Crakers out of the Paradice Dome, Jimmy reflects on the scientific imperialism of Crake: "Sitting in judgment on the world . . . but why had that been his right?" (341). If in *Oryx and Crake* Atwood focuses on the lives of the male elite in her futuristic world, in *The Year of the Flood* she retells her apocalyptic story from the point of view of two female inhabitants of the pleeblands, Ren and Toby, who are former members of the God's Gardeners, a group that has warned of a "waterless flood" that will destroy humanity. In *The Year of the Flood,* as she does in *Oryx and Crake,* Atwood invokes the imagery of the Garden of Eden in admonitory/prophetic and parodic/satiric ways as she depicts the God's Gardeners, a cult of people who seek to blend religion and science, live sustainably, and practice egalitarianism and cooperation as they show respect for nature.

"Ours Is a Fall into Greed": *The Year of the Flood*

The Year of the Flood is told through three narrative strands that alternate between the perspectives of two women, Ren and Toby, and the sermons of Adam One, leader of the God's Gardeners. Ren and Toby lose their tenuous places in society through economic and social displacements, and, consequently, suffer a variety of oppressions that compel them to use their bodies as commodities when trying to survive in the underground economy in the lawless, teeming pleeblands. When Ren and Toby live for a time with the Gardeners, they both maintain a mixture of belief and skepticism while participating in the cult activities and learning the egalitarian, ecofriendly, and practical Gardener values that help them to survive and that hold promise for the future inhabitants of the postapocalypse world.

Toby's family is impoverished by her mother's mysterious lingering illness and death, likely caused by HelthWyzer pharmaceutical company's supposedly health-promoting supplements. Toby then ekes out a meager living, first through selling parts of her body. She sells her long hair, then two of her eggs. When her second egg extraction causes an infection that renders her infertile, she finds a job in a fast food restaurant selling burgers made of suspect ingredients (ground up animal and likely even human parts) where the manager, Blanco, abuses her and demands sexual services.

Ren first works at a health spa that caters to pampered Compound wives, but then becomes a sex worker at an upscale brothel called Scales and Tails where she is one of the prized "regular girls" because of her skills as a trapeze artist. The less fortunate "temporaries" are hired for life-threatening "plank work" with Painballer vets (newly released vicious criminals) who "could go berserk and . . . break a lot more than the furniture" (130). These temporaries, young minority and illegal immigrant women, are considered expendable because the brothel gets "a big-time extra bonus" for servicing these violent men (130).

The God's Gardeners, one of the marginalized religious cults that arise during the time of social unrest, aspires to an ethic that is in marked contrast to the acquisitive, consumption-driven, status-seeking societies of the wealthy Compounds. The Gardeners seek to practice and promote ecofeminist values of nonhierarchical communalism and caring that encompass the entirety of living beings. Instead of gated Compounds, the Gardeners live in abandoned buildings in the midst of the pleeblands, such as the Edencliff apartment building. Whereas the pleebland children, the pleebrats, scavenge for clothing and trinkets that they quickly tire of or trade, the Gardeners warn their children to avoid such shiny baubles. The Compound residents dine at restaurants, eat meat from a variety of animals, including endangered species, and dress fashionably; the Gardeners are vegetarians who grow their own food and wear dark clothing that does not show the dirt. Whereas the Compound scientists in *Oryx and Crake* produce pills that make people sick and then sell them expensive cures, the Gardeners learn to grow and harvest healing herbs, and practice healing rituals, such as meditation and vigils. Whereas the Compound societies pay well for scientific and technological prowess, the Gardener society participates in an underground economy, selling or trading recycled materials. The nonworking Compound wives amuse themselves by shopping, playing golf, and enjoying spa beautification treatments; the Gardener women share both the routine daily tasks and the group leadership on an equal basis with the men. The Gardeners prize practical skills, such as foraging, recycling, and making clothing and furniture out of found materials. The group's leaders, the Adams and Eves, are chosen because of their practical knowledge, such as beekeeping or herbal healing. And they pass down their knowledge and beliefs to Gardener children, who are expected to participate in the food-gathering and other activities of the group. Ren recalls some of the "useful lessons" they are taught: "Nothing should be carelessly thrown away, not even wine from sinful places [used by the Gardeners to make vinegar]. There was no such thing as garbage, trash, or dirt, only matter that hadn't been put to a proper use. And, most importantly, everyone, including children, must contribute to the life of the community" (69).

As Adam One in his sermons addresses his "Fellow Gardeners in the Earth that is God's Garden," he warns against human greed. "Ours is a fall into greed: Why do we think everything on Earth belongs to us, while in reality we belong to Everything? . . . God's commandment to 'replenish the earth' did not mean we should fill it to overflowing with ourselves, thus wiping out everything else" (52–53). Unlike Crake, who has an arrogant belief that he can get rid of the "design faults" of the human "primate brain" that mars humanity by causing greed, prejudice, and jealousy (see *Oryx* 305), Adam One celebrates the human connection to all animals, including primates:

"We affirm our Primate ancestry. . . [W]e are closely related to our fellow Primates . . . Our appetites, our desires, our more uncontrollable emotions—all are Primate! . . . We pray that we may not fall into the error of pride by considering ourselves as exceptional, alone in all Creation in having Souls; and that we will not vainly imagine that we are set above all other Life, and may destroy it at our pleasure, and with impunity (51–53).

The Gardeners espouse an ethic of stewardship for the natural world and its inhabitants. Adam One explains that God "bequeathed [the animals who survive extinction] anew to our care" (90). He laments the "wholesale slaughter of ecosystems," and warns that his followers "must be ready for the time when those who have broken trust with the Animals—yes, wiped them from the face of the Earth where God placed them—will be swept away by the Waterless Flood" (91).

Yet while the Gardeners are taught to respect nature and that killing even worms and ants is wrong, the children "re-locate" snails from the plants in their gardens by tossing them off the roof. Adam One addresses his followers with a combination of exalted rhetoric and banalities. After praising them for "covering . . . barren rooftops with greenery [and] doing our small part in the redemption of God's Creation from the decay and sterility that lies all around us, and feeding ourselves with unpolluted food into the bargain," he then remarks, "I am glad we have all remembered our sunhats" (11). Thus, the Gardeners are portrayed with an Atwoodian mix of humor and satire, and the Gardeners' theology is "scrambled" as Adam One strives to interpret the Bible both literally and scientifically. While the Gardeners are not perfect people, they do aspire to live according to principles of social and environmental justice. Their peaceable value system tends toward passivity, for they choose to "bear witness . . . and to guard the memories and the genomes of the departed" rather than to be more active agents (253).[2]

Although Adam One insists that the Gardener life is one of "peace," to Zeb "peace goes only so far. There's at least a hundred new extinct species since this time last month. They got fucking eaten! We can't just sit here and watch the lights blink out" (252). When Zeb and his, MaddAddam followers commit acts of bioterrorism, they are intent on using "bioform resistance," hoping that if they can "destroy the infrastructure" of the wasteful and greedy corporate society "then the planet could repair itself" (333). Blamed for the MaddAddam acts, the Gardeners are ruthlessly hunted down and those who are not killed, including Adam One and his remaining followers, are forced into hiding. After the Waterless Flood—Crake's pandemic virus—kills off most of humanity, Adam One prepares his followers to leave their hiding pace—their sheltering Ararat. Initially, he is hopeful that "the Waterless Flood has cleansed as well as destroyed, and that all the world is now a new Eden. Or, if it is not a new Eden yet, that it will be one soon" (345). But when Adam One and members of his group begin to show symptoms of the virus, he prepares them for their end. "It is not this Earth that is to be demolished: it is the Human Species. Perhaps God will create another, more compassionate race to take our place" (424).

But while some of the Gardeners, at the end, appear destined to die of the plague, Ren, Amanda, Toby, and several others do survive. Unlike the friendship of Jimmy and Crake, which is based on status and competition and which leads Jimmy to kill Crake, the friendship of Ren, Amanda, and Toby promotes survival.[3] Ren and Amanda survive the Waterless Flood only to be taken captive by the Painballers—hardened condemned criminals who have survived the Painball arena where they were imprisoned and forced to engage in a savage, web-broadcast game of predator and prey. To the Painballers, Ren and Amanda are female objects and sexual slaves to be sexually consumed and brutally tortured. When Ren escapes the Painballers, Toby comes to her aid and heals her, seeing her as someone to "cure" and "cherish" even though she is well aware that having another person to feed will use up her limited supplies more quickly (360). And then Ren and Toby risk their own lives to save Amanda who, in a gruesome example of the consumerist, masculinist ethos Atwood is critiquing in the novel, is viewed by the Painballers as "disposable," an object to be traded for food and ammunition (389). At the end of *Oryx and Crake*, Jimmy, who believed himself perhaps the only surviving human, discovers two men and a woman and is trying to decide whether or not to shoot them. *The Year of the Flood* revisits this scene, and depicts Ren shouting out to Jimmy not to shoot Amanda, who is being used as a human shield by the Painballers.[4] Ren and Toby's acts of bravery and loyalty save Amanda, and afterwards Ren feels fortunate, despite all the horrors she has endured: "We're lucky, I think. To be here. All of us, even the Painballers" (428). As Jimmy, Amanda, Toby, Ren, and the Painballers (who have been tied up to keep them from committing more violence) share a meal together, Toby enjoins them, at least for the moment, "to forget the past" and be "grateful for this food that has been given to us" (430–31).

After Amanda's rescue from the violent and brutal Painballers, the novel's mood becomes elegiac, as the concluding section focuses on nurturance and forgiveness. Adam One's last sermon exhorts his remaining followers to forgive "the killers of the Elephant" and to pray for "All Souls" including "the Souls of those who have persecuted us" (425). Toby's generous sharing of their meager meal with the Painballers[5] echoes these themes of nurturance and forgiveness. Similarly, Ren forgives Jimmy for his mistreatment of her when they were young, and observes that she feels happier after forgiving him: "something heavy and smothering lifts away from me, and I truly do feel happy" (431). Does the novel perhaps suggest that forgiveness can redeem past misdeeds? Does forgiving possibly promise a new beginning?[6] As Atwood offers in her novel a stark contrast between the killing and masculinist ethos of the Painballers and the nurturing and ecofeminist ideals of Ren and Toby, she also holds out some hope, slim though it may be, for the future.

Conclusion

In *Oryx and Crake* and *The Year of the Flood*, destruction is more widespread than in *The Handmaid's Tale*; most of the world's humans have succumbed to the viral pandemic. Atwood's critique has grown more pointed and more complex. Shannon Hengen points out that in these works Atwood's "voice has become admonitory as she uses her writings to urge us to curb the godlike power of science before it is too late" (139–40). In her futuristic, dystopian works, Atwood demonstrates the dangers of social systems that devalue women and nature, and she also suggests that we may change our ways and thus avert disaster.

Atwood frequently employs genre conventions to structure her texts, while using parody, irony, satire and inversion to both stretch the boundaries of and to critique those conventions. *Oryx and Crake* and

The Year of the Flood work within the genre of apocalypse to promulgate an ecofeminist ethic and to "examine both the limitations and possibilities of apocalyptic rhetoric" (Jennings 18). The novels deploy the metaphor of apocalypse, which has been aptly described as "the single most powerful master metaphor that the contemporary environmental imagination has" (Buell 285). Lawrence Buell argues that apocalyptic narratives "create images of doom to avert doom" (295). If, as some claim, the use of apocalyptic rhetoric to speak of imminent disaster in our real world can lead to a numbing fatalism or apathy (Hambrick), apocalyptic fiction is designed to provide enough distance to allow readers to open imaginative spaces, to test new possibilities, and to engage imaginatively with environmental issues. As Buell argues, apocalyptic fiction may become a powerful voice to avert catastrophe:

> As ecocatastrophe becomes an increasingly greater possibility, so will the occasions for environmental apocalyptic expression, and the likelihood that it will suffuse essay, fiction, film [and other arts] . . . in unprecedentedly powerful, mind-haunting ways. Can our imaginations of apocalypse actually forestall it, as our fears of nuclear holocaust so far have? Even the slimmest of possibilities is enough to justify the nightmare (308).

Even as *The Year of the Flood* puts forward a critique of apocalyptic rhetoric, the culture of the God's Gardeners, however imperfect and off-kilter it may be, points toward an alternative, ecofeminist, value system of communality, frugality, and respect for the environment and for living beings. "Ours is a fall into greed: Why do we think everything on Earth belongs to us, while in reality we belong to Everything?" as Adam One says, voicing Atwood's concerns about our heedless destruction of the planet (52–53). Atwood also uses Toby to give voice to her environmental concerns in the scene in which Toby recalls how she heard people warn, *"We're using up the Earth. It's almost gone"* (239). At first Toby tuned them out: "I knew there were things wrong in the world. . . . But the wrong things were wrong somewhere else" (239).

Perhaps Atwood's "unprecedentedly powerful, mind-haunting" apocalyptic fictions may motivate people to realize how close "the wrong things" are. Perhaps her ecofeminist novels may lead us not only to rethink our consumerist, exploitative behavior as we "use up the Earth" but also to formulate more balanced and egalitarian approaches to nature and society, and thus ensure the continuing survival of the planet and humanity.

Notes

My thanks to J. Brooks Bouson for her perceptive editing that improved and helped to shape this essay.

1. Françoise d'Eaubonne coined the term *eco-feminism* in 1974 to recognize the related oppressions of a patriarchal social system that seeks to dominate nature and beings that are "other," or different. See Anne Primavesi's "Ecofeminism" in the *Encyclopedia of Science and Religion.*

2. According to Hope Jennings, "The Gardeners' overall passivity . . . allows them to abnegate all meaningful responsibility" (14–15). Jennings is more critical of the Gardeners than I am. She argues that the Gardeners are dangerous in their "tragic apocalyptic" beliefs, for such beliefs lead to hopelessness and despair. But I do agree with Jennings' reading of *The Year of the Flood* as more optimistic than *Oryx and Crake* largely because of its more "feminine" vision. As Jennings explains, *The Year of the Flood* is "grounded in a (skeptical) faith in the possibility of human survival and/or redemption. Toby's pragmatic integrity and Ren's resilient optimism allows them to view others as well as themselves through a critical but also forgiving lens. This distinguishes them from the predominantly pessimistic and self-absorbed perspectives of Jimmy and Crake" (16).

3. The contrasting friendships of the men in *Oryx and Crake* and the women in *The Year of the Flood* are another key to their survival. The friendship of Jimmy and Crake is based on status and competition; Jimmy measures himself against Crake, and feels that his friend wins all their arguments. They share the sexual services of Oryx, but never discuss this with each other. In fact, Jimmy wonders if Crake knows about his affair with Oryx, or if possibly Crake orchestrated this love triangle for his own strategic purposes. At a crucial plot juncture, Jimmy kills Crake. Does he act out of anger? Jealousy? Or did Crake set him up to do this, as Jimmy comes to believe?

   In contrast, the female friendships in *The Year of the Flood* promote the women's survival. They take personal risks to rescue each other from danger. As Paula Anca Farca explains: "While [in Atwood's novels] women's relationships with men usually fail and contribute to the women's defeats or deaths, the network of female relationships is more powerful and effective" (18). This analysis of women's friendships rings true for *The Year of the Flood*, but is only partly true of *The Handmaid's Tale*. In the earlier novel female friendship is important, but less efficacious. Lee Briscoe Thompson points out that Offred's friendship with Moira is the longest-lasting relationship in that novel, and one that figures prominently in Offred's story. However, it is through men and male networks that Offred is rescued from her handmaid role in Gilead (293–95).

4. Jimmy is on the verge of physical and emotional collapse at the end of the two novels. In *Oryx and Crake* he spends a lot of time in "pointless repining," and in erotic fantasies about former lovers and especially about the sex worker Oryx. He is slowly starving, and depends for his sustenance on weekly donations of a cooked fish from the Crakers, on scavenging whatever remains he can find of the processed synthetic foods he was used to eating, and on plants that he sometimes finds still growing nearby. Ren and Toby, on the other hand, due in part to their training by the Gardeners, remain skeptical but hopeful at the end of *The Year of the Flood*, and act positively to further their survival. The practical Toby manages to maintain a garden and to grow herbs and vegetables. Toby, Ren, and her friend Amanda spend little time in negative fantasies, but move along with the business of living in the present, for as Amanda points out, "Being discouraged is a waste of time" (*Year of the Flood* 76). Similarly, in *The Handmaid's Tale* Offred focuses on survival.

5. The shared meal occurs on the Gardener feast night devoted to Saint Julian and All Souls (428–30). The, Gardeners' calendar of "saints" includes people who have been notable for their egalitarian and environmental values. Julian of Norwich was a fourteenth-century mystic, who wrote in her *Revelations of Divine Love* that God is both a nurturing mother as well as a powerful father.

6. See Kuribayashi for a further discussion of forgiveness in the novel.

Works Cited

Atwood, Margaret. *The Handmaid's Tale*. 1985. New York: Random, 1998.

_____. *Oryx and Crake*. Toronto: McClelland, 2003.

_____. *Payback: Debt and the Shadow Side of Wealth*. Toronto: Anansi, 2008.

_____. *The Year of the Flood*. New York: Doubleday, 2009.

Buell, Lawrence. *The Environmental Imagination: Thoreau, Nature Writing, and the Formation of American Culture*. Cambridge, MA: Harvard UP, 1995.

Carr, Glynis. Introduction. *New Essays in Ecofeminist Literary Criticism*. Ed. Glynis Carr. Cranbury, NJ: Associated UP, 2000. 15–25.

Cudworth, Erika. *Developing Ecofeminist Theory: The Complexity of Difference*. New York: Palgrave, 2005.

Eisler, Riane. *The Chalice and the Blade*. Rev. ed. San Francisco: Harper, 1995.

Farca, Paula Anca. "*The Year of the Flood* and the Garden of Limited Choices." *Margaret Atwood Studies* 3:2 (Aug. 2010): 18–21.

Gaard, Greta. "Toward a Queer Ecofeminism." *New Perspectives in Environmental Justice: Gender, Sexuality, and Activism.* Ed. Rachel Stein. New Brunswick, NJ: Rutgers UP, 2004. 21–44.

Hambrick, Keira. "Imagining Sustainability: Speculative Environmentalism in *The Windup Girl.*" Northeast Modern Language Society, Rutgers University, New Brunswick, NJ. 8 Apr. 2011. Conference Presentation.

Hengen, Shannon. "Moral/Environmental Debt in *Payback* and *Oryx and Crake.*" *Margaret Atwood: The Robber Bride, The Blind Assassin, Oryx and Crake.* Ed. J. Brooks Bouson. London: Continuum, 2010. 129–140.

Jennings, Hope. "The Comic Apocalypse of *The Year of the Flood.*" *Margaret Atwood Studies* 3:2 (Aug. 2010): 11–18.

King, Ynestra. "The Ecology of Feminism and the Feminism of Ecology." *Feminist Theory: A Reader.* Eds. Wendy K. Kolmar and Frances Bartkowski. Boston: McGraw, 2010. 407–13.

Korten, David C. *The Great Turning: From Empire to Earth Community.* Bloomfield, CT: Kumarian, 2006.

Kuribayashi, Tomoko. "Women, Nature, and Forgiveness in *The Year of the Flood: An Exploratory Consideration.*" *Margaret Atwood Studies* 3:2 (Aug. 2010): 22–38.

Primavesi, Anne. "Ecofeminism." *Encyclopedia of Science and Religion.* eNotes, n.d. Web. 30 May 2011.

Thompson, Lee Briscoe. *Scarlet Letters: Margaret Atwood's The Handmaid's Tale.* Toronto: ECW, 1997.

Postapocalyptic Vision: Flood Myths and Other Folklore in Atwood's *Oryx and Crake* and *The Year of the Flood*_____

Sharon R. Wilson

In *Oryx and Crake* (2003) and *The Year of the Flood* (2009), Atwood dramatizes dangerous trends in contemporary society, in particular the increasing destruction of the natural environment, the extinction of animal species, and the heedless use of biotechnology to create new species and even to tamper with the human genome. *Oryx and Crake* and *The Year of the Flood* are speculative fictions about a possible end of the world for which human beings seem to be heading. The books highlight the question of whether or not people really are at the center of the universe. Contrary to some readers' expectations, rather than dictating what people ought to be doing, Atwood uses characteristic comic, parodic, and ironic techniques, multiple unreliable narrators, and other literary devices including intertexts—that is, texts such as myths within other texts such as novels—to explore these questions. Because intertexts are embedded stories that effect theme, structure, characterization, and every aspect of the work in which they are embedded, *Oryx and Crake* and *The Year of the Flood*, like most of Atwood's work, do suggest ways out of the dystopia, underworld, maze, or self-created traps that these novels depict. Atwood's characters frequently trap themselves by disconnecting from their senses: vision, taste, smell, touch, speech, and hearing. *Oryx*'s Crake, Jimmy, and Oryx, and *Flood*'s Adam One, Ren, Toby, and other God's Gardeners primarily suffer from varying kinds and degrees of blindness. Atwood uses folkloric and other intertexts not only to illuminate blindness but also to suggest what postapocalyptic vision could be like. In both novels, Atwood also demythologizes what is, in many ways, a comic apocalypse (Jennings 11).[1]

Frankenstein and Faust Legends and the "Fitcher's Bird" Fairy Tale in *Oryx and Crake*

In *Oryx and Crake,* in which the Frankenstein and Faust legends and the Grimms' "Fitcher's Bird" fairy-tale intertexts are dominant, the master storyteller is Jimmy—also known as Snowman and, on the Internet, Thickney. He even begins the second chapter of the book with "Once upon a time." Glenn (Crake on the Internet) ironically thinks he will create a perfect world by killing *Homo sapiens* and developing a new humanoid species. However, "both Crake and Jimmy are monsters in their contrasting ways of seeing without seeing. It is no accident that Crake's dome complex [for scientific research] is described as a 'blind eyeball' and that it has only slits for windows" (*Oryx* 297 as qtd. in Wilson, *Myths* 48). Even the video screens of the complex have only "blind eyes" (*Oryx* 276). Crake's pseudolove, Oryx, who represents the powerless victims of human trafficking in the book, intensifies Crake's and his world's blindness by ironically admiring his "vision" (322). Recalling other scientific geniuses, such as mad scientists in movies of the 1950s and classic fairy-tale wizards, Crake is a Dr. Frankenstein, "a demi-autistic 'brainiac' who functions as a mutant on another planet as he proceeds toward exterminating humanity on this one" (*Oryx* 174, 193 as qtd. in Wilson, *Myths* 48; see also Wilson, "Frankenstein's" passim). Since her early rare book, *Speeches for Doctor Frankenstein* (1966), and her untitled watercolors published as *Frankenstein I and II*, Atwood has been interested in Dr. Frankenstein (see Wilson, *Margaret* Plates 6 and 7; Wilson "Frankenstein's" 398). Like Dr. Frankenstein, Atwood's Crake does the unthinkable: he creates a living being, in this case a humanoid species that will supposedly never rape or engage in war, has natural sun repellant, and neatly drops dead at age thirty. For similar reasons, he creates the BlyssPluss pill. While the people who take Crake's pill think that its sole purpose is to offer sexual enhancement, Crake, in fact, embeds his hemorrhagic virus in the BlyssPluss pill, and thus, he uses the ruse of promising enhanced sexual libido to kill off humanity. In his blind quest for the

Absolute—the creation of life—Crake is also like the legendary Dr. Faust or Faustus, who sells his soul to the devil, first to attain total scientific knowledge and then ultimate beauty. Significantly, people exposed to the BlyssPluss virus in this blind society end up with ruptured and empty eye sockets, as do Crake and Oryx, who bear the names of extinct or nearly extinct animals from the Extinctathon Internet game Jimmy and Crake play as students.

Crake is also a Fitcher wizard from the Grimms' "Fitcher's Bird" fairy tale, a tale Atwood embeds in most of her work, including *Power Politics* (1971), *Bluebeard's Egg* (1983), *Alias Grace* (1996), *Bodily Harm* (1981), *The Blind Assassin* (200), and *The Robber Bride* (1993) (Wilson, *Myths* 35–36). Even one of Atwood's watercolors features Fitcher's Bride (see *Fitcher's Bird* in Wilson, *Margaret Atwood's*). "Fitcher's Bird," "Blue Beard" in Perrault's version, is a story about the power a person and his group can exercise over a whole society. Fitcher is rich, magnetic even to those who fear him, and lives far away from ordinary people. Atwood's watercolor depicts a skeleton bride in a wedding dress. Because Fitcher kills his brides, they literally marry death. Regarding the third sister, who later disguises herself as a magnificent bird in order to escape, this time Fitcher symbolizes marriage as death; ironically, against expectation, including that of his friends as well as his own.

Oryx and Crake uses especially the "Fitcher's Bird" motif of the door to the forbidden room, which in the fairy tale hides chopped up bodies of Fitcher's former wives. In the novel, Crake, the Fitcher figure, keeps his plans for a new "paradise" secret and locks up the scientists and the created species, the Crakers, in the Dome, which is inaccessible to ordinary people. The grandmasters' section of the Extinctathon website is also a forbidden room (Wilson, "Frankenstein's" 402). Although Jimmy sees women as doors to be unlocked with unmeant words such as "I love you," doors hide numerous kinds of menace such as "bad" microbes and viruses, the forbidden knowledge his society fears, possibly Oryx's past, and "the hidden thing at the core of life" (314). Doors open Jimmy to the world of words, to recognition of Crake's role as Fitcher, to his complicity in "Fitcher's games," and near the end of the book, when he sees the Robinson Crusoe footprints on the beach, to a possible future (Wilson, *Myths* 41–42).

Other fairy-tale and folk allusions in *Oryx and Crake* include "The Robber Bridegroom,"[2] "The Wolf and the Kids," "Red Cap," "The Water of Life," "Hansel and Gretel," "Cinderella," "Beauty and the Beast,"[3] "The Three Pigs" (Wilson, *Myths* 39), and *The Arabian Nights*. These references, among those to self-help books, colonial narratives, and other "voices" from Jimmy's past at HelthWyzer High and the Martha Graham Academy, suggest the extent to which Jimmy has absorbed cultural stories quite unlike the technological ones to which he is subjected at Crake's Watson-Crick Institute and the Rejooven-Esense Compound.

Mythology, another kind of folklore, is also important in the two Atwood novels. Although some critics loosely refer to Atwood's novels as myth and also discuss science fiction, nonmimetic narratives, and fabulation as "myth,"[4] these novels are not myths. Mythology, as discussed by folklorists, is etiological and believed. It cannot be defined as an untrue story, as in general parlance. As a type of folklore, a story that is presented as having actually occurred, myth explains "the cosmological and supernatural traditions of a people, their gods, heroes, cultural traits, religious beliefs, etc." (Leach 778).

Both *Oryx and Crake* and *The Year of the Flood* use such myths as intertexts, which includes their effect on theme and structure in moving from destruction to rebirth. Crake attempts to ban mythology from his created species, the Crakers, because he wants to alter "the ancient primate brain" of humans and thus get rid of racism, hierarchy, and territoriality in his creatures. His Crakers, he insists, will have no need "to invent any harmful symbolisms, such as kingdoms, icons, gods, or money" because he has used bioengineering to get rid of such behaviors: "That stuff's been edited out," he remarks (305, 311). Crake thinks that the raison d'être for religion is misery, and he insists that

"*God is a cluster of neurons*" (157). But he is defeated by the Crakers' curiosity and by being a mythmaker himself. When the Crakers ask Oryx who "made" them, she tells them that the "clever and good" Crake made them (311). Indeed, although Crake violently disrespects plant, animal, and human life, he *literally* engages in creation mythology by creating a new species and a horrific new world.

Left alive by Crake so he can act as the guide of the Crakers, Jimmy rebelliously creates myths centering on Crake for the Crakers, but he has trouble keeping his stories straight. After the apocalypse, Jimmy thinks of himself as the Abominable Snowman, a legend about the Yeti, and imagines that in this alter ego he embodies what might have been the Crakers' human ancestral past: "On some nonconscious level Snowman must serve as a reminder to these people, and not a pleasant one: he's what they may have been once. . . . *I'm your ancestor, come from the land of the dead. Now I'm lost, and I can't get back*" (106). In this persona, Jimmy thinks of himself as an Other species, lonely, monstrous, and cold.

One of Jimmy's creation myths involves Crake's making the bones of the Crakers out of coral on the beach and their flesh out of mangoes. Jimmy also tells the Crakers that the Children of Oryx—that is, the animals, birds, and fish—were hatched out of an egg laid by Oryx, and that she also laid one full of words which the Children of Crake ate up, which explains why animals are unable to talk. The Crakers demand that Jimmy repeat the stories, including the creation myth of their origins. Like the Chinese creation myth referred to here (see note 5), Jimmy's "in the beginning" story starts when everything was chaos, and Crake made the Great Rearrangement and the Great Emptiness to save the Crakers from being eaten by the people of the chaos (102–03). Oryx's story of the world being created out of an egg—an act that again creates order out of chaos—also resembles the Indian and numerous other creation myths (see note 6).Thus Crake is deified in Jimmy's stories, even coming down from the sky, and Jimmy is his prophet. Not only do the Crakers participate in liturgies, but they also make "lore" about Jimmy, conjecturing that he was once a bird but forgot how to fly, that he's cold because his feathers fell out and he eats fish, and that he has wrinkles because he once lived underwater. Perceptively, they speculate that "*Snowman is sad because the others like him flew away over the sea, and now he is all alone*" (8). Like Jimmy, their ability to create stories reveals their growth, particularly in attempting to explain and understand their world.

Jimmy's myths, as Carol Osborne remarks, "have established a communal code that is radically different from the ideology governing interactions in the old world," for he teaches the Crakers to avoid the "bad things" that occurred in the chaos, and, anticipating the God's Gardeners of *The Year of the Flood,* his myths also show the primacy of love and respect for all life and for the natural environment. "What seems the most important aspect of the mythology Snowman has invented," writes Osborne, "is the sense of community that results from the ritual telling of the stories, for it sets a precedent for how stories may function when Snowman goes to meet the humans" at the end of the novel ("Mythmaking" 40). This possibility not only creates a more hopeful ending than many readers construct for this novel but is a preview of the exchanging of tales that occurs in *The Year of the Flood.* Ultimately, Snowman begins to overcome both the "thickness" and coldness associated with his names and the blindness that kept him hooked into Crake's fake vision.

Flood Myths and Folklore in *The Year of the Flood*

The Year of the Flood, described by Atwood as a "simultane-quel" rather than sequel to *Oryx and* Crake (see Atwood "Review"), overlaps the action of the previous novel, including brief meetings with or references to Jimmy, Oryx, and Crake, but tells other aspects of the story from different points of view. Again, many of the characters have double or triple names, suggesting their fragmentation. Like most of Atwood's work, *The Year of the Flood* uses various kinds of creation folklore to convey her social criticism, culminating in warnings of an

---

approaching apocalypse for the world outside the novel. Drawing upon sometimes parodied folk tales, folk songs, oral histories, legends, fairy tales, myths, and the Bible, *The Year of the Flood* is about a flood, this time waterless, destroying the earth. Flood stories, including the Babylonian and Sumerian *Gilgamesh*; Chinese, Navajo, Pre-Incan, and Greek tales; and the Genesis vi–ix story in the Bible, occur all over the world. They are generally creation or fertility myths that explain fundamental questions about existence. Floods are often only one of the means of apocalypse. The Chinese creation myth, "The Creation of the Universe and Human Beings,"[5] the Indian "Creation, Death, and Rebirth of the Universe, Gods, and Human Beings,"[6] and the Genesis story of the flood[7] are creation myths that explain basic questions about existence. They all also depict how rebirth follows apocalypse.

Atwood's tale of a waterless flood draws from flood tradition and related folklore intertexts, most significantly the Genesis tale. Karen Stein notes that the "originating myth of Paradise," which is used in both *Oryx and Crake* and *Frankenstein*, is "one of the central stories of Western civilization" (151–52). Clearly, Crake's "Paradice Project," a blind gamble aimed at destroying human life on Earth, is a parody of the biblical myth, satirizing overreaching scientific attempts to create paradise on Earth. In *The Year of the Flood*, a religious environmental group called the God's Gardeners represent Noah and his family and constitute a "plural Noah" (91), for they feel responsible for replenishing the earth after a second "flood" caused by shortsighted as well as corrupt human beings. The ark of the biblical apocalyptic story is generally thought to land on Mount Ararat. In Atwood's book, the God's Gardeners take shelter during the waterless flood in one of their Ararats, the cellars of the Buenavista Condo Complex, where Adam One hopes for a new Eden. In the preflood world, the Gardeners, at the Festival of Arks, are enjoined to construct their Ararats carefully and to provision them with foresight as well as canned goods. Children launch their handmade little arks on Arboretum Creek, and one of the Gardeners' hymns refers to the body as an "earthly Ark" (93). The novel begins with a hymn from *The God's Gardeners Oral Hymnbook*—"The Garden"—which draws on the biblical story of the Garden of Eden as it tells of the destruction of nature's trees, waves, and birds, which have been ruined by the greedy Spoilers. The song calls for the Gardeners, devoted to preservation of the Garden and life, to tend the Garden and restore it to life. But while the Tree of Life is important in various mythologies and religions, in Atwood's futuristic world it has become the Natural Materials Exchange flea market, which sells jewelry made of paper clips and cabbages from the edges of sprayed golf courses—an excellent illustration of the irony and parody with which the book's various groups, including green ones, are treated.

In *The Year of the Flood,* the world Atwood depicts, initially through Toby, lacks respect for life, including the environment, the integrity of animal species, and human life. Greed, racism, sexism, classism, and irresponsibility abound, and numerous houses of all flesh proliferate. Seasons no longer occur, species such as tigers and lions have disappeared, mice have attacked cars, and microbes have eaten asphalt. Great dead zones proliferate in now warm oceans. Food choices range from SecretBurgers, partly made up of dead human bodies, to exotic dishes in the Rarity Restaurant, a gourmet restaurant that serves nearly extinct species as food. In the first chapter, taking place in the year 25, referred to as the year of the waterless flood but sometime after the "flood," the air smells of burning and Toby (known as Inaccessible Rail on the Internet) sees vultures, towers devoid of life, hybrid green rabbits, and rakunks (a combination of raccoons and skunks). Most people have been killed by Crake's virus. As in the Indian myth, the world has become a wasteland. Even in Year 5, twenty years before the waterless flood kills off humanity, Adam One invokes the Genesis story as he explains that the purpose of the Gardner Creation Day celebration is to help redeem the earth from decay and sterility by creating a Rooftop Garden. Adam One's sermon—which is about the Big Bang creation myth, God creating light, Adam naming the creatures, and Adam, or mankind, possessing free will—suggests that life will continue after the flood, but one must wonder how long it will do so.

Since *The Year of the Flood* literally depicts no flood, and does not even give many details about the plague that kills all but a few *Homo sapiens*, the title of the book is significant: it links this disaster to the whole tradition of the world being destroyed because of human deficiency and error. Although *The Year of the Flood* has less explicit vision imagery than *Oryx and Crake*, the expanding perspectives of its two female narrators—Toby and Ren—make us perhaps even more aware of the characters' and humanity's blindness. Not unlike Jimmy in *Oryx and Crake*, Toby comes to recognize her own "blindness" during the preflood years, remembering how she "tuned" out other people when they discussed the "wrongness" of the world: *"We're using up the Earth. It's almost gone"* (239). But while Atwood's character voices her increasing environmental concerns, this does not mean that Atwood has assumed an "admonitory voice" in recent works, as some critics claim, which implies that she is directly preaching to her readers (Hengen 139). Nor does this mean that Atwood in these works is pointing toward "a notion of God as humankind's essential reason for pursuing the good, the true, and the just," or that "God has come to represent, for her, the core of meaning itself" (Hengen 129).[8] Indeed, readers of Atwood's novels, in particular *Oryx and Crake* and *Year of the Flood*, must be careful about confusing the narrators' views with authorial comment.

Because Atwood's acknowledgments to *Year of the Flood* deceptively invite those who wish to use the Gardeners' hymns "for amateur devotional or environmental purposes . . . to do so" (433), and because Atwood has herself participated in public performances of the hymns, readers who look for easy messages may be lured into a briar patch. As Ursula Le Guin states, "any affirmation by this author will be hedged with all the barbed wire, flaming swords and red-eyed rottweilers she can summon" (6). Jeanette Winterson notes that the Gardeners sing "terrible hymns," lack any "dress sense," and have a "bolted-together theology" (2). Marcel Theroux says that Atwood "plays with" parts of the Gardener religion "for laughs": "their hymns have a comically bouncing, churchy rhythm, and we learn that both Ren and Toby have been drawn toward the sect for nonreligious reasons" (119).

Despite the Gardeners' sometimes effective healing techniques and their lip service to respect for Earth, their actions often contradict their words and Adam One's commandments. As Hope Jennings remarks:

> The text's satirical portrayal of the Gardeners is located in the inherent contradictions of their beliefs and discourse, as Atwood playfully, riotously intersperses Adam One's sermons and the Gardeners' corresponding hymns with the narrative (and skeptical) viewpoints of Toby and Ren. Adam One's sermons are a comedic hodgepodge of "high" and "low" language, as he mixes lyrical (albeit biblically parodic) passages with mundane observations. (13)

The Gardener hymns often have a singsong rhythm, Adam One's sermons make use of homilies such as "It is better to hope than to mope" (89), there is a silent prayer on a timer (246), and there is even a dumpling containing a turnip Noah" (89). Thus, even as Atwood wears her environmental politics "on her sleeve," she, nevertheless, does not "shy away from showing the Gardeners' tendency toward self-righteous foolishness" (Kirkus 24). Adam One admits that all religions are foolish and directs his followers, on April Fish Day, to make fun of one another: "To be an April Fish is to humbly accept our own silliness, and to cheerfully admit the absurdity—from a materialist view—of every Spiritual truth we profess" (196). While we recognize the book's comic satire of cults, this does not, of course, mean that we should disregard the dangers to which the Gardeners are responding or the blindness of our culture's single-minded worship of science and technology without a grounding in ethics and an understanding of the interdependence of all life.

Rather than Atwood directly voicing her concerns over genetic splicing, species extinction, apocalypse, and general blindness, *The Year of the Flood* consists of the oral histories of various characters, especially Toby's and Ren's, and, as a whole, it purports to be an oral history of the year of the flood and events before and soon after it. As Ren says, the Gardeners taught her "to depend on memory, because nothing written down could be relied on" (6). A third-person central consciousness or reflector, Toby (Tobiatha) and the first-person narrator Ren (Brenda) are familiar Atwoodian Scheherazades, that is, narrator-characters who tell their stories partly as a survival technique. Like Jimmy-Snowman of *Oryx and Crake,* Toby initially believes that she is the last human being on earth, and certainly this book dramatizes the dystopia that contemporary humanity seems to be reaching toward. Toby and Ren, like Adam One, Zeb, and the other characters who "narrate" through dialogue, are, of course, again unreliable or untrustworthy narrators. The Crakers see Glenn, inventor of the BlyssPluss pill, as God; Zeb's MaddAddams think they will preserve life by planting bioform bombs; and Adam One's Gardeners think that they will create a new Eden by being vegetarians and following other rules of their religion. As evidence of their unreliability, Zeb disguises himself through black-market procedures; Ren thinks that Jimmy has "trashed [her] life" (307), and she imagines that Toby, who is very attracted to Zeb, knows and cares nothing about romantic love.

Toby works at the AnooYoo Spa, one of the places responsible for conditioning women to think that glamour is a main value. The Spa attempts to stop time and to make each woman "feel like a princess" (264). Thus, the Spa's minivans sport winking-eye logos, and Toby, like so many of Atwood's previous narrators, including Jimmy who wears one-eyed sunglasses through much of the earlier book, looks at "reality" through binoculars even though she knows that "everything is different up close" (4). Initially, Ren, a trapeze dancer, is locked inside the double virus barrier, the "Sticky Zone" of Scales and Tails, which is part of the SeksMart, another business that commodifies women and thus blinds humanity. She watches injured coworkers, CorpSeCorps minders, and Painballers in the "Snakepit" main room through cameras and the video screen, she sees one-eyed Mordis (who has saved her life) through a window, and then she cannot see outside at all. Ironically, both Toby and Ren survive in or alongside places, including SecretBurgers and the Sewage Lagoon, which are antilife.

When characters like Ren, Toby, and Zeb meet again after the "flood," they exchange oral histories. While these become part of the plot that informs readers of happenings, it is important to recognize that, unlike *Oryx and Crake,* which focuses on the male point of view in telling the stories of Jimmy and Crake, *The Year of the Flood* focuses on the female point of view as it tells the stories of Ren and Toby. Thus, the histories presented in the first two novels, which occur simultaneously, do not constitute the final "facts," and, indeed, Atwood's plan to write a third volume of this trilogy reveals that there are more revelations to come.

In this second volume, we primarily feel what God's Gardener females feel and experience during the apocalypse, which is not at all what Jimmy-Snowman and the privileged people in the Compounds experience. As unprotected pleeblander women, Ren, Amanda and Toby all experience rape and thus the violence in these novels is gendered. And yet, Toby's story—her horrific sexual torture at the hands of Blanco—becomes part of the Gardner oral history, as is the story of her rescue by Adam One and the Gardeners. In a similar way, stories about the bee cyborg spy, the "flood," the CorpSeCorps, the pleebs, and the Gardeners are also "part of oral history," and Zeb is admired because he has "lore" (250, 140). The narrative emphasizes that these stories are, in fact, *stories.* Toby hears "the story" of Lucerne and Zeb (116). When Ren and Amanda meet, they tell each other "the stories" of why they are still alive. Like Jimmy in the earlier novel, Amanda tells Ren that she survived against the zombie people by sleeping in trees (318, 322–23). Former God's Gardeners Shackie, Croze, and Oates, who become part of Zeb's MaddAddam ecoterrorist group, tell stories about their acts of bioform resistance as they attempted to destroy the infrastructure so that people would think about their actions. Later, pausing to mention her concern for Amanda, Ren "tells her story" to Toby (362).

Amanda's outdoor art landscape installation series, which she calls "The Living Word," is part of her oral history. Amanda's folk art—as she explains, she spells out words "in giant letters, using bioforms to make the words appear and then disappear" (304)—also emphasizes how important words and stories are in this novel. Using syrup and ants and later vultures and bones, her artwork makes viewers pay attention to how their actions affect life forms. It is also important that her next installation is supposed to be about love. In this novel, despite the background of death and violence, many of the characters care about one another. Along with seeing, sharing their oral histories, and thinking, this caring appears to be one of the qualities necessary for growing beyond the apocalypse. As Lauren A. Rule Maxwell observes, *The Year of the Flood* "provides an alternative frame of reference in which people who make efforts to live in greater harmony with the world around them really do make a difference" (9).

The Year of the Flood also makes use of legends, fairy-tale allusions, animal folklore, folk remedies, sermons, stories about the saints, and songs as folk allusions or intertexts. The Gardeners' Pollination Day Festival, devoted to the mysteries of plant reproduction, discusses legends of fruit, such as the Golden Apples and the Fruit of the Tree of Knowledge. To Croze, even the sex club Scales and Tails is "a legend" and so he wants to "see it" (335). Atwood has frequently remarked that fairy-tale characters' ignorance almost seems evil, and her fairy-tale allusions here ironically suggest that kind of ignorance. The AnooYoo Spa uses "The Ugliest Duckling" fairy tale as an advertising slogan, and the "Little Pink Riding Hood" uniforms the employees wear make ineffective, gender-marked disguises. In imagining herself as a predator of the pigoons, as Zeb taught, Toby envisions one of "The Three Pigs" vulnerable in front of its dwelling made of straw that only appears to be brick (327). In an extension of Canada's tradition of doomed animals in tales following those of Charles G. D. Roberts,[9] sections of both *Oryx* and *Year* focus on hybrid animals such as rakunks, liobams, pigoons, and funeral-holding pigs. After taking one of Pilar's plant potions, which is supposed to resolve her doubts about becoming an Eve by trusting Nature, Toby has a Vigil vision of a peaceful golden animal. One of the most interesting aspects of the book are bee and serpent lore and folk remedies, such as the use of willow, poppy, honey, maggots, molds, spider webs, and mushrooms. Willow is an analgesic (176) and poppy induces sleep (356). According to Pilar, who is Eve Six, "All the bees of a hive are one bee," honey is an antibiotic and heals an open wound, and "if the beekeeper dies, the bees must be told" (99), as they are told when Pilar herself dies. While bees are the messengers to the dead, mushrooms are "roses in the garden of that unseen world" and help people through "Fallow states" (100). They may be used to boost the immune system (357). Atwood reveals her considerable knowledge of this lore, including kinds of mushrooms and the healing, renewal, wisdom, immediacy, wholeness of being, and cycle of life associated with serpents (234–35). As Adam One points out in one of his sermons, earthworms, nematodes, and ants till the soil, maggots and molds have antibiotic properties, spider webs stop the flow of blood from an open wound, and even flora, bacteria, and carrion beetles have their uses (160).

Adam One's sermons, usually addressed to fellow creatures as well as Gardeners—and one to "Friends, dear Fellow Creatures, Fellow Sojourners on this dangerous road that is now our pathway through life" (403)—recount the history of the flood, other creation myths, and the Gardeners' activities. Some are legends about various new ecological "saints" (e.g. Dian Fossey, Euell Gibbons, Farley Mowat, Rachel Carson, Sojourner Truth), and Atwood even gives three of her characters her saint's names: Shackleton, Crozier, and Oates.[10] Each sermon is followed by a song from *The God's Gardners Oral Hymnbook*. Since the Crakers' singing is "beyond the human level, or below it. As if crystals are singing" (*Oryx* 105), the singing that Amanda, Toby, Jimmy, Ren, and the two Painballers hear at the end of *The Year of the Flood* probably comes from the Gardeners, so music begins and ends the novel pair.

The Gardners' hymns, influenced by William Blake, John Bunyan, and hymn books from the Anglican Church of Canada and the United Church of Canada (Acknowledgments 433), all connect to Adam One's sermons and also are folkloric. Most of the hymns are sensory, referring to the body, vision, taste, the splendor of the earth, and to specific creatures and plants. What might seem comic rhyme, rhythm, or juxtaposition in the written text is not very noticeable in the folk/country recording of the hymns, which notably sounds like popular rather than reverent church music (Hymns). "My Body Is My Earthly Ark" advances the idea of the body itself as "proof against the Flood /. . . . / With Creatures all, in harmony" (93). In "Oh Sing We Now the Holy Weeds," even the dandelion, burdock root, acorn, bark of spruce and birch, and nettles are "beautiful to see" (127), and moles and carrion beetles make their contributions in "We Praise the Tiny Perfect Moles" (162). "The Peach or Plum" is especially sensuous in its description of the way that the birds, bees, and bats sip nectar "hour by hour" (278). In "When God Shall His Bright Wings Unfold," God appears as dove, raven, swan, hawk, cockatoo, owl, waterfowl, and even vulture.

Following Adam One's "On the Fragility of the Universe" for Saint Julian and All Soul's Day, *The Year of the Flood* ends with a hymn, "The Earth Forgives," and the folklore suggests, as the book has demonstrated, that, despite the human tendency to be violent, human beings are capable of changing, forgiving, and attaining vision. Julian was a fourteenth-century mystic and one of the earliest known women writers: "Julian's success in removing or reducing the stigma long attached to the (female) body in the Christian tradition must have been one major factor that led to Atwood's choice of the historical figure and name for the final day of her narrative" (Kuribayashi 25). The "dynamic tension" between opposite ideas at the same time (Osborne "Compassion" 36–39) that Atwood's characters and books usually maintain erases the possibility of a resolved ending, but the atmosphere of joy and singing here offers more hope than the "Zero Hour" ending of *Oryx and Crake* does. Like Jimmy in *Oryx and Crake*, Toby and Ren leave their locked spaces, go outside to see and act in the forbidden ruined world, and tell their stories. In the second book's final Ren section, Jimmy is rapturous at the sound of many people singing and he says, "You can't kill the music. . . . You can't!" (431). Ren sees the new moon rising, a mythic sign of rebirth; remembers making balls of the Julian Cosmos as a child; and realizes that, despite their pain, Toby, Amanda, Jimmy, and the two Painballer rapists, who have just shared a meal, are lucky. We don't know what the next day will bring, but so far, they and Earth have survived. As in traditional flood stories like the Chinese "The Creation of the Universe and Human Beings," the Indian "Creation, Death, and Rebirth of the Universe, Gods, and Human Beings," and the biblical flood story, we hope and expect that life within and outside Atwood's novels will continue.

Notes

1. Jennings uses the word "myth" to refer to the "grand tradition" of the apocalypse in literature (12). The framework and the tone of the novel present "a comic vision" partly because of the text's comic distance from religious and secular myths (13, 18).

2. Many other fairy tales are referenced or alluded to briefly in the novel. Most important is "The Robber Bridegroom" (Zipes 153–57), which, like "Fitcher's Bird," also suggests marriage to death, this time through cannibalism as well as dismemberment of the Robber's female victims. Men (the robbers) marry death too, however, in that the wedding guests of the female victim either turn the Robber and his band over to the magistrate or execute him themselves. In *Oryx and Crake*, instead of providing pleasure, taking BlyssPluss does marry victims to death. This fairy tale is also behind other real or symbolic cannibalism in the book and *The Year of the Flood*, including SecretBurgers and capitalism. Before taking Jimmy to the pleeblands, Crake warns him that Compound people are a feast there: it's "like having a big sign on your forehead saying, Eat Me" (287).

3. The wolves in "The Wolf and the Kids" and "Little Red Cap" are suggested by the elite Compound scientists who "use disguise and deception, including false

advertising and products, in order to open the doors of their victim's defenses so that they may be eaten, in this case by microbes that produce this novel's apocalypse" (Wilson, *Myths* 40). Instead of the Fountain of Youth sought in the Grimms' "The Water of Life" (Zipes 356–61), the pleeblanders find only death. In *Oryx and Crake*, Oryx is folklore's "sold child," still an abused Cinderella orphan obsessed with the trappings of beauty (or Gretel greedy for "candy," but here she is also a reversed one in that her "prince" kills her). Like "The Girl Without Hands" and Beauty of "Beauty and the Beast," but unlike the women in *The Year of the Flood,* father figures make her passive, an "object of exchange" (Sedgwick 524).

4. See Osborne ("Mythmaking" n. 1, 43–44) and Doty (19).

5. In the Chinese creation myth, "The Creation of the Universe and Human Beings," a monster causes world destruction, including a flood. This myth cannot be accurately dated since most books were burned on 213 BC, but it is found in books written between 200 and 500 AD. Pangu breaks open the world egg to separate the heavens from the earth and to create order out of chaos, including mountains, the sun and moon, oceans, plants, and animals. After the Mother Goddess Nugua creates people, the monster Gong-gong becomes angry and rips up mountains, causes the sky to crash, and floods the land. Although some of the land remains lower than the rest of China, the Goddess repairs most of the damage (Rosenberg 390–92).

6. The Indian "Creation, Death, and Rebirth of the Universe, Gods, and Human Beings," probably written down between 300 and 500 AD, moves from one great age to another in eternally repetitive cycles, with each age worse than the one that precedes it. At the end of 1000 Maha Yugas or Great Ages, that constitute one day in the life of the world, the god Vishnu, in the form of Shiva-Rudra, destroys all life on earth. Great heat, drought, and scorching fire create a wasteland and famine. Just before a great flood buries all life, a golden egg that contains the seeds of all life appears and floats on the ocean. Then Vishnu as Brahma, Creator of Life on Earth, awakens, a lotus flower emerges from his navel, and life begins again (Rosenberg 354–57).

7. The best-known flood story is the biblical tale, which ends with the etiological myth of the rainbow and God's covenant to living beings that no further destruction of all life by water is to occur. One version includes a disinterred Father Adam, and sometimes the Devil boards the ark with the ass (Leach and Fried 395, 795–96). In Genesis, shortly after the fall of humankind and the exile from Eden (3:24) when God sees the wickedness of human beings and their continuous evil thoughts, God repents having created them and decides to destroy not only human beings, but "beast, and the creeping thing, and the fowls of the air." The earth is filled with violence and "all flesh had corrupted his way upon the earth." Thus, "everything that is in the earth shall die." Noah and his family and two of each kind of animal board the ark, it rains for forty days, the water stays on the earth for 150 days before it dries up, and God restores the seasons and makes a covenant with all living beings. Humans are not to kill all flesh again,

and Noah and his family offer burnt sacrifices. Related motifs include escape in an ark, bird scouts, and the ark coming to rest on a mountain. Ironically, in the same chapter of Genesis as the world begins again, Noah loses no time getting drunk on wine, lying nude in his tent, and punishing the son who sees him naked and covers him (Chap. 6–9). The Bible continues with human beings being fruitful and multiplying on the earth.

8. According to Stephen Dunning, "the relationship between [sic] Crake, Snowman, and Oryx unmistakably suggests the Christian trinity whose authority science has effectively displaced" (95). Readers who may miss the irony and parody of Adam One's sermons and of God's Gardeners' hymns in *The Year of the Flood* (or simply use "preaching" for a more accurate word) speak of Atwood's preaching there, too. Osborne even suggests that Atwood shares many of her readers' New Age beliefs (Osborne, "Compassion" 32, 34).

9. Charles G. D. Roberts's animal tales constitute part of Canada's classic or canonical literature and are important texts in illustrating the theme Atwood investigates in *Survival: A Thematic Guide to Canadian Literature* (1972)—how frequently Canada's people and even animals do not survive against nature. In Roberts's "Strayed," readers know from the beginning that the young ox "of a wild and restless nature" will not survive when he leaves his yokemate for the woods (10).

10. According to the acknowledgments, one character, Amanda Payne, is a name "courtesy of an auction for the Medical Foundation for the Care of Victims of Torture (U. K.)" (*Year of the Flood* 434).

Works Cited

Atwood, Margaret. Acknowledgments. *The Year of the Flood.* By Atwood. New York: Doubleday, 2009. 433–34.

———. *Oryx and Crake.* New York: Doubleday, 2003.

———. "A Review of Margaret Atwood's *The Year of the Flood.*" *Libdig101library.* Vanderbilt U, n.d. Web. May 6, 2011.

———. *Speeches for Doctor Frankenstein.* Bloomfield Hill, MI: Cranbrook, 1965.

———. *The Year of the Flood.* New York: Doubleday, 2009.

Doty, William G. *Mythography: The Study of Myths and Rituals.* Tuscaloosa: U of Alabama P, 1986.

Dunning, Stephen "Margaret Atwood's *Oryx and Crake:* The Terror of the Therapeutic." *Canadian Literature* 186 (2005): 86–101.

Hengen, Shannon. "Moral/Environmental Debt in *Payback* and *Oryx and Crake.*" *Margaret Atwood: The Robber Bride, Alias Grace, Oryx and Crake.* Ed. J. Brooks Bouson. London: Continuum, 2010. 129–40.

The Holy Bible. King James Version. New York: World, 1954.

Hymns of the God's Gardeners. Comp. Orville Stoeber (music) and Margaret Atwood (lyrics). Earthly Ark Music, 2009. MP3.

Jennings, Hope. "The Comic Apocalypse of *The Year of the Flood.*" *Margaret Atwood Studies* 3.2 (Aug. 2010): 11–18.

Kirkus Reviews. Rev. of *The Year of the Flood.* 77.15 (1 Aug. 2009): 24.

Kuribayashi, Tomoko. "Women, Nature, and Forgiveness in *The Year of the Flood.*" *Margaret Atwood Studies* 3.2 (Aug. 2010): 22–30.

Leach, Maria, and Jerome Fried, eds. *Funk and Wagnalls Standard Dictionary of Folklore, Mythology, and Legend.* San Francisco: Harper, 1984.

Le Guin, Ursula K. Rev. of *The Year of the Flood* by Margaret Atwood. *The Guardian.* Guardian News and Media, 28 Aug. 2009. Web. 23 Jan. 2012.

Maxwell, Lauren A. Rule. "Desperate Times. Desperate Measures: Atwood's Speculative Fiction and Environmental Activism." *Margaret Atwood Studies* 3.2 (Aug. 2010): 4–10.

Osborne, Carol. "Compassion, Imagination, and Reverence for All Living Things: Margaret Atwood's Spiritual Vision in *The Year of the Flood.*" *Margaret Atwood Studies* 3.2 (Aug. 2010): 30–42.

_____. "Mythmaking in Margaret Atwood's *Oryx and Crake.*" *Once Upon a Time: Myth, Fairy Tales and Legends in Margaret Atwood's Writings.* Ed. Sarah A. Appleton. Newcastle upon Tyne: Cambridge Scholars, 2008. 25–46.

Rev. of *The Year of the Flood* by Margaret Atwood. *Kirkus Reviews* 77.15 (1 Aug. 2009): 24.

Roberts, Charles G. D. "Strayed." *Canadian Short Stories.* Ed. Robert Weaver. Toronto: Oxford UP, 1966. 10–14.

Rosenberg, Donna. *World Mythology: An Anthology of the Great Myths and Epics.* Lincolnwood, IL: NTC, 1993.

Sedgwick, Eve Kosovsky. "Gender Asymmetry and Erotic Triangles." *Feminisms: An Anthology of Literary Theory and Criticism.* Eds. Robyn Warhol and Diane Price Herndl. New Brunswick, NJ: Rutgers UP, 1997. 524–31.

Stein, Karen F. "Problematic Paradice in *Oryx and Crake.*" *Margaret Atwood: The Robber Bride, Alias Grace, Oryx and Crake.* Ed. J. Brooks Bouson. London: Continuum, 2010. 141–55.

Theroux, Marcel. Rev. of *The Year of the Flood* by Margaret Atwood. *Publishers Weekly* 256.29 (20 July 2009): 119.

Wilson, Sharon R. "Frankenstein's Gaze and Atwood's Sexual Politics in *Oryx and Crake.*" *Margaret Atwood: The Open Eye.* Ed. John Moss and Tobi Kozakewich. Ottawa: U of Ottawa P, 2006. 397–406.

_____. *Margaret Atwood's Fairy-Tale Sexual Politics.* Jackson, Mississippi: UP of Mississippi, 1993.

_____. *Myths and Fairy Tales in Contemporary Women's Fiction.* New York: Palgrave, 2008.

Winterson, Jeanette. "Strange New World." Rev. of *The Year of the Flood* by Margaret Atwood. *The New York Times.* The New York Times Company, 17 Sept. 2009. Web. 23 Jan. 2012.

RESOURCES

Chronology of Margaret Atwood's Life_____

1939	Margaret Eleanor Atwood is born in Ottawa, Canada, on November 18. During Atwood's childhood, her family divides its time between Ottawa and the wilderness of northern Canada, where Atwood's father, an entomologist, does research on forest insects.
1946	When Atwood's father accepts a faculty position at the University of Toronto, the Atwood family moves to Toronto, though they continue to spend summers in the Canadian north woods.
1951–1957	Atwood begins attending school regularly in 1951. While at Leaside High School, she writes for the school newspaper.
1957–1961	Atwood studies at the University of Toronto's Victoria College and earns an honors BA in English. During her university years, Atwood writes poems and stories for the campus literary journal and designs posters and programs for campus theater productions.
1961	Atwood's first poetry collection, *Double Persephone*, appears in 1961 and wins the University of Toronto's E. J. Pratt Medal for Poetry.
1961–1963	Atwood studies at Radcliffe College (which becomes part of Harvard University in 1963) with the support of a Woodrow Wilson Fellowship. She earns an MA in English in 1962 and begins working toward a doctorate at Harvard.
1963–1964	Atwood leaves Harvard to return to Toronto where she takes a job at a market research company and begins working on a novel that remains unpublished. During the summer of 1964, she travels to England and France.
1964–1965	Atwood moves to Vancouver when she becomes a lecturer in English at the University of British Columbia. She writes a draft of *The Edible Woman* and numerous short stories and poems.
1965	Atwood returns to Harvard to continue work on a doctorate. She does not finish a thesis.

1966	*The Circle Game* is published and it wins the Governor General's Literary Award the following year.
1967–1968	In 1967, Atwood marries James Polk, an American and a fellow graduate student during her years at Harvard. The couple moves to Montreal when Atwood takes a job teaching Victorian and American literature at Sir George Williams University, which is today Concordia University. In 1968, *The Animals in That Country* is published, and in the fall of 1968, Atwood and Polk move to Edmonton, Alberta, where Polk takes up a teaching position at the University of Alberta.
1969	*The Edible Woman* is published, and Atwood teaches creative writing at the University of Alberta.
1970	*The Journals of Susanna Moodie* and *Procedures for Underground* are published. Atwood and Polk live abroad in England and France.
1971	*Power Politics* is published. Atwood and Polk return to Canada and settle in Toronto. In 1971, Atwood becomes a member of Anansi Press's board of directors, a position that she holds until 1973, and from 1971–72, she is an Assistant Professor at York University.
1972	*Surfacing* and *Survival: A Thematic Guide to Canadian Literature* are published. Atwood is the writer-in-residence at the University of Toronto's Massey College from 1972–73.
1973	Atwood and Polk divorce and Atwood moves to a farm in Alliston, Ontario, with Graeme Gibson, a novelist. Trent University, Ontario, grants her an honorary doctorate.
1974	*You Are Happy* is published. Atwood becomes a cartoonist for *This Magazine* and writes a TV script, *The Servant Girl*, for the Canadian Broadcasting Corporation. She is awarded an honorary doctorate from Queen's University.
1976	*Lady Oracle* and *Selected Poems, 1965–1975* are published. Atwood gives birth to a daughter, Eleanor Jess Atwood Gibson.

1977	*Dancing Girls* and *Days of the Rebels: 1815–1840* are published. *Dancing Girls* wins the City of Toronto Book Award and the Canadian Booksellers Association Award.
1978	*Two-Headed Poems* and *Up in the Tree* are published and Atwood receives the St. Lawrence Award for Fiction. During the first part of the year, Atwood and her family spend six weeks traveling around the globe. In the spring, Atwood travels through the United States on a book tour and then the Atwood family travels to England. They spend the remainder of the year in Edinburgh, Scotland, and Gibson serves as the writer-in-residence at the University of Edinburgh.
1979	*Life Before Man* is published.
1980	*Anna's Pet* is published. The family moves from their Alliston farm back to Toronto, and Atwood is elected as the vice president of the Writers' Union of Canada. Atwood is awarded an honorary doctorate from Concordia University and is a recipient of the Radcliffe Graduate Medal.
1981	*Bodily Harm* and *True Stories* are published. Atwood wins a Guggenheim Fellowship and is president of the Writers' Union of Canada from May 1981 to May 1982.
1982	*Second Words: Selected Critical Prose* is published. Atwood is awarded the Welch Arts Council International Writer's Prize.
1983	*Murder in the Dark* and *Bluebeard's Egg* are published. The family lives in Norfolk, England, from September 1983 through March 1984.
1984	*Interlunar* is published. The family lives in West Berlin for three months, beginning at the end of March, and returns to Toronto late in the summer of 1984. Atwood begins a two-year term as president of the International PEN, Canadian Centre.
1985	*The Handmaid's Tale* is published. Atwood serves as the Endowed Chair in Creative Writing at the University of Alabama and receives honorary degrees from the University of Guelph, the University of Waterloo, and Mount Holyoke College.

1986	*Selected Poems II: Poems Selected and New, 1976–1986* is published. From February to May of 1986, Atwood teaches creative writing at New York University, where she holds the Berg Chair. Atwood wins the Governor General's Award for *The Handmaid's Tale* and also receives the Toronto Arts Award, the *Los Angeles Times* Fiction Award, and the *Ms.* Magazine Woman of the Year Award.
1987	The Royal Society of Canada inducts Atwood as a Fellow and she receives an honorary degree from Victoria College. Atwood wins the Arthur C. Clarke Award for Best Science Fiction for *The Handmaid's Tale* and also receives the Humanist of the Year Award and is the regional winner of the Commonwealth Literary Prize.
1988	*Cat's Eye* is published. Atwood receives a YWCA Women of Distinction Award and a National Magazine Award for Environmental Journalism, First Prize.
1989	Atwood wins the City of Toronto Book Award, the Coles Book of the Year Award, and the Canadian Booksellers' Association Author of the Year Award for *Cat's Eye*, which is also short-listed for the Booker Prize. Atwood spends a term as writer-in-residence at Trinity University in San Antonio, Texas.
1990	*Selected Poems, 1966–1984* and *For the Birds* are published. Atwood attends the premier of Volker Schlondorff's film adaptation of *The Handmaid's Tale* at the Berlin Film Festival. She receives the Order of Ontario Award and Harvard University's Centennial Medal.
1991	*Wilderness Tips* is published and Atwood is awarded an honorary degree from the Université de Montréal. In the summer of 1991, Atwood delivers the Clarendon Lectures at the University of Oxford, and her lectures are published by Clarendon Press in 1995 as *Strange Things: The Malevolent North in Canadian Literature*. She spends the winter of 1991–92 with her family in France.
1992	*Good Bones* is published. Atwood receives the Trillium Award for Excellence in Ontario Writing and the Book of the Year Award from the Periodical Marketers of Canada for *Wilderness Tips*.

1993	*The Robber Bride* is published and it wins the Canadian Authors' Association Novel of the Year award.
1994	*The Robber Bride* wins the Trillium Award for Excellence in Ontario Writing, the Commonwealth Writers' Prize for the Canadian and Caribbean Region, and the *Sunday Times* Award for Literary Excellence. Atwood receives an honorary degree from the University of Leeds and wins the Government of France's Chevalier dans l'Ordre des Arts et des Lettres.
1995	*Morning in the Burned House* and *Strange Things: The Malevolent North in Canadian Literature* are published, and Atwood wins the Trillium Award for Excellence in Ontario Writing for *Morning in the Burned House*.
1996	*Alias Grace* is published and it wins the Giller Prize and is short-listed for the Booker Prize. Atwood's honors include the Norwegian Order of Literary Merit, the Canadian Booksellers Association Author of the Year Award, and an honorary degree from McMaster University.
1997	*In Search of Alias Grace* is published. Atwood receives the Premio Mondello and the Salon Magazine Best Fiction of the Year Award for *Alias Grace*.
1998	*Eating Fire: Selected Poetry, 1965–1995* is published. The University of Oxford awards Atwood an honorary doctorate.
1999	Atwood receives the London Literature Award.
2000	*The Blind Assassin* is published and it wins the Booker Prize. Atwood delivers the Empson Lectures at the University of Cambridge and attends Poul Ruders's operatic adaptation of *The Handmaid's Tale*, which premiers in Copenhagen.
2001	The University of Cambridge awards Atwood an honorary doctorate, and she secures a place on Canada's Walk of Fame.
2002	*Negotiating with the Dead: A Writer on Writing* is published.

2003	*Oryx and Crake* is published and is short-listed for the Man Booker Prize, the Giller Prize, and the Governor General's Award for Fiction. Atwood receives the Radcliffe Medal and the Harold Washington Literary Award.
2004	*Bottle and Moving Targets: Writing with Intent, 1982–2004* are published. Harvard University awards Atwood an honorary doctorate.
2005	*The Penelopiad* and *Curious Pursuits: Occasional Writing, 1970–2005* are published. Atwood receives an honorary doctorate from the Université de la Sorbonne Nouvelle, Paris. She wins the Banff Centre's National Arts Award, Edinburgh's International Book Festival Enlightenment Award, and the *Chicago Tribune* Literary Prize.
2006	*The Tent* and *Moral Disorder and Other Stories* are published.
2007	*The Door* is published and is a finalist for the Governor General's Literary Award. Atwood receives a Kenyon Review Literary Achievement Award.
2008	*Payback: Debt and the Shadow Side of Wealth* is published. Atwood wins Spain's Prince of Asturias Award for Letters.
2009	*The Year of the Flood* is published.
2010	Atwood wins the World Economic Forum's Crystal Award and the Dan David Prize.
2011	*In Other Worlds: SF and the Human Imagination* is published.

Works by Margaret Atwood _____

Novels
The Edible Woman, 1969
Surfacing, 1972
Lady Oracle, 1976
Life Before Man, 1979
Bodily Harm, 1981
The Handmaid's Tale, 1985
Cat's Eye, 1988
The Robber Bride, 1993
Alias Grace, 1996
The Blind Assassin, 2000
Oryx and Crake, 2003
The Penelopiad, 2005
The Year of the Flood, 2009

Short Stories and Short Fictions
Dancing Girls and Other Stories, 1977
Bluebeard's Egg and Other Stories, 1983
Murder in the Dark: Short Fictions and Prose Poems, 1983
Wilderness Tips, 1991
Good Bones, 1992
Good Bones and Simple Murders, 1994
Bottle, 2004
Moral Disorder and Other Stories, 2006
The Tent, 2006

Poetry
Double Persephone, 1961
The Circle Game, 1964 (single poem), 1966 (collection)
Kaleidoscopes Baroque: A Poem, 1965
Talismans for Children, 1965
Expeditions, 1966
Speeches for Dr. Frankenstein, 1966
The Animals in That Country, 1968
What Was in the Garden, 1969
The Journals of Susanna Moodie, 1970
Procedures for Underground, 1970

Power Politics, 1971
You Are Happy, 1974
Selected Poems, 1965–1975, 1976
Two-Headed Poems, 1978
True Stories, 1981
Snake Poems, 1983
Interlunar, 1984
Selected Poems II: Poems Selected and New, 1976–1986, 1986
Selected Poems, 1966–1984, 1990
Poems, 1965-1975, 1991
Poems, 1976-1989, 1992
Morning in the Burned House, 1995
Eating Fire: Selected Poetry, 1965–1995, 1998
The Door, 2007

Nonfiction
Survival: A Thematic Guide to Canadian Literature, 1972
Days of the Rebels: 1815–1840, 1977
Second Words: Selected Critical Prose, 1982
Margaret Atwood: Conversations, 1990
Deux sollicitudes: Entretiens, 1996 (with Victor-Lévy Beaulieu; *Two Solicitudes: Conversations*, 1998)
Strange Things: The Malevolent North in Canadian Literature, 1995
Negotiating with the Dead: A Writer on Writing, 2002
Moving Targets: Writing with Intent, 1982–2004, 2004
Writing with Intent: Essays, Reviews, Personal Prose, 1983–2005, 2005
Curious Pursuits: Occasional Writing, 1970–2005, 2005
Payback: Debt and the Shadow Side of Wealth, 2008
In Other Worlds: SF and the Human Imagination, 2011

Edited
The New Oxford Book of Canadian Verse in English, 1982
The Oxford Book of Canadian Short Stories in English, 1986 (with Robert Weaver)
The CanLit Foodbook: From Pen to Palate, a Collection of Tasty Literary Fare, 1987
The Best American Short Stories 1989, 1989 (with Shannon Ravenel)
The New Oxford Book of Canadian Short Stories in English, 1995 (with Robert Weaver)

Children's

Up in the Tree, 1978
Anna's Pet, 1980 (with Joyce Barkhouse)
For the Birds, 1990 (with Shelly Tanaka)
Princess Prunella and the Purple Peanut, 1995 (illustrated by Maryann Kowalski)
Rude Ramsay and the Roaring Radishes, 2003 (illustrated by Dušan Petričić)
Bashful Bob and Doleful Dorinda, 2004 (illustrated by Dušan Petričić)

Bibliography

Appleton, Sarah A. "Canadian Characters at King Arthur's Court: Arthurian Legend and Margaret Atwood's *The Blind Assassin.*" *Margaret Atwood Studies* 1.2 (Dec. 2007): 3–10.

_____. "Myths of Distinction, Myths of Extinction in Margaret Atwood's *Oryx and Crake.*" Appleton, *Once Upon a Time* 9–23.

_____, ed. *Once Upon a Time: Myth, Fairy Tales and Legends in Margaret Atwood's Writings.* Newcastle upon Tyne, England: Cambridge Scholars, 2008.

Barzilai, Shuli. "The Bluebeard Syndrome in Atwood's *Lady Oracle*: Fear and Femininity." *Marvels and Tales: Journal of Fairy-Tale Studies* 19.2 (2005): 249–73.

_____. "'If You Look Long Enough': Photography, Memory, and Mourning in *The Blind Assassin.*" Bouson, *Margaret Atwood* 103–23.

_____. "'Say That I Had a Lovely Face': The Grimms' 'Rapunzel,' Tennyson's 'Lady of Shalott,' and Atwood's *Lady Oracle.*" *Tulsa Studies in Women's Literature* 19.2 (Fall 2000): 231–54.

_____. "'Tell My Story': Remembrance and Revenge in Atwood's *Oryx and Crake* and Shakespeare's *Hamlet.*" *Critique* 50.1 (Fall 2008): 87–110.

Bloom, Harold, ed. *Margaret Atwood.* Bloom's Modern Critical Views. New York: Bloom's Literary Criticism, 2009.

Bosco, Mark. "The Apocalyptic Imagination in *Oryx and Crake.*" Bouson, *Margaret Atwood* 156–71.

Bouson, J. Brooks. *Brutal Choreographies: Oppositional Strategies and Narrative Design in the Novels of Margaret Atwood.* Amherst: U of Massachusetts P, 1993.

_____. "'A Commemoration of Wounds Endured and Resented': Margaret Atwood's *The Blind Assassin* as Feminist Memoir." *Critique* 44.3 (2003): 251–69.

_____, ed. *Critical Insights: The Handmaid's Tale by Margaret Atwood.* Pasadena, CA: Salem, 2010.

_____. "'It's Game Over Forever': Atwood's Satiric Vision of a Bioengineered Posthuman Future in *Oryx and Crake.*" *Journal of Commonwealth Literature* 39.3 (2004): 139–56.

_____, ed. *Margaret Atwood: The Robber Bride, The Blind Assassin, Oryx and Crake.* London: Continuum, 2010.

_____. "Slipping Sideways into the Dreams of Women: The Female Dream Work of Power Feminism in Margaret Atwood's *The Robber Bride.*" *LIT: Literature Interpretation Theory* 6.3–4 (1995): 149–66.

_____. "'We're Using Up the Earth. It's Almost Gone': A Return to the Post-Apocalyptic Future in Margaret Atwood's *The Year of the Flood.*" *Journal of Commonwealth Literature* 46.1 (Mar. 2011): 9–26.

Cooke, Grayson. "Technics and the Human at Zero-Hour: Margaret Atwood's *Oryx and Crake.*" *Studies in Canadian Literature/Études en Littérature Canadienne* 31.2 (2006): 105–25.

Cooke, Nathalie. *Margaret Atwood: A Biography.* Toronto: ECW, 1998.

_____. *Margaret Atwood: A Critical Companion.* Westport, CT: Greenwood, 2004.

_____. "Turning the Pages: Rereading Atwood's Novels." *English Studies in Canada* 33.3 (Sept. 2007): 89–93.

Dancygier, Barbara. "Narrative Anchors and the Processes of Story Construction: The Case of Margaret Atwood's *The Blind Assassin.*" *Style* 41.2 (2007): 133–152.

Darroch, Heidi. "Hysteria and Traumatic Testimony: Margaret Atwood's *Alias Grace.*" *Essays on Canadian Writing* 81 (Winter 2004): 103–21.

Davies, Madeleine. "Margaret Atwood's Female Bodies." Howells, *Cambridge Companion* 58–71.

Davis, Roger. "'A White Illusion of a Man': Snowman, Survival and Speculation in Margaret Atwood's *Oryx and Crake.*" *Hosting the Monster.* Ed. Holly Lynn Baumgartner and Roger Davis. Amsterdam: Rodopi, 2008. 237–58. At the Interface 52.

DeFalco, Amelia. "Haunting Physicality: Corpses, Cannibalism, and Carnality in Margaret Atwood's *Alias Grace.*" *University of Toronto Quarterly: A Canadian Journal of the Humanities* 75.2 (Spring 2006): 771–83.

DiMarco, Danette. "Paradice Lost, Paradise Regained: *Homo Faber* and the Makings of a New Beginning in *Oryx and Crake.*" *Papers on Language and Literature: A Journal for Scholars and Critics of Language and Literature* 41.2 (2005): 170–95.

Dunning, Stephen. "Margaret Atwood's *Oryx and Crake*: The Terror of the Therapeutic." *Canadian Literature* 186 (2005): 86–101.

Dvorak, Marta. "The Right Hand Writing and the Left Hand Erasing in Margaret Atwood's *The Blind Assassin.*" *Commonwealth Essays and Studies* 25.1 (Autumn 2002): 59–68.

Fand, Roxanne J. "Margaret Atwood's *The Robber Bride*: The Dialogic Moral of a Nietzschean Fairy Tale." *Critique: Studies in Contemporary Fiction* 45.1 (Fall 2003): 65–81.

Hengen, Shannon. *Margaret Atwood's Power: Mirrors, Reflections, and Images in Select Fiction and Poetry.* Toronto: Second Story, 1993.

_____. "Moral/Environmental Debt in *Payback* and *Oryx and Crake.*" Bouson, *Margaret Atwood* 129–40.

_____. "Strange Visions: Atwood's *Interlunar* and *Technopoetics.*" Wilson, *Textual Assassinations* 42–53.

Hengen, Shannon, and Ashley Thomson. *Margaret Atwood: A Reference Guide, 1988–2005.* Lanham, MD: Scarecrow, 2007.

Howells, Coral Ann, ed. *The Cambridge Companion to Margaret Atwood.* New York: Cambridge UP, 2006

_____. *Margaret Atwood*. 2nd ed. New York: Palgrave, 2005.

_____. "Margaret Atwood: *Alias Grace*." *Where Are the Voices Coming From? Canadian Culture and the Legacies of History*. Ed. Coral Howells. Amsterdam: Rodopi, 2004. 29–37.

_____. "Margaret Atwood's Dystopian Visions: *The Handmaid's Tale* and *Oryx and Crake*." Howells, *Cambridge Companion* 161–75.

_____. "*The Robber Bride*; or, Who Is a True Canadian?" Wilson, *Textual Assassinations* 88–101.

_____. " 'We Can't Help but Be Modern': *The Penelopiad*." Appleton, *Once Upon a Time* 57–72.

Ingersoll, Earl. "Flirting with Tragedy: Margaret Atwood's *The Penelopiad* and the Play of the Text." *Intertexts* 12.1–2 (Spring–Fall 2008): 111–28.

_____, ed. *Margaret Atwood: Conversations*. Princeton: Ontario Rev., 1990.

_____. "Margaret Atwood's *The Blind Assassin* as Spiritual Adventure." Perrakis, *Adventures of the Spirit* 105–25.

_____. "Survival in Margaret Atwood's Novel *Oryx and Crake*." *Extrapolation: A Journal of Science Fiction and Fantasy* 45.2 (2004): 162–75.

_____. "Waiting for the End: Closure in Margaret Atwood's *The Blind Assassin*." *Studies in the Novel* 35.4 (Winter 2003): 543–58.

_____, ed. *Waltzing Again: New and Selected Conversations with Margaret Atwood*. Princeton, NJ: Ontario Rev., 2006.

Jennings, Hope. "The Comic Apocalypse of *The Year of the Flood*." *Margaret Atwood Studies* 3.2 (Aug. 2010): 11–18.

Kapuscinski, Kiley. "Negotiating the Nation: The Reproduction and Reconstruction of the National Imaginary in Margaret Atwood's *Surfacing*." *English Studies in Canada* 33.3 (Sept. 2007): 95–123.

Kuhn, Cynthia. " 'Clothes Would Only Confuse Them': Sartorial Culture in *Oryx and Crake*." *Styling Texts: Dress and Fashion in Literature*. Ed. Cynthia Kuhn and Cindy Carlson. Youngstown, NY: Cambria, 2007. 389–410.

Kuribayashi, Tomoko. " 'A Mouse in the Castle of Tigers . . . Might Become a Tiger': Victims, Survivors, and Narratives in *Alias Grace* and *The Blind Assassin*." *Margaret Atwood Studies* 1.1 (Sept. 2007): 16–27.

_____. "Women, Nature, and Forgiveness in *The Year of the Flood*: An Exploratory Consideration." *Margaret Atwood Studies* 3.2 (Aug. 2010): 22–30.

Macpherson, Heidi. *The Cambridge Introduction to Margaret Atwood*. New York: Cambridge UP, 2010.

McWilliams, Ellen. *Margaret Atwood and the Female Bildungsroman*. Farnham, UK; Burlington, VT: Ashgate, 2009.

Michael, Magali Cornier. "Narrative Multiplicity and the Multi-layered Self in *The Blind Assassin*." Bouson, *Margaret Atwood* 88–102.

_____. "Rethinking History as Patchwork: The Case of Atwood's *Alias Grace*." *MFS: Modern Fiction Studies* 47.2 (Summer 2001): 421–47.

Moss, John, and Tobi Kozakewich, eds. *Margaret Atwood: The Open Eye*. Ottawa: U of Ottawa P, 2006.

Murray, Jennifer. "Questioning the Triple Goddess: Myth and Meaning in Margaret Atwood's *The Robber Bride*." *Canadian Literature* 173 (2002): 72–90.

Nicholson, Colin, ed. *Margaret Atwood: Writing and Subjectivity: New Critical Essays*. New York: St. Martin's, 1994.

Niederhoff, Burkhard. "The Return of the Dead in Margaret Atwood's *Surfacing* and *Alias Grace*." *Connotations: A Journal for Critical Debate* 16.1–3 (2006–2007): 60–91.

Nischik, Reingard M. *Engendering Genre: The Works of Margaret Atwood*. Ottawa: U of Ottawa P, 2009.

_____, ed. *Margaret Atwood: Works and Impact*. Rochester, NY: Camden, 2000.

_____. "*Murder in the Dark*: Margaret Atwood's Inverse Poetics of Intertextual Minuteness." Wilson, *Textual Assassinations* 1–17.

_____. "Nomenclatural Mutations: Forms of Address in Margaret Atwood's Novels." *Orbis Litterarum: International Review of Literary Studies* 52.5 (1997): 329–51.

Osborne, Carol. "Mythmaking in Margaret Atwood's *Oryx and Crake*." Appleton, *Once Upon a Time* 25–46.

Perrakis, Phyllis Sternberg, ed. *Adventures of the Spirit: The Older Woman in the Works of Doris Lessing, Margaret Atwood, and Other Contemporary Writers*. Columbus: Ohio State UP, 2007.

_____. "Atwood's *The Robber Bride*: The Vampire as Intersubjective Catalyst." *Mosaic: A Journal for the Interdisciplinary Study of Literature* 30.3 (1997): 151–68.

Potts, Donna L. "'The Old Maps Are Dissolving': Intertextuality and Identity in Atwood's *The Robber Bride*." *Tulsa Studies in Women's Literature* 18.2 (1999): 281–98.

Rao, Eleonora. "Home and Nation in Margaret Atwood's Later Fiction." Howells, *Cambridge Companion* 100–13.

_____. *Strategies for Identity: The Fiction of Margaret Atwood*. New York: Lang, 1993.

Raschke, Debrah, and Sarah Appleton. "'And They Went to Bury Her': Margaret Atwood's *The Blind Assassin* and *The Robber Bride*." Perrakis, *Adventures of the Spirit* 126–52.

Ridout, Alice. "Temporality and Margaret Atwood." *University of Toronto Quarterly: A Canadian Journal of the Humanities* 69.4 (Fall 2000): 849–70.

_____. "'Without Memory, There Can Be No Revenge': Iris Chase Griffen's Textual Revenge in Margaret Atwood's *The Blind Assassin*." *Margaret Atwood Studies* 2.2 (Dec. 2008): 14–25.

Rogers, Janine. "Secret Allies: Reconsidering Science and Gender in *Cat's Eye*." *English Studies in Canada* 33.3 (Sept. 2007): 145–70.

Rule, Lauren. "Not Fading into Another Landscape: Specters of American Empire in Margaret Atwood's Fiction." *MFS: Modern Fiction Studies* 54.4 (Winter 2008): 627–53.

Shapira, Yael. "Hairball Speaks: Margaret Atwood and the Narrative Legacy of the Female Grotesque." *Narrative* 18.1 (Jan. 2010): 51–72.

Staels, Hilde. "Atwood's Specular Narrative: *The Blind Assassin*." *English Studies: A Journal of English Language and Literature* 85.2 (2004): 147–60.

_____. "Intertexts of Margaret Atwood's *Alias Grace*." *MFS: Modern Fiction Studies* 46.2 (Summer 2000): 427–50.

_____. *Margaret Atwood's Novels: A Study of Narrative Discourse*. Tübingen, Ger.: Francke Verlag, 1995.

_____. "Parodic Border Crossings in *The Robber Bride*." Bouson, *Margaret Atwood* 36–49.

_____. "*The Penelopiad* and 'Weight': Contemporary Parodic and Burlesque Transformations of Classical Myths." *College Literature* 36.4 (Fall 2009): 101–18.

Stein, Karen F. "A Left-Handed Story: *The Blind Assassin*." Wilson, *Textual Assassinations* 135–53.

_____. *Margaret Atwood Revisited*. New York: Twayne, 1999.

_____. "Margaret Atwood's Modest Proposal: *The Handmaid's Tale*." *Canadian Literature* 148 (Spring 1996): 57–73.

_____. "Problematic Paradice in *Oryx and Crake*." Bouson, *Margaret Atwood* 141–55.

_____. "Talking Back to Bluebeard: Atwood's Fictional Storytellers." Wilson, *Textual Assassinations* 154–71.

Sullivan, Rosemary. *The Red Shoes: Margaret Atwood Starting Out*. Toronto: Harper, 1998.

Tolan, Fiona. *Margaret Atwood: Feminism and Fiction*. Amsterdam and New York: Rodopi, 2007.

_____. "Situating Canada: The Shifting Perspective of the Post-Colonial Other in Margaret Atwood's *The Robber Bride*." *American Review of Canadian Studies* 35.3 (2005): 453–70.

_____. "Sucking the Blood Out of Second Wave Feminism: Postfeminist Vampirism in Margaret Atwood's *The Robber Bride*." *Gothic Studies* 9.2 (2007): 45–57.

_____. "'Was I My Sister's Keeper?': *The Blind Assassin* and Problematic Feminisms." Bouson, *Margaret Atwood* 73–87.

VanSpanckeren, Kathryn. "Atwood's Female Crucifixion: 'Half-Hanged Mary.'" Appleton, *Once Upon a Time* 151–78.

_____. "Atwood's Space Crone: Alchemical Vision and Revision in *Morning in the Burned House*." Perrakis, *Adventures of the Spirit* 153–80.

_____. "Humanizing the Fox: Atwood's Poetic Tricksters and *Morning in the Burned House*." Wilson, *Textual Assassinations* 102–20.

VanSpanckeren, Kathryn, and Jan Garden Castro, eds. *Margaret Atwood: Vision and Forms*. Carbondale: Southern Illinois UP, 1988.

Vickroy, Laurie. "Seeking Symbolic Immortality: Visualizing Trauma in *Cat's Eye*." *Mosaic: A Journal for the Interdisciplinary Study of Literature* 38.2 (June 2005): 129–43.

_____. "You're History: Living with Trauma in *The Robber Bride*." Bouson, *Margaret Atwood* 50–65.

Wilson, Sharon Rose. "Blindness and Survival in Margaret Atwood's Major Novels." Howells, *The Cambridge Companion to Margaret Atwood* 176–90.

_____. "Fairy Tales, Myths, and Magic Photographs in Atwood's *The Blind Assassin*." Appleton, *Once Upon a Time* 73–93.

_____. "Magical Realism in *The Robber Bride* and Other Texts." Bouson, *Margaret Atwood* 23–35.

_____. "Margaret Atwood and the Fairy Tale: Postmodern Revisioning in Recent Texts." *Contemporary Fiction and the Fairy Tale*. Ed. Stephen Benson. Detroit: Wayne State University Press, 2008. 98–119.

_____. *Margaret Atwood's Fairy-Tale Sexual Politics*. Jackson: University Press of Mississippi, 1993.

_____, ed. *Margaret Atwood's Textual Assassinations: Recent Poetry and Fiction*. Columbus: Ohio State UP, 2003.

_____. *Myths and Fairy Tales in Contemporary Women's Fiction: From Atwood to Morrison*. New York: Palgrave, 2008.

_____. "Quilting as Narrative Art: Metafictional Construction in *Alias Grace*." Wilson, *Margaret Atwood's Textual Assassinations* 121–34.

Wright, Laura. "National Photographic: Images of Sensibility and the Nation in Margaret Atwood's *Surfacing* and Nadine Gordimer's *July's People*." *Mosaic: A Journal for the Interdisciplinary Study of Literature* 38.1 (Mar. 2005): 75–92.

_____. "Orwellian Animals in Postcolonial Contexts: Margaret Atwood's *Oryx and Crake*." *Margaret Atwood Studies* 2.1 (Aug. 2008): 3–13.

Wyatt, Jean. "I Want to Be You: Envy, the Lacanian Double, and Feminist Community in Margaret Atwood's *The Robber Bride*." *Tulsa Studies in Women's Literature* 17.1 (1998): 37–64.

York, Lorraine M., ed. *Various Atwoods: Essays on the Later Poems, Short Fiction, and Novels*. Concord, ON: Anansi, 1995.

Zimmerman, Barbara. "Shadow Play: Zenia, the Archetypal Feminine Shadow in Margaret Atwood's *The Robber Bride*." *Pleiades* 15.2 (1995): 70–82.

CRITICAL
INSIGHTS

About the Editor

J. Brooks Bouson is a Professor of English at Loyola University Chicago. In her book on Margaret Atwood, *Brutal Choreographies: Oppositional Strategies and Narrative Design in the Novels of Margaret Atwood* (1993), Bouson makes use of both feminist and psychoanalytic theory as she investigates the psychological and political concerns expressed in Atwood's novels, and she also shows, through an analysis of the critical conversations surrounding Atwood's novels, that Atwood's works have the power to disturb and compel readers while calling attention to their preoccupation with form and design. Since the publication of *Brutal Choreographies,* Bouson has published book chapters and essays on Atwood, including an essay on Atwood's invocation of third-wave "power feminism" in *The Robber Bride* (1993); on Atwood's borrowing from a popular genre, the confessional memoir, in *The Blind Assassin* (2000); on Atwood's satiric vision of a bioengineered and posthuman future in *Oryx and Crake* (2003); and, on Atwood's critique of contemporary society's unbridled consumption and environmental destruction as she returns to the postapocalyptic future of *Oryx and Crake* in *The Year of the Flood* (2009). Bouson also has published two critical collections on Margaret Atwood: *Margaret Atwood: The Robber Bride, The Blind Assassin, Oryx and Crake* (2010) and *Critical Insights: Margaret Atwood, The Handmaid's Tale* (2009). In addition to her work on Atwood, Bouson has published essays and book chapters on a variety of authors (including Dorothy Allison, Saul Bellow, Emily Dickinson, Ted Hughes, Franz Kafka, Jamaica Kincaid, Toni Morrison, Edwin Muir, George Orwell, Richard Russo, and Christa Wolf) and she is the author of *Embodied Shame: Uncovering Female Shame in Contemporary Women's Writings* (2009); *Jamaica Kincaid: Writing Memory, Writing Back to the Mother* (2005); *Quiet As It's Kept: Shame, Trauma and Race in the Novels of Toni Morrison* (2000); and *The Empathic Reader: A Study of the Narcissistic Character and the Drama of the Self* (1989). She is the editor of *Critical Insights: Emily Dickinson* (2010).

Contributors

J. Brooks Bouson is a professor of English at Loyola University Chicago. She has published essays and book chapters on a variety of authors (including Dorothy Allison, Margaret Atwood, Saul Bellow, Emily Dickinson, Ted Hughes, Franz Kafka, Jamaica Kincaid, Toni Morrison, Edwin Muir, George Orwell, Richard Russo, and Christa Wolf) and she is the author of *Embodied Shame: Uncovering Female Shame in Contemporary Women's Writings* (2009); *Jamaica Kincaid: Writing Memory, Writing Back to the Mother* (2005); *Quiet As It's Kept: Shame, Trauma and Race in the Novels of Toni Morrison* (2000); *Brutal Choreographies: Oppositional Strategies and Narrative Design in the Novels of Margaret Atwood* (1993); and *The Empathic Reader: A Study of the Narcissistic Character and the Drama of the Self* (1989). In addition, she is the editor of critical collections on Margaret Atwood and Emily Dickinson: *Margaret Atwood: The Robber Bride, The Blind Assassin, Oryx and Crake* (2010); *Critical Insights: Margaret Atwood, The Handmaid's Tale* (2009); and *Critical Insights: Emily Dickinson* (2010).

Shannon Hengen is a professor of English at Laurentian University in Sudbury, Ontario, Canada, where she has taught the writings of Margaret Atwood in such courses as "The Writer's Voice," "Canadian Thought and Culture," and "Science Fiction," and where her department hosts the annual Margaret Atwood Birthday Dinner, which Atwood herself attends. Hengen has published articles on Atwood, Canadian theater, and comedy and is the author of *Margaret Atwood's Power* (1993); the editor of *Performing Gender and Comedy: Theories, Texts, Contexts*, two volumes (1998); the coeditor of *Approaches to Teaching Margaret Atwood's* The Handmaid's Tale *and Other Works* (MLA, 1996); and she has also copublished a comprehensive bibliography of works by and about Atwood, entitled *Margaret Atwood: A Reference Guide* (2007). With Ashley Thomson, she publishes in *Margaret Atwood Studies* the "Annual Checklist of Works by and About Margaret Atwood." From 1999 to 2000, she was president of the Margaret Atwood Society. Hengen's other scholarly interests include the work of De-ba-jeh-mu-jig Theatre Group, the writings of Louise Erdrich, and the work of South African poet-journalist Antjie Krog.

Heidi Slettedahl Macpherson is a pro vice-chancellor of research and innovation at De Montfort University in Leicester, England. She is the author of *The Cambridge Introduction to Margaret Atwood* (2010); *Transatlantic Women's Literature* (2009); *Courting Failure* (2007); and *Women's Movement* (2000), as well as the editor of a number of books on transatlantic studies. She has published widely on topics such as women, drama, and the law; transatlantic literature; women's travel narratives; American studies in Britain; and women and the law in twentieth-century fiction. She has published numerous articles on women authors, including Eva Hoffman, Sarah

Dunant, Amy Tan, Anne Tyler, Joan Barfoot, Gail Anderson-Dargatz, Tillie Olsen, Ann Tracy, Paule Marshall, and Bharati Mukherjee.

Coral Ann Howells is a professor emerita of English and Canadian literature, University of Reading, England, and Senior Research Fellow, Institute of English Studies, University of London. She has lectured and published extensively on contemporary Canadian women's fiction in English. Her books include *Private and Fictional Words* (1987); *Margaret Atwood* (2005); *Alice Munro* (1998); and *Contemporary Canadian Women's Fiction: Refiguring Identities* (2003). She is editor of the *Cambridge Companion to Margaret Atwood* (2006), which won the Atwood Society prize for best book in 2007, and coeditor with Eva-Marie Kröller of the *Cambridge History of Canadian Literature* (2009). She is a Fellow of the Royal Society of Canada and is currently coediting a volume of the *Oxford History of the English Novel*.

Earl G. Ingersoll is a distinguished professor (scholarship) and distinguished teaching professor emeritus at the State University of New York at Brockport. He is the author of several books on twentieth-century writers, including *Engendered Trope in Joyce's "Dubliners"* (1996); *D. H. Lawrence, Desire, and Narrative* (2001); and *Waiting for the End: Gender and Ending in the Contemporary Novel* (2007). Among his dozen other books are three collections of essays on Lawrence and single-author interview books on well-known authors, including Doris Lessing, Lawrence Durrell, Anthony Burgess, May Sarton, Rita Dove, and Li-Young Lee, as well as two interview books on Atwood: *Margaret Atwood: Conversations* (1991) and *Waltzing Again: New and Selected Conversations with Margaret Atwood* (2006). He is also the author of over a dozen articles, chapters, and essays on Atwood's fiction.

Shuli Barzilai is a professor of English at the Hebrew University of Jerusalem. Author of *Lacan and the Matter of Origins* (1999) and *Tales of Bluebeard and His Wives from Late Antiquity to Postmodern Times* (2009), she has published articles in *Canadian Literature*, *Critique: Studies in Contemporary Fiction*, *Marvels & Tales*, *PMLA*, and *Signs*, among other journals. She has been the recipient of the Canadian Government Faculty Research Award for "Of Stumps and Other Vanquished Things: Emily Carr, Margaret Atwood, and Landscape as Archive" (*Word & Image* 2007) and the Canadian Government Faculty Enrichment Award for her course, "Margaret Atwood: Literature and Ideology."

Kathryn VanSpanckeren, a professor of English and writing at the University of Tampa in Florida, has been reading Atwood's poetry since graduate school at Harvard. Like Atwood, she won a Woodrow Wilson Fellowship, and her thesis advisor was Jerome Buckley, Atwood's thesis advisor and fellow Canadian. Frustration with the critical neglect of Atwood in the United States led her to publish *Margaret Atwood: Vision and Forms* (1988) with Jan Castro; since then, she has published seven essays on Atwood's works, especially the poetry. Trained in Folklore and Mythology at University of California Berkeley, she has collected folklore in the Himalayas, Indonesia, and elsewhere, and has lectured and taught abroad, especially in Asia. Her *Outline History of US Literature*, written for non-Americans, has been translated into over twenty-five languages and is maintained on the web by the US State Department. Her poetry has appeared in various journals, including *American Poetry Review* and *Ploughshares*; she coedited a book on the late John Gardner, focusing on his play with traditional narrative genres in poetry and prose, and his powerful ethical commitment; and she has published essays on contemporary authors who draw on oral tradition, including Leslie Marmon Silko and Maxine Hong Kingston.

Tomoko Kuribayashi, a professor of English at the University of Wisconsin–Stevens Point, earned her BA and first MA, both in English, from University of Tokyo, and then obtained a second MA and a PhD, also in English, from the Universities of Alberta and Minnesota. She is the coeditor of two collections of articles, *Creating Safe Space: Violence and Women's Writing* (1997) and *The Outsider Within: Ten Essays on Modern Japanese Women Writers* (2003), as well as the translator of *The Rape of the Nation and the Hymen Fantasy: Japan's Modernity, the American South, and Faulkner* by Mizuho Terasawa. Kuribayashi has published articles on Atwood's *Alias Grace, The Blind Assassin*, and *The Year of the Flood*, and her study of contemporary Japanese writer Yoko Tawada is included in an edited collection, *Traversing Transnationalism: The Horizons of Literary and Cultural Studies*, published by Rodopi Press.

Reingard M. Nischik is a professor and chair of North American literature at the University of Constance in Germany. She has published some twenty-five books as well as numerous book chapters and articles on Canadian, American, and Comparative Literature and was managing editor of the *Zeitschrift für Kanada-Studien* from 1992 to 2005. Nischik is the two-time recipient of the Best Book Award of the Margaret Atwood Society, which she won for her edited collection *Margaret Atwood: Works and Impact* (2000/2002) and for her monograph *Engendering Genre: The Works of Margaret Atwood* (2009). Her other books include *History of Literature in Canada: English-Canadian and French-Canadian* (ed., 2008) and *The Canadian Short Story: Interpretations* (ed., 2007, 2010).

Carol Margaret Davison is a professor of English literature at the University of Windsor. A specialist in gothic and Victorian literature, African-American literature, women's writing, and cultural teratology, she is the author of *History of the Gothic: Gothic Literature, 1764–1824* (2009); *Anti-Semitism and British Gothic Literature* (2004); and the editor of *Bram Stoker's Dracula: Sucking Through the Century, 1897–1997* (1997). She edited a special issue of *Gothic Studies* on the Gothic and Addiction (2009) and coedited a special issue devoted to Marie Corelli for *Women's Writing* (2006). She is currently at work, with the assistance of a SSHRC Standard Research Grant, on *Gothic Scotland/Scottish Gothic*, a theoretical examination of the Scottish gothic tradition.

Laura Wright is an associate professor and the director of graduate studies in English at Western Carolina University. Her work focuses on postcolonial literature and theory, ecocriticism, and animal studies, and her publications include *Writing "Out of All the Camps": J.M. Coetzee's Narratives of Displacement* (2006); *Wilderness into Civilized Shapes: Reading the Postcolonial Environment* (2010); and *Visual Difference: Postcolonial Studies and Intercultural Cinema* (2010). She is the lead editor, with Elleke Boehmer (Oxford University) and Jane Poyner (Warwick) of the approved MLA volume, *Approaches to Teaching Coetzee's Disgrace and Other Works*, and she has published work on Margaret Atwood in *Mosaic* and *Margaret Atwood Studies*.

Michael P. Murphy is the author of *A Theology of Criticism: Balthasar, Postmodernism, and the Catholic Imagination* (2008). An adjunct professor of social ethics and educational leadership at the University of San Francisco, he received his doctorate in theology and literature from the Graduate Theological Union, Berkeley, and he currently lives in the Bay Area with his wife and two daughters.

Laurie Vickroy is a professor of English at Bradley University. Her scholarship and teaching have focused on trauma studies, particularly the interrelationship of trauma, culture, and women's identity. She is the author of *Trauma and Survival in Contemporary Fiction* (2002) and coeditor of *Critical Essays on the Works of Dorothy Allison* with Christine Blouch (2005). She has written on a number of contemporary authors including Margaret Atwood, Toni Morrison, Dorothy Allison, Jeanette Winterson, Pat Barker, Marguerite Duras, Reinaldo Arenas, and Larry Heinemann, among others. Her work has appeared in the following journals: *Mosaic, The Comparatist, MELUS, Modern Language Studies, Women and Language, Obsidian II,* and *CEA Critic*. Recent publications include: "That Was Their Deal: Trauma Narratives' Ethical Reframings" in *Between the Urge to Know and the Need to Deny: Trauma and Ethics in Contemporary British and American Literature* (2011) and "You're History: Living with Trauma in *The Robber Bride*" in *Margaret Atwood: The Robber Bride, The Blind Assassin, and Oryx and Crake* (2010).

Sarah Appleton, professor of literature at Murray State University for many years, now teaches at Old Dominion University. She is the author of *The Bitch Is Back: Wicked Women in Literature* (2001) and, most recently, is the editor of the collection *Once Upon a Time: Myth, Fairy Tales and Legends in Margaret Atwood's Writings* (2008). She has published articles on Margaret Atwood in critical collections and in scholarly journals, including in *Margaret Atwood Studies*. She is currently working on a manuscript dealing with archetypal women in literature.

Alice Ridout is a visiting assistant professor at Algoma University in Canada, where she teaches Canadian literature, popular literature and culture, and an upper-year seminar in the contemporary woman's historical novel. She is author of *Contemporary Women Writers Look Back: From Irony to Nostalgia* (2011) and coeditor of

Doris Lessing: Border Crossings (2009). She has published on Margaret Atwood in *Margaret Atwood Studies* and the *University of Toronto Quarterly*. She is book reviews coeditor for the Oxford journal, *Contemporary Women's Writing*, and vice president of the International Doris Lessing Society. In her leisure time, she enjoys running with her energetic dog along forest trails.

Karen F. Stein is a professor of English and women's studies at the University of Rhode Island. Her research focuses on contemporary North American women writers, especially Margaret Atwood and Toni Morrison. She is especially interested in the ways that contemporary women writers inflect gothic themes and motifs. She was honored with the Woman of the Year award from the University of Rhode Island Association of Professional and Academic Women in 1993 and from the Rhode Island Commission on Women in 2007. She is the author of *Margaret Atwood Revisited* (1999) and of articles about Atwood and other North American women writers, including "It's About Time: Temporal Dimensions in Margaret Atwood's *Life Before Man*," which appeared in *Once Upon a Time: Myth, Fairy Tales and Legends in Margaret Atwood's Writings,* edited by Sarah Appleton (2008). She received a sabbatical and a Humanities Faculty Fellowship from University of Rhode Island in 2008–2009, during which she wrote *Reading, Learning, Teaching Toni Morrison* (2009).

Sharon R. Wilson is a professor of English and women's studies at the University of Northern Colorado. She has published *Margaret Atwood's Fairy-Tale Sexual Politics* (1993); *Myths and Fairy Tales in Contemporary Women's Fiction* (2008); *Margaret Atwood's Textual Assassinations* (2003); and, with Thomas Friedman and Shannon Hengen, *Approaches to Teaching Atwood's* The Handmaid's Tale *and Other Works* (1996). Wilson's published articles have focused on Margaret Atwood, Doris Lessing, Rosario Ferre, Jean Rhys, Samuel Beckett, E. R. Eddison, and the film *Citizen Kane*. She has been president of the Doris Lessing Society and was founding copresident of the Margaret Atwood Society.

Index

Abominable snowman, 338
Adam One (*Year of the Flood*), 21, 313, 324, 326–28, 340
    sermons, 341, 343, 347, 348
Adams and Eves (*Year of the Flood*), 325
afterlife, 115
Alias Grace (Atwood), ix, xvi, 45, 75–87, 294–99, 299–301, 302–04, 307, 309, 336
"All Bread" (Atwood), 143
All Souls Day (*Year of the Flood*), 348
"Alternate Thoughts from Underground" (Atwood), 204
American identity, 219
Americans, 27
Amnesty International, 50
Anansi Press, House of, 26
Ancient Mariner, 110–13
    stories, 5, 13
Antonia. *See* Tony
Animals in That Country, The (Atwood), 130, 134, 200
AnooYoo Spa (*Year of the Flood*), 344, 346
"Another Visit to the Oracle" (Atwood), 149
Apocalypse, 100, 313
Apollo, 160
Aphrodite. *See* Venus
April Fish Day (*Year of the Flood*), 343
Arabian Nights, The, 337
Ararats (*Year of the Flood*), 340
Arboretum Creek (*Year of the Flood*), 340
Arthur, 14
Artist as shaman, 138
"Art of Cooking and Serving, The" (Atwood), 188–90
"Asparagus" (Atwood), 146

Athena. *See* Minerva
Atwood, Margaret
    awards, 27, 30
    biography, 25–31
    Canadian nationalism of, 221
    Canadian writer, 6, 7, 26, 27
    career, 6–13, 30–31, 55, 101
    celebrity, 11–13, 40, 68
    childhood, 6, 28–29
    creating characters, 41–43, 276, 278
    dystopian novels of, 234, 262
    ecofeminist novels of, 329–331
    education, 6, 7, 27
    female protagonists of, 254
    feminism, 8–10, 29, 40–44, 51, 154, 156, 277, 278
    feminist works, 17
    feminist writer, 153, 167, 277
    gothic literature and, 193
    humor of, 31
    interviews, 39–41, 43, 44, 126, 193
    literary criticism, 37–38, 197
    media portrayals of, 39
    papers of, 55
    poetry of, xi, 27, 125–50, 153–68
    political causes, 29, 31, 50, 144
    political power, 255
    prose poem, 179
    romantic poet, 149
    sexism, 7, 8
    short prose, 171
    studies and criticism of, 54–71
    vocabulary, 125
    watercolors, 335, 336
    woman writer, 7–9, 38, 42
    writers/writing, 5, 21, 29, 31, 277, 278
    writing process, 129
Aunt Lydia. *See* Lydia, Aunt

Gothic literature, 14
  Atwood and, xiii
  Atwoodian, 200–09
  Canadian, 193, 197
  history of, 194–96
  New World, 193
  Old World, 193
  sociological, 199
  southern Ontario, 139
  wilderness, 193, 197
Governor General's Award, 130
"Great Unexpectations: An Autobio-
  graphical Forward," 6–8
Griffen, Iris Chase (*Blind Assassin*),
  ix, xv, xvi, 14, 18, 87–96, 254, 257,
  270–73, 277, 285–88, 296
Griffen, Richard (*Blind Assassin*), x, 19,
  89, 296

Haggard, H. Rider, Primary, 193
Hammer, Mike, 76
Handmaids (*Handmaid's Tale*), 232,
  262, 279, 316
Handmaid's Tale, The (Atwood), xiv,
  16, 51, 56, 59, 60, 62, 68, 130, 144,
  230–50, 254, 262–66, 276, 313,
  316–17
  Beatitudes (Bible), 232
  Genesis (Bible), 232
  language in, 231
  neologisms in, 233
  pollution in, 316–17
  religion in, 232
  transignifications in, 233, 240
Hansel and Gretel, 337
Harvard University, 27, 238
"Heart" (Atwood), 148
Helen of Troy, 43, 146, 158, 165
"Helen of Troy Does Counter Dancing"
  (Atwood), 146, 154, 165

Helen of Troy (*Morning in the Burned
  House*), 165, 167
HelthWyzer High, 337
HelthWyzer (*Year of the Flood*), 324
Hera. *See* Juno
"High Summer" (Atwood), 144
Historical fiction
  postcolonial, 308
  postmodern, 306
Historiographic metafiction, 297, 306
Hite, Molly, 282
Howells, Coral Ann, 46
Hyde, Lewis, 31

Imagined Communities (Anderson), 222
Inaccessible Rail. *See* Toby
"In Search of *Alias Grace*: On Writ-
  ing Canadian Historical Fiction"
  (Atwood), 44, 45, 294
Interlunar (Atwood), 131, 145
Intertexts, 334, 337
Island of Doctor Moreau, The (Wells),
  99–105, 106, 108–18
I-Thou encounter (Buber), 248

Jesus Christ, 243
Jezebel's (*Handmaid's Tale*), 239
Jimmy-Snowman
  Oryx and Crake, 20, 103, 108, 319,
    322, 335, 336, 338
  Year of the Flood, 349
Joan Foster, 14
Jordan, Dr. Simon (*Alias Grace*), 75, 76,
  296, 300
Journals of Susanna Moodie, The
  (Atwood), 130, 137, 197, 201–05

Karen (*Robber Bride*), 289
Kinnear, Thomas, 75
Kinnear, Thomas (*Alias Grace*), 77
Künstlerroman, 4